THE U-BOAT WAR

OSPREY
PUBLISHING

Dedicated to Opus

THE U-BOAT WAR
A GLOBAL HISTORY 1939-45

LAWRENCE PATERSON

OSPREY PUBLISHING
Bloomsbury Publishing Plc
Kemp House, Chawley Park, Cumnor Hill, Oxford OX2 9PH, UK
29 Earlsfort Terrace, Dublin 2, Ireland
1385 Broadway, 5th Floor, New York, NY 10018, USA
E-mail: info@ospreypublishing.com
www.ospreypublishing.com

OSPREY is a trademark of Osprey Publishing Ltd

First published in Great Britain in 2022

A catalogue record for this book is available from the British Library.

ISBN: HB 978 1 4728 4825 3; PB 978 1 4728 4843 7; eBook 978 1 4728 4827 7;
ePDF 978 1 4728 4826 0; XML 978 1 4728 4824 6

22 23 24 25 26   10 9 8 7 6 5 4 3 2 1

All uncredited images form part of the author's collection.
Index by Alan Rutter

Typeset by Deanta Global Publishing Services, Chennai, India
Printed and bound in Great Britain by CPI (Group) UK Ltd, Croydon CR0 4YY

Osprey Publishing supports the Woodland Trust, the UK's leading woodland conservation charity.

MIX
Paper from
responsible sources
FSC® C171272

To find out more about our authors and books visit www.ospreypublishing.com. Here you will
find extracts, author interviews, details of forthcoming events and the option to sign up for our
newsletter.

Contents

Acknowledgements

There are many that should be mentioned, but my word-count is unforgiving. I would like to express my thanks to the U-boat veterans that it has been my pleasure to know over the years. Among them, I would especially like to mention Horst Bredow, Georg Seitz, Volkmaar König, Gerhard Buske, Herbert Waldschmidt, Hans-Rudolf Rösing, Jürgen Oesten, Hans-Joachim Krug, Georg Högel, Ludwig Stoll, Wolfgang Pohl, Wolfgang Hirschfeld, Bernard Geissman and Ernst Göthling. Thanks to my wife Anna, Megan, James and 'Mumbles and Mr Mumbles' Paterson, Maggie Bidmead and Paul Milner, for access to his incredible photo collection.

List of Illustrations

The Type IIB *U23* before the war. Numbers on the conning tower and small bow plaques were removed before the outbreak of hostilities.

Type VII *U33*, with the external stern torpedo tube clearly visible; the tube was integrated internally from the VIIB onwards.

U33 in Wilhelmshaven on 28 September 1939 at the end of its first patrol, with souvenirs from the British steamer *Olivegrove*, the first of three ships sunk during this baptismal war patrol.

Georg Högel, radio operator aboard Lemp's *U30* and *U110*, was a gifted artist. So too was Guy Griffiths, who was taken prisoner aboard *U30* at the outbreak of hostilities. He formed a lifelong friendship with Högel. This illustration taken from a letter from Griffiths to Högel dated 6 January 1980 shows Griffith's Skua attack on *U30*.

Günther Prien (with binoculars), his ears wadded with cotton wool as crewmen prepare to test fire an MG34 from *U47*'s conning tower.

Fritz-Julius Lemp, who had recently been awarded the Knight's Cross, with Karl Dönitz aboard *U30* in Kiel at the end of its final war patrol, 30 August 1940.

Otto Kretschmer (in leather jacket), the highest-scoring U-boat 'Ace' of the Second World War.

Schnurzl photographed aboard *U30* by Georg Högel.

Lemp's *U110* with 'Schnurzl' emblem and Schepke's *U100*

with splinter camouflage and his crouching panther
emblem, Kiel, 9 March 1941. Both captains wear the
traditional white caps. This was to be *U100*'s last patrol.

The Type IID *U139* being commissioned by *Oberleutnant
zur See* Robert Bartels in Kiel on 24 July 1940.
The small size of the coastal Type II is immediately
apparent. Bartels was killed in action near Madagascar
on 20 August 1943 as captain of the Type IXD-2 *U197*.

The forward torpedo compartment of *U43*. (Paul Milner)

Victor Oehrn was tasked with restarting the Atlantic U-boat
offensive after disastrous torpedo performance caused
morale to crash. Here he celebrates the award of his Knight's
Cross following *U37*'s return to Lorient in October 1940.
At left is Günther Prien; second from right Joachim Schepke.

The charismatic Joachim Schepke speaking at the Berlin
Sportspalast to thousands of young schoolchildren in a
state-sponsored recruitment drive.

Horst Degen, Engelbert Endrass and Erich Topp. Degen was
IWO on Topp's *U552* when this photograph was taken.

Victor Oehrn (left) and Eberhard Godt (centre); the latter
headed BdU Ops.

Karl Dönitz (seated in car) with Hans-Rudolf Rösing
(centre) at the latter's Angers FdU West headquarters.

Size comparison of a Type VIIC and a Type XB minelaying
U-boat, moored in Kiel.

The cook ('*Smutje*') aboard *U43* in his cramped galley. U-boat
provisions were among the best issued by the Wehrmacht,
though fresh food was soon either eaten or disposed of as
rotten, replaced by tinned and preserved items. (Paul Milner)

Hans-Heinz Linder's *U202* docks in the Penfeld River, Brest,
used for mooring before the construction of U-boat
pens. (Paul Milner)

The forward gun of *U111* during severe winter conditions
on the boat's patrol near Newfoundland. (Paul Milner)

Jost Metzler, commander of *U69*, the first Type VIIC to be
launched. He sank the first American ship of the war

when he torpedoed freighter *Robin Moor* on 21 May 1941, after stopping the ship and discovering cargo considered contraband under prize rules.

Adalbert 'Adi' Schnee and men aboard *U201* taking advantage of the mid-Atlantic 'air gap' for coffee, cake and music.

Trainee captains of the 21st U-Training Flotilla aboard *U141*. Standing left to right: Horst Geider (*U61*, *U761*); Hans Döhler (*U21*, *U606*, killed 22 February 1943); Jürgen Krüger (*U141*, *U631*, killed 17 October 1943); Kurt Eichmann (*U151*, *U98*, killed 15 November 1942); Wolfgang Leimkühler (*U4*, *U225*, killed 22 February 1943); Siegfried Koitschka (*U7*, *U616*). Seated: Hardo Rodler von Roithberg (*U24*, *U71*, *U989*, killed 14 February 1945).

Dönitz – known to his men as *Der Löwe* (The Lion) – maintained as close personal contact with the men under his command as possible. Here he inspects a crew of the 7th U-Flotilla at La Baule, 30 November 1942. The *Obermaat* nearest the camera wears the Spanish Cross, signifying his involvement in patrols during the Spanish Civil War.

The time-consuming task of moving a torpedo from its under-deck storage to inside the forward torpedo room – only practical in areas safe from air attack. The external storage canisters were discontinued once Allied air power became preeminent; the containers were easily damaged by depth charge.

Certificate for the award of the U-boat Badge to Edmund Prochnow. Somewhat curiously, it is undated, though Prochnow was a member of the 'Weddigen' Flotilla before transfer as part of Otto Kretschmer's *U23* crew to *U99* (7th U-Flotilla). He had been hospitalised with severe rheumatism in 1940, reassigned to the 3rd U-Flotilla for a recovery period until 1941, and had returned to the 7th U-Flotilla aboard *U93*. He survived the boat's sinking by HMS *Hesperus* on the early morning of 15 January 1942.

U203 enters the first completed U-boat bunker pens at Saint Nazaire, 30 June 1941.

Helmut Rosenbaum in La Spezia, 5 September 1942, after being awarded the Knight's Cross for sinking HMS *Eagle*. He later headed the 30th U-Flotilla before being killed in a flying accident on 10 May 1944.

Hitler awards the Oak Leaves to Rolf Mützelburg (*U203*) and Adalbert Schnee (*U201*), 15 July 1942.

Wolfgang Lüth, one of the two most highly decorated men of the U-boat service, was awarded the Knight's Cross with Oak Leaves, Crossed Swords and Diamonds on 9 August 1943. He survived the war and was accidentally shot by a German sentry at the naval school, Flensburg-Mürwik, on 13 May 1945.

The stern of the Type VIIC *U737* in the North Atlantic. Possessing excellent seakeeping qualities, they could be uncomfortable in heavy swell. (Paul Milner)

Helmut Möhlmann, here as commander of *U571* returning to La Pallice (whose activities bear no resemblance to Hollywood's 'vision' of events). Möhlmann later served at BdU before taking command of the 14th U-Flotilla in Narvik.

The bridge watch aboard *U737*, which mounted nine war patrols as part of the Norwegian 13th U-Flotilla before being sunk on 19 December 1944 in Vestfjord following collision with a Kriegsmarine minesweeper. Thirty-one men were killed and 20 rescued from the freezing water. *U737* sank no ships. (Paul Milner)

Reinhard Reche's *U255* returns to Narvik victorious after the attack on PQ17. Reche had sunk four ships, boarding abandoned Liberty ship *Paulus Potter* and retrieving much material as well as the ship's flag, seen here streaming from the periscope.

Werner Hartenstein, commander of *U156*, which opened the *Neuland* attack on Caribbean oil traffic and installations.

Christmas 1942 aboard *U604*.

An unexploded torpedo from *U67* ashore in Curaçao, with

the badly damaged Dutch tanker *Rafaela* being towed
into St Anna Bay where it later broke in two.

The Metox 'Biscay Cross' is mounted at the front of this
Type IX conning tower.

U20 (left) and *U19* of the 30th U-Flotilla in Constanta harbour.

Reichsminister Josef Goebbels visits 6th U-Training Flotilla
in Danzig during 1942, signing the flotilla guest book.
On the right is flotilla commander *Kapitänleutnant*
Georg-Wilhelm Schulz, formerly of *U124*. He
later joined the staff of FdU *Ausbildungsflottillen*
(Commander Training Flotillas) in Gotenhafen,
becoming the last commander of 25th U-Training
Flotilla in April 1945.

U43 refuelling from the Type XIV *U461*, July 1942.

The Type3 XIV *U462* photographed from *U604* during
resupply near the Azores on 27 February 1943. The
tanker's octopus *Wappen* is just visible on the conning tower.

One of nine Type VIIC U-boats handed over for
commissioning into the Italian Navy during 1943.
None would leave the Baltic training grounds before
the Italian armistice in September. They were reclaimed
by the Kriegsmarine and use solely for training purposes.

U43's *Oberleutnant zur See* Hans-Joachim Schwantke
bringing a bottle aboard *U109* during a mid-Atlantic
meeting. The man in the background is wearing a
Tauchretter. Schwantke was killed on 30 July 1943
with his entire crew when *U43* was sunk by an Avenger
launched from USS *Santee*. (Paul Milner)

U511 – codenamed 'Marco Polo I' – arrives off the Japanese-
occupied harbour of Penang, July 1943.

U271 was sunk with all hands by depth charges during this
attack by a USAAF Liberator bomber on 28 January 1944.

The lower extended *Wintergarten* of a Type VIIC with
37mm flak weapon. Steel helmets became common
among bridge and flak crews as the danger from aircraft
became paramount.

Looking from the conning tower hatch at crewman manning the
FuMB-26 Tunis radar detector aboard *U861* in the Indian
Ocean. Tuned to the 3cm wavelengths used by American
radars, Tunis was introduced into service in June 1944.

Oberleutnant zur See Helmut Herglotz bringing *U290* into
Bergen, 16 June 1944.

U441 showing the fearsome array of weaponry for this
original 'flak boat'.

U290 showing the round dipole antennae of the FuG 350
Naxos radar detector. The large rectangular opening
housed the FuMO 61 Hohentwiel radar when not in use.

U43 making a surfaced torpedo attack. While *Oberleutnant zur
See* Hans-Joachim Schwantke stands at right and maintains
overall control, the UZO targeting device is manned (third
from left) by another for surface firing. (Paul Milner)

The Brest U-boat pens after the fall of the city to Allied troops,
September 1944. On the hill behind is the French naval
academy that was the headquarters of the 1st U-Flotilla.
From the left the first five 'pens' were 'wet pens' that could
hold two boats; the remainder were dry docks.

U802 after its surrender showing (from left) the snorkel,
radio DF loop, observation periscope, and attack
periscope. The helical wires around the periscope heads
reduced vibration.

The Type XXIII *U4709* leaving Kiel. It was commissioned on
3 March 1945 and scuttled on 4 May.

The Type XXI *U2519*, captained by Peter 'Ali' Cremer, formerly
of *U333*. This boat was commissioned on 15 November
1944 but never saw action. Cremer left the boat in February
1945 to become commander of a naval tank destroyer unit
that was in combat near Hamburg. (Paul Milner)

Kapitänleutnant Heinrich-Andreas Schroeteler of *U1023*
(though pictured here as captain of *U667*). He was
one of the last U-boat skippers to sink an enemy ship
on 7 May 1945. (Paul Milner)

Glossary

ASDIC Term applied to the sonar equipment used for locating submerged submarines. A powerful and effective weapon, it emitted a distinct 'ping' when locating the target. ASDIC is an acronym for 'Anti-Submarine Detection Committee', the organization that began research into this device in 1917.

ASW Anti-Submarine Warfare.

AZ (German) *Aufschlagzündung*; impact trigger for the Pi1 pistol fitted to both G7a and the G7e torpedoes.

BdU (German) *Befehlshaber der Unterseeboote*; Commander U-boats.

Eel (German) *aal*; slang expression for torpedo.

EK (German) *Eisernes Kreuz*; the Iron Cross, awarded in either First or Second Class.

Enigma Coding machine used by German armed forces throughout the Second World War.

FdU (German) *Führer der Unterseeboote*; Flag Officer for submarines, responsible for a particular geographical region.

G7a German torpedo propelled by compressed air.

G7e German torpedo propelled by electric motor.

HF/DF High Frequency Direction Finding; radio direction finder for locating high-frequency U-boat transmissions (colloquially known as being 'DFed').

IWO See *Wachoffizier* below.

KG (German) *Kampfgeschwader*; Luftwaffe bomber group.

Kriegsmarine (German) Navy of the Third Reich.

KTB (German) *Kriegstagebuch*; War Diary. Kept by the commander during a U-boat's patrol and later entered into official records.

LI (German) *Leitendre Ingenieur*, Chief Engineer.

Luftwaffe (German) Air Force.

MGK (German) *Marinegruppenkommando*; geographic command posts (e.g. MGK West, MGK Nord etc) for naval surface and land-based forces.

MZ (German) *Magnetzündung*; magnetic trigger for the Pi1 pistol fitted to both the G7a and the G7e torpedoes.

OKM (German) *Oberkommando der Marine*; Supreme Navy Command.

OKW (German) *Oberkommando der Wehrmacht*; Supreme Armed Forces Command.

RK (German) *Ritterkreuz*; Knight's Cross. Highest level of the Iron Cross award for valour, augmented with Oak Leaves, Swords and Diamonds for further meritorious award.

SKL *Seekriegsleitung*; Naval High Command.

UZO *U-Boot-Ziel-Optik*; surface targeting device introduced in 1939 that electrically transmitted targeting information from a pair of mounted binoculars to the torpedo calculator.

Wachoffizier (German) Watch Officer. There were three separate U-boat watch crews, each consisting of an officer or senior NCO, Petty Officer and two ratings. The ship's First Watch Officer (IWO) would be the Executive Officer (second in command); the Second Watch Officer (IIWO), the ship's designated Second Officer; and the Third Watch Officer (IIIWO), often the *Obersteuermann* (Navigation Officer). The duties of the IWO included torpedo and firing system care and maintenance as well as control of surface attacks; the IIWO handled administration regarding food and supplies as well as the operation of deck and flak weapons.

Wehrmacht (German) Armed Forces.

Wintergarten (German) Nickname given to the open railed extension astern of the conning tower, *Eisbbuilt*, to accommodate increased flak weaponry. Known to the Allies as a 'bandstand'.

Introduction

The crews of five merchant ships and three escorting armed trawlers that comprised convoy EN491 could have been forgiven for some level of complacency. The date was 7 May 1945, and the small cluster of ships had departed the Scottish port of Methil shortly after 2000hrs that evening, an interim stop in the voyage from Hull to Belfast, expected to take three days. The month had begun with unsettled weather; frequent rain showers and thunderstorms had swept across the United Kingdom until the evening of departure from Methil, when a fresh high-pressure system brought a warmer breeze to the British eastern seaboard. In Europe, the war that had raged since 1939 was but hours from ending. Hitler was dead, and partial surrender documents had already officiated over the preceding days for various geographical combat areas, before the final instrument of complete unconditional German surrender was signed earlier that day at SHAEF headquarters within the red brick building housing the *Collège Moderne et Technique de Reims*. The final capitulation would come into effect at 2301hrs (Central European Time) the following day, 8 May. U-boats had already been ordered to cease offensive operations four days previously on 4 May.

Captain Johannes Lægland's 23-year-old Norwegian merchant ship *Sneland I* carried 2,800 tons of coal bound for Northern Ireland, sailing as Number 2 ship in the small starboard column and also serving as the convoy commodore's ship for what would be one of the last wartime convoys. Immediately ahead rode the newer Canadian merchant ship *Avondale Park*, skippered by Captain James Cushnie and also carrying coal to Belfast.

As the ships sailed into the Firth of Forth, it is thought likely that the defensive Indicator Loop System comprising two sets of electric cables laid a mile apart on the estuary may have registered the passing of an unexpected large metal object that evening, but the trace had been disregarded as no credible threat at this extremely late stage of the war. If so, it was a grievous mistake. Indeed, at 2145hrs that evening, the war at sea had claimed another victim in the English Channel when a Norwegian minesweeper was torpedoed and sunk by the ageing Type VII U-boat *U1023* with only ten of its 32-man crew rescued in Lyme Bay.

The unidentified craft that had activated the magnetic loop and was steadily approaching EN491 was the small electro-U-boat *U2336*, captained by *Kapitänleutnant* Emil Klusmeier. This 32-year-old officer had started his naval service in 1930, three years before the accession of the National Socialist Party to power in Germany and five years before the Reichsmarine was renamed Kriegsmarine. Serving as a senior non-commissioned officer within U-boats from 1937, he received promotion to officer one year later. By October 1940, he was transferred to Dönitz's operational staff where he remained until 1944 and his return to sea as commander-in-training aboard Karl Boddenberg's *U963*; their single war patrol together aborted due to the D-Day landings. Klusmeier had then returned to shore and wrote the operating manual for the newly developed and technologically advanced Type XXIII U-boat expected to shortly enter service, Klusmeier volunteering to take one to sea as commander and prove his theoretical instructions correct. Circumstances prevented active operations until, on 1 May, *U2336* finally slipped from Larvik bound for the British east coast.

A little before 11 o'clock, the first of two fired torpedoes slammed into the *Avondale Park*'s laden hull. The ship's 17-year-old cabin deck boy Sydney Rapley later recalled the unexpected attack: 'We had come down through the Pentland Firth and on the evening of May 7 I took the helmsman a cup of cocoa and biscuits. I went back to my cabin to sleep. I was reading the *Readers' Digest* when the torpedo hit. I got blown up out of my bunk. I was on the top so hit the roof. We got to the lifeboat and were picked up by a Royal Navy vessel minutes later.'[1] The stricken ship began to go down; Chief Engineer Anderson and Donkeyman William Harvey were both killed after being trapped below decks while on engine room watch. Captain Cushnie and 35 other survivors abandoned ship and were rescued by HMT *Valse* (T-151) and *Leicester City* (FY-223). Fearing a mine strike and to avoid collision with the sinking Canadian vessel, Captain Lægland swung *Sneland I* to port when the second torpedo struck the starboard side near No. 2 hatch. Fatally holed, the ship was gone within two minutes, taking Lægland and six others to the bottom and leaving 22 survivors to be rescued. *Avondale Park* took longer to sink, finally going down on an even keel in 51 metres of water, thereby becoming the last vessel to be destroyed by aggressive U-boat action of the Second World War.

Klusmeier – his boat's small weapon load exhausted – departed stealthily as desultory depth charges were dropped far behind. *U2336* was detected twice more as it passed over the Indicator Loops while circling the Isle of May following the attack. No doubt he was testing the exceptional submerged capabilities of his new vessel, returning unscathed to Kiel on the night of 14 May to find the port already occupied by British troops.

Accused of breaking international law following Dönitz's order to cease fire, Klusmeier was interrogated by British authorities before they accepted his denial of having received such instructions due to proceeding largely submerged, his U-boat capable of three consecutive days underwater. After two months, he was released from British captivity and returned to his hometown of Bochum.

Emil Klusmeier belonged to a minority group in that he successfully sank at least one single ship. Despite common assertions to the contrary, the U-boats of Hitler's Kriegsmarine were largely ineffectual in their allotted role as predators of Britain's commercial trade routes. Despite localized and brief successes, they were constantly hamstrung by rigid tactical doctrine that became increasingly reliant on outmoded and flawed technology. Combined with a fatal misplaced belief in the impregnability of German codes, the U-boats were doomed to fail at their second attempt to force the United Kingdom to its knees through an effective blockade. However, Allied fear of U-boat predation always loomed large through the early years of the war, and subsequently in the various retellings of the tumult that has come to be known as the 'Battle of the Atlantic'. Customary essays on this struggle tell us that Karl Dönitz admitted defeat within the Atlantic in May 1943. This is not true, as he refused to concede the struggle and always intended to return to the *Schwerpunkt* – the central focus – of his operations, diverting his strength to peripheral areas of combat in which his boats already fought.

For, though Dönitz's vaunted tonnage war was considered fought and lost within the Atlantic battleground, U-boats sailed in every theatre of action in which German forces were present, ranging from the Arctic seas of northern Russia to waters touched by the icy Antarctic currents swirling towards New Zealand. All these theatres of action were deeply interconnected, even if only by the allocation of resources to one starving others of valuable tools for the job at hand. The U-boat war fought between 1939 and 1945 may have been of most crucial importance within the Atlantic Ocean but was an imperative of the Kriegsmarine in each of its geographic settings once its major surface forces had been decimated and effectively neutralized after only two years of fighting.

Chapter One

Genesis

*'I cannot say that I was altogether pleased. The idea of a cruise
to the Far East had been very alluring, while in the formation
of the new balanced fleet which we were planning, the U-boat
would represent only a small and comparatively unimportant
part. I saw myself being pushed into a backwater.'*

Karl Dönitz[1]

Fregattenkapitän Karl Dönitz arrived in Kiel to take command of
fledgling U-boat combat flotilla 'Weddigen' during July 1935.[*] He
had captained *Emden* during a cruise around Africa and the Indian
Ocean and was expecting another long voyage to Japan and China
before his surprise posting. The light cruiser, the first to be built
in Germany after the First World War, was used to train cadets
and midshipmen for the Reichsmarine – a shadow of the former
Imperial German Navy due to armament restrictions imposed by
the Versailles Treaty after the war's end. Dönitz had served during
that conflict on surface ships until 1916, when he requested transfer

---

[*] The early U-boat flotillas were named after First World War U-boat 'Aces' – in this
case, Otto Weddigen, who cemented his place in history when, as captain of *U9*, he
torpedoed and sank three old British cruisers – HMS *Aboukir*, *Cressy* and *Hogue* – within
less than one hour on 22 September 1914. Weddigen was immediately awarded the Iron
Cross, a copy of which he had attached to the conning tower of *U9*. One month later,
he received Prussia's highest military order, the *Pour le Mérite* and was killed in action on
18 March 1915.

to the U-boat service, going on to command minelayer *UC25* and attack boat *UB68* from which he was captured on 4 October 1918 after technical difficulties forced its scuttling.

Kiel also harboured a new U-boat school headed by veteran submariner Kurt Slevogt, which boasted six Type IIA U-boats (*U1–U6*) and functioned under the umbrella of the Naval Torpedo Inspectorate. Promoted to *Kapitän zur See* on 1 September, Dönitz was charged with raising a new U-boat service, beginning with 'Weddigen's' three improved Type IIB U-boats: *U7*, *U8* and *U9*.

The Type IIA was a single hull design, meaning that the bulkhead was the external pressure hull and all diesel was stored internally. A single 20mm anti-aircraft gun could be mounted on the forward deck. The conning tower was small, with two periscopes protruding from it: an aerial (navigation) periscope towards the front and a smaller-headed attack periscope in the middle of the tower. Possessing no watertight compartments, it carried three bow-mounted torpedo tubes, capable of carrying three loaded torpedoes and two reloads under the interior decking, or an alternative load of torpedo mines. Interior space was extremely limited, the small control room (*Zentrale*) that was the nerve centre of every U-boat positioned below the tower. The majority of the 24-man crew lived in the forward area, sharing 12 bunks between them, while a further four for the engineering crew were provided in the absolute stern of the boat, past the engine room and single WC. Cooking and sanitary facilities were basic. Two six-cylinder diesel engines were capable of 13 knots surfaced; two electric motors were able to reach 6.5 knots submerged. While the small boat possessed certain advantages – such as ability to operate in shallow coastal water, quick diving time and low-surfaced silhouette – its disadvantages quickly became apparent. Not only was its maximum pressure rating limited to 150 metres deep and its weapon load relatively light, but the IIA possessed an operational radius of only 1,050 nautical miles if running at 12 knots – barely capable of reaching northern Scotland from Kiel.

An improved Type IIB was soon produced, 20 models rolling out of three different shipyards. This model had three additional frame spacings inserted amidships, allowing an additional oil bunker beneath the control room, increasing operational range to 1,800 nautical miles at 12 knots. The diving time was also slightly improved to 30 seconds.

Strictly forbidden by the Treaty of Versailles, development of this new generation of U-boat designs had been undertaken in secret by a complicated network of fake business fronts, illegal money and design and testing on behalf of 'client' nations outside of Germany. However, Commander-in-Chief of the Reichsmarine, *Admiral* Erich Raeder, had established a clandestine U-boat department as early as 1927 under the cover-name 'Au' (Anti-U-boat Defence Questions). Through a series of prototypes built for Spain, Turkey and Finland, three different U-boat types in increasing size gradients were chosen for the Reichsmarine: a 250-ton coastal type, and 500- and 750-ton ocean-going models. These became the Type II, Type VII and Type I respectively. Raeder finally gave the order to begin assembly of the first six Type II U-boats on 8 February 1935, and after years of covert building, the Kriegsmarine replaced the Reichsmarine as one of three Wehrmacht branches; rearmament was officially announced by Adolf Hitler on 16 March 1935, a little under two years after he had taken full dictatorial control of Nazi Germany.

In 1935 Dönitz exerted little control over future U-boat development, which remained in naval command's hands, the U-boat regarded as merely one component of a balanced fleet. Its potentially war-winning capability demonstrated in 1917 appears to have been forgotten, thought to have been nullified by British anti-submarine sonar technology, ASDIC. Effectiveness of this active sonar had been deliberately inflated by the British Admiralty via carefully worded press stories and 'intelligence leaks'.

However, ASDIC had limitations, its efficacy deteriorating rapidly in water turbulence created by high speeds (above 20 knots) and rough weather (as frequently encountered in the North Atlantic), proving unreliable in water with steep temperature gradients and strong thermoclines (as in the Mediterranean). It possessed both a maximum range of 1,500 yards and a minimum range, meaning contact was lost immediately before depth-charge attack. Bearings were inexact, target depth impossible to ascertain, and estimated ranges carried a 25-yard margin of error – crucial given that early British depth charges possessed a lethal range of only 7 yards.

Though many German naval officers' views of U-boat value were diminished by their perception of ASDIC, Dönitz was not one of them. While exerting little control above his station, he exercised considerable influence over his subordinate command and, assisted by experienced U-boat engineer Otto Thedsen, energetically set about their task. Existing operational doctrine was revised. Previously, trainee commanders had been taught to attack submerged, from 3,000 metres' distance, with a salvo of torpedoes. Dönitz amended this to 600 metres maximum. The art of 'shadowing' was also strenuously taught, relying on a steely nerve to constantly open and close distance between U-boat and target, alternating between submerging, surfacing, then pursuing at speed, all while transmitting location information and avoiding counterattack by any escort vessels alerted by the radio signals.

Furthermore, he urged surfaced attacks under cover of darkness, thereby negating ASDIC and allowing the U-boats' surface speed, manoeuvrability and low silhouette to be maximized. Dönitz emphasized the importance of aerial reconnaissance reports, the visible horizon from low conning towers providing only a short radius of vision, and advocated group attacks against a single objective, a principle known as *Rudeltaktik*, now most commonly called the 'wolfpack'.

The concept of a 'pack' attack had originated with *Kommodore* Hermann Bauer, U-boat commander-in-chief 1914–17. Responding to defensive convoying, Bauer advocated grouping U-boats via radioed instructions from a large 'headquarters' U-boat stationed beyond enemy patrol range, which carried wireless and cypher experts, fuel, and weapon stocks for combat boats as its staff plotted enemy convoy traffic and directed the battle. Fortunately for the Allies, Bauer's proposal was dismissed by the Imperial Navy

Staff, who preferred to rely on large numbers of individual U-boat operations.

Dönitz acknowledged tactical questions posed by Bauer's method. Should the group be coordinated by a tactical commander within one of the U-boats, a surface vessel, or a land-based headquarters equipped with powerful radio equipment and immediately privy to the latest intelligence information? Furthermore, to what degree would individual commanders be granted freedom of action within what should be a tightly coordinated offensive operation? The complex and purportedly impenetrable Enigma machine at least seemed a fine solution to the question of how information could be encoded, decoded, transmitted and received between U-boat and controller.

In training, prospective commanders and crew undertook 66 surfaced and 66 submerged simulated attacks using compressed air 'water slugs', before graduating to practice torpedoes with dummy warheads. Emergency dives, deep dives, surfaced and underwater navigation drills were relentlessly repeated within the Baltic, while academic study in all aspects of submarine warfare provided a firm grasp of theoretical war at sea, as well as weapons maintenance and capabilities.

Despite their strength as torpedo carriers, the mine would unexpectedly become the most effective U-boat weapon of the early war. Three types of mines could be launched by torpedo tube: TMA, TMB and TMC. *Torpedomine* A was a moored mine that detached from its weighted plate after launching. Two could be carried within each torpedo tube, and they were capable of being moored in water up to 270 metres deep, the 215 kg warhead attached by chain to float just below the water's surface, to be detonated by its magnetic influence trigger. However, the mine proved to have too little buoyancy and too thin a mooring rope; after usage during the early months of war, it was redesigned late in 1939, eventually becoming the TMC mine.

Phasing out the TMA was the TMB, a ground mine and therefore only able to function to a maximum 20 metres' depth. Measuring only 2.3 metres in length, up to three TMBs could be carried in each torpedo tube. The magnetic fuse was timer activated, allowing the U-boat to move out of range before going live. The TMB warhead comprised 576kg of TNT, twice that of period torpedoes. Like magnetically fused torpedoes, it was triggered by a ship's metal hull, designed to explode beneath the keel, the resultant shock wave amplified through incompressible water. More effective than any contact hit against a hull side or bottom, it exerted huge stresses on the hull and would snap the ship's spine. The TMC – derived from the original TMA – was a later development following concerns that the TMB was insufficient to sink capital ships. Measuring 3.4 metres in length, only one TMC could be carried in each tube, but the warhead was packed with 1,000kg of explosive, effective from depths of up to 36 metres.

The two torpedo types with which U-boats were equipped were the G7a (TI) and G7e (TII). The 'G' was a hangover from early naval weaponry days before the term 'torpedo' was in common usage, standing for '*Geradelaufapparat*', literally 'straight running device'. The '7' denotes the 7-metre length of the weapon, and 'a' or 'e' either 'air' or 'electric'. The former (known as an 'Ato') was the standard pre-war German torpedo, powered by a mixture of fuel, hot air and steam burning within a four-cylinder combustion engine giving a maximum speed of 40 knots and theoretical range of 75km. Due to this mechanism, the torpedo left a small trail of bubbles in its wake. The G7e (known as an 'Eto'), by contrast, was fully electric with lead-acid batteries powering the motor, slower at 30 knots and a range of 50km, but leaving no tell-tale wake.

Dönitz's tenure as 'Weddigen' commander ended at the beginning of 1936, when he relinquished the position to Otto Loycke and was promoted to the post of *Führer der Unterseeboote* (FdU). Despite his advancement, Dönitz still exercised no influence over any aspect of U-boat development, holding only operational control.

During June 1936, the first medium U-boat, the 500-ton Type VII *U27*, was launched; three months later, the 'Saltzwedel' Flotilla formed in Kiel before moving west to the North Sea base at Wilhelmshaven.* Two prototype heavier boats, Type Is *U25* and *U26*, were also attached to 'Saltzwedel', though they ultimately proved an unsatisfactory design.

The first-generation Type VII was a single-hulled, single-rudder U-boat with four bow torpedo tubes and one external stern tube. Despite remaining relatively spartan and cramped internally, the Type VII proved popular with crewmen, it being agile and relatively fast on the surface as well as carrying an 88mm fast-firing deck gun. However, its radius of action was limiting for an ocean-going U-boat – 4,300 nautical miles at 12 knots – and it proved slightly unstable when submerged.

Internally, the pressure hull was divided into three separate compartments by two pressure-proof bulkheads, watertight bulkheads further subdividing the internal space into six rooms. The stern compartment was the stern torpedo and electric motor room, housing the emergency helm that was locked in place to the hull wall, but could be swung into action if required. Headed forwards, next was the diesel engine room, then petty officers' accommodation (*Unteroffizierraum*) with eight bunks, the tiny aft WC, and the small galley that was the domain of the cook (who was known as the *Smutje* within the German Navy) before reaching the central compartment. This control room held navigation and diving controls and access to the conning tower, which was ellipsoid in its aft section and the arc of a circle in the lateral and forward sections, joined together without flat spots, which served to decrease any potential drag during submerged travel. The tower was enclosed within an outer casing, its top crowned with the bridge deck fabricated from 30mm-thick steel plate, welded to the conning tower walls. Within the pressure hull portion of the conning tower were the aft (attack) periscope with hydraulic driving motor, which was used for submerged attacks, the main rudder steering station, and torpedo fire control installation. Externally, the bridge was manned by four lookouts

---

* Named after Reinhold Saltzwedel, who sank 111 ships, totalling 170,526 tons, before being killed in action on 2 December 1918.

with their own 90° quadrant and a Watch Officer who maintained the overview. During torpedo attacks, the First Watch Officer (*I Wachoffizier*, generally abbreviated to 'IWO') would man the surface targeting sight – the *U-Boot-Ziel-Optik* or UZO – while the captain held overall control of events. The stern section of the tower hosted the 20mm flak weapon.

Immediately forward was the tiny commander's 'cabin' to port, separated from the rest of the boat by a simple green curtain, lying opposite the information nerve centre of small radio/telegraphy and hydrophone rooms. The officers' and chief petty officers' quarters (*Oberfeldwebelraum*) were next, and the forward WC. Finally, the forward torpedo room with four tubes also doubled as enlisted men's quarters, where the majority of the crew slept, 'hotbunking' between 12 bunks, with one man rolling into the cot to sleep as its previous occupant rose to go on watch. Each man had a small wooden locker in which to store his few personal belongings aboard the boat.

Though the medium U-boat had shown far greater potential than its larger counterparts, it possessed a relatively modest radius of action and displayed difficult handling characteristics when submerged. Thedsen initiated a series of design augmentations which added 2 metres to its length as well as additional 'saddle tanks' of self-compensating fuel bunkers each side of the hull; these were open at the bottom, allowing diesel oil to float on heavier seawater that entered the tank as fuel was consumed. With expended fuel volume replaced by seawater, potential air pockets that could affect stability were eliminated. This Type VIIB U-boat was capable of a range of 6,500 nautical miles at a surface speed of 12 knots and 90 nautical miles at 4 knots submerged; maximum surface speed increased from 16 to 17.2 knots by adding superchargers to the MAN (Maschinenfabrik Augsburg-Nürnberg) diesels. Furthermore, the single external torpedo tube was removed and placed internally, firing between the new twin rudder arrangement that immediately improved the boat's underwater stability and handling. Torpedo stowage was also increased from 11 to 14, with two pressure-tight canisters between the outer deck casing and pressure hull and a further reload stored beneath the decking for the stern tube. Though only 24 of this Type VIIB were constructed between 1936 and 1940, they would swiftly become a mainstay of the early U-boat offensive.

By contrast, the Type I had proved highly unsatisfactory. Both models, constructed by Deschimag in Bremen, proved to have mediocre turning circles due to a single rudder resting between the prop wash of dual screws. Its diving time was poor, rated at 40 seconds to reach 10 metres when running at full speed with 6 tons of negative buoyancy. Furthermore, depth keeping proved difficult, as the boat's centre of gravity was not in the control room but would be placed, dependent on speed, up to 6 metres forward. The fuel bunkers' vent system also proved unreliable, with air bubbles running forward and aft, further complicating depth keeping as they changed volume with the ambient pressure.

Despite failure of the Type IA, the need for a 'cruiser' U-boat remained, and a new design based on its principles but with improved performance across the board yielded the superior 740-ton Type IX design. This incorporated similar improvements that had upgraded the Type VII to VIIB; the first four were contracted to Deschimag on 21 November 1936 (*U41–U44*).

Roomier than the medium boat, the Type IX still carried four forward torpedo tubes, but two in the stern compartment. Nicknamed the 'sea cow', the large boats were more difficult to handle than their smaller cousins, with a slower diving time that rendered them vulnerable in close-quarter convoy actions. However, the Type IXA was fractionally faster on the surface and had a range of 8,100 nautical miles at 12 knots, increased to 8,700 miles with the Type IXB, and vastly improved with the IXC to 11,000 miles.

In July 1936, a military coup mounted by right-wing General Francisco Franco in Spain led to all-out civil war. Franco appealed to fascist Italy and Germany for assistance, Mussolini despatching immediate military aid, including two submarines. These were the vanguard of the covert *sottomarini legionari* (Legionnaire Submarines), soon an open secret internationally. Ideologically opposed to a communist-controlled Spain, and informed of

Italy's naval commitment, Hitler soon authorized covert military intervention, which led to the formation of the Condor Legion. Among the German commitment were two 'Saltzwedel' U-boats assigned to the clandestine Operation *Ursula*, *U33* and *U34* – codenamed *Triton* and *Poseidon* respectively – slipping from Wilhelmshaven on 20 November 1936. Once at sea, all national markings were removed, the boats passing through the Strait of Gibraltar a week after leaving Germany.

They awaited cessation of Italian submarine operations before beginning their own missions. Italian submarine *Torricelli* had torpedoed Republican cruiser *Miguel de Cervantes*, the damaged cruiser yielding torpedo fragments clearly of Italian origin, igniting an international furore over 'foreign submarines' operating for the Nationalists. Once activated, the U-boat had several attempted attacks foiled by torpedo malfunction, effective target manoeuvring and a lack of positive target identification. Communications with Germany proved laborious, and though they remained undetected, mounting fears of a security breach prompted *Ursula*'s cancellation on 10 December, with both boats ordered back to Germany, their patrol areas being returned to the Italians.

Ironically, it was at this point that *U34* intercepted Republican submarine *C3* near Malaga. *C3* was proceeding surfaced a little after 1400hrs when Harald Grosse mounted a submerged attack with a single G7a torpedo, fearing at first that he had missed as there was no explosion after the expected length of run, until hydrophones detected the unmistakeable sounds of a ship breaking up underwater. Only three of the Spanish crew survived, and despite Republican press reports blaming foreign submarines, naval investigators concluded it was more likely an internal explosion. There had been no explosion betraying torpedo or mine impact, but rather eye-witness reports of a huge cloud of steam or white smoke. The probability is that *U34*'s torpedo failed to explode but sliced through the submarine's pressure hull, causing a battery explosion, the boat breaking in two and sinking rapidly to the seabed 67 metres below. After dark, Grosse surfaced and transmitted: 'Poseidon, 1603 K: AQ 14:19 Sunk red sub type C off Malaga.' It was the first combat success of the Kriegsmarine's

U-boats; both *U33* and *U34* were back in Wilhelmshaven by the third week of December.

Torpedo malfunctions reported by both U-boats caused concern in Berlin. Between the wars, torpedo testing and development rested solely in the hands of the TVA (Torpedo Test Institute) in Eckernförde until Raeder established an independent Testing Command (TEK) to investigate the issue further. Interdepartmental friction between competing agencies subsequently impeded matters, and although the TEK did discover potential irregularities from fresh firing tests, its results were channelled through the TVA to Berlin and their importance downplayed.

Ursula did not mark the end of a Kriegsmarine U-boat presence in Spanish waters, as 15 U-boats visited the country overtly, painted in bold national colours somewhat cynically as part of the Non-Interventionist Committee's multi-national naval presence near Spain's Atlantic coast. These U-boat cruises to Spanish waters provided valuable handling experience for captains and crews, though the civil war prevented planned Atlantic exercises proposed in 1937 by Dönitz to fully test his *Rudeltaktik* methods outside of the relatively cramped Baltic Sea.

Meanwhile, Dönitz pushed for construction emphasis on Type VIIs, which he believed the perfect *Rudeltaktik* weapon. However, naval command disagreed, holding the strategic view that possible future hostilities with Poland and potentially France would require the Kriegsmarine to protect the Baltic and North Seas, suitable for Type IIs, bolstered at the other extreme by larger cruiser U-boats suitable for Atlantic operations and minelaying within the eastern Mediterranean. During 1937, an enlarged Type II carrying improved communications equipment and increased fuel bunkerage yielded the Type IIC (*U56–U63*). Further refinements, notably the addition of saddle tanks that increased the U-boat's beam by 3.8 metres and gave a range of 3,450 nautical miles at 12 knots, would later produce the IID (*U137–U152*).

Frustrated, Dönitz stated unequivocally in 1938 that to successfully wage war against a naval power likely to institute defensive convoys he required 300 operational U-boats, 75 per cent of which should be

Type VII medium boats. With 100 at sea at any given time, 100 could be either inbound or outbound to its operational zone, while the last 100 were overhauled in port. Though supported in his conclusions by Fleet Commander *Admiral* Hermann Boehm, Kriegsmarine leadership doubted the likelihood of defensive convoying, as U-boat operations were already tied to adherence to Prize Law, in which a merchant vessel could not be sunk 'without having first placed passengers, crew and ship's papers in a place of safety'. In this instance, lifeboats were not regarded as such, and German naval instructions stipulated that any merchantman sailing without naval escort had to be brought to a stop, a prize crew placed aboard to determine whether it carried material considered contraband. If so, once the crew and passengers were placed in a 'place of safety', the ship could be sunk. This convoluted process robbed U-boats of the element of surprise and placed them in danger, as the British Admiralty began arming merchant ships, fitting some with naval guns that converted them to 'armed merchant cruisers' or the dreaded Q-ships of the previous war.*

Following assurances from Hitler that war with Britain was unlikely, Raeder had pushed ahead with construction of a balanced fleet, favouring surface vessels over U-boats. The final draft of the so-called 'Z-Plan' was not presented to Hitler until 17 January 1939, intended for completion by 1948. According to this plan, the Kriegsmarine would increase to a size of approximately 800 units centred on an impressive number of capital ships, and the U-boat fleet would increase to a strength of 249 by 1947, including 27 planned Type XB minelayers and a Type XI artillery cruiser (with twin turrets and stored aircraft) and a 2,000-ton Fleet U-boat Type XII, neither of the latter ever progressing past paper.

By 10 March 1939, 72 U-boats had either been built or were in construction, only 48 of them having been commissioned. Just

---

* The Q-ship was a merchant ship heavily armed with concealed weapons designed to lure surfaced U-boats into range before opening fire. However, though feared by U-boat crews, the effectiveness of the Q-ship was somewhat exaggerated. During the First World War, from a total of 150 engagements, British Q-ships destroyed only 14 U-boats and damaged 60 for a loss of 27 of their own.

over a month later, during a bellicose speech given in the Reichstag, Hitler repudiated the Anglo-German Naval Agreement of 1935 that had sought to curb a naval arms race. As international tension increased and the war of words between Berlin and other European states escalated, *Kommodore* Dönitz (promoted on 28 January) spoke directly to Raeder regarding his inability to wage an effective war against Great Britain with so few U-boats, asking that his fears be passed on to Hitler himself. Some of his captains harboured the same view, such as Werner Lott of *U35*:

> Hitler had been impressed on his state visit to Italy in May 1939 by a rather static display of submerged power in Naples Bay and now Hitler wanted to impress him [King] with daring and very mobile manoeuvres. All went well on this exercise around Hitler's Aviso *Grille* and thereafter we all entered Swinemünde Harbour. There the U-boat captains were invited to lunch with him aboard *Grille* where C-in-C Raeder presided and Dönitz was also present. After lunch a most unusual thing happened: Raeder rose, made a few complimentary remarks and then said 'Have you any questions?' I knew him personally well and shot without a second's hesitation the question at him: 'We cannot help feeling that we are drifting towards war – is that really unavoidable?' And he also answered without hesitation: 'Hitler has so far achieved so much in his six years in power that I do not think he will risk all the positive achievements in a hazardous war.' Well, that was in 1939.[2]

By August Dönitz controlled six U-boat flotillas from his FdU command ship *Erwin Wassner* in Kiel:

1st 'Weddigen' Flotilla (Kiel): seven Type IIBs.
2nd 'Saltzwedel' Flotilla (Wilhelmshaven): *U25* (training boat), *U26* (Type IA), nine Type VIIs.
3rd 'Lohs' Flotilla (Kiel): eight Type IIBs.
5th 'Emsmann' Flotilla (Kiel): six Type IICs.

6th 'Hundius' Flotilla (Kiel): seven Type IXAs.
7th 'Wegener' Flotilla (Kiel): eight Type VIIBs.*

Furthermore, the Neustadt U-boat school (relocated from Kiel in May 1937) possessed nine Type II U-boats that could be pressed into active service if required.

Each combat flotilla provided a purely administrative structure, while U-boat command and control were refined beneath the FdU office in Kiel.† From there, Dönitz exercised operational control in outer home waters and the Atlantic, and two geographic sub-commands were created, responsible for localized organizational concerns, including transit to and from German coastal waters and logistics: FdU Ost (based in Kiel) and FdU West (based in Wilhelmshaven), each covering the needs of four flotillas. Commander of the 'Saltzwedel' Flotilla, Hans Ibbeken was appointed FdU West on 18 August, his chief of staff the 'Weddigen' commander Hans Looff. In the Baltic, Oskar Schomburg, a veteran of the previous war, took charge of the post of FdU Nord.

With Dönitz on long overdue leave in Bad Gastein on 15 August, his chief of staff received a telephone call from naval command informing him that a 'party for U-boat officers was to be held on Saturday 19 August and as many as possible were to attend'. This innocuous message warned of likely hostilities and was coded notice for training exercises to cease and 18 Atlantic U-boats prepared for departure to pre-determined patrol stations west of the British Isles. Dönitz opened his FdU War Diary that day: 'The very confident

---

* The remaining flotillas were named after: Johannes Lohs, who sank 76 ships totalling 148,677 tons before killed in action by a mine on 14 August 1918; Hans Joachim Emsmann, who sank 27 ships totalling 9,221 tons (the majority fishing vessels) and was killed on 28 October 1918 while trying to enter Scapa Flow in command of *U116*; Paul Hundius, who sank 67 ships totalling 95,280 tons before killed in action on 16 September 1918; Bernd Wegener, who sank 29 ships totalling 29,402 tons before killed on 19 August 1915, when *U27* was sunk by gunfire from British Q-ship *Baralong*. *Kapitänleutnant* Wegener and ten crewmen survived the sinking but were summarily executed under orders from *Baralong*'s captain, Lieutenant Godfrey Herbert.
† On the other hand, as the number of training flotillas increased during the war, it is worth noting that each fulfilled a specific purpose.

attitude of the crews deserves special mention. In my opinion it is a sign that the broad masses of the people have great faith in the government.'[3]

However, morale alone would not win the war. On 16 August Dönitz was informed that there were insufficient stocks of operational torpedoes despite his 'urging the matter for nearly 4 years'.[4] Furthermore, a profusion of code-words and a flood of orders created some manner of confusion as the Kriegsmarine shifted from peace to a wartime footing. With North Sea patrols not yet ready to begin, Atlantic boats made way towards their stations with 'Hundius' Flotilla commander Werner Hartmann placed in command of *U37*, intended to operate as group tactical commander. 'Wegener' senior officer, Ernst Sobe, was scheduled to reach the Atlantic aboard *U53*, enabling any potential U-boat group operations to be divided into north and south sub-groups.

Dönitz lamented the paucity of his forces. Having desired 300 U-boats before war with England, he possessed only 57. Further raising Dönitz's ire were orders for Type VII minelaying over torpedo patrols. Dönitz vehemently opposed the diversion of any of his slender forces away from a strike at Britain's ocean commerce, but Type VII minelaying was now ordered within the English Channel against strongly defended British troop embarkation ports; French targets not yet sanctioned at the war's beginning. Smaller Type II U-boats, eminently suitable for inshore operations, had already been earmarked for minelaying along the British North Sea coast, and Operation *Ulla* – a rather fluid measure covering patrols at the eastern entrance to the English Channel, later extended to northern harbours and the Great Fisher Bank plus minelaying before British harbours. An interim compromise resulted in only the large *U26* being tasked with sailing around the north of England towards the West Channel to lay mines off either Spithead, the Needles, Portland, Plymouth or in the Bristol Channel, the exact target to be determined later. *U26* put to sea under the command of Klaus Ewerth at midday on 29 August.

With conflict against Great Britain now inevitable, Dönitz submitted yet another proposal – for an emergency building programme of Type VII and Type IX U-boats, with an emphasis on the former. Raeder would not fully read the submitted plans until after the war had broken out, and although he finally agreed, this was a small consolation as war began and, in his memoirs, Dönitz would later write, 'Seldom indeed has any branch of the armed forces of a country gone to war so poorly equipped.'

On the last day of August 1939, *U31* reported three Polish destroyers that were the key target for Baltic U-boats sailing into the North Sea. All available Type IIs of the 'Lohs' and 'Emsmann' flotillas had been assigned patrol areas off the Gulf of Finland and within the Irben Strait, and three 'Saltzwedel' Type VIIs were tasked with minelaying and patrolling off Hela. In the Kattegat, three training Type IIs of Neustadt's U-boat school watched for potential British intervention, standing by to operate defensively against the Soviet Baltic Fleet if conflict in Poland prompted hostilities with the Soviet Union.

However, the Russo-German non-aggression pact rendered the Baltic relatively secure and deployment of the 'Saltzwedel' boats redundant. *U31*, *U32* and *U35* began their return to port to resupply and form a small 'reserve' for relieving the Atlantic force, though *U32* would first be diverted to minelaying in British waters. This left ten small Type IIs to sail into the Baltic.

Before dawn on 1 September, the obsolete battleship *Schleswig Holstein* opened fire on Polish positions at Danzig, and German troops crossed the border. At sea, young captain Fritz-Julius Lemp recorded the event within his War Diary aboard *U30*: 'Negotiations failed. Hostilities against Poland.'* With the British response as yet uncertain, all U-boats were ordered to hold position. At 1550hrs on 3 September they received a new transmission: 'Open hostilities against England immediately, do not wait to be attacked first.'

---

* The U-boat's War Diary was intended to maintain a complete record of the boat concerned. Standing Orders stated that they were to be completed immediately after return from each operation and a new one begun straight away, beginning with the lay days in harbour or dock and continuing until after the next operation.

Chapter Two

War

'*Keep a watch for subs.*'
Captain James Cook to Third Officer Colin Porteous,
Athenia, 3 September 1939[1]

Prize Regulations, based on Article 22 of the 1930 London Naval Treaty, remained enforced by OKM (*Oberkommando der Marine*) on U-boats. However, Dönitz had already noted that enemy convoying, instructions by the British Admiralty for merchants to radio the position of any sighted U-boats and the arming of merchant ships already displayed British willingness to contravene the same treaty rules.

Nevertheless, OKM directed adherence to 'stop and search' warfare, forcing Dönitz to deploy his few Atlantic boats further west of the British Isles than the choke points of shipping bound for ports and harbours. Those assigned coastal water missions, particularly the small Type IIs, were ordered to concentrate on targets clearly permissible to be sunk without warning: troopships, vessels under military escort, or those participating in military actions by, for example, transmitting information.

Aboard *U30*, Lemp and his men had already been at sea for 13 days when war was declared, and the course was set for his operational area northwest of Ireland. Lemp was a popular man among both peers and crew, a jovial, even-tempered 26-year-old who had been born in the Chinese port city Tsingtau. His father was a junior army officer, and the family returned to Germany before Tsingtau fell to Japanese troops in 1914. Lemp enlisted at age 18 as a Reichsmarine officer cadet, appointed commander of *U28* in October 1938. Taking command of *U30* only one month later, he skippered his new U-boat to Spain as part of the overt Kriegsmarine presence and soon gained a reputation as an extremely able seaman who was calm under pressure, evidenced by his coolness and control when *U30* collided with a sister U-boat while running submerged, much of the conning tower torn away and upper deck casing ripped off.

Lemp was also responsible for beginning what would become almost an immediate custom among U-boats. One of *U30*'s radio crew was gifted artist Georg Högel, who Lemp requested adorn the conning tower with a portrait of the captain's beloved dog Schnurzl.* Other U-boats followed suit with emblems (*Wappen*) of choice; some, such as *U47*'s 'Bull of Scapa Flow' and *U96*'s 'Laughing Sawfish', were later adopted by flotillas.

In calm weather, *U30* lookouts spotted prominently marked Norwegian motor tanker *Knute Nelson* during the afternoon, *U30* passing surfaced as tanker crewmen kept a wary eye upon them. Later that afternoon, still some time before a hazy dusk lowered over the horizon, a distant large ship was sighted only ten degrees off the U-boat's starboard bow. Lemp summoned First Watch Officer Hans Peter Hinsch to the conning tower where they studied the approaching vessel, sailing alone on a westerly course. Though unable to discern its identity, as dusk settled it displayed no lights and was steering clearly visible zigzags. Of little doubt of its military nature, Lemp ordered *U30* submerged to periscope depth. *Funkmaat* (Telegraphist) Georg Högel later described what happened next:

> Because of its frequent change of course, the captain already believed that he probably had a troop transport in front of him and ordered an attack with a double shot.

---

* A familiar sight in Wilhelmshaven as he awaited the return of *U30* from patrol, Schnurzl was killed in action on 22 February 1940 when he leapt aboard either destroyer *Z1* or *Z3* as they departed harbour, sunk in error by Luftwaffe bombing and mines.

At this time I was on watch... and I was curious to see our first sharp shots. The first torpedo left the tube and the bright crack of an explosion told us: Hit! But what was wrong with the second torpedo? Except for the torpedo mechanics, all comrades had left the room in a hurry. It was running while still in the tube!

Why? We didn't know, but it had to be released as soon as possible. It carried the newest magnetic warhead! Since our boat was not demagnetized, there was a high risk of explosion. The noise it caused was so loud that it was impossible to report it through the mouthpiece. So, the *Mechanikersmaat* [Torpedo Petty Officer] himself hurried to the *Zentrale* while Gustav [Gentzler] was trying hard between the tubes to get rid of the danger.

Lemp fired a third torpedo. He missed the target.

Gustav asked for more internal air pressure to put pressure behind the tube runner. Only on the second attempt was there finally silence. It had left the tube. A few seconds later there was a huge bang, an explosion in the depths. What happened? When the tube was opened, the rudder rod was found still there, it must have been bent when the torpedo was loaded and jammed in the tube when pushed in. We had every reason to take a deep breath.

But the next surprise awaited me in the radio room. On the international steamer distress frequency an SOS went into the ether: '1,100 passengers on board – *Athenia* – SOS SOS – location ...'

We had hit the 14,000-ton passenger steamer *Athenia* because the commander had got it wrong! And this on the first day of the war![2]

Lemp had torpedoed 13,465-ton *Athenia* of the Donaldson Atlantic Line in direct contravention of operational instructions and in violation of international law. As well as 1,103 passengers – including about 500 Jewish refugees, 469 Canadians, 311 US citizens and 72 UK subjects – *Athenia* was crewed by 315 men and had departed Liverpool the previous day. Captain James Cook was bound for Canada when one of Lemp's torpedoes exploded in No. 5 hold and against the engine room bulkhead on *Athenia*'s port side. The liner began settling by the stern but remained afloat for more than 14 hours as both military and merchant vessels came to her aid, before finally sinking stern first at 1040hrs the following morning. Of the 1,418 people aboard, 98 passengers and 19 crew members were killed.* Controversy still surrounds exactly what happened after the torpedo hit, with eyewitnesses reporting *U30* surfacing and opening fire with its deck gun though German sources dispute this.

Undoubtedly, Lemp had committed a grievous error based almost entirely on his observation that the ship was darkened and steering an irregular course. It was an inauspicious beginning to Dönitz's U-boat war. To compound his error, Lemp, apparently deeply shaken, departed the scene without either providing aid or reporting to FdU. By doing so, German authorities remained ignorant of the event and strongly denied responsibility, as the spectre of the *Lusitania* sinking that had propelled the United States into war in 1917 appeared all too real. Hitler furiously ordered all passenger ships off limits until further notice, and Dönitz falsely assured OKM that all U-boats had reported and disavowed knowledge of the sinking.

Lemp's remaining patrol was of mixed fortune; one merchant was torpedoed, and its survivors assisted with food, water and sailing directions for land, while another, *Fanad Head*, was sunk by scuttling charges. Stopped by gunfire, *Fanad Head* was abandoned, and a boarding party led by First Watch Officer Hinsch searched the vessel for provisions before setting charges in its cargo hold. *U30* had been found short of bread due to a loading error in Wilhelmshaven; once the fresh loaves had been exhausted, canned bread was unpacked and found instead to be powdered milk.

---

* Ironically, she was the second Donaldson Atlantic Line ship of that name to be torpedoed and sunk off Inishtrahull by U-boat; the original *Athenia* was sunk by a torpedo from *U53* on 16 August 1917.

As the German boarders prepared *Fanad Head* for destruction, three Skua aircraft from HMS *Ark Royal,* responding to the freighter's first hurried 'SSS' transmission, attacked and forced *U30* to submerge. Unfortunately, for two of the three Skuas, their shallow diving attacks resulted in the 100lb bombs bouncing off the water's surface and exploding, bringing them down. While both air gunners were killed, the pilots were subsequently rescued by *U30*'s boarding party once the final aircraft departed after causing minor damage and casualties aboard the U-boat and seriously wounding *Maschinenmaat* (Engineering Petty Officer) Adolf Schmidt of the boarding party.

Lemp surfaced and retrieved his boarding party and British prisoners, their task incomplete, as he fired all four bow tubes at the stationary freighter to finish it off; inexplicably, every single shot missed. Finally, the last stern torpedo hit and sent the ship to the bottom.

Of the two Britons, Lieutenant Thurston had suffered severe burns and lacerations, rescued by a German who leapt off *Fanad Head* to save him. Lieutenant (Royal Marines) Guy Griffiths had escaped serious injury and swam unaided to the freighter. He subsequently forged a lasting friendship with Georg Högel:

> We were both very lucky to survive the war, and I still remember your *U30* Captain Lemp and your First Lieutenant [sic] Eichelborn with the black beard, shooting down a cockroach by flicking a lady's garter at the ceiling. 'Another bomber hit,' he called out joking. I lay at night, if you remember, on a bunk near the curtain behind which was, I think, your radio post and noted each evening how contact and messages were received and sent. Lemp allowed me, later on to go up at night on the conning tower to get a bit of fresh air.[*]

---

[*] Letter from Guy Griffiths to Georg Högel, 5 January 1988. It was Chief Engineer Hans-Joachim Eichelborn that was fond of hunting cockroaches with a garter he had 'retrieved' from a French chorus girl. Both Griffiths and Lieutenant R.P. 'Thirsty' Thurston returned to flying duty post-war, though Thurston was killed when the engine on his Seafire cut out as he attempted to land on a carrier deck.

Hunted for seven hours by *Ark Royal*'s destroyer escort, *U30* finally slipped away after being battered by depth charges. Lemp requested and received permission to deliver Schmidt to the German consul at Reykjavik for emergency surgery, the young sailor sworn to secrecy regarding *Athenia*'s sinking.* *U30* departed neutral Iceland with fresh supplies, including a live turkey the crew subsequently named 'Alfons' and who remained within the electric motor room until return to Wilhelmshaven on 27 September. The crew, two prisoners and Alfons were disembarked, and Lemp – debriefed behind closed doors by Dönitz – revealed the truth about *Athenia*. Dönitz accepted Lemp's assertion that he believed he was attacking an armed merchant cruiser as did officers at OKM after Lemp was flown immediately to Berlin to report in person. Deciding that he had acted in 'good faith', no punishment was prescribed, as it may have sent the wrong message to other commanders to curb their aggressiveness and exercise undue caution. He was, however, confined to barracks in Wilhelmshaven and made to study foreign shipping silhouettes.

By 7 September, ten Atlantic U-boats of the 'Hundius' and 'Wegener' flotillas were ordered withdrawn to refit, their return to action planned for October. German intelligence indicated a likely drop in British merchant traffic as convoying was properly established; coastal trade convoys between the Firth of Forth and Thames were established on 6 September, ocean-going trade convoys from Liverpool, two days later.† These initially departed via the South Western Approaches, escort ships attached to a radius of 200 nautical miles west of Ireland (15° West) or to the middle of Biscay for those Gibraltar-bound, whereupon they detached and made rendezvous with inbound convoy traffic. Cruisers and

---

* Schmidt was later captured when British troops occupied Iceland in May 1940 and kept rigidly to his oath of silence.

† Each convoy series received coded designation, these first convoys being: FN for Forth North, i.e., from the Thames to the Forth; FS for the reciprocal Forth South; OA, 'Outward A', from Southend via the English Channel; OB, 'Outward B', from Liverpool and the Bristol Channel; and OG, 'Outward Gibraltar'. The first British convoy to sail was actually OG1 that formed at sea off Gibraltar on 2 October.

armed merchant cruisers occasionally escorted convoys to North America, while in the Western Atlantic the Royal Canadian Navy escorted within a few hundred miles of Halifax, Nova Scotia. However, apart from Gibraltar convoys and until August 1940 and the introduction of the 'SC' (Slow Convoy) route, there was no provision made for merchant ships that travelled at less than 9 knots; instead, they were compelled to sail independently.

Though convoying had helped defeat U-boats of the previous war, during the interwar years the organizational apparatus to create and manage such convoys was dismantled. From 1935 Britain once again began precautionary plans to recreate a new Admiralty Trade Division and Naval Control Service (NCS), the Trade Division officially reconstituted in May 1939 to control the movements and logistical support of all merchant ships and convoys.

Like Dönitz's U-boats, Royal Navy anti-submarine forces had been starved of resources. As late as April 1939, the Admiralty had planned only ten new anti-submarine warfare (ASW) patrol vessels, though Hitler's denouncement of the Anglo-German Naval Treaty led to last-minute orders made in July and August for 56 more. Based on the whale catcher *Southern Pride*, they were built by specialist fishing boat designers Smiths Dock Company of Middlesbrough and led to the creation of the 'Flower' class corvette. By the year's end, 145 had been ordered.

Armed with a single 4-inch bow gun, 40 depth charges on stern racks, a 2-pdr 'pom-pom' (sometimes substituted with a Lewis gun if supplies were short), and a minesweeping winch, the 'Flower'-class corvette proved extremely seaworthy, though capable of a top speed that could not match a surfaced U-boat and incredibly uncomfortable for crewmen; it was cramped, cold and prone to burying its forecastle in oncoming waves, leaving both above and below decks soaking wet and cold. The vessels also rolled almost uncontrollably up to 40 degrees either side of the upright centreline in heavy seas.

A new destroyer designed specifically for escort service – the Type I 'Hunt' class – began launching between December 1939 and September 1940 but soon proved unsatisfactory for ocean-going service and was relegated to home waters. The burden of initial convoy escort duty would fall to the corvettes and whatever craft could be made available.

British warship dispositions were known to the Kriegsmarine thanks to the cryptanalysis department of SKL's (*Seekriegsleitung*) naval intelligence unit known as the *Beobachtungsdienst*, shortened to *B-Dienst*. Created during the mid-1930s, one of its most gifted operatives, cryptanalyst Wilhelm Tranow, had broken the Royal Navy's most widely used five-digit Naval Administrative Code during the autumn of 1935 after working on messages from the Royal Navy's Mediterranean fleet; it remained comprehensively decrypted until 1943. German codebreakers had also broken the merchant navy's cypher system – the British and Allied Merchants Ships (BAMS) code – which remained unchanged for months.

The gathering of convoy OB4 was therefore known to Dönitz; Johannes Habekost's *U31* was directed to intercept, sighting OB4 after passing through the English Channel and into the Western Approaches. Habekost surfaced out of visual range of OB4 and raced ahead of the convoy's predicted path, attacking what he believed was its leading ship from periscope depth the following morning. A single torpedo hit 4,060-ton *Aviemore*, which broke in two and rapidly sank, though the freighter was simply in the wrong place at the wrong time and not part of OB4. Three other U-boats Dönitz had directed towards OB4 also failed to make contact.

As those U-boats ordered to do so withdrew, Dönitz concentrated the remainder to cover the North Channel and Western Approaches. Many ships continued to sail independently, and by the end of September, 43 of these had been sunk. In return, two U-boats had been lost in action northwest of Scotland: Type IX *U39* was sunk on 14 September by destroyers of 8th Destroyer Flotilla following an unsuccessful attack against the aircraft carrier HMS *Ark Royal*, in which premature torpedo detonation betrayed its presence; and Johannes Franz's *U27* was depth charged and sunk also by destroyers of the same Home Fleet flotilla five days later. Franz had attacked what be believed to be British cruisers with three torpedoes, two exploding after reaching arming distance while the third corkscrewed away into the darkness. Franz was shocked to discover that the 'cruisers' were in fact destroyers of the 8th Destroyer Flotilla, and depth charges brought the hastily dived boat to the surface, where it was scuttled. As the entire German crew were rescued, a boarding party from HMS *Fortune* reached *U27* but found nothing of value, as the Enigma machine, secret documents and cypher material had been thrown overboard.

Repetitive torpedo failure quickly became a cause for concern. Doubts regarding the functionality of the newly developed magnetic influence detonator that had been added to the standard electrical contact pistol (Pi1) had been brusquely dismissed by TVA Director Oskar Wehr who implied that 'war nerves' among young commanders were responsible.* But during mid-September, Dönitz was infuriated to learn that, despite previous dockyard assurances that all issued G7e torpedoes had been adapted for angled shots, while gyro-angling gear had indeed been fitted, the tailfins had not received required modifications and therefore would malfunction. Immediate instructions were issued to boats at sea to refrain from angle shooting.

On 14 September, Otto Schuhart reported two torpedoes from *U29* exploding prematurely after reaching minimum safety distance. Initially, Wehr's department blamed navigation error on behalf of the U-boat crew – the magnetic pistol (MZ) set for high sensitivity and the U-boat probably further north than reckoned, thereby under greater effect from the Earth's magnetic poles. Pistol settings were recommended desensitized, suitable for operations in northerly latitudes but uncertain to fire if passing beneath ships less than 3,000 tons. Such vessels would instead require contact pistols (AZ).

Despite this imperfect primary weapon, torpedoes and shellfire were still successful against merchant and military targets. The most impressive of the latter was the sinking of aircraft carrier HMS

---

* The magnetic trigger was based on the British Sinker Mk 1 magnetic mine from the last war, deployed too late in 1918 to prove its worth. The firing circuit was complete apart from a small gap that could be closed by a pivoting magnetic needle. Under external magnetic force, this calibrated needle was attracted by the magnetism, 'dipped' and closed the circuit, firing the weapon by the small electrical current from a generator driven by the five-bladed nose propellor.

Courageous by Schuhart in *U29* on 17 September by a fan of three G7e torpedoes fired at just under 3,000 metres. The carrier was a converted First World War battlecruiser serving with the Home Fleet, and two torpedoes impacted against *Courageous*, which went down in 20 minutes; 518 of her 1,200 complement were killed, including Captain W.T. Makeig-Jones. Escorting destroyers fixed *U29* with ASDIC and pummelled the area with depth charges for four hours, though Schuhart went to 105 metres – below the shallow-set depth charges – and escaped. Hitler would later decorate Schuhart and his crew personally during a visit to Wilhelmshaven, the captain receiving the Iron Cross, First Class, and his entire crew the Iron Cross, Second Class.

Despite France being at war with Germany, U-boats were instructed to refrain from hostile action against French shipping, except in self-defence. Raeder believed that Germany may yet re-establish peace with the French government and U-boats were to 'avoid incidents with France at all costs'. This suspension of action against a major European belligerent remained in force for several weeks, virtually ruling out night attacks, as it was nearly impossible to positively identify ship nationalities. During this period, merchants under military charter shuttled British troops across the Channel unhindered. Following frequent appeals by Dönitz for these restrictions to be removed, SKL relented slightly and allowed enemy convoys to be attacked north of Brittany's latitude, even if under French or French and British escort. Confusingly, however, U-boats were forbidden to act against passenger ships even if escorted, in fearful knee-jerk reaction to public opinion following the *Athenia* sinking. This prohibition lasted until 1 November, when Berlin allowed all ships sailing darkened and in convoy to be attacked without warning.

Prize Regulations had already relaxed in the North Sea, perhaps hastened by the sinking of the neutral Danish *Vendia* by Joachim Schepke in *U3* after he alleged that the Dane had attempted to ram his boat. Though vehemently denied by the Danish captain and crew, OKM upheld Schepke's claim and rejected Danish protests, giving permission to attack any darkened ship sighted near the

English and French coasts.* Finally, Hitler issued Directive No. 5, in which naval warfare against France was authorized to be conducted 'exactly in the same manner as against Great Britain'.

The British Admiralty further played into Dönitz's hands at the beginning of October, when they warned British merchant shipping that, due to several merchant ships firing defensive weapons at U-boats, German retaliation was likely to classify every British merchantman as 'military'. British vessels were therefore ordered to ram any sighted U-boat. 'Thus, the British Admiralty has issued an official and open request to merchantmen for direct participation, in operations by offensive action against warships. The report affords Naval Staff a welcome pretext for preparing further propaganda for an intensification of the U-boat war against merchant shipping.'[3]

By 4 October, the zone in which Prize Regulations had been removed was extended to 15° West, well into the Atlantic Ocean. Greater numbers of British merchant ships were armed in response, and Dönitz subsequently designated several British coastal zones as open to unrestricted submarine warfare, although this emotive phrase remained strictly forbidden by Hitler. At the end of December, OKW issued a directive allowing U-boats to sink all ships without warning in those areas off the enemy coasts where the use of mines was considered possible, believing that torpedoes could not be proved responsible. At the outbreak of hostilities, considerable U-boat strength had been concentrated within the North Sea, the majority Type IIs. These were particularly unsuited to operating within the constraints of Prize Law, possessing inadequate surface armament that was difficult to man in even moderate seas. Correspondingly, they were predominantly directed

---

* Schepke later that same day reported that the Swedish freighter *Gun* attempted to also ram *U3* after a prize crew had boarded and determined it was carrying contraband. During confusion caused by an attack on the stationary U-boat by HMS *Thistle*, Schepke's boarding party unsuccessfully tried to scuttle the Swede before *U3* sank it with a single torpedo.

to act against Royal Navy forces that had relocated to the Hebrides or to undertake minelaying.

Restrictions gradually eroded until, by January 1940, U-boats were free to operate at maximum efficiency, torpedoing suspected enemy ships without warning. It had taken only four months for the Kriegsmarine to reach a state of unrestricted submarine warfare, for which Dönitz would later be charged with 'crimes against peace' at the Nuremberg trials. Amid his defence was an affidavit from Admiral Chester Nimitz who, in his role as Commander-in-Chief, United States Pacific Fleet, had ordered unrestricted submarine warfare on the first day of conflict with Japan.

On 19 September, the position of *Führer der Unterseeboote* was changed to *Befehlshaber der Unterseeboote* (Commander U-boats, BdU). Beneath this new umbrella, Dönitz divided his staff into two distinct branches: BdU *Operationsabteilung* (BdU Ops.), headed by Eberhard Godt (Dönitz's former chief of staff); and BdU *Organisationsabteilung* (BdU Org., known as 2. *Admiral der Unterseeboote* until September 1941), headed by Hans-Georg von Friedeburg. To the latter department went Otto Thedsen as Chief Engineer and head of the Technical Department. Godt's department would handle tactical command of operational U-boats, while von Friedeburg oversaw training, logistics and all personnel matters, both the Neustadt U-boat school and the anti-submarine school placed immediately under his control. Both officers would head these posts until the war's end.

The end of the first wave of combat patrols had highlighted weaknesses within the U-boat service. While pre-war training had generated considerable daring, imagination and ability – any commanders thought hesitant or lacking aggression were immediately removed – some U-boats had not withstood the test. While most limitations of the Type IA had already been established, the Type VII had suffered a number of unexpected constructional weaknesses after several engine beds had failed to withstand prolonged running, and engine exhaust valves were found to be weak and badly designed as they closed *against* external water pressure. Previously forbidden to test dive below 50 metres during pre-war trials, they leaked badly at any greater depth, and subsequent bilge pumping generated unacceptable noise. With a shortage of both dockyard capacity and specialist engineers, repair times frequently became unacceptably extended, and most Type VII boats were subsequently relegated to minelaying missions in British waters.

The Type VIIB had already proved the almost perfect vehicle for Atlantic operations, though an improved model – the Type VIIC – displayed even greater promise. Initial stimulus for the upgrade was installation of new active sonar sound-detection equipment (*S-Gerät*) to augment existing passive *Gruppen-Horch-Gerät* in use since 1935. To do so required the *Zentrale* to be lengthened by 60cm. This allowed enlargement of the conning tower, inclusion of two pressure-tight negative buoyancy tanks to improve diving time, enlargement of the interior fuel bunkers by 5.4 cubic metres and engine enhancements. The Type VIIC would soon become the workhorse of the U-boat arm, the first keel laid down on 11 November 1939 at Kiel's Germaniawerft and launched as *U69* on 19 September 1940.

Equipment also improved. Early U-boats' sighting column for surfaced attacks, known as a TUZA (*Torpedo-U-Boot-Zielapparat*, U-boat Torpedo Target Apparatus) comprised a pair of mounted Zeiss binoculars that transmitted target bearing information to the control room by means of the Bowden cable. Combined with course information, the angle on the bow to target was then calculated and passed verbally to the bridge and the officer at the TUZA. Once the Zeiss binoculars were set atop the sighting column to the prescribed angle, the U-boat was turned to fix its target in the crosshairs, and the launch order was passed to the torpedo room where the weapon was fired manually. A salvo spread of torpedoes was launched by firing torpedoes while the U-boat was still turning.

An early disadvantage of the TUZA was the necessity to demount the instrument before the U-boat submerged; this was rectified when Zeiss developed the TUZA 3, which was pressure-proof up to a depth of 100 metres. However, the TUZA was superseded by the UZO (*U-Boot-Ziel-Optik*) introduced from 1939 onwards, which electrically transmitted target information directly to the torpedo calculator by means of a synchro link rather than verbally from man to man.

The U-boat service quickly identified crucial deficiencies and worked to rectify faults over which it could exert at least advisory control. However, the solution to torpedo malfunction was beyond BdU's control and persisted unchecked as the Torpedo Inspectorate continually deflected responsibility for repetitive malfunctions to commander and crew error. However, premature detonations remained widespread, and by mid-September, the Torpedo Inspectorate began new investigations.

At the beginning of October, they declared that premature detonation in G7e torpedoes had been traced to bad internal cabling, creating an unexpected magnetic field, which could be rectified with a new internal wiring layout. Once more they declared the G7e torpedo suitable for use with magnetic pistols. By contrast TVA engineers declared that G7a premature detonations resulted from unidentified 'mechanical disturbances' and they were not to be used until the issue was identified, and solutions found.

Dönitz expressed strong doubts in the coincidence of both torpedo types suffering different problems. Nonetheless, he cleared the G7e for operational use with magnetic pistols again. Two weeks later, *U46* reported another G7e premature detonation during an attempted convoy attack – one of seven definite failures that left the entire crew visibly depressed upon their return to Germany. Dönitz immediately ordered impact firing only for the G7e torpedo and a cut out switch fitted that disabled the magnetic pistols converting them to contact fuse only. As Dönitz lamented, 'We were thus back where we were in 1914/18. But I had to make this difficult decision to abandon the much-vaunted, much-discussed magnetic firing in order to avoid losing boats, directly or indirectly, through our own weapons and in the interests of U-boat successes.'

The contact pistol was an unnecessarily complicated interwar design reliant on correct depth keeping to function, and Wehr telephoned Dönitz on 20 October with the serious news that in recent tests, both steam and electric torpedoes had run 2 metres deeper than set, thereby passing under their targets when set for impact firing. This issue of fluctuating depth keeping had already been noted by the TVA but thought of little importance with the advent of the magnetic trigger. This problem would remain unsolved until February 1942 during maintenance by the crew of Otto Ites' *U94* during a North Atlantic patrol.* The torpedo crew had been routinely venting their electric torpedoes; periodic battery recharging released hydrogen gas, which required evacuation from mechanical spaces lest sparks from the e-motor cause an explosion after the torpedo was fired.

During this process they discovered a design flaw that leaked air into the weapon's balance chamber that housed a hydrostatic valve controlling the torpedo's depth setting. The valve was therefore subject to ambient air pressure, and submerged U-boats accrued excess internal air pressure through the frequent releases of compressed air for ballast trim and weapon use. The longer the period of submersion, the greater the ambient air pressure passed into the torpedo depth setting, subsequently sending them deeper than expected.

Compounding the issue, the safety device in impact pistols that prevented a torpedo arming near the firing boat was faulty. A small four-bladed propeller at warhead tip was spun by water movement, which brought two detonator contacts together when a set number of revolutions had occurred, putting the torpedo 300 metres from its launch tube. This small propeller also then acted as 'whiskers' of the contact pistol, pushed back by impacting a solid object and firing the explosive charge. However, the propeller blades were of significantly smaller diameter than the torpedo itself. A hit on a flat target – such as Baltic target ships or deep draught vessels – would result in detonation, but striking a curved hull could result in the blades not touching the target, the torpedo then sliding

---

* Ites had served as Watch Officer aboard *U48* under three different commanders before taking his own boat. A fast-rising star of the U-boat service, he was later captured, his interrogators recording, 'Daring and nerveless, he was admired by his crew as a fighter. Friendly and talkative, he made himself one of his men, who referred to him as "Unser Otto" and "Onkel Otto".' He was awarded the Knight's Cross and credited with a confirmed 15 ships sunk, totalling 76,882 tons.

underneath to pass beyond the target ship. The torpedo with this new 'improved' contact fuse that replaced the reliable fuses of the previous war had been tested only twice during 1937 by TVA test firing before being passed for operational use.

Though this second issue was not yet understood, deep-running torpedoes explained several unexplained misses from perfectly aligned impact shots. Torpedoes with contact pistols were ordered set at a maximum depth of 4 metres, ideally 2 metres or less than the draft of the target. To avoid 'surface runners', the minimum depth setting was fixed at 3 metres, or 4 if in an Atlantic swell. The cumulative effect resulted in an inability to attack targets with a draught of less than 5 or 6 metres – for example, small merchants or enemy destroyers. Furthermore, the shallower settings for contact-fused torpedoes also lessened the effect of detonation, higher up a ship's side. By the end of October, the situation was critical as recorded within the BdU War Diary:

> The problem of torpedo failures is unfortunately still far from being solved. *U25* reports four failures at one stopped ship, shots at short range. The Torpedo Inspectorate's instructions were observed. There is therefore no longer any doubt that the Torpedo Inspectorate themselves do not understand the matter. At present torpedoes cannot be fired with non-contact firing units, as this has led to premature detonation... Exact instructions are given for setting the safety range and these are observed. Nevertheless at least 30 per cent of the torpedoes are duds. They either do not detonate at all or they detonate in the wrong place. There does not seem to be any sense in issuing new instructions to the boats as they never lead to the desired results. The Commanding Officers must be losing confidence in their torpedoes. In the end their fighting spirit will suffer. The torpedo failure problem is at present the most urgent of all the problems of U-boat warfare.[4]

The first month of war had highlighted deficiencies of the U-boat service, both expected and unexpected: torpedoes were unreliable, the quantity of combat boats woeful, with older models barely handling the strain of Atlantic operations. To highlight the necessity of an intense building programme, Dönitz offered his resignation as BdU and requested appointment as Director General of a U-boat expansion programme. Wisely, Raeder refused the idea, instead ordering a new U-boat Directorate formed at OKM: SKL-U, under command of *Vizeadmiral* Leopold Siemens. This new department decided future U-boat development paths, construction details and training programmes with no input sought from Dönitz, despite Raeder's contention that it would be 'to all intents and purposes' subordinate to BdU. Though accepting the wisdom of remaining at his post, Dönitz emphatically voiced doubts that such influence could be exercised from below. In this he was to be proven correct, as he was largely excluded from U-boat development and construction until 1943. In fact, as early as November he received a terse memorandum from Raeder, informing him, 'The Commander-in-Chief U-boats is to devote his time to conducting battles at sea and he is not to occupy himself with technical matters.' Albert Speer later wrote in his memoirs that after being appointed Armaments Minister (in February 1942) and also assuming control of the Organisation Todt – Nazi Germany's civil and military engineering organization – following the death in a flying accident of Fritz Todt, Raeder 'tartly forbade Dönitz to discuss technical matters with me.'[5]

However, his training regime had produced skilled submariners – young commanders almost unfailingly aggressive in attack and independently intelligent in all aspects of command and control. The sense of elan with which Dönitz had intended to imbue his arm of service had taken root, and among the first wave of commanders and First Watch Officers were men who would soon become household names, none more feted during those early months than Günther Prien. Prien had been assigned the special mission to penetrate British defences at Scapa Flow on 14 October and attack elements of the Home Fleet. Prien breached the Flow with *U47* running surfaced under cover of darkness, firing a salvo of three bow torpedoes, a fourth lodging in its tube. Two apparently missed, while the third struck battleship HMS *Royal Oak*'s bow and exploded, sending vibrations through the ship and waking the crew. Believing it to be a minor on-board incident, the majority returned to sleep and Prien fired his stern tube, which also missed. Reloaded, he launched a second three-torpedo attack, all three hitting *Royal Oak*, which sank within 13 minutes; 835 men were killed or later died from injuries, the second-largest loss of life from a British warship in the Second World War. By the time British authorities realized it was a U-boat attack, Prien had slipped out of Scapa Flow and was returning to Germany, where Goebbels' propaganda network exploited the success, which even Churchill called 'a remarkable exploit of professional skill and daring', within the House of Commons.* The defences of Scapa Flow had been badly neglected between wars and, combined with harassing Luftwaffe raids that highlighted a woeful lack of anti-aircraft protection, led to the Royal Navy's Home Fleet temporarily abandoning Scapa Flow for the distant anchorages of Loch Ewe, the Clyde and Rosyth until defences could be improved.

Within little over a month, Germany's U-boats had cemented their place in worldwide consciousness, first for the barbarity of the *Athenia* sinking that, despite continuing denials, most believed to have been a German torpedo, and then, for Prien's spectacular attack. By way of counterpoint, Werner Lott's *U35* was even featured on the cover of *Time* magazine during October after Lott rescued the crew of the Greek freighter *Diamantis*. Panicked by a warning shot across their bow, the Greeks hastily abandoned ship and were taken aboard *U35* from lifeboats unsuited for the heavy weather conditions while their abandoned ship carrying iron ore was sunk despite two G7a torpedoes exploding prematurely. Sailing 35 hours out of his way, Lott deposited the crew in neutral Ireland's Dingle Harbour before resuming his patrol, ending in Wilhelmshaven on 12 October with four ships destroyed and a fifth damaged. Lott was reprimanded for endangering his boat by his unauthorized detour to Ireland.

---

* While his entire crew received the Iron Cross in various grades, Prien became the U-boat service's first recipient of the Knight's Cross, awarded on 18 October.

Subsequently ordered on torpedo patrol near the Orkneys in search of Royal Navy targets, Lott's next voyage in November lasted only 12 days at sea. Sighted while running surfaced by destroyer HMS *Icarus* northwest of Bergen, *U35* made an emergency dive as the destroyer approached out of the blinding morning sun, hammered by depth charges as *Icarus* was joined by HMS *Kingston* and *Kashmir* for the hunt. The boat was severely damaged, Lott ordering it surfaced and abandoned; the entire crew of 43 was rescued as their U-boat was successfully scuttled.

Though the only U-boat sunk during November, Lott's was the eighth lost since the war's beginning – five by enemy warships, the remainder by defensive minefields. In return, by the end of November, 108 merchant vessels had been sunk by either mines or torpedoes, totalling over 400,000 tons, the majority sailing independently or straggling from convoys. Furthermore, after September's first wave of attacks, BdU managed a monthly average of ten U-boats at sea during October, 16 in November but only eight during December.

With the impossibility of strangling Britain's trade routes through its inadequate surface fleet, U-boats and aircraft remained Germany's best chance. During October, details of an 'Enlarged U-boat Construction Programme' were laid, which, by March 1943 could be expected to have put at BdU's disposal 308 U-boats, including 75 for training, and accounting for a yearly 10 per cent rate of loss. However, such a plan required complete curtailment of merchant ship construction, abandoning current warship construction of anything above destroyer size, and ceasing all construction of destroyers, torpedo boats, minesweepers and motor-minesweepers. Furthermore, it was conditional of increased numbers of skilled workmen and dedicated service of several building yards and ancillary ammunition and parts suppliers to U-boats alone.

Predictably, given the competing demands of the three main Wehrmacht service arms, and to a lesser degree the Waffen SS, these requirements could not be met, least of all while Hitler had already commanded army expansion for an invasion of France. Instead, the 'Restricted Construction Programme' would come into effect during 1940. Between the outbreak of war and the end of 1939, only six new U-boats were launched: two Type IICs (*U62*, *U63*), two Type VIIBs (*U50*, *U55*) and two Type IXBs (*U64*, *U65*), four of which would complete trials and be commissioned into service before the new year.

Despite lacking Atlantic strength, U-boats had made two attempts at coordinated 'pack' operations. Dönitz had endeavoured to group U-boats for an attack tactically controlled by Werner Hartmann aboard *U37*. After weighing the likelihood of convoy contact against strong ASW surface and air forces, Dönitz opted to gather his group southwest of Ireland, allowing Hartmann operational choice whether to move onwards to the northwest of Spain or west of Portugal due to prevailing weather conditions. The option allowed Hartmann to avoid increasingly bad weather and stronger British forces in the Western Approaches and instead send his group towards Gibraltar, where British merchant traffic funnelled into a constricted area. However, two of the proposed boats were delayed in dockyard repairs, Prien's *U47* diverted to Scapa Flow, and three others – *U40*, *U42* and *U45* – sunk. Wolfgang Barten's *U40* had been ordered to attempt passage through the English Channel if at all possible, striking a mine of British minefield C3 east of Dover. Only nine men managed to escape the U-boat using *Tauchretter* escape gear after it hit the bottom, still lying upright in 22 metres of icy cold water. U-boat crews were trained in the terrifying ordeal of waiting as their boat flooded until the internal water level rose and equalized external water pressure, allowing the opening of the conning tower hatch and egress of the U-boat interior. One man died during the ascent, while three survivors were later rescued by British destroyers which also recovered five bodies. Barten's was the third U-boat lost to British mines laid across the Strait of Dover, causing outbound U-boats to cease using the English Channel as a transit route to the Atlantic, passing instead north of the British Isles, significantly increasing time spent to and from operational areas.

Hartmann's remaining slim force of three boats nevertheless engaged the unescorted northbound convoy HG3 after it was sighted by Herbert Sohler's *U46*. Having departed Gibraltar on 12 October, the 27 merchants were unescorted, and Hartmann vectored *U37* and Herbert Schultze's *U48* towards the target. Hartmann opened his attack at 1535hrs on 17 October, sinking 10,183-ton passenger ship *Yorkshire*; the master, Victor Smalley, 24 crew members and 33 passengers were lost, while 105 crew members and 118 passengers were rescued and later landed at Bordeaux. Twenty minutes after *U37*'s torpedoes had exploded, *U46* fired a G7e torpedo at the *City of Mandalay*, which Sohler had unsuccessfully tried to stop with artillery fire. One torpedo hit amidships in the engine room, the second detonating prematurely, though the steamer had taken enough damage to slowly sink.

Contact with HG3 was briefly lost, Werner ordering a hastily organized patrol line to catch dispersing steamers fleeing north. Herbert Schultze was able to attack one of two sighted steamers that night, sinking 7,256-ton *Clan Chisholm* and unsuccessfully pursuing the second ship, *Sagaing*, before being driven away by destroyers answering urgent distress calls. On 18 October, all three U-boats homed on *U48*'s last reported sighting of HG3, though they were subsequently driven away by British destroyers and aircraft as they neared the Western Approaches. Several torpedo failures were reported by each U-boat as the group was disbanded; and *U48* was ordered back to Germany.

Though Dönitz felt that the value of his *Rudeltaktik* theory had been vindicated, a lack of U-boats had failed to capitalize on this first attempted 'pack' attack. A second in November was also pared down by availability from an expected five U-boats to three. This time, Ernst Sobe aboard *U53* was unable to act as tactical controller, though it was lookouts aboard that boat that spotted convoy traffic to which *U41*, *U43* and *U49* were directed. The latter was forced to break off operations after suffering depth-charge damage, while the other pair achieved some successes against two separate convoys and straggling ships. However, grouping what few U-boats he had at sea allowed vast swathes of uncovered sea through which shipping passed and, penalized by his lack of boats, Dönitz reluctantly cancelled group operations, opting instead to despatch each of his few Atlantic U-boats to different sectors immediately after they were operationally ready.

Three U-boats were also assigned to open a new theatre of operations within the Mediterranean. Although Dönitz would come to resist any diversion of his U-boat strength to this 'peripheral' theatre, he initially favoured the idea. He intended to use the large Type I U-boats for dual minelaying at Gibraltar and torpedo patrol between Oran, where intelligence had reported much convoy traffic. Furthermore, the relatively constricted sea area could engender a certain level of cooperation between U-boats and also force reallocation of Royal Navy and French ASW forces, thereby drawing them away from the Atlantic battleground.

Raeder also possessed a strategic naval view that included control of the Mediterranean, which Hitler consistently failed to grasp. Realizing from the outbreak of war that the Kriegsmarine could not seriously threaten British dominance on the world's oceans, he believed that only by utilizing collaborative strength with the Imperial Japanese Navy, the material supremacy of the Royal Navy could be diluted by necessity to maintain a presence within disparate geographically areas. Raeder had anticipated Japan's likely struggle against British Asian colonialism since Japan and Germany had signed the Anti-Comintern Pact during 1936 to form a united front against Communism. This slowly morphed into Japan's burgeoning antipathy with Britain and the United States, eventually resulting in the Tripartite Pact signed on 27 September 1940. In the interim, Raeder had requested permission to lease some of Japan's large cruiser submarines, alongside bases within the Far East, with which to strike at the trade arteries traversing the Indian Ocean and keeping alive British interests in the Middle East and North Africa. Indeed, although Hitler failed to grasp this most fundamental of issues, German domination of the Mediterranean could lead to control of North Africa and the Middle Eastern oil fields, potentially spreading as far as the southern borders of the Caucasus. From there India, and ultimately the entire Indian subcontinent, lay vulnerable to attack and exploitation. The course of war against Britain thus could have been altered dramatically by

German naval success in the Mediterranean Sea and land victory in Egypt. On 8 December 1939, OKM had formally requested Japanese bases for Kriegsmarine units, but protracted negotiations in Tokyo remained initially inconclusive.

Within the Mediterranean, the new deployment began badly. After attacking French convoy K20 northwest of Finisterre and, despite torpedo failures, sinking 5,874-ton steamer *Baoulé*, Victor Schütze reported failure of *U25*'s main deck gun in action. Furthermore, concussion from the weapon firing had cracked the supporting crosspiece of the forward torpedo hatch, rendering the boat unable to submerge beyond shallow depths. Following unsuccessful attempts to effect repairs, the boat lingered in Biscay, where *Bootsmaat* Wilhelm Lützeler was washed overboard and lost in heavy weather. Disappointed, Schütze returned to Wilhelmshaven.

Left to breach the Mediterranean were *U26* and *U53*, the former tasked with first laying mines across the entrance to Gibraltar harbour but prevented by bad weather, strong searchlights and numerous ASW patrols. Klaus Ewerth aborted the minelay and instead reloaded with torpedoes and eased through the Strait of Gibraltar under cover of darkness and with the eastward surface current adding as much as 4 knots to the U-boat's speed. Once within the Mediterranean, *U26* roved south of Almeria where Ewerth reported sinking 4,285-ton *Loire* carrying 5,588 tons of pyrite and 416 tons of wine, with a single stern shot after one torpedo failure. The French ship was lost with all 39 men aboard, nothing but debris found by French warships four days after *Loire* disappeared. It was Ewerth's sole success, and after ten days within the Mediterranean, *U26* returned to the Atlantic; the only U-boat of the Second World War to successfully traverse the Strait of Gibraltar in both directions.

The third of the planned Mediterranean boats, *U53*, achieved little, shadowing a convoy off Lisbon for 36 hours and issuing constant position reports before being driven off by escorting destroyers. Returning to Germany without attempting to pass into the Mediterranean, Ernst-Günter Heinicke sank nothing and was judged by Dönitz to have acted with insufficient aggression and relieved of his command, posted to the auxiliary cruiser *Widder*. The U-boats' first Mediterranean foray had been a dismal failure.

Meanwhile, torpedoes continued to vex the few U-boats in action. On 5 November, a newly adapted magnetic pistol was issued, the Pi(A-B), which sought to stabilize the dipping needle, preventing premature detonation. However, after *U28* and *U49* were equipped with the new pistol, they both reported continued malfunctions either through premature detonations or a failure to fire. The premature detonations of two torpedoes fired by Kurt von Gossler's *U49* had also resulted in severe depth charging, during which the boat sank to a perilous depth of 170 metres before slipping free.

Despite repeated vehement denials of having issued faulty weaponry, Oskar Wehr was dismissed from directorship of the TVA and replaced by the more energetic *Admiral* Oskar Kummetz, with torpedo specialist Dr E.A. Cornelius appointed 'Torpedo Dictator'. The two instigated fresh test firing against U-boat tender *T123* that proved magnetic pistols failed to fire when shot under the ship's keel. Complicated interim operating instructions to potentially minimize failures were passed via BdU to commanders, although none were successful. Dönitz recorded that:

> Commanding Officers' and crews' confidence in the torpedo is very much shaken. Again, and again the boats have tried, in the face of strong enemy activity, to fire their torpedoes under the best possible conditions and often when they have made a daring attack they have been rewarded with failures and even danger to themselves. At least 300,000 tons, which might have been sunk, can be reckoned lost through torpedo failures... It is very bitter for Commanding Officers and the executive control to find that the U-boat Arm cannot achieve the success expected of it, despite a thorough peacetime training, because of torpedo failures.[6]

Chapter Three

The Myth of the 'Happy Time'

'So, this is called the happy time? I don't know why.'
Otto Kretschmer, U99[1]

The issue of maintaining U-boats within the Atlantic operational area occupied BdU as Dönitz tried to maximize his available U-boats. After difficult negotiations, one potential solution emerged when the Spanish government begrudgingly allowed German resupply points to be established in Cadiz, Vigo and El Ferrol. Franco's declaration of strict neutrality negated open resupply in Spanish harbours, despite German Naval Attaché in Madrid Kurt Meyer-Döhner having amassed enough stores to provide a healthy supply network for U-boats. Unwilling to flagrantly breach the laws of neutrality, Spanish authorities instead allowed covert resupply points to be established. Five German merchant ships were strategically 'interned' in mainland Spain and within the Canary Islands, each laden with supplies and part of Meyer-Döhner's secret supply service that comprised just one facet of the German *Ettapendienst.*[*] In Vigo lay the ship *Bessel* (codenamed *Bernardo*); *Max Albrecht* in El Ferrol (codenamed *Arroz*), *Corrientes*

---

[*] Established in 1896, the *Ettapendienst* (Supply Service) was broadly charged with supplying the raw materials with which Germany could wage war, drawing on the combined resources of the navy, diplomatic corps, business and industry. Also tasked with supplying ships at sea – notably Germany's commerce raiders – the service operated dummy companies and bank accounts in virtually every country in the world.

(codenamed *Lima*) and *Charlotte Schliemann* (codenamed *Culebra*) in Las Palmas; and *Thalia* (codenamed *Moro*) in Cadiz. A sixth – *Lipari* – was refitted for the task in Cartagena, but never used. It was to Cadiz that Dönitz despatched his first U-boat to resupply.

Initially planned for *U44*, which had already mounted a successful patrol sinking seven ships thus far and an eighth shortly after, the idea was aborted when it became apparent that should *U44* fail to successfully refuel, it would lack sufficient fuel to return to Germany. Instead, Schütze's *U25* was directed to refuel from *Thalia*, which it did successfully on the night of 30 January, the first of six U-boats that the tanker would replenish. The boat entered the harbour under cover of darkness, trimmed down with decks awash and, despite an offshore breeze and slight swell, within six hours it was ready to depart with fresh food and fuel aboard.

On 23 February, Raeder proposed in conference with Hitler that two U-boats armed with torpedoes and mines operate off Halifax, Nova Scotia, though the Führer refused due to the potential psychological effect upon the United States. Instead, Raeder asked for a decision on whether the operation of U-boats in the Mediterranean would be politically practicable, Hitler wanting first to obtain Mussolini's agreement. Hitler directly asked whether such a deployment would have a 'decisive effect on the conduct of the war', Raeder stating that, in his estimation, the cumulative effect of *all* U-boat operations against unescorted and unprotected ships would be decisive and that denial of U-boats in the Mediterranean or near Halifax would limit the effect of the U-boat war appreciably.

Meanwhile, waters west and northwest of Spain were allocated to a small number of new Type VIIBs whose training had been cut short by difficulties with ice in the Baltic. The harsh winter of 1939/40 caused severe icing of harbours and channels in and around the Baltic, delaying training regimens as well as inflicting some measure of damage to U-boats in transit, despite the use of obsolete battleships and tugs as icebreakers. A wooden 'shoe' fitted over U-boat bows helped protect torpedo tubes and forward hydroplanes, but unexpected dockyard repairs became relatively frequent. Rather than postpone active deployment of freshly trained commanders until scheduled working up and firing practice was completed, BdU instead directed them to operate west of Spain where Allied ASW forces were judged to be relatively thin. Despite some success, three of these new boats were among the eight sunk between January and March.

Otherwise, the first months of 1940 were dominated by minelaying outside major British harbours. Faith in torpedoes had been badly shaken, and when Lemp's *U30* skilfully penetrated the destroyer screen around HMS *Barham* and *Repulse* as they sailed near the Flannan Isles to re-join the Home Fleet's 2nd Battle Squadron, a near-perfect submerged attack resulted in three out of four G7e with magnetic pistols malfunctioning or missing. Only one hit battleship *Barham* forward on the port side in the vicinity of 'A' and 'B' shell rooms, killing four men and wounding another. Escorting destroyers failed to make ASDIC contact with *U30*, which departed to continue its planned minelaying off Liverpool. The damaged *Barham*, meanwhile, trimmed down by the bows by 10 feet, also made its way to Liverpool where it faced three months of repairs. From there, *Barham* would later sail for Gibraltar and Mediterranean service. Lemp's 12 TMB mines that he laid with great precision later succeeded in sinking a tanker and three freighters, further damaging a fourth and forcing a brief closure of Liverpool harbour until it could be effectively swept.

During January, BdU restructured and reorganized the six existing combat flotillas. Plans that referenced the modified U-boat construction programme envisioned a future total of 14 front-line flotillas, each of 25 U-boats. With this in mind, Dönitz focussed available U-boats into fewer flotillas – six condensed to three – that now bore solely numerical designations rather than the illustrious names of the previous war's U-boat heroes: 'Weddigen' Flotilla (Kiel – Type II) was redesignated 1st U-Flotilla; 'Saltzwedel' Flotilla (Wilhelmshaven – Type VII) redesignated 2nd U-Flotilla; 'Lohs' and 'Emsmann' Flotillas (Type II) were disbanded and their boats transferred to 1st U-Flotilla; 'Hundius' Flotilla (Type IX) was disbanded and all boats transferred to 2nd U-Flotilla; 'Wegener' Flotilla (Kiel – Type VII) was redesignated 7th U-Flotilla.

On land the war appeared to have largely stagnated following the fall of Poland. While the Soviet Union embarked on its ill-considered invasion of Finland, in France Allied troops manned emplacements opposite the German border with little direct action between the combatants. However, behind the scenes, Hitler had already agreed a refined plan to invade France through Belgium while also occupying The Netherlands. Codenamed *Fall Gelb*, this final version entailed a main thrust made through the inhospitable terrain of the Ardennes, proving dramatically successful when launched in May.

However, while Wehrmacht attention was directed west, fears of a surprise British occupation of Norway threatening Germany's northern flank steadily increased in Berlin. On 15 February, the Royal Navy ignored Norwegian neutrality to rescue 299 captive British sailors from the German ship *Altmark* moored within Norwegian territorial waters. Hitler rightly believed that this demonstrated Allied ambivalence towards Norwegian neutrality rivalling even his own and promptly ordered the occupation of Norway and Denmark to take priority over France and the Low Countries. The invasion, codenamed *Weserübung*, was confirmed; *Wesertag* was set for 9 April, fully endorsed by Raeder, convinced that Great Britain would sever Scandinavian exports to Germany, bar access to the Atlantic and hinder operations within the North Sea. By British occupation of Norway, pressure could be applied on Sweden, choking the flow of merchant shipping to Germany and possibly even forcing Sweden into the war on the side of the Allied powers.

In this instance, Raeder was correct, as Allied planning to neutralize Norway was already well advanced. The Allied Supreme War Council had met in Paris on 5 February to discuss sending an expeditionary force to aid Finland against Soviet aggression. Any such force could only reach Finland after disembarkation in Norway, passing through Sweden once permission had been secured. By landing in Narvik, the all-important Swedish Gällivore iron-ore mines could be occupied while troops moved east, under the guise of maintaining Allied communication lines. Despite potential confrontation with Russia, plans were finalized, and British forces gathered in Scotland as French transport ships assembled in Brest and Cherbourg.

As news of the Allied application for transit rights to Finland, and Sweden's subsequent refusal on 12 March, became known internationally, Scandinavian countries urged Finland to accept armistice terms offered by the Soviet Union. Despite Britain's continued encouragement to resist, Finland sued for peace with the Soviet Union on 13 March. The pretext for the Allied plan now lost, an alternative was adopted. To frustrate the flow of trade to Germany through Norwegian territorial waters, British and French ships would lay mines along the Norwegian coast, forcing German shipping offshore and outside neutral waters where they could be attacked by the Royal Navy. This was in contravention of an agreement signed between Great Britain and Norway on 11 March 1940, by which exports to Germany, even of contraband, were permitted providing they did not exceed the levels of 1938 trade.

The mining operation was set for 5 April. The second stage was Operation *R4*, the landing of the 18,000 Anglo–French troops originally earmarked for Finland at Stavanger, Trondheim, Bergen and Narvik in response to the expected German reaction to Allied infringement of Norwegian neutrality. The troop convoys were scheduled to begin sailing on 8 April, and at 0600hrs that morning, the Norwegian government was informed of the minelaying within Norwegian territorial waters. In Berlin this was greeted with a certain degree of satisfaction, providing a small measure of public justification for the impending German invasion, now labelled a reaction to Allied intentions.

On 4 March, BdU received orders to cancel all further U-boat departures, those already at sea instructed to avoid proximity to the Norwegian coast. The planned transfer of some older boats to the Neustadt U-boat school was cancelled as was major repair work, those U-boats in shipyards patched up to enable functionality. Training boats were brought to operational readiness, as every available U-boat would be utilized to assist the Kriegsmarine's ambitious *Weserübung* strategy. Due to dockyard delays, only 12 Type VII and Type IX U-boats were operationally ready as well as one of the unsatisfactory Type IAs. Twelve smaller Type II U-boats were utilized, six of them from Neustadt, disrupting training exercises in the Baltic. For personnel that were in Neustadt awaiting transfer to a combat unit, during February, the *Unterseeboots-Ausbildungsabteilung* (UAA) was formed in Plön under the command of former First World War U-boat commander, and holder of the *Pour le Mérite*, Hans Rose.

The U-boats' task was threefold: they were to cover warships and troop landings along the Norwegian coast, counter the expected Allied invasion force, and drive off enemy naval forces threatening maritime communication lines to Germany. An insufficient number of U-boats necessitated stationing in open sea within reach of multiple threatened areas. To this end, Dönitz divided his forces into nine separate groups:

> Group One (deep echelon covering Narvik, Harstad, Westfjord, Vaagsfjord): *U25*, *U46*, *U51*, *U64* (initially acting as escort for commerce raider *Orion* heading for the Atlantic), *U65*
>
> Group Two (inner approaches to Trondheim, Namsos, Romsdalsfjord): *U30*, *U34*
>
> Group Three (two boats in deep echelon at each harbour entrance, a fifth directly off Bergen): *U9*, *U14*, *U56*, *U60*, *U62*
>
> Group Four (one boat immediately before Stavanger, the other covering outer approaches and Haugesund): *U1*, *U4*
>
> Group Five (east of the Shetland Islands to intercept Allied troop ships and cover Vaagsfjord and Trondheim): *U37* (initially relieving *U64* of *Orion* escort duties), *U38*, *U47*, *U48*, *U49*, *U50*
>
> Group Six (Pentland Firth, Orkney Islands, Shetland Islands to intercept enemy warships): *U13*, *U57*, *U58*, *U59*
>
> Group Seven (planned to patrol the eastern entrance to the English Channel, but never assembled)

Group Eight (Stavanger, Lindesnes, Egernsund): *U2*, *U3*, *U5*, *U6*
Group Nine (Bergen, Shetland Islands) *U7*, *U10*, *U19*

The first U-boats began departing on 3 April, all commanders unaware of *Weserübung* but carrying sealed orders to be opened on receipt of the code-word 'Hartmut' from BdU. There were also four U-boats – *U17*, *U23*, *U24*, *U61* – unavailable at the outset but beginning patrols once *Weserübung* was under way. Generally operating near Bergen or the Orkney and Shetland Islands, none were successful. The larger boats *UA*, *U26*, *U29*, *U32* and *U43* would be used for running fuel and ammunition to German troops ashore, when they became operationally ready. The 1,128-ton minelayer *UA* had been built to a modified Type IX specification as the Ay-class for the Turkish Navy and was intended to be named *Batiray*. The third of four ordered – the first two already in Turkish service – with every possible boat of value to Dönitz, *Batiray* was instead taken over by the Kriegsmarine, its mineshafts converted to fuel tanks and commissioned as *UA* into the 'Wegener' Flotilla on 20 September 1939.[*]

In due course, *Weserübung* was, for U-boats, an unmitigated disaster. Four directly involved in 'Hartmut' were lost: *U1* and *U50* both to a British minefield north of Terschelling; *U64* bombed and sunk in the Herjangsfjord northeast of Narvik by an aircraft from HMS *Warspite*; *U49* sunk northeast of Harstad by depth charges from British destroyers HMS *Fearless* and *Brazen*.

In return, *U37* sank three solo sailing merchants, *U13* another pair during its patrol, *U59* a single Norwegian freighter, and *U34* torpedoed Norwegian minelayer *Frøya*, which had already been damaged and beached at high speed near Søtvika. The only Royal Navy vessel destroyed was submarine HMS *Thistle*, sunk with all hands by Hans-Peter Hinsch's *U4* who hit it near Skudenes with a G7e in the early hours of 10 April.

---

[*]   Of the two Turkish boats, *Atilay* was commissioned in 1940, while *Yildiray* was only completed post-war. *Atilay* was lost with all hands after accidentally striking a mine from the First World War Dardanelles campaign on 14 July 1942.

As a means of preventing Allied counterattack against Kriegsmarine surface forces, the U-boats' failure was absolute. No more so than at Narvik, where the Royal Navy sank eight German destroyers and the ammunition ship *Rauenfels* in two separate attacks with no loss to themselves. Where U-boats intercepted warships or troop transports and pressed home desperate attacks, they were rewarded with perpetual torpedo failures. Dönitz had despatched his most experienced commanders to the furthest battlefield points, and among the multiple torpedoes launched by U-boats, Günther Prien in *U47* recorded multiple close-range torpedo attacks in which torpedo malfunction foiled every shot. At one point *U47* ran aground and was prepared for scuttling as an enemy trawler approached flashing Morse signals, apparently awaiting reply. Narrowly escaping identification and attack, with one diesel failing with a loud bang at the most inopportune moment as the engines strained to move *U47*, Prien finally managed to free his boat from its predicament and narrowly escaped into deeper water.

The battle for Narvik remained Germany's most precarious of the Norwegian campaign and a successful attack by Prien on Allied troop transports may well have had severe consequences for the Allies whose landings were unmolested. Dönitz was furious and recorded in the BdU War Diary on 16 April:

> At 0410 a report was received from *U47* [Günther Prien] that she had found the transports at anchor in Bygden (Vaagsfjord). Four misses! *U65* had already fired a double shot (most probably at close range therefore) without success. I am now beginning to suspect that even the use of impact firing is not preventing torpedo failures. Either the G7e is keeping a much greater depth than hitherto known or the pistol does not arm. A second report from *U47* confirms this idea: in a second attack on the transports another four torpedoes failed to fire. This means a total of eight unsuccessful shots by our best U-boat commander. It is quite clear to me that these failures are responsible for the commanding officer's lack of success.

U-boats were clearly unsuited to the task of coastal defence against enemy warships due to restricted vision and speed. Although constricted Norwegian waterways funnelled the enemy into potential killing grounds, over 40 separate torpedo attacks were launched against warships and troop transports without any success. Though Norway capitulated on 10 June, U-boats returned to port with the morale of officers and men at its lowest ebb.

Although OKM released U-boats from Norwegian commitment on 26 April, Dönitz questioned committing them to action anywhere with proven faulty weaponry. Conversely, he reckoned incalculable harm would be inflicted on the U-boat service were it to be suddenly demobilized. Immediate enquiries were held, headed by Kummetz. These appeared to confirm that the Earth's magnetic field at northern latitudes (referred to as 'Zone O') interfered with the MZ trigger, desensitized to counteract British degaussing of ships. Hastily arranged experiments at TVA also proved that the AZ unit of the Pi1 pistol suffered a high percentage of failures, primarily the premature release of the firing pin. Furthermore, reliance on contact pistols was foiled by deep-running torpedoes. The frustration at BdU was expressed within the War Diary:

> The results are staggering. After twenty years of peacetime work one might have expected a torpedo better than the one used in the last war, a torpedo, for instance, capable of sinking a battleship with one shot (like that shot at *Barham* on 28 December) ... I do not believe that ever in the history of war men have been sent against the enemy with such a useless weapon.[2]

Dönitz demanded a simplified pistol built, the recent capture of British submarine HMS *Seal* having provided working examples of such a device, which was immediately copied.

The end of *Weserübung* and heavy damage to surface ships caused severe overcrowding in German shipyards and, correspondingly, Dönitz's men played little part in the successful invasion of The Netherlands, Luxembourg and Belgium (*Fall Gelb*) launched on 10 May and the subsequent conquest of France (*Fall Rot*), accomplished with a speed that surprised even the Germans. On the eve of *Fall Gelb*, rising star Wolfgang Lüth in *U9* – adorned with a copy of Otto Weddigen's 'Iron Cross' on the conning tower – sank French submarine *Doris* during a patrol of the Dutch and Belgian coasts.

Luxembourg was subdued in one day, and within four The Netherlands had surrendered, Belgium following suit two weeks later. Britain's troops and some allies were evacuated from Dunkirk and its environs in Operation *Dynamo*, swiftly followed by Operation *Aerial* from the French Western Atlantic ports. It was a stunning defeat, fought primarily on land and in the air, with the Kriegsmarine playing at best a peripheral part, even during the Allied maritime evacuation.

The perilously slim strength of the Kriegsmarine after its severe losses in Norway left naval action against the Dunkirk evacuation traffic in the hands of U-boats and S-boats (*Schnellboote*, equivalent of a Royal Navy Motor Torpedo Boat), though use of the former within the shallow-water region was constrained by navigation difficulties and strong British defensive measures. Both *U29* and *U101* outbound to the Atlantic west of the Orkneys and Hebrides had been ordered to operate in the English Channel towards the end of May. Cross-channel traffic was expected to increase from Le Havre and Cherbourg with potentially larger ships, but the western approach to the Channel proved perilous due to constant fog. Both boats were ordered to the Finisterre area instead, and plans to send other boats to the Channel were cancelled. Hans-Bernhard Michalowski's *U62* scored the sole U-boat success against *Dynamo* on 29 May, when it torpedoed HMS *Grafton*. The destroyer had come to the aid of HMS *Wakeful* that had been steaming along 'Route Y' used for *Dynamo* traffic before being torpedoed and sunk by *S30*.

On 10 June Norway capitulated following the Allied withdrawal from Narvik, with Italy plunging its tiny ineffectual dagger into France and declaring war on the Allied powers that same day. Border skirmishes followed in faraway North Africa between British forces in Egypt and Italian troops within the Libyan Cyrenaica province, an Italian colony since 1912. Four days later Paris was surrendered to the Wehrmacht, and on 22 June France signed an armistice that came into force three days later. U-boats received radioed instructions that hostilities with France would cease from 0135 on 25 June, German summertime, although 'French ships which continue to proceed under escort or without lights or are obviously making for British ports are still to be treated as enemy.'[3]

Following the capitulation of the French Atlantic coastal cities, only the Ouessant Islands remained in Allied hands, with over 2,500 French and English troops that had evacuated the mainland gradually trickling away to England aboard any available vessels. Finally, on 5 July 1940, three days after the surrender of the last French soldiers still manning the redundant Maginot Line, a single German *Kapitän zur See* supported by 15 sailors arrived to take the surrender of Ouessant and its remaining 224-man garrison, marking the definitive end of the battle for France.

With many British destroyers and escort vessels suffering damage during the withdrawal from France, and the fact that war with Italy meant increased Mediterranean activity, the pressure on the Royal Navy became extreme. As German forces began visible preparations for a cross-channel invasion of Great Britain, many of the overworked British destroyers were held in the 'Narrow Seas', acting as a potential anti-invasion barrier and thereby depriving Atlantic convoys of crucial escort vessels.

For Dönitz, U-boat construction was not keeping pace with promises made by Hitler in conference with Raeder on 21 May. Raeder had enquired whether the likelihood of a long war justified the withdrawal of some older combat U-boats to training purposes alongside disengagement of those U-boats from the Neustadt school in action against Norway. Otherwise, new U-boats constructed faced the prospect of having no trained crews. Hitler agreed, intending to have construction emphasis moved to U-boats and the Junkers Ju 88 programme following the end of hostilities in France and a proposed partial army demobilization. The emphasis failed to materialize, and by the end of June considerable delays in U-boat construction were primarily due to a shortage of allocated labour and materials. With increased use of subsidiary shipyards overseen by a central construction office at Germaniawerft, a lack of naval supervisory personnel to advise many yards inexperienced in the high tolerances demanded by U-boat construction, and a subsequent 'loaning' of specialized personnel between yards added to delays. By the end of June, only 12 new boats had been commissioned thus far in 1940, while 18 had been lost.

Accelerated U-boat construction with new shipyards was creating its own problems, as evidenced by an interrogation report of crewmen from *U76*, built at Vulkan Werke, Vegesack, and sunk on its first patrol in 1941.

> Prisoners stated that a defect occurred in the compressed air system in the Control Room; this was said to have been caused by a fractured bolt in a coupling between the high pressure and low-pressure systems. Another defect mentioned was bad welding near the exhaust, which was said to have become defective owing to exhaust pressure. An E.R.A. stated that the cap over the exhaust would not function, so that water entered the U-Boat while submerged. Trouble with the Diesels was also mentioned. During discussion on the subject of defects, prisoners severely criticised the construction and hasty commissioning of new U-Boats.[4]

To restore the flagging morale of U-boat crews, Dönitz chose one of 'Weddigen's' earliest commanders and now BdU staff officer Victor Oehrn to restart the Atlantic campaign. He replaced *U37*'s veteran commander Werner Hartmann, Hartmann 'cursing like a tugboat captain' at being posted ashore to replace Oehrn at BdU, though perhaps mollified by the award of the Knight's Cross for the destruction of nearly 80,000 tons of enemy shipping in action.

Hopes that torpedo pistol adjustments would yield positive results were dashed after a report from *U37* on 22 May listing four failures from five torpedoes fired; two exploding prematurely, two failing to fire. It was the last straw for Dönitz: 'The latest explanations and theories of the technical branches to account for these failures henceforth carried no weight with me at all. I refused any longer to burden U-boats with these wretched things, and forthwith forbade all use of magnetic pistols.'[5] Despite this discouraging start, Oehrn sank ten ships, totalling 41,146 tons, through a combination of torpedoes, shellfire and scuttling charges, and damaged one other before returning to Germany on 9 June, going a long way to breaking the negative spell cast by *Weserübung* and kickstarting in earnest the Battle of the Atlantic.

Newly occupied territory promised enormous possibilities. While Belgium and The Netherlands were dismissed as potential U-boat bases due to proximity to Britain, in Norway Trondheim and Bergen began operating as staging and repair bases, extending the range of outbound U-boats into the Atlantic and relieving some pressure on German shipyards. Narvik would later become an important centre for operations within the Arctic Ocean. Crucially, the fall of France provided U-boats with Atlantic ports, and before the armistice had been signed BdU had already despatched staff officers to scout likely locations. With U-boats stationed on the edge of the Atlantic, laborious – and potentially dangerous – circumnavigation of Great Britain would no longer be required for every patrol and, resupplied in France, U-boats could reach further into the Atlantic beyond British air cover. Furthermore, given Dönitz's 'hands-on' style of command in which he met his U-boat skippers to fully grasp the situation in action, a suitable site was sought for BdU headquarters which would allow this kind of face-to-face command that had forged such a strong bond between him and his men.

Ultimately, five ports were selected: Brest, Lorient, Saint Nazaire, La Pallice (the port for La Rochelle, the only deep-water port of the French Atlantic coast) and Bordeaux. Each had already hosted French naval forces; the first two were perhaps the most significant naval installations of the French Atlantic coast. Anti-aircraft guns were installed in preparation, and two French admirals remained on official duty in Brest and Lorient, their cooperation with German officials noted as 'satisfactory' by SKL. Local French workers from the state dockyards and dockyard control declared themselves willing to work under Kriegsmarine direction, and in France, some 2,000 men worked for the Kriegsmarine, greatly relieving pressure on oversubscribed repair and refitting within German shipyards.

A freight train carrying 24 torpedoes, air pumps, torpedo maintenance material and technicians departed Wilhelmshaven for Paris under the command of Wilhelmshaven Naval Dockyard's Torpedo Director, Clamor von Trotha. From Paris it could be quickly directed to any point on the French coast as required, as engineers of the MAN (Maschinenfabrik Augsburg-Nürnberg) were immediately despatched to Lorient to begin reinforcing fishing boat shipways and the central turntable within the *Port de Commerce* for Type II U-boat tonnage.

The centre of the Lorient U-boat base lay within the French military arsenal nearly 5 kilometres from the narrow entrance channel between Port Louis and Larmor Plage, upstream along the Scorff River. Past the small fishing port of Kéroman that lay at the junction of the Le Ter waterway and the Scorff, the arsenal already housed two large dry docks, each capable of accommodating a pair of Type IXs, though dangerously exposed to British air attack. Also lying on the Scorff River, past the Gueydon Bridge, a degaussing range was scheduled for construction opposite disused French building yards, allowing demagnetizing of U-boats and small Kriegsmarine vessels. Mines and torpedoes arrived via Paris, stored initially within dockside buildings on the Scorff's southern bank, to be loaded aboard U-boats by barge. While French naval accommodation existed, it was soon found to be almost uninhabitable as it was littered with refuse and human waste. Instead, men would be accommodated in small hotels.

Initially, relations with the local Breton inhabitants appear to have been relatively cordial, as Bernard Geismann of *U107* later recalled: 'We were actually warmly received by French civilians, and we soldiers were under strict instructions to behave well towards the population.'[6]

Minesweeping protection was provided by newly arrived *Räumboote* (motor minesweepers) of 2nd R-Flotilla, and the first U-boat to enter Lorient was Lemp's *U30*, which arrived after nearly a month in the

Western Approaches during which he had sunk five ships. For six days, the boat received minor repairs as the crew lived in the small Breton hotel *Le Pigeon Blanc*, enjoying bars, cafes and brothels only recently vacated by French and British troops. Georg Högel, one of *U30*'s radio operators, was among those first German sailors in Lorient:

> July! It was hot. In the naval barracks, we searched the room for useable uniforms. With our journey our clothes were in no fit state, so oily and greasy after weeks of sailing... We found combs, toothbrushes, hats (with the red pompoms), white and blue striped shirts, shoes; everything was there, piled high, as if the French wanted to annoy us with it all... We also found closets and looked for suitable blue gear; trousers, a jacket. We buttoned the black, white and red Iron Cross ribbon into the button hole, put on our side caps and were almost German – half French but at least neatly dressed... Lemp came back from Brest. The officers of the boat had brought wonderful fur vests from captured booty for the crew. We made a trip to Rennes in several cars, but we no longer wore the dark blue, thick navy clothes, but English battle dress... We came across stacks of English battle dress, khaki-coloured, light and easy to wear within the barracks area.[7]

Despite the retreating British troops having poured acid over piles of abandoned battledress, enough remained useable, and with German clothing still en route in the flotilla transport train, it was in this distinctive khaki uniform that Lemp and his crew took *U30* back to sea to patrol north of Spain before forced to return to Lorient with one diesel engine malfunctioning.

A second U-boat, Wilhelm Rollmann's *U34*, sailed into Lorient on 18 July after having sunk seven merchants and the destroyer HMS *Whirlwind* in the Western Approaches. During Rollmann's stay in port, Dönitz arrived in Lorient and talked to both him and Lemp, who uniformly pointed out that the obsolete Type VIIs were plagued by mechanical faults and not up to the rigours of Atlantic patrols. Dönitz decided to retire the remaining Type VIIs to training duties, returning to Germany after their next patrols. The 2nd U-Flotilla would henceforth operate solely larger Type IX cruiser U-boats after the two Type Is had both been lost in action – *U25* sunk by a British minefield near the West Frisian Islands and *U26* scuttled southwest of Ireland after being disabled by heavy depth-charge and bomb damage from British corvette HMS *Gladiolus* and an RAAF Sunderland aircraft.[*]

Dönitz settled on the spacious Villa Kerillon in Kernéval, facing the Kéroman foreshore where U-boat bunkers would be constructed. To the left and right, Villas Margaret and Kerozen would house officers working within U-boat command and the all-important communications centre within bomb-proof bunkers constructed to the villa's rear. On 29 August, Dönitz transferred his headquarters temporarily from Wilhelmshaven to Boulevard Souchet 18, Paris, while he awaited bunker completion and installation of communication equipment. This headquarters complex – soon christened 'Berlin' – would be ringed to landward by formidable defences that eventually included an anti-tank ditch, three bunkered 50mm cannon, an embedded French obsolete tank turret and observation bunkers with machine-gun positions. The coastline was fringed by further anti-tank weapons, 105mm and smaller calibre anti-aircraft guns, machine-gun positions and searchlights. Dönitz would finally declare the new headquarters operational at 0900hrs on 11 November 1940.

On 22 August, *U65* became the first U-boat to use Brest harbour after an aborted mission to land two IRA men in Ireland, IRA Chief of Staff Seán Russell and Frank Ryan, the former dying from a burst gastric ulcer while nearing Galway during a voyage beset by

---

[*] Rollmann's return voyage to Wilhelmshaven netted a further four merchant ships, totalling 29,900 tons sunk and the submarine HMS *Spearfish*, from which a single survivor, Able Seaman William Pester, was rescued and taken prisoner. This made Rollmann the highest-scoring U-boat commander thus far, with 24 enemy ships totalling 100,064 tons sunk, including a destroyer, minelayer and submarine. He was awarded the Knight's Cross, the fifth of the U-boat service. Rollmann was then put ashore as an instructor before returning to active service in 1943 when he commissioned the large type IXD-2 *U848*. This boat was sunk with all hands southwest of Ascension Island on 5 November 1943.

Force 8 gale winds. *Kapitänleutnant* Hans-Gerrit von Stockhausen brought *U65* into port where the boat was placed in dry dock on the Penfeld River, draped in camouflage netting during repair and refit.

During the first calendar year of the war, 30 U-boats had been lost – nearly 50 per cent of the operational U-boat force – the last being Erich Topp's *U57* accidentally rammed and sunk with six men killed at Brunsbüttel locks, though subsequently raised and returned to service in 1941. During that same period, 28 new U-boats had been commissioned. Against this, U-boats claimed a battleship, an aircraft carrier created from a converted battlecruiser (*Courageous*), three destroyers, two submarines and five auxiliary cruisers sunk, as well as 440 ships, totalling 2,330,000 tons; this differs from the Admiralty figures of 353 ships sunk, totalling 1,513,390 tons.[8]

U-boat use of Lorient caused the Admiralty Trade Division to divert convoy traffic to use of the North Channel; 'OA' convoys that had originated in Southend stopped in October 1940 after being briefly routed north of Scotland. Both 'OB' and 'OG' convoy series were redirected to use the North Channel, avoiding the Western Approaches and pushed further north from the autumn.

Despite not yet utilizing group tactics, U-boats accrued significant tonnage sunk. Among those most successful at that point were two new Type IID boats, *U137* and *U138*, captained by rising stars Herbert Wohlfarth and Wolfgang Lüth respectively. Both U-boats reached Lorient towards the end of the month after expending all ammunition in action. As Lüth's *U138* approached the port trailing behind inbound *U47*, two torpedoes from submarine HMS *Tribune* narrowly missed, Lüth avoiding them by throwing the port diesel full ahead and turning hard to starboard. The first torpedo passed under the U-boat near the 20mm deck gun, the second 10 metres ahead. Lieutenant Edward Balston had been ordered to patrol Biscay and originally sighted *U47*, planning a five-torpedo attack before Prien fortuitously turned away, presenting *Tribune* with the slender stern target. At that point, *U138* was sighted and attacked and missed. Escorting submarine hunters (*U-Boot Jäger*) arriving from Lorient depth charged the area briefly, though well wide of their mark.* British submarines became commonplace dangers before the port entrances.

Prien was returning from a particularly successful patrol in which he sank six ships and damaged another. Four of his victims were from slow convoy SC2, exact details of the convoy route provided by B-Dienst at the end of August. *U47*, *U65*, *U101* and *U124* were ordered by BdU to lie in wait along the expected route before SC2 made rendezvous with its local escort. According to German reckoning, SC2 would be in grid-square AL 0216 (57°N 19°50'W) at midday on 6 September, and *U65* was ordered to station itself at that point, the remainder in radio silence quarter line astern, covering a total breadth of 40 miles.

As expected, von Stockhausen's *U65* contacted SC2 on schedule but was prevented from attacking by gale winds and bad visibility. Aboard the convoy commodore's vessel, *Harpoon*, likely U-boat detection was reported, and the 54 ships placed on high alert, whereupon lookouts aboard *Canford Chine*, carrying iron ore to Newport, briefly sighted and reported 'U-boat near'. Despite the fierce weather, a British Sunderland aircraft complicated matters for approaching U-boats, and not until the following day did Prien launch his first attack, sinking three ships in three separate approaches as an ad hoc assembly of escort ships arrived during the course of the day.

Despite periodically losing the convoy, Prien sank a fourth freighter, while Günter Kuhnke's *U28* destroyed another in what was the first 'pack' attack coordinated purely by BdU transmissions as opposed to a senior officer aboard one of the attacking U-boats.† Of those others originally detailed to intercept, *U101* was forced to break away to Lorient with engine problems, *U65* failed to hit anything, and *U124* reluctantly detached for weather reporting

---

* Lüth's next patrol in *U138* sank another 5,317-ton ship and damaged another, leading to his award of the Knight's Cross, the only such award for a Type II U-boat commander. He was soon transferred to the 2nd U-Flotilla to command the Type IXA *U43*.

† By Dönitz's reckoning, this placed Kuhnke's claimed tonnage at over 100,000 tons, and he was awarded the Knight's Cross on 19 September. In reality, he had destroyed 56,272 tons.

duties after some damage to its bow caps, the reports vital for pending Luftwaffe operations over England.

Georg-Wilhelm Schulz was at the end of his maiden patrol aboard *U124*, the boat having replaced *U64* that had been sunk in Narvik, its conning tower displaying a large painted *Edelweiss* in honour of the *Gebirgsjäger* that had rescued *U64*'s crew. During the relatively dull routine of his weather reporting duty, Schulz ordered routine maintenance carried out; *U124* faced unexpected jeopardy when a machinist unwittingly removed the stopcock of 'Tube 7', the aft toilet. Panicked by the sudden deluge of water, the machinist ran for the *Zentrale*, before *E-Maschinist* Karl Rode snatched the stopcock from the terrified man and jammed it back in place with only minor flooding of the bilge. Fortunately, the boat was running surfaced; if submerged below anything but shallow depths, the outside water pressure would have prevented Rode from replacing the stopcock. Schulz's anger was expressed to the hapless crewman in terms 'eloquent, forceful, and 100 per cent Navy'.[9]

Among extra boats vectored on to SC2 was the relatively new *U99*, which had already completed two war patrols under the command of the gifted Otto Kretschmer, sinking 11 ships and awarded the Knight's Cross by Raeder in Lorient on 8 August. Now he followed beacon signals from *U47*, the onset of a fresh bout of bad weather coinciding with Kretschmer's arrival at SC2, rain squalls lashing the boat ploughing through heavy swell.

Three separate attacks resulted in three failures for *U99*, each 'eel', as torpedoes were known to U-boat men, visibly breaking the surface between swell peaks and careering off course. The perfectionist Kretschmer was disappointed and angry, pondering likely gyroscopic failure caused by the high sea in which the torpedoes were fired. Yet another defect to the U-boats' primary weapons, and three valuable 'eels' wasted. To pique his annoyance, *U99* carried an Italian passenger that he had been tasked with showing how a decorated U-boat 'Ace' and his crew fought within the Atlantic. Primo Langobardo was a 38-year-old Italian submarine veteran, decorated with the *Medaglia d'argento al valor militare* (Silver Star for valour) as captain of the *Galileo Ferraris* during the Spanish Civil War. He was there to learn the ropes as Italy lay poised to enter the Atlantic battle.

Italy entered the war with one of the largest submarine fleets in the world at 115 operational vessels, and on 24 July formally requested German agreement to transfer submarines from the Mediterranean Sea to the Atlantic. Under German direction, the three submarine classes deployed in the Atlantic – *Marcello*, *Marconi*, and *Calvi* – were considerably larger and more unwieldy than their German counterparts, crew comfort of greater concern to the Italian Navy than the German. Correspondingly, Dönitz directed the first three submarines transferred to the weakly defended area south of Lisbon, while the Germans remained responsible for the seas north of the Portuguese capital. This dividing line avoided the potential complication of coordinating fully the activities of the two navies and offered the Italians favourable climatic conditions.

After an Italian military commission toured the Atlantic ports, they chose to base their forces in the inland port of Bordeaux, in the southern reaches of Biscay along the Gironde River. The river was connected to a sophisticated system of navigable canals leading to the Mediterranean, though Italian submarines managed to traverse the Strait of Gibraltar in this case. The new Italian base was designated 'BETASOM'; a telegraphic address that comprised 'B' (Beta, for Bordeaux) and 'SOM' as an abbreviation for *Sommergibile* (submarine). Guarded by 250 marines of the 1° *Reggimento* 'San Marco', BETASOM occupied a harbour basin that included two dry docks, officially inaugurated on 30 August 1940 by Admiral Angelo Perona.

To streamline relations between the two navies, Hans-Rudolf Rösing was appointed liaison officer to the Italians, and several Italian officers were sent on patrol aboard combat U-boats to observe German practices and get a sense of environmental differences to familiar Mediterranean waters. Langobardo later took command of *Luigi Torelli*, which had left La Spezia on 31 August 1940 in the first group of BETASOM boats.

Dönitz did not expect much from the Italians but hoped at least that their presence would enhance reconnaissance tasks. It was, however, to prove disappointing to Dönitz. By December,

BdU had received no reliable reconnaissance, only tardy, almost incomprehensible messages or inaccurate reports, as German radio operators had not been attached in deference to Italian national sensibilities. Italian crews were trained for patrols of shorter duration, generally targeting enemy harbours using submerged attacks. Even weather reporting duties proved inefficient, and valuable U-boats were still required for the task. Italian performance in action had yielded few sinkings and, due to what Dönitz considered clumsy operational procedures, he judged their presence not only futile, but prejudicial to U-boat operations.

The main reasons for their failure are:

1. They do not know how to attack unnoticed or to remain unseen.
2. They do not understand how to haul ahead of a slower enemy.
3. They have no idea of night surface attack.
4. They understand nothing of shadowing and reporting.

… I think that in the end the real reasons for their failure lies with the personnel. They are not sufficiently hard and determined for this type of warfare. Their way of thinking is too long-winded and lacking in initiative to allow them to adapt themselves readily and simply to the changing conditions of war. Their personal conduct lacks discipline, and they cannot keep calm in face of the enemy. In view of all this, I am forced to detail and operate the German boats without regard for the Italians. It is to be hoped that the Italians will benefit with time to an increasing extent from opportunities arising for them out of this.*

---

* Indeed, German opinion of their Italian allies was low even within U-boat crews. Within the Admiralty interrogation report of survivors of *U110* sunk in May 1941, the crew 'referred to their Italian allies in terms of the utmost contempt, special scorn being reserved for Italian U-boat crews. One man indignantly described the Italian U-boats as usually sinking an intercepted vessel by gunfire after rescuing as many of the crew as possible. After hastily returning to port the Italians then triumphantly exhibited the unfortunate prisoners and spent weeks celebrating their achievement.' BdU KTB 4 December 1940.

In the meantime, the U-boats had been experiencing what is now frequently referred to as their 'Happy Time'. It was most definitely a time of the 'Aces', as Prien, Kretschmer, Joachim Schepke in his Type VIIB *U100* and Heinrich Bleichrodt aboard the veteran *U48* were made famous by action against the Atlantic convoys. Eastbound Halifax convoy HX72 was attacked by eight U-boats between 20 and 22 September, BdU direction aided by B-Dienst intelligence and regular sighting reports from *U47*, now bereft of torpedoes after action against SC2 and on weather reporting duty.

The convoy lost 11 ships in total – three to Kretschmer, one to Bleichrodt, and seven to Schepke – before reaching the Western Approaches escort that curtailed the U-boat operation. The German willingness to close the enemy and actually pass through any escort screen and attack from within the columns of merchant ships was, as yet, unappreciated by the Admiralty, who believed U-boats attacked by 'browning': making distant attacks against a mass of shipping, requiring neither high-speed torpedoes nor good shooting. This dovetailed with previous orthodox training using the 'fan-shot' of torpedoes but, thanks to Dönitz's training, was everything that younger, more aggressive captains railed against. It is telling that only the three U-boats that attacked at point-blank range scored torpedo hits, while those making distant fan shots all missed.

Chief of Staff to the First Lord of the Admiralty, the highly experienced ex-destroyer commander George Creasy, doubled as Director of Anti-Submarine Warfare and underestimated the new U-boat commanders. He believed their preferred attack method was to strike at night, approach the convoy, fire a full bow salvo, then turn about and fire the stern torpedo before retreating to reload. Correspondingly, general orders to merchant convoys were for escorts to turn *outward* if attacked, with star shells fired into the sky away from the convoy body. To make matters worse, star shells were virtually useless until replaced in May 1941 by 'Snowflake' rockets that deployed 28 white star lights of some 300,000 candlepower. Descending slowly by parachute, 'Snowflake' effectively turned night into day. Creasy's standing advice played into the hands of

U-boat skippers willing to penetrate a convoy and attack from within, while also aiding convoy location for approaching U-boats.

If SC2 and HX72 served to further vindicate BdU's 'wolfpack' attacks directed from Dönitz's headquarters by radio, the massacres of SC7 and HX79 during October proved their greatest triumphs.

On 16 October Claus Korth's *U93* shadowed an outbound convoy sighted two days previously, though of seven other U-boats and one Italian submarine, only *U38* was in a suitable position to attack. With contact sporadic at best, several U-boats began plotting likely intercept courses for Korth's convoy, until BdU was electrified by fresh reports from *U48* of a large inbound convoy: SC7. Bleichrodt identified what he took to be 25 merchant ships under escort by only three gunboats, and Dönitz immediately ordered all available boats to operate against Bleichrodt's convoy, seven assembled in a rough patrol line northeast of Rockall Bank.

Bleichrodt opened the initial attack, sinking the convoy's largest ship, 9,512-ton tanker *Languedoc* (scuttled by gunfire from HMS *Bluebell*) and 3,843-ton *Scoresby*, before forced to dive by depth charges and losing contact. Dönitz and Godt in Paris nervously reshuffled the line to locate SC7, several of the searching U-boats encountering each other in the frustrating hunt until Godt issued orders to instead work independently against Korth's outbound convoy.

Barely had they begun to turn towards *U38*'s estimated position when *U101* found SC7 and began to shadow. The slow convoy to Liverpool had found the planned speed of 8 knots unable to be matched by several older, smaller ships, lowering the pace throughout. Thirty-five ships departed Nova Scotia, but some immediately began to straggle, and bad weather helped separate several others from the main body, two of them subsequently sunk. For three-quarters of the journey only sloop HMS *Scarborough* provided escort, joined immediately before Bleichrodt's attack by sloop HMS *Fowey* and the new corvette HMS *Bluebell*. However, *Scarborough* spent so long hunting Bleichrodt that the sloop was unable to catch up with SC7, reducing the escort to two.

Approaching U-boats pounded through a short sea towards *U101*, the first torpedoes fired by *U46*. Finn Skage, Master of Norwegian freighter *Snefjeld*, later reported:

> On Friday 18 October… convoy was in 9 columns. First ship was torpedoed (rear of outside Port column) at about 1930hrs. Convoy made emergency turn to Starboard when a ship in one of the Starboard Columns was torpedoed. At approximately 1945hrs an emergency turn to Port was made and immediately afterwards a third ship was attacked. After this, formation of convoy became ragged and U-boats appeared on surface using flares and gunfire. I think there were at least four U-boats.[10]

It quickly became a virtual massacre, Kretschmer doing his best to penetrate the convoy columns and attack from within.

> I tried to get through the escorts into the convoy, which was my own peculiarity of attacking, and failed the first time. They saw me and shot star shells so that I had to go away again. But the second time I succeeded and got inside the convoy, going up and down the lanes and looking for the most important valuable ships and had the opportunity to expend all my torpedoes, I had twelve in all.[11]

During a six-hour period, despite the arrival of additional escorts sloop HMS *Leith* and corvette HMS *Heartsease*, 16 ships were sunk, seven of them by Kretschmer alone. Combined with four that had been lost before the main attack, SC7 suffered 20 ships destroyed with four others severely damaged. Defensive efforts were uncoordinated and ineffective, and Royal Navy reliance on the collective strength of convoying combined with excessive faith in ASDIC – useless against surfaced U-boats – had been their undoing. The bloody battle was a disaster for the Allies; 141 merchant sailors were killed in what the Germans had already begun calling 'The Night of the Long Knives'. Only a lack of torpedoes and diversion of U-boats towards convoy HX79 relieved the pressure on SC7. Prien in *U47* sighted this new inbound convoy on the morning of the 19th, and BdU directed *U28*, *U46*, *U47*, *U48* and *U100* to attack, sinking 12 ships and damaging two others. As German propaganda trumpeted the triumph, in Paris Dönitz was ecstatic with what he called 'a colossal success'.[12] The principles on which U-boat tactics and training had been based since 1935 had been proven correct, although reliant on sufficient U-boats within the operational area – an infrequent situation thus far in the war. Ironically, U-boat successes against SC7 and HX79 once again denuded the North Atlantic of U-boats, as all that had taken part in the actions were forced to return either for repair or ammunition.

Dönitz, as was his custom, was present to personally debrief each of the returning commanders where their War Diary entries were examined and analysed in depth. Kretschmer – known as 'Silent Otto' due to his aversion to excessive radio transmissions – was once again admonished for his meagre communication, though remained unapologetic as he had a hearty respect for British radio direction finding. Though Kretschmer's silence sometimes complicated BdU's tight planning of patrol lines, the young commander was correct. He believed that excessive transmissions either attracted anti-submarine forces or caused convoy traffic to divert from gathering U-boats. For example, between 0106hrs on 18 October and 2119hrs on 19 October (attacks against SC7 and HX79), Prien's *U47* and Schepke's *U100* sent 82 radio transmissions between them. During the same period, Kretschmer sent two. Later, long after the war had ended, he would comment, 'I have the opinion today that much of the U-Boat war's success had been lost because of those damn radio transmissions.'[13]

This, then, was the apparent 'Happy Time' of the U-boats. Though sometimes bloodily successful, it was fleeting and by no means as one-sided as frequently represented, and ships sailing independently remained primary U-boat victims. It is worth noting the Admiralty's own figures for shipping losses specifically to U-boat attack during 1939 and 1940 as recorded in *The Defeat of the Enemy Attack on Shipping*, published by the Admiralty's Historical Section in 1947:

1939
Ships convoyed: 3,500
Ships sunk in convoy: 5
Convoy stragglers sunk: 3
Independently sailing ships sunk: 90
Total merchant shipping crew casualties (including DEMS gunners) from U-boat action: 260
Total: 98

1940
Ships convoyed: 17,900
Ships sunk in convoy: 102
Convoy stragglers sunk: 66
Independently sailing ships sunk: 288 (plus 5 in theatres other than the Atlantic)
Total merchant shipping crew casualties (including DEMS gunners) from U-boat action: 3,375
Total: 461[14]

For the Royal Navy, attempts at establishing an anti-submarine force within the North West Approaches had failed, leading to relocation in February 1941 of Western Approaches Command combined headquarters from Plymouth to Liverpool, improving cooperation between British air and sea forces and the Trade Division. Dedicated ASW naval forces were lacking, and during 1940 dozens of trawlers were adapted for anti-submarine use, bolstering weak escort forces. The principle espoused since the war's beginning by Admiral Martin Dunbar-Nasmith, Commander-in-Chief Western Approaches, was that once located, a U-boat should be hunted to exhaustion, submersion limited by battery life. However, scarcity of escort vessels made this an impossibility lest convoys be left unprotected. Increasing the number of craft available began making this theory more feasible and formation of escort groups began; each group was trained to work as a coordinated team, attached to a convoy and under the command of a single group leader. Increased ship numbers permitted the required extensive anti-submarine training, which, combined with the fitting of effective radio-telegraphy equipment, allowed surface escorts to operate efficiently in pairs, with one holding ASDIC contact while the other attacked. Depth-charge use was also improved, with newer escorts now able to deliver an increased full salvo of ten depth charges.

On 2 September, Britain signed a deal with the United States for the exchange of 50 obsolete First World War destroyers in exchange for 99-year leases on eight British possessions in the Caribbean and Western Atlantic for establishment of US air and naval bases. Though the terms were highly disadvantageous to Britain, Churchill had achieved the first open American support in the war against the Axis powers, the destroyers not compromising the neutrality act as they were deemed 'surplus' vessels. Six were assigned to the Royal Canadian Navy and the remainder to the Royal Navy where they were reclassified 'Town' class. However, this did not prove the quick fix for bolstering convoy escorts, as they were soon found to be in extremely poor shape after having been neglected and mothballed for several years. Only nine were in service by the end of 1940, 30 by May 1941; deeply unpopular with commanders and crews, they were uncomfortable and displayed poor handling characteristics.

Nevertheless, the United States had provided substantive support for Britain at war. On 29 December, Roosevelt spelt it out via his 'Fireside Chat', a series of informal evening radio broadcasts to the American people:

This is not a fireside chat on war. It is a talk on national security... As planes and ships and guns and shells are produced, your Government, with its defense experts, can then determine how best to use them to defend this hemisphere... We must be the great arsenal of democracy... We have furnished the British great material support and we will furnish far more in the future.

By October, the Luftwaffe had failed to destroy the Royal Air Force, and the likelihood of an attempted invasion of Great Britain diminished greatly. While British ships damaged at Dunkirk began returning to service, they were no longer stringently held back for anti-invasion duty. Neither were Coastal Command aircraft, which were instead more readily deployed on anti-submarine duties. Likewise, British submarines were released for service away from home waters and regularly stationed in Biscay, establishing what became known as the 'Iron Ring' outside of the Biscay ports, albeit more in hopes of catching German capital ships than U-boats. Nonetheless, Dietrich Knorr's *U51* was the first U-boat sunk by British torpedo in Biscay; it was destroyed with all hands on 20 August west of Saint Nazaire following a 12-day voyage from Kiel.

Strengthening British anti-submarine forces pushed U-boat operations further west. During the extraordinarily successful October operations, Atlantic U-boats were gathered between 10° and 15° West, moved beyond 15° during the following month. Though the greater sea space allowed U-boats increased freedom of movement, convoy location became the primary problem. Coupled with only four to six U-boats operating within this area between November 1940 and January 1941, there was little success for Dönitz. Bad winter weather complicated both location and weapon use, though transferring Atlantic boats to potentially more settled regions seemed a retrograde step.

I am always reconsidering whether it would not be more profitable in winter to transfer the theatre of operations further south into calmer areas and I always conclude that in spite of the bad weather, as enemy traffic is more concentrated in the north, more can be sunk within any given time than in the south. Only the amount of tonnage is of real importance for the final outcome of the war and I have therefore stuck to the north as the primary centre of U-boat operations. It is of course desirable to worry the enemy in other areas and achieve a diversionary effect. This would relieve pressure in the main theatre of war, but it is no way to defeat the enemy… However, the central Atlantic operations area must not be neglected altogether and knowledge of conditions and potential operational success must be obtained. *U37* and *U65* will be quite sufficient for this purpose at present. For the time being, all other boats will go north.[15]

Despite isolated attacks by individual boats against convoy traffic and independents, the only 'wolfpack' convoy battle of that period occurred after *U101* sighted HX90 on 1 December. With *U101* shadowing and sending regular position reports, HX90 came under sustained attack by *U43*, *U47*, *U52*, *U94*, *U95* and *U101*, which between them sank nine merchant ships and damaged three others before the convoy reached the safety of the North Channel minefields. Italian boats *Argo*, *Giuliani* and *Tarantini* joined the battle but achieved no success.

Requests from Dönitz for Luftwaffe reconnaissance support repeatedly butted against Göring's intransigence regarding the release of any of *his* aircraft to naval control. The Luftwaffe continuously claimed a lack of available aircraft for BdU reconnaissance; single flights were occasionally made, providing vague reports of dubious value. Even the reverse use of U-boats to guide aircraft to targets had failed, as shown by Wolfgang Lüth's attempt to have the 10,350-ton New Zealand merchant *Orari* finished off by Luftwaffe attack. Lüth, in his new Type IXB *U43*, had hit the ship in the stern southwest of Ireland with one of his last two torpedoes. Unable to use deck guns due to bad weather, Lüth followed for six hours while transmitting beacon signal and weather reports for a planned KG40 mission.* With no other U-boats in the area, Dönitz was enthusiastic about the opportunity to consolidate cooperation with the Luftwaffe, but the aircraft's early-morning departure was delayed until 1100hrs, meaning it would only reach the target three hours later. Meanwhile, Lüth

---

* KG40 – *Kampfgeschwader* 40 – was a bomber unit soon to be designated maritime specialists.

was forced to continue his return passage due to a dangerously low level of lubricating oil. The plan was stillborn, and *Orari's* crew covered the torpedo hole with tarpaulins and reached the Clyde where the ship was repaired.

Though Göring generally prevailed in the tug-of-war over Luftwaffe maritime operations, on 6 January 1941 a Führer directive was issued that 12 Condor aircraft of I/KG40 (Fw 200) be assigned to operate directly under BdU control. Hitler's decision was a boost for Dönitz, albeit one requiring hurdles of technicalities to be overcome before truly bearing fruit. The rate of Condor serviceability was extremely low, as the civilian airframe was not up to the rigours of Atlantic military service. Plus, while BdU was pleased, Göring was far less so, as it transpired that Hitler's decision had been made while the Luftwaffe chief enjoyed one of his many holiday periods vacationing in Paris. Göring was furious at what he saw as an attempt to subvert part of his domain to Kriegsmarine control and summoned Dönitz to his headquarters train lying in a siding between Paris and Dieppe. This marked the first meeting of the two men, and Göring attempted to alternately persuade and threaten Dönitz to return KG40 to Luftwaffe control. When the two parted as what Dönitz later described as 'bad friends', the matter remained unchanged, and I/KG40 was retained by U-boat headquarters.

Though a stopgap measure, the Fw 200 had already begun to prove its worth. By the end of 1940, KG40 had lost two aircraft but been credited with sinking 800,000 tons of enemy shipping, though this estimate was far higher than the reality. The most successful single attack had taken place on 26 October, when the 42,348-ton liner *Empress of Britain* was bombed 70 miles northwest of Donegal Bay. The liner carried 224 military personnel and civilians, plus a crew of 419 men, returning from troop transport to Suez via Cape Town, and the explosions caused fire that rapidly spread, overwhelming all efforts by the crew to contain the blaze. The ship was abandoned by all but a skeleton crew remaining to fight the blaze. Hull plates visibly glowed red when the stricken ship was sighted by Hans Jenisch in *U32* and finished off by torpedoes. Fortunately for Jenisch, nearby destroyers remained unaware of his presence and believed the explosions to have been the liner's diesel bunkers.*

Operationally, Dönitz was soon unsatisfied with Luftwaffe performance, aircrews' reported ship-sighting information relayed to individual U-boats via an extremely ponderous route; the aircraft could not communicate directly by radio due to differing radio procedures and a lack of equipment and trained personnel. Instead, aircraft shadowed while transmitting long-wave homing signals via a trailing aerial, this beacon picked up by U-boats and retransmitted by short signal to BdU, who plotted the various beacon signals and attempted to eliminate navigational errors, before retransmitting a corrected position to the U-boats at sea. This procedure took valuable time, the aircraft frequently having shifted location or departed due to a lack of fuel. Additionally, location of convoy traffic itself was difficult for the Luftwaffe crews. In a typical mission to the sea area west of Ireland, a Condor possessed enough fuel to stay on station for approximately three hours before forced to return. During this time, crewmen would be sweeping the sea with binoculars, the aircraft tending to fly at around 500 metres altitude, which allowed a search radius of around 20 kilometres in bright clear weather, frequently not the case within the Atlantic.[†]

Compounding the deficit of dedicated reconnaissance aircraft, convoys were re-routing further north, pushing intercepting U-boats towards Iceland, which had been occupied by the British on 10 May to counter possible German occupation. Though Hitler had no plans to invade, Britain feared the occupation of Denmark – whose King was Iceland's Head of State, despite remaining a sovereign country – and strong German diplomatic presence would lead to inevitable German occupation. Hitler subsequently expressed interest in such a move, providing Iceland as an airbase for the protection of U-boats. The feasibility study for

---

* Jenisch himself was sunk two days later by destroyers HMS *Harvester* and *Highlander*.
† On-board radar was still some time in the future for the Condors. Experiments with the air-to-sea *Atlas* and *Neptun-S* systems produced disappointing results later in 1941, and it was not until 1943 that the first effective radar sets began to be carried.

Operation *Ikarus* concluded that, though invasion and occupation was possible, resupply of garrison troops and Luftwaffe units would be prohibitively difficult.* Bordeaux-based KG40 aircraft could only effectively cover the southeastern corner of northerly U-boat dispositions, even if the long-range Condors departed France and flew a circular route to land in Stavanger or Aalborg for refuelling. Barely able to provide information on shipping traffic in the southern sector, only BETASOM boats of dubious value patrolled that area.

Almost inevitably, by March 1941, aircraft of I/KG40 reverted to Luftwaffe control once more. After intense lobbying of OKW by the highest echelons of the Luftwaffe, Hitler issued a new order in which the Luftwaffe retained dominion over the majority of naval aviation, including Atlantic reconnaissance. However, by counterpoint, Göring was ordered to establish the post of *Fliegerführer Atlantik*, who would control reconnaissance missions for BdU as well as meteorological flights, support for Kriegsmarine surface forces within the Atlantic and such offensive operations against maritime targets as were agreed between the Luftwaffe and Kriegsmarine.

In France, veteran former naval officer Martin Harlinghausen was appointed to the new post, his headquarters in the grand requisitioned Château de Kerlivio, Brandérion, 14 kilometres west of Lorient. In Harlinghausen, Dönitz had an efficient and experienced officer with whom to deal, later describing him as 'a man of exceptional energy and boldness', and the two endeavoured to create a good working relationship.[16]

During February, cooperation between U-boat and aircraft finally reached fruition. After cruiser *Admiral Hipper* left Brest following routine maintenance, five Focke-Wulf Fw 200s attacked HG53 in cooperation with Nicolai Clausen's *U37*, which had reported the convoy off Cape St Vincent while headed to Freetown. Clausen sank two ships before shadowing and transmitting position reports for both the Luftwaffe and *Admiral Hipper*. Condors bombed and

* A similar German idea regarding the Azores was also investigated but dismissed for the same reasons, though American fears of the latter led to occupation by US forces in 1943 (Operation *Alacrity*).

sank four ships, heavily damaging a fifth, while one Fw 200 hit by anti-aircraft fire crash landed in Portugal. Though *U37* sank British freighter *Brandenburg* the following day, attempts to bring *Admiral Hipper* into action against HG53 failed although the cruiser sank a straggler on 11 February. Instead, *Hipper* abandoned the chase and attacked SL64, destroying seven of its 19 ships. For the first time, a capital ship, a U-boat and aircraft had cooperated in action with degrees of success.

A single Condor returning from Stavanger during February reported convoy traffic southeast of Lousy Bank, and two merchant ships were sunk before OB288 reached the North Channel. BdU coordinated several U-boats within the area into a patrol line of *U69*, *U73*, *U95*, *U96*, *U107* and Italian *Bianchi*, Helmut Rosenbaum's *U73* making first contact, confirming convoy course and speed and bringing the other boats into action. A concentrated night attack was then made after escorts had departed, and merchants began dispersing following Admiralty information that they were being shadowed by at least one U-boat. The gathered U-boats sank nine ships; Convoy Commodore, Rear Admiral Richard Plowden, was killed aboard *Sirikishna*, sunk by *U96*. During the afternoon of the following day, 25 February, Günther Prien's *U47* contacted OB290 in the North Channel, attacking and sinking four ships early the next morning before Udo Heilmann's *U97*, empty of torpedoes, assumed responsibility for maintaining contact and guided Condors to the convoy where they sank a further eight ships. This marked a distinct high point in U-boat–Condor cooperation, not to be repeated for the foreseeable future.

Chapter Four

Diverging Objectives

'I was well aware that I had hit Malaya… *she played hell, firing star shells all over the horizon…'*

Jürgen Oesten, *U106*[1]

Kapitänleutnant Hans-Gerrit von Stockhausen's *U65* had departed Lorient on 15 October 1940 for the Sierra Leone port of Freetown and nearly three months at sea. Dönitz had been directed by SKL to send at least one U-boat to the area around Freetown, an expansive natural harbour with a malarial township along its southern edge, bordered by thick, humid jungle. Though possessing no real shore facilities, merchant ships bound from South America, South Africa and the Indian Ocean travelled independently to Freetown from where they could be combined as an 'SL' convoy for the final leg of the voyage to Liverpool. Royal Navy staff were accommodated aboard the elderly liner *Edinburgh Castle* which lay offshore alongside a hospital ship and smaller merchants carrying refuelling diesel and coal from Britain.*

Inaugural SL1 had departed Freetown on 14 September 1939, and no ship was lost on any of the convoys that followed until *U28* sank *Royston Grange* from SL8 on 25 November, the 5,144-ton

---

* Before construction of a dedicated W/T station, Freetown naval communications from Britain were via cable sent to the Colonial Secretariat, from which a messenger walked to hand deliver a transcript to naval officers. The speed of this service was increased somewhat by colonial authorities authorizing the purchase of a bicycle.

freighter taking its cargo of grain, cereals and meat from Buenos Aires to the bottom though with no loss of life. By the end of 1940, only eight ships from the 'SL' convoys had been sunk, all by U-boats waiting near the North Channel towards Liverpool.

Thus far, British control of the South Atlantic sea lanes faced its greatest potential threat from Vichy forces controlling French West Africa, particularly after an ill-fated British attempt to capture Dakar by force in November 1940. Indeed, by June 1941, German plans were firmly under way to utilize Dakar as a U-boat supply point for South Atlantic operations. On 28 May, Admiral François Darlan and the German ambassador to Vichy, Otto Abetz, signed the Paris Protocols that granted Germany military facilities in Syria, Tunisia and French West Africa; U-boats were to be stationed in Dakar from 15 July 1941 with surface and air forces to follow. Freetown thereby remained the most important colonial outpost between South Africa (which had declared war on Germany on 6 September 1939) and Great Britain. As it was relatively poorly defended, Dönitz decided that, despite reluctance to divert U-boats from the North Atlantic, a 'surprise operation should lead to considerable actual success in sinking valuable units, in addition to the desired diversionary effect'.[2]

Stockhausen's was not the first U-boat to have been directed to the South Atlantic, Hans Cohausz taking the ex-Turkish *UA* from Kiel bound for Freetown during June. In transit, he was ordered to attack the Royal Navy's blockading 'Northern Patrol', stationed within the choke point of the 'Greenland, Iceland, and United Kingdom (GIUK) Gap', through which all German vessels attempting to break into the North Atlantic must pass. *UA* subsequently sank auxiliary cruiser HMS *Andania*, before heading south meeting with German raider *Schiff* 33 '*Pinguin*' on 18 July to replenish fuel, provisions and ammunition, by which time serious engine trouble had afflicted *UA*. Cohausz rendezvoused with *Pinguin* as planned near Cape Verde Islands, though bad weather forced both to head south for two days to calmer waters. For refuelling, the U-boat was positioned astern of the tanker, whose motorboat was lowered to assist in passing a hawser and the diesel fuel hose, plugged and filled with air to prevent it sinking. The hawser was then secured to the U-boat's bow, hose connected, and diesel pumped through. On average, fuelling took approximately two hours; however, the replenishment of *UA* took five days to complete, with stores and 11 torpedoes laboriously ferried from the raider to *UA* on rubber floats, towed by the motorboat. Only one torpedo could be carried at a time, hoisted by a davit aboard the U-boat and loaded through the torpedo hatch.

To conserve the U-boat's fuel, *Pinguin* towed *UA* to the shipping lanes off Freetown, where Cohausz unsuccessfully pursued a tanker. By 3 August, engine defects had become critical and Cohausz headed back to Germany, sinking four further ships before docking in Wilhelmshaven just over three weeks later. Following Cohausz's debriefing, Dönitz was unconvinced that his lack of success within the South Atlantic was the result of insufficient targets. Furthermore, he was disappointed that *UA* did not strike the 'Northern Patrol' again on its return voyage after Cohausz had been instructed to do so based on solid B-Dienst intelligence revealing target ships' locations.

> Operation in the tropics did not present any unforeseen difficulties regarding materiel or personnel, and with additional air-conditioning apparatus even our present types of boats should be fit for use in the tropics. Taken as a whole, this patrol was not altogether satisfactory. Not all opportunities to attack were exploited and lack of perseverance can be seen.[3]

For the second attempt, Stockhausen sank eight ships, four of them tankers, and damaged a ninth. He was later criticized by BdU for not supplying regular progress reports, requests for information indicating few ships had been sighted by late November. Dönitz weighed the alternatives of either withdrawing *U65* or reinforcing its potential, and with B-Dienst providing further information of the trade routes tracing Africa's west coast, he decided on the latter course of action and despatched *U37*; Clausen instructed to operate initially off Portugal before proceeding south to refuel tankers and operate off Freetown. *U37* resupplied twice from the disguised

German supply ship *Nordmark* sailing near the Cape Verde Islands in support of raider *Admiral Scheer*.

At the beginning of December, *U37* encountered convoy OG46, sinking two ships in convoy and two stragglers. On 16 December, Clausen missed with a single torpedo shot on the small Spaniard *San Carlos* travelling in ballast unescorted south of Fuerteventura. He elected to surface and attack the vessel with gunfire, one man aboard killed before the remaining crew and passengers abandoned ship. The Spaniard stubbornly refused to sink, and Clausen sent a small scuttling party in the U-boat's dinghy to set charges, the men noting that the 20cm strong wooden hull had not been penetrated by the U-boat's 105mm gunfire. The scuttling charges, however, did not fail, and *San Carlos* sank.

Clausen's decision to sink the Spaniard appears dubious, but his next was potentially disastrous. On the afternoon of 19 December, *U37* torpedoed Vichy French oiler *Rhône* and Agosta-class submarine *Sfax* 7 miles off Cape Juby, Morocco. The two vessels were sailing from Casablanca for Dakar, and Clausen appears to have realized his error, as the U-boat's War Diary lists only: 'DJ 9285 – Nothing to see.' Curiously, this grid square listed is located on land in the Sahara Desert. Twice, planned resupply in the Canary Islands was prevented by enemy activity, and by 21 December Dönitz revoked his decision.

U65 reported that she had no further success. Little traffic in her operational area.

Supply of *U37* in the Canaries has again had to be postponed because of enemy activity.

My view that U-boat operations in the Southern area do not lead to success which can be achieved in the North is again confirmed. Operation in the Southern area is also subject to the possibility of supplying with material and ammunition. As the present case shows difficulties can arise here, which can mean uncertainty and delay for the boats and reduce their chances of success, which are already rather meagre. I have therefore decided to recall both the boats and afterwards send to the more promising Northern area. It is intended to operate the three large Italian boats in the Freetown area, starting with *Capellini* who will arrive there at the end of the year.[4]

Though he would again revise his decision, Dönitz clearly believed that the South Atlantic merely distracted from the northern logical centre point of convoy operations. His was a tonnage war, akin to accountancy with its 'simple' profit and loss spreadsheet: merchant tonnage sunk versus merchant tonnage built; U-boats lost versus U-boats commissioned. As an example, taking into consideration the time spent in dockyard before and after patrol, as well as the patrol itself, *U65* was occupied for the best part of half a year, in return for eight ships sunk. Though Stockhausen was considered to have commanded the boat well, the return for such a period, when every combat U-boat was required, was not considered viable in Dönitz's reckoning. Nonetheless, Stockhausen was believed to have passed the magic 100,000 tons of shipping sunk (in reality 87,278 tons) and was awarded the Knight's Cross on 14 January. Like many veteran officers, he was then posted ashore, later to take charge of the 26th U-Training Flotilla but was killed in Berlin on 14 January 1943 when he was struck by a car while crossing the road.

Between February and April, U-boats were pushed further west past the 20° meridian, Hitler on 25 March ordering the war zone be extended to Greenland and southwest to the 38° meridian of longitude, as steadily improving British escort and ASW strength compelled U-boats to operate further from the British Isles. Individually, U-boats found it increasingly difficult to penetrate thickened convoy escort screens, leading to an increased reliance on U-boat groups and patrol lines. Within open sea, U-boats used daylight to move at surface speed towards reported convoy traffic, maximizing their offensive power by attacking surfaced under cover of darkness. If forced to submerge, visual target contact and all speed advantages were lost.

On 26 January, the state of the U-boat arm made deceptively happy reading in Berlin. A total of 379 boats existed on paper. However, of these 48 were in training, 52 with U-Boat Acceptance Command (U.A.K.) and 231 still under construction, leaving only 48 operational. U-boat production as yet proved incapable of substantially reinforcing combat strength, and the problem of convoy location had grown acute. Hopes pinned on aerial reconnaissance had distinctly faded after repeated failures. Senior Kriegsmarine officers baldly stated that a major obstacle in cooperation with U-boats was the Luftwaffe's unwillingness to attack escort ships and thereby leave the merchants to be torpedoed by U-boats. Göring's desire for 'headlines' sent his aircraft in to wage his own tonnage war, attacking merchants and frequently scattering a convoy while U-boats were depth charged by unchecked escort ships and unable to keep pace. On the other side of the coin, *Fliegerführer Atlantik* also experienced frustration, as on at least one occasion aircraft transmitted detailed and accurate bearings to shadowed convoy traffic, only to later learn that no U-boats were within the area – a fact of which neither Harlinghausen nor his staff had been made aware.

The flagging U-boat service then suffered a succession of disasters within the North Atlantic. As U-boats pushed progressively north towards Iceland, and following a series of abortive convoy interceptions based on inexact Luftwaffe reports, on 6 March Prien's *U47* sighted OB293 of 37 ships bound for North America. He began shadowing while BdU directed *U70*, *U99*, *UA* and the distant *U37* to close on Prien's location. *U99* sighted *U47* at about 1800hrs but was forced to dive by destroyers emerging from mist at only 1,000 metres and heading directly for them. As *U99* submerged, warship screws passed overhead more than once, with a scattering of depth charges nearby though not posing any danger. *U47* later resurfaced to report depth-charge attacks, before heading back towards OB293.

At 0424hrs on 7 March, Prien signalled once more convoy speed, position, and course before opening his attack. Forty minutes later, two torpedoes hit the 20,638-ton British whaling factory ship *Terje Viken*, credited to *U47* although according to the exhaustive research completed by German historian Axel Niestlé, possibly fired by Joachim Matz in *U70*. The huge ship was the largest vessel of its kind in the world and being used as a tanker though travelling in ballast. The first torpedo hit the starboard side approximately

30 metres from the bow, passing through the ship and also holing the port hull, the second torpedo striking forward of the first, wrecking the forward hold. Meanwhile, of Prien there was no more sign.

What exactly happened to Günther Prien and the crew of *U47* remains unknown to this day. Originally, he was claimed sunk by HMS *Wolverine* on 8 March, but we now know for certain that the boat *Wolverine* depth charged was *UA*, now under the command of Hans Eckermann, and returning damaged to Lorient. *U47* disappeared, lost somewhere near OB293 – possibly to depth charges, floating mines that had broken loose from defensive minefields and not been rendered safe, a diving accident because of new and inexperienced crew or, the most popular theory and one to which Otto Kretschmer also subscribes, a victim of its own torpedo. If the gyroscope failed within an active torpedo, it habitually began to circle and became a danger to the firing U-boat. Somewhere, thousands of metres below the surface in this area, the wreck of *U47* lies undisturbed on the seabed and is unlikely to ever give up the secret of what caused its destruction.

Kretschmer, meanwhile, had caught up with OB293, helped by distress rockets fired by ships already attacked and on fire. Closing on the convoy's starboard column, Kretschmer finished off *Terje Viken* and another damaged freighter with gunfire and torpedoes. However, both *U99* and *U70* came under extreme pressure, having fallen behind the convoy and vulnerable to counter-attacks from 'sweepers' trailing the merchants. Dawn was breaking and the two U-boats briefly sighted each other, *U70* damaged after being rammed by Dutch tanker *Mijdrecht* that Matz had just torpedoed. A pair of corvettes sighted the boats, and both made rapid alarm dives to escape, Matz continuing his course while Kretschmer moved under the drifting wreckage of *Terje Viken*. For Matz it was too late to evade, as corvettes HMS *Arbutus* and *Camellia* hounded *U70* with depth charges, sending the U-boat into a chaotic uncontrolled descent that exceeded 200 metres, only checked by both electric motors set at full speed ahead, hydroplanes on maximum rise and all tanks blown. *U70* broke the surface and came under immediate fire before sinking; 25 of the crew, including Matz, were rescued by their attackers.

While *U70*'s fate was confirmed shortly thereafter, Prien's boat was not officially declared lost – *Vermisst Zwei Stern* – until 26 April, when there was no chance of the boat still being at sea. Feldpost number 18837 was no longer accepting correspondence. However, so great was the likely blow to German national morale that his loss was not publicly acknowledged by OKW until 23 May 1941. Prien's popularity in Germany was equalled perhaps only by Otto Kretschmer's and Joachim Schepke's. All three had received the Oak Leaves to their Knight's Crosses, Kretschmer the leading tonnage 'Ace' of the Kriegsmarine. While Kretschmer was taciturn and private by nature, Schepke was tall, blond and handsomely charismatic and had been widely feted by Goebbels' propaganda machine. Despite showing the strain of almost constant patrolling and his tonnage claims becoming ever more exaggerated, he had still managed to sink 36 ships totalling 153,677 tons.

During the days immediately following Prien's disappearance, and the departure of *UA* for France, Dönitz acerbically pondered the farcical situation by which, of only four U-boats stationed within the North Atlantic (*U37*, *U74*, *U95* and *U99*), two were detailed for weather reporting service, one of which, *U37*, was still at sea without torpedoes exclusively for meteorological work. Reinforcements were urgently required, and Lemp took his new Type IXB boat *U110* from Kiel on 9 March.

Six days later he reported an eastbound convoy south of Iceland, HX112 of 41 merchants, the cruiser ocean escort handing over to 5th Escort Group – HMS *Walker, Vanoc, Volunteer, Bluebell* and *Hydrangea* – reinforced by HMS *Sardonyx and Scimitar.* Lemp immediately attacked, hitting tanker *Erodona* and setting her cargo of fuel ablaze, killing 36 of the 57 crew. Lemp's G7a torpedo track had been sighted, and though HMS *Vanoc* failed to find *U110*, it forced Lemp to retreat, and he temporarily lost contact. At 1220hrs *U37* found the convoy, followed by *U99*. Kretschmer positioned himself carefully until darkness fell, and he slipped between two escorts on the port wing and opened fire. Kretschmer missed with only a single torpedo and had fired one dud. Though racing at high surface speed between merchant columns, he had been rarely glimpsed as escort ships fired star shells outwards from the convoy body. This single most successful convoy attack of *U99*'s career sank five ships totalling 34,505 tons and damaged another, bringing Kretschmer's patrol total to a staggering 61,711 tons destroyed in 24 days at sea. With no torpedoes remaining, Kretschmer ordered course laid for Lorient.

Schepke's *U100* had also sighted HX112 but was in trouble, as surfaced attack attempts had been foiled by the small fluorescent bow wave, *U100* forced to dive and depth charged by destroyers HMS *Walker* and *Vanoc*. Severely damaged, *U100* sank to 230 metres before Schepke used what little compressed air remained to blow tanks and surface, no more than 500 metres from HMS *Vanoc*. Travelling at 15 knots, *Vanoc* made immediate contact and swung towards *U100*. Schepke became flustered when diesels refused to fire, electric motors engaged, and the young captain ordered astern on the starboard motor, where he should have ordered ahead. Seconds later, he realized his error and ordered his men to prepare to abandon ship just before *Vanoc*'s bow hit *U100* almost at right angles to the conning tower, running up and over *U100*, which passed beneath 'B' gun. The hull flank of *U100* and her conning tower were crushed, Schepke caught and wedged between the smashed bridge combing and periscope housing as *U100* sank. Siegfried Flister, a prospective commander under instruction aboard *U100*, was standing immediately behind his captain and later told British interrogators that Schepke was stuck and dragged under by the sinking U-boat.

Aboard *Vanoc* there was jubilation. Despite the ship's ASDIC dome being wrecked by the impact and leaking, damage was light, and the destroyer immediately began to rescue German crewmen. Only six had been hauled from the water when the situation became 'somewhat awkward and confused' and *Vanoc* was forced to move off.[5] A second U-boat had appeared out of nowhere only 1,000 yards away and HMS *Walker* opened fire. It was *U99*. Kretschmer later recalled the disaster that followed:

> Through the fault of my starboard forward lookout… who had not seen anything of the approaching HMS *Walker*, we had

almost run into the destroyer. Only the vigilance of the officer on watch, who from time to time took a look around covering also the quarter of the Petty Officer, saved the boat from that fate, but unfortunately, he sounded [the] diving alarm in contrast to my standing order not to dive in such a situation, but to show the stern with high speed and call me onto the bridge, whereupon I would take command of the situation. So, the boat became stationary in the midst of the hunting destroyers. *U99* got a full load of depth charges from HMS *Walker* which effected an inrush of water and dropping of the boat like a stone.[6]

Walker had been circling *Vanoc* protectively as the latter picked up survivors from *U100* before obtaining an ASDIC contact, though commander Donald Macintyre was at first sceptical that their luck could be that good. *U99* reached 120 metres before depth charges exploded beneath it, plunging to 140 metres and sinking well below the official crush depth. Electric motors were disabled and the propellers no longer capable of maintaining *U99*'s place in the water column, the boat listing heavily as water entered the aft torpedo room. Kretschmer ordered main ballast tanks blown and *U99* rocketed upwards, bursting nose first through the surface as *Walker* fired all weapons.

A final radioed message was despatched in plain language, while the Enigma machine and its code books were thrown overboard: 'Bombed, boat sunk, Heil Hitler. Kretschmer 2 destroyers, 53 tons.' Chief Engineer Gottfried Schröder flooded ballast tanks, but was never seen again, going to the bottom with his boat, posthumously awarded the German Cross in Gold on 19 March 1942. Two men of Schröder's engine room crew were also lost, one having lost his lifebelt and unable to swim, while the other fell from the destroyer's scrambling net. Kretschmer was the last to leave the water, his seaboots so full of water and his limbs so tired that he could not move. As *Walker* began to get under way and Kretschmer was increasingly buffeted by the wake, he was spotted and dragged aboard by German and British sailors. In the space of less than two weeks, Dönitz had lost his three most celebrated captains.

After HX112 convoy traffic in the northern route dropped, only isolated steamers were sighted, while the Luftwaffe reported lively traffic southwest of the North Channel near Rockall Bank. With unexpectedly heavy losses, Dönitz prudently evacuated the northern area, redispersing U-boats to the south and, for the first time, west of the 25° meridian. For Dönitz this was a retrograde step, as it lessened time available on station for U-boats facing longer transits from base. Lengthier spring hours of daylight also forced U-boats to submerge more often, robbing them of the visible horizon and manoeuvrability. Shadowing while surfaced became exponentially more hazardous as Coastal Command changed tactics and began escorting at greater distance from convoys to force U-boats underwater.

This withdrawal marks an important milestone in the U-boat war, as Dönitz admitted temporary defeat following heavy losses, opting to retreat. Thus, the vaunted 'Happy Time' was over, its greatest successes achieved by men now dead, held prisoner or transferred ashore. The age of the North Atlantic 'Aces' had waned, and evermore Dönitz would concentrate on patrol lines and 'wolfpacks'.

His decision to move into the greater ocean expanse was risky but appeared vindicated when *U74* found eastbound SC26 on the first day of April, bringing seven other boats to begin attacking the following night. Between the first torpedoes fired by *U46* and the last by *U76* two nights later, ten ships were sunk and three damaged; surprised by destroyers while charging batteries, Friedrich von Hippel's *U76* was depth charged and scuttled.

This attack on SC26 was, however, a lucky accident for the Germans, and no other convoys were found until towards the end of the month when HX121 was sighted south of Iceland, attacked by five U-boats and five ships sunk. In return, veteran *U65*, under new commander Joachim Hoppe, was depth charged and destroyed by destroyer HMS *Douglas* with all 50 crewmen killed. Reports from captains returning from south of Iceland appeared to contradict Dönitz's assumptions of a strong enemy patrol presence in the northern area. Some encountered very few enemy forces above the accepted increase in British ASW activity since 1940. Coastal Command Hudson (269 Squadron) and Sunderland

(204 Squadron) aircraft had begun relocating to Iceland and, following establishment of a Royal Navy advanced fuelling depot, three newly formed escort groups (B3, B6 and B12) were likewise centred. These were intended to relieve outbound convoy escorts at about the 20° West meridian and accompany the convoy to 35°, approximately 900 nautical miles' distance, whereupon they would detach and rendezvous with inbound traffic. The sudden German losses had therefore been no more than 'normal' operational hazards, and U-boats began to return eastwards to waters south of Iceland, while the smaller Type IIs took up the offensive in the Faroes-Hebrides passage and the North Channel; Eberhard Wetjen's Type IID *U147* was lost with all 26 hands on 2 June after depth charging by destroyer HMS *Wanderer* and corvette HMS *Periwinkle*.

On 19 May, HX126 was sighted by Herbert Kuppisch's *U94*, Dönitz ordering the convoy shadowed as all western boats hastened to his beacon signals. Ultimately 11 U-boats took part in the action that followed, six of them succeeding in sinking nine ships, four after the convoy had scattered. The convoy had been attacked south of Greenland in the gap still not covered by escort forces, and as a result the Admiralty finally introduced 'end-to-end' surface escorts in conjunction with the Royal Canadian Navy. Long-distance Catalina flying boats had increased air cover to 700 miles from the British Isles, 400 miles from Iceland and 500 miles from Newfoundland, though an 'air-gap' remained in the mid-Atlantic. However, with enough escort ships finally constructed in both British and Canadian yards, as well as the aged American four-stack destroyers and the transfer of ten ocean-going US coastguard cutters to the Royal Navy, Canadian escort ships based at St John's, Newfoundland, could cover convoys to 35° West where they handed over to Iceland-based Royal Navy ships. The first inbound convoy to benefit from this new arrangement was HX129 that sailed on 27 May, though its defences remained untested as it travelled unmolested. Not until June was HX133 intercepted by a U-boat group that swelled to ten, sinking seven ships and damaging another in a controlled 'wolfpack' attack that trailed over five nights, although two U-boats were also lost. The 'Ace' Herbert

Wohlfarth's *U556* and Peter Lohmeyer's *U651* were both severely depth charged and brought to the surface, where their crews scuttled and abandoned ship. All Lohmeyer's crew were rescued, while five men were lost from *U556*. All survivors underwent detailed interrogation, which shows revealing comments made by Royal Navy officers. While accepting an inherent anti-German bias, the reports provide an interesting snapshot of two of Dönitz's U-boat crews. Wohlfarth was colourfully described as:

> ... extremely security-conscious... rather a bully, and arrogant; his success had made him conceited, but he showed a certain sense of humour. He was adequately educated and reasonably polite, but in conversation he betrayed occasional streaks of callousness and cruelty.

The chief and petty officers included a very few trained and experienced men who had previously served in *U137* under Wohlfarth but most petty officers were men of limited experience who had been hastily promoted after inadequate promotion courses. Discontentment with their lot and with the lack of prospects was coupled with criticism, not so much of their own officers, as of the naval authorities, service conditions, and what they considered the absence of realisation on the part of higher authorities of the conditions and requirements of the lower deck.

The ratings were the usual propaganda-fed, sheep-like Nazis of about 19 to 22 years of age; many were typical products of the '*Hitler Jugend*' organisation, had joined the Navy because they had been attracted by clever propaganda, and had been drafted without option to U-boats. Some were men of poor brain and had lived the simplest peasant lives until they found themselves, almost to their surprise, in the Navy. The petty officers were extremely critical of these recruits and expressed much apprehension as to the results to be feared from entrusting work of any importance to such men. There seemed to be an atmosphere of suppressed anxiety and an incipient fear which they themselves could not define.[7]

The officers and crew of *U651* received even stronger condemnation from their captors.

> The six officers and thirty-nine Petty Officers and men of *U651* formed one of the most fanatically Nazi and truculent crews interrogated for many months. Some of the more than usually unpleasant characteristics were thought to have been due partly to the teaching and example of the Captain, and partly to the extent to which Nazi propaganda had been applied and the hold which it had obtained upon the imagination of these men... The deterioration since the beginning of the war in the type of U-boat officer was more marked in the case of *U651* than in any batch of naval prisoners recently examined.[8]

Meanwhile, Dönitz reinvigorated his South Atlantic operations. Three large Type IXB U-boats – *U105*, *U106* and *U124* – had departed Lorient during February bound for Freetown, refuelling from the tanker *Charlotte Schliemann* (codenamed *Culebra*) in Las Palmas, Spanish Canary Islands, between 4 and 6 March. At 1410hrs the following day, BdU received notice that northbound convoy SL67 had been sighted by battleships *Scharnhorst* and *Gneisenau*, who maintained contact unobserved and without attacking due to the presence of battleship HMS *Malaya*, as major German surface units were under instructions not to engage British capital ships. The large convoy was escorted by *Malaya*, destroyers HMS *Faulknor* and *Forester*, armed merchant cruiser HMS *Cilicia* and corvette HMS *Asphodel*. Georg-Wilhelm Schulz's *U124* made contact with *Scharnhorst* and *Gneisenau*, and between the three commanders plans were made for both *U124* and *U105* to attack SL67 with the intention of sinking or at least damaging *Malaya*, clearing a path for the two German battleships.* With Jürgen Oesten's *U106* a few

---

* Schulz's Second Watch Officer, Werner Henke, spotted the distant German battleships first, originally taking them to be British. Schulz prepared an attack while radioing BdU for confirmation that no German ships were in the area. After hurried telephone calls between Kernéval and Berlin, the two battleships started zigzagging, informed a U-boat was stalking them while the message was relayed to *U124*.

days behind the other boats, he was to position himself to pick up remnants of the convoy later.

During early morning on 8 March, both U-boats attacked, sinking five merchant ships – Schulz penetrating the convoy and firing all six tubes over the course of a 20-minute attack which destroyed four of the merchants with a single salvo – but failing to hit *Malaya*. Later that day, the British sighted the two German ships, which were briefly chased but outpaced pursuit and withdrew west away from the convoy.

Schulz replenished from the raider *Schiff 41 'Kormoran'*, meeting the successful cruiser *Admiral Scheer* and transferring spare quartz crystals in a disused cigar box to the cruiser for repair of a damaged radar before *Scheer* headed north to the Denmark Straight and passage back to Germany. Transfer of torpedoes, provisions and fuel from *Kormoran* took three days, during which time *U124*'s medical officer, Dr Hubertus Goder, and a dangerously ill crewman were taken aboard for emergency surgery, replaced by an engineer from *Kormoran*.

U124 then headed east towards Freetown to join *U105* and *U106*, but suffered catastrophic failures of both diesels, drifting and helpless as engineers struggled to replace eight bearings which had collapsed. Without spares, temporary bearings were fashioned of compacted foil from cigarette packets by Chief Engineer Rolf Brinker.

While Schulz remained out of the picture near Freetown, both Georg Schewe's *U105* and Oesten's *U106* had encountered convoy SL68, though unable to bring *Scharnhorst* and *Gneisenau* back to the fray. Oesten's lookouts sighted the mass of 58 merchant ships, transmitting beacon signals to bring Schewe to the scene, whereupon, over the next few nights, they sank seven ships. Oesten severely damaged one other as well as hitting HMS *Malaya* on the port side. With damage to the boiler room, *Malaya* assumed a 7° list and broke away for repairs in Trinidad. After temporarily repaired in Port of Spain, *Malaya* moved on to the Brooklyn Navy Yard, where it remained until August, the first Royal Navy vessel of the war to be repaired and refitted in the USA. One step closer to open belligerency, the United States had already pledged aid to Great Britain during March 1941 when it opened American naval and private shipyards to damaged British warships, lend-lease funds paying for the cost of their repair.

Oesten received the Knight's Cross on 26 March for his combined tonnage and the successful strike against *Malaya*, Schewe later receiving the award on 23 May while returning to Germany from what would be the second most successful single patrol by a U-boat and the sinking of 12 ships, accumulating 71,450 tons.* Success in the South Atlantic – coinciding as it did with declining fortunes in the North – prompted reinforcement of cruiser U-boat operations around Freetown, and *U107*, *U103*, *U38* and *UA* sailed for this area during April, which would bring Dönitz's forces in the region to seven. However, to his chagrin, OKM ordered both *U105* and *U106* withdrawn from their rich hunting ground and redirected to the waters off Rio di Janeiro to cover the imminent sailing of the blockade-breaker/minelayer *Lech* that had been lying in the Brazilian harbour with a valuable cargo including nickel, hides, castor oil, mica and coffee, bound for France. Schewe and Oesten were instructed to immediately resupply from *Nordmark* and proceed south.

I consider the U-boats' task of getting the ship out is difficult and not certain to be successful. The disadvantage of sending boats to this remote area lies in the fact that it means scattering our few available forces. It means that the Freetown Groups will be broken up. There will only be one boat there (*U124*) until the beginning of May. The same thing is happening at present in the northern area owing to the withdrawal of *U94* and *U108* for attacks on warships northwest of Ireland [the Royal Navy's 'Northern Patrol'].†

---

* Schewe's remarkably successful 111-day voyage was later surpassed only by Günter Hessler in *U107*, when he undertook a 913-day patrol between March and July to the same operational area and sank 14 ships totalling 86,699 tons.
† *U108* sank auxiliary cruiser AMC *Rajputana* of the Northern Patrol on 13 April, four days after the 16,568-ton ship parted company with convoy HX117; BdU KTB 5 April 1941.

Both boats waited pointlessly in the waters off Natal, the expected departure of *Lech* postponed until 28 April. Both Schewe and Oesten had been instructed to avoid Rio to prevent prematurely breaking the ban on attacks within the USA Neutrality Zone that had been extended to include South America. Before the outbreak of war, the United States had committed itself to defending the entire land area of the Western Hemisphere against military attack from the 'Old World', the hemisphere defined as all land masses of North and South America plus Greenland, Bermuda and the Falkland Islands in the Atlantic area, and all islands east of the 180th meridian and the Aleutians in the Pacific. During April 1941, President Roosevelt had extended the hemispheric 'American Security Zone' within the North Atlantic to include waters west of 26° longitude, effectively putting 'defensive' American warships within U-boat operational areas.

Meanwhile, in mid-April fuel shortages forced *U124* to begin its return journey, leaving Freetown bereft of U-boat presence.* In response OKM relented and allowed Schewe's *U105* to return from Brazil, while Oesten's *U106* was given permission to operate aggressively outside the 300-mile neutrality limit. However, Oesten soon reported his boat unable to comply due to limited fuel and lubricating oil. Dönitz seethed at the enforced hiatus of attacks against Sierra Leone:

> The whole operation has miscarried… This means a useless period of waiting for the boats which they could have spent more profitably in the operations area off Freetown. In addition, they cannot be given freedom to attack enemy ships outside the scope of their escort duty for *Lech*, although originally assurances were received from Naval War Staff that this would be allowed. They have therefore not only been withdrawn from

---

* Georg-Wilhelm Schulz had sunk 11 ships, totalling 53,297 tons, during the 68-day patrol and was awarded the Knight's Cross while still at sea on 4 April. Aware that Rolf Brinker had saved the boat through his ingenious use of cigarette foil, he requested the Knight's Cross for him too, though Brinker was instead awarded the German Cross in Gold, the fourth Kriegsmarine man to receive the medal.

a good area for several weeks, but they will have been a total loss to the war against merchant shipping during this time and their long passage will make demands on their engines which will eventually mean a longer period repairing when they return.[9]

U105 sank a single ship in the mid-Atlantic during the entire month of April, while *U106* achieved nothing. Oesten finally rendezvoused with *Lech* on 29 April and successfully escorted it towards the Azores, laboriously refuelling and resupplying from the merchant before parting company. Eventually, the entire mission was proved futile; *Lech* subsequently scuttled itself on 28 May after it was intercepted by light cruiser HMS *Edinburgh* 400 miles north of the Azores. To add insult to injury, SKL enquired whether *U106* could also escort blockade breaker *Windhuk* out of Santos, although this second escort was soon cancelled; *Windhuk*'s departure was indefinitely delayed and the ship later seized by Brazilian authorities in January 1942 after two years in the harbour. Oesten was released from this second obligation on 7 May; but low on fuel and suffering engine problems, he was ordered to rendezvous with the supply ship *Egerland*, one of several that had been positioned to support the maiden sortie of Germany's newest battleship, *Bismarck*.

Despite delays in the sailing of *UA* and *U103* due to mechanical problems, the new wave of West African U-boats found further rich pickings among both unescorted merchants and convoy traffic. Furthermore, Dönitz despatched *U69* to the region – the first Type VIIC launched and the first to attempt such an ambitious journey, carrying eight torpedoes and 12 mines from Lorient on 5 May. Even the small amount of personal space allocated to each man had been reduced. *Kapitänleutnant* Jost Metzler later wrote of the noticeable changes to the Type VII and it preparation for sea:

The armament was far heavier than before. A considerable amount of the crews' personal belongings and dispensable articles on board had been put ashore. All the chests and corners on board in which the men kept writing materials, books or pictures were commandeered for provisions and ammunition. Behind the bunks and bulkheads, in the bilges, between the torpedo tubes and behind the diesel engines were piled tins, crates, canisters and ammunition. The cook guarded all these treasures with an eagle eye. In the control room, next to the periscope and between the manometers, hung magnificent sausages and a few Westphalian hams. There was not a single spot left in which something had not been stored. Even the men's pockets were full of cigarettes and chocolates which had been issued for their spell in harbour.[10]

Metzler aimed to stretch his fuel supply by creeping south on one diesel, until rendezvousing with the tanker *Egerland* two weeks later in the Central Atlantic west of Freetown. Heading almost due East, Metzler then encountered on 21 May a ship that would mark another turning point of the war, vividly described in *U69*'s War Diary. After sighting the steamer which carried a conspicuous covered deck cargo and on which no illuminated neutrality markings could be seen, Metzler suspected it to be a Q-ship.[*]

0525: Take position 2,000 meters off and ask the name via Morse lamp. Steamer gives: *Robin Moor*.

Name is not to be found in any catalogue, my suspicion increases.

0535: Order steamer to stop and ask for boat with Captain and papers. Steamer stops immediately and simultaneously puts boat into the water. Lie with sharp silhouette on the

---

[*] The so-called 'Q-ship' had been developed during the First World War. Q-ships were small tramp steamers, outwardly dishevelled and unworthy of a torpedo, but equipped with hidden guns and designed to entice a U-boat into approaching surfaced to sink the ship with gunfire or by scuttling. Once within range, the camouflaged guns would be revealed, and fire opened. They possessed a reputation enduringly feared by U-boat crews, though of approximately 150 such ships that served between 1914 and 1918, ten U-boats were sunk for the loss of 27 of their own. Originally referred to by the Royal Navy using the broad term 'Special Service Vessels', they were only officially designated 'Q-ships' for a period during 1916, apparently in relation to the majority basing at Queenstown (now Cobh) in Ireland.

steamer. I am ready for a stern shot and – if necessary – crash dive.

0600: Boat with the First Officer of the ship is alongside. Papers were not brought. Find out from the First Officer that because it was sold 14 days ago the ship's name was changed from *Exmoor* to *Robin Moor*. Allegedly an American ship on the way from New York to South Africa; cargo allegedly engines and semi-finished motor vehicles, as well as general piece goods. Explain to the First Officer, that on the basis of his information, the steamer carries absolute contraband and therefore must be sunk. Request the abandonment of the ship and at the same time for the Captain to bring over the papers. The First Officer raises no objection, he and his crew note my explanation calmly. A willingness which is all the more suspicious! Observe that after return of the boat to the steamer a mass confusion ensues, doors fly up and the boats go to water in a panic and retreat from the steamer.

0815: (ESE 1-2, Sea 1, light swell, Vis. medium, light tropical rain). Boat with Captain and cargo papers alongside. The papers prove banned goods perfectly, even weapons are listed. Explain to the Captain personally that steamer must be sunk because cargo is exclusively and absolutely banned goods against which nothing is objected. Hand over to the Captain more provisions, cognac and dressings. Captain and crew call 'Heil Hitler!' Set off and moved away quickly. Most remarkable behaviour! Expect a surprise attack at any moment from the enormous deck cargo.

0949: To avoid surprises, gave the steamer a stern shot: Bow left, target angle 90°, depth 2 meters, Eto tube runner ejected with mine gear.

Crash dive. Running time 127 seconds – 1900 meters.

Hit centre.

Observe from periscope depth. Steamer sinks very slowly. Nothing remarkable noted on deck.

1045: Surfaced and sank ship with 30 rounds of artillery ammunition from 3000 meters… Entire deck cargo floats off.

Boxes do not sink after MG C30 bombardment, through bullet holes aluminium parts can be recognized. Because aircraft tires float among the boxes, it is an aircraft cargo.[11]

Metzler had obeyed standing orders regarding contraband material, though once suspicions that *Robin Moor* may have been a Q-ship were allayed by its sinking without incident, he began to regret what he knew would become a diplomatic incident. Despite carrying banned goods to and from a belligerent nation, the ship was genuinely American – the first to be sunk of the Second World War. Nevertheless, *U69* continued its patrol, sinking another unescorted steamer and successfully mining both Takoradi and Lagos harbours, approaching the narrow harbours by night, trimmed down in shallow water and undetected despite strong phosphorescence. On 4 June, the 2,879-ton British dredger *Robert Hughes* was sunk by one of the five mines dropped at Lagos, with 14 crewmen killed.

By the time that Metzler docked once again in Lorient on 8 July, he had sunk seven ships, totalling 33,868 tons, two of them from convoy SL78 during the return voyage and another from OB337; the convoy commodore's armed ship *Robert L. Holt* engaged in an artillery duel with *U69* in which the U-boat expended considerable ammunition. Given the British ship's firepower, it was mistaken for an auxiliary cruiser; the master, John Alexander Kendall, commodore, Vice-Admiral N.A. Wodehouse, 41 crew members, eight gunners and five naval staff members were all lost with their ship.

In fact, during mid-1941 the West African theatre yielded the three most successful patrols of the entire war: *U107* (86,699 tons), *U105* (71,450 tons) and *U103* (65,172 tons). Furthermore, every U-boat commander involved was highly decorated either during or immediately after these voyages: Günter Hessler (*U107*), George Schewe (*U105*), Jürgen Oesten (*U106*), Georg-Wilhelm Schulz (*U124*), and Jost Metzler (*U69*) all received the Knight's Cross, while Heinrich Liebe (*U38*) and Viktor Schütze (*U103*) were awarded the Oak Leaves to their existing Knight's Crosses.

In Britain there was grave concern over such heavy losses near Freetown, and the number of unescorted solo sailings dramatically reduced and convoying subsequently increased. The decision was taken to introduce 'end to end' convoying, whereby each convoy departing Freetown was escorted to Gibraltar by a planned five corvettes, requiring extra escort vessels to be diverted from the North Atlantic, and the anti-submarine contingent bolstered by the attachment of armed trawlers from Northern Ireland. Once near Gibraltar the merchants would then merge with convoys already leaving the 'Rock'.

Upon Metzler's return, he was commended for his courageous minelaying and exceptional patrol during which he faced and overcame numerous mechanical problems. However, despite support from his fellow officers for his sinking of *Robin Moor*, Dönitz officially noted that the ship's destruction was 'contrary to standing orders'. In the United States, although newspapers decried 'Nazi brutality', there was a relatively moderate political response, with Representative John William McCormack quoted as saying, 'It was very unfortunate but there is no reason now to get unnecessarily excited over this incident.' Nevertheless, Roosevelt condemned the sinking in the strongest terms and, using the foray of the *Bismarck* into the Atlantic Ocean as a reason to align more closely with Great Britain, German assets were frozen on 12 June, the State Department instructing Germany and Italy to close all of their consulates in the United States two days later, prompting Germany to retaliate in kind.

Ratcheting tension yet further was the American occupation of Iceland during July, freeing British forces previously garrisoning the island for service elsewhere. Roosevelt had declared in a speech that successful hemispheric defence depended upon the salvation of Great Britain and its oceanic lifeline across the North Atlantic, effective control of Iceland therefore integral to the national security of the United States. On 6 August, the US Navy established an air base at Reykjavik with the arrival of Patrol Squadron VP-73 PBY Catalinas and VP-74 PBM Mariners. United States Army personnel also began arriving that month, including the P40 Warhawk fighters of USAAF 33rd Pursuit Squadron.

American ships had been considered hostile by German submariners for some time; shadowing U-boats while broadcasting coordinates for British ships as pursuant to provisions provided by the US Navy's 'Western Hemisphere Defense Plan No. 2', declared active from 24 April. This US Navy's 'Neutrality Patrol' invited challenge, and on 20 June Rolf Mützelburg in *U203* sighted darkened cruiser USS *Texas* and its destroyer screen zigzagging within the prescribed German blockade zone and requested permission to fire. BdU denied the request, though Dönitz later modified his permission to allow operations against American warships once they had passed the western boundary of the blockade area by 20 or more miles. This too was, however, reversed by unequivocal instructions from Hitler, immediately transmitted to all U-boats at sea:

> The Führer has ordered, for the next weeks, avoidance of any incident with the USA. Proceed accordingly in any doubtful case. Further, attacks on warships within and outside the blockade area until further notice only cruisers, battleships and aircraft carriers and only if these are definitely recognized as enemy vessels. If warships are proceeding without lights this is not to be taken as an indication that they are hostile.[12]

The reason for this restrictive order became clearer the following day. Hitler wished to avoid any further provocation of the United States while he focussed the strength of the Wehrmacht elsewhere, as recorded within Metzler's War Diary for 22 June:

> 0000: 'Perseus' in effect.
> 0400: Beginning of the war with Russia.

Chapter Five

The Descent

'*I have always thought that Lemp committed suicide…*'
David Balme, HMS *Bulldog*[1]

The Kriegsmarine played little role in *Barbarossa*. The potential for using the Baltic as a troop-carrying 'highway' into Russian territory appears valid on paper but would have faced the powerful Red Banner Baltic Fleet, and the Kriegsmarine had been visibly diminished by two years of war.

Bismarck, pride of the German fleet, had slipped from Gotenhafen on 19 May and sailed in company with heavy cruiser *Prinz Eugen* for Operation *Rheinübung*, an Atlantic sortie to pillage the Allied merchant convoy routes. Despite dramatically sinking HMS *Hood*, *Bismarck* took damage, forcing the two ships to separate with the battleship making for France. Harried by British forces, while Dönitz formed two U-boat patrol lines to potentially ambush pursuing ships, *Bismarck* was finally cornered in terrible weather conditions, disabled by gunfire and scuttled by the German crew. From 2,221 men, only 114 survived, the majority rescued by British ships, three by *U74* and another two by a *Vorpostenboot* (patrol boat, typically an armed trawler). Meanwhile, *Prinz Eugen* refuelled from tankers near the Azores before discovering a chipped propellor blade and serious engine defects, abandoning the mission to travel to Brest.

The blow to national prestige led Hitler to forbid further capital ship forays into the Atlantic, and pocket battleships *Gneisenau* and *Scharnhorst* as well as the heavy cruiser *Prinz Eugen* remained effectively penned in Brest. Elsewhere, heavy cruiser *Lützow* (ex-*Deutschland*) was scheduled for six months of repair, having suffered a British torpedo hit in Norwegian waters, while *Admiral Hipper* and *Admiral Scheer* were also in shipyards. Light cruiser *Nürnberg* had been relegated to training duties, *Köln* still undergoing modification and *Leipzig* and *Emden* the only pair in active service. The Kriegsmarine's destroyer arm had taken severe casualties in the invasion of Norway during April 1940 and would also play little part in the opening of the Russian campaign.

Instead, a relatively sparse naval force was assembled for *Barbarossa*, whose primary offensive cutting edge comprised 28 S-boats, supported by six minelayers and the smaller craft of the minesweeping and patrol flotillas as well as a small number of U-boats. Dönitz later stated:

> When war against Russia broke out, eight boats were dispatched to operate in the Baltic. There they found practically no targets and accomplished nothing worth mentioning. They were accordingly returned to me at the end of September.
>
> In the same way, from July 1941 onwards four to six boats had to be detached for operations against the Russians in the Arctic, although of course at that time there were not yet any Allied convoys carrying supplies to Russia. These U-boats, too, roamed the empty seas... the decisive factor in the war against Britain is the attack on her imports. The delivery of these attacks is the U-boats' principal task and one which no other branch of the Armed Forces can take over from them. The war with Russia will be decided on land, and in it the U-boats can play only a very minor role.[2]

He was, of course, correct. Raeder had ordered U-boats to the Arctic in anticipation of a British attempt to open a northerly supply route to the Soviet Union, but in this he was premature. Much against Dönitz's advice, Type VIICs *U81* and *U652* arrived first, while *U451* and *U566* were scheduled to leave Trondheim for the Arctic on 23 July. Georg-Werner Fraatz's *U652* sailed from Kiel to Horten on 19 June, administratively attached to Kiel's 3rd U-Flotilla but operating not under direction from BdU but rather directly beneath the command umbrella of Hermann Boehm, Admiral Commanding Norway. Fraatz and his crew spent nine days in Horten before heading north to Trondheim and eventually the polar seas, docking in Bøkfjorden, Finnmark, on 22 July. There, within the 23-kilometre fjord, Fraatz moored at the small town of Kirkenes, designated Kriegsmarine operational centre for the northern Arctic coast. The large depot ship *Black Watch* was commissioned into service there during 1941, later joined by *Stella Polaris* as U-boats proliferated. Not until 6 August would any of the Arctic boats draw blood, when Fraatz sank 558-ton Russian ASW trawler *RT70* 7 miles off Cape Teriberka with a single G7e torpedo.

The extent of *Barbarossa*'s Baltic U-boat employment saw a handful of small Type II U-boats shifted from training duties to offensive operations, testing new commanders and crew alike and yielding several small successes. On 21 June, the SKL War Diary recorded the dispositions of the *Barbarossa* boats – *U140*, *U142*, *U144*, *U145* and *U149* – in the Gulf of Riga and Gulf of Finland, while three others – *U137*, *U143* and *U146* – were assigned to the North Sea to patrol near the Orkney and Shetland Islands in case of British intervention. With BdU attention required on the commerce war, the Baltic boats were removed from BdU control, passing instead into the jurisdiction of Commander-in-Chief Cruisers, Hubert Schmundt who, subordinate to *Generaladmiral* Rolf Carls' *Marinegruppenkommando Nord* (MGK Nord), exercised operational control over all naval craft employed in *Barbarossa*.*

---

* Carls was not widely liked by U-boat officers, who christened him the 'Blue Tsar' because, as Jürgen Oesten later put it to me, 'his manners were Tsar-like, but his intelligence and capability were medium only' (16 June 2002).

During June and July, three of the Baltic boats each sank a Soviet M-class submarine.*

The three North Sea boats remained with BdU, transferred to the administrative strength of Kiel's 3rd U-Flotilla, under the command of Hans-Rudolf Rösing at that time, during their relatively uneventful forays into the North Sea. Somewhat ironically, the sole combat sinking they made as part flanking force for *Barbarossa* was the torpedoing of 3,496-ton Finnish steamer *Pluto* on 28 June northwest of the Butt of Lewis. The cargo ship was sailing from Buenos Aires for Petsamo, carrying a cargo of 4,000 tons of grain, 1,114 tons of coal and 237 tons of oil. Three of the 39 crew were killed.

In June 1941, Dönitz possessed only 38 boats in action, 28 of them within the North Atlantic. While total U-boat strength lay at 150, 112 of these were either training vessels or in the process of trials before active deployment. As a result, June was a particularly barren month for North Atlantic U-boat success. Thinly spread, they were further hampered by thick fog as warm Gulf Stream air and Arctic cold fronts collided south of Greenland. With no Halifax convoys sighted, Wilhelm Kleinschmidt's *U111* on its maiden patrol was authorized to refuel from *Belchen* and then penetrate Newfoundland waters as far as the entrance to the Belle Isle Strait, the first U-boat foray into North American waters. Kleinschmidt was under firm instructions to fire at nothing except 'exceptionally valuable' targets, lest the United States be provoked further, though he found nothing, suffering damaged torpedo tube caps caused by drifting ice. Only a single convoy, HX133, had been successfully intercepted and engaged by a group of boats from Brest with six ships sunk from a total of 64 merchants and 20 escorts. However, it was not solely U-boat numbers that inhibited success.

While the Wehrmacht considered its Enigma code to be of such complexity that it was unbreakable, the main Luftwaffe cypher had been broken in May 1940 and was consistently read by Allied

* *U144* (Gert von Mittelstaedt) sank *M78* on 23 June, *U149* (Horst Höltring) sank *M99* on 27 June, and *U140* (Hans-Jürgen Hellriegel) sank *M94* on 21 July. *U144* was sunk with all hands on 10 August by Soviet submarine *ShCh-307*.

intelligence until the war's end. The Kriegsmarine proved more difficult as, instead of the army and Luftwaffe choice of three out of five supplied rotors for the encryption machine, giving 60 possible wheel orders, Kriegsmarine operators were supplied with the normal five, plus three extra 'double notched' rotors, producing 336 potential wheel orders, the 'double notched' rotors turning the next wheel in line twice per revolution. The answer was a carefully orchestrated series of Allied raids targeting patrol vessels and weather reporting ships which yielded significant documents and cypher material. Three Enigma rotors – including Kriegsmarine rotors VI and VII that were unknown to Allied intelligence at that time – had also been recovered from a survivor of *U33*, sunk by the minesweeper HMS *Gleaner* on 12 February 1940. Hans von Dresky's boat had been attempting to lay mines in the Firth of Clyde when it was sunk by *Gleaner*, Dresky distributing the Enigma rotors between three crewmen to dump overboard once he surfaced and ordered the crippled U-boat scuttled. In freezing waters, only 17 men survived, one of them clearly failing to follow instructions regarding the rotors, probably due to shock and disorientation. Dresky was not among the survivors.

Due to the efforts of an extraordinary group of cryptanalysts that the British had gathered at Bletchley Park, by March 1941 several signals that had been transmitted in the Kriegsmarine's 'home waters' code during February – known as *Heimisch*, codenamed 'Dolphin' by the British – were broken. While not of immediate tactical value, this intelligence, known as 'Ultra', provided precious insight into German naval operations. However, the Allies required a continuous and reliable break of the codes. During the same period, the simpler 'hand-cypher' used by dockyards and minor vessels in German and Norwegian waters (*Werftschlüssel*) was also broken. With many messages transmitted in both this cypher and via the Enigma, they provided valuable cross-references in the struggle to fully crack the Enigma. In May, the weather ship *München* was captured, providing the *Heimisch* settings for June, and a few days later a major breakthrough occurred during a U-boat attack against convoy OB318 southwest of Iceland.

Kuppisch's *U94* sighted OB318 during late afternoon on 7 May, and was ordered by BdU to attack if possible or otherwise shadow for the benefit of six other U-boats deployed in the Northwest Atlantic, named 'West' group. As Kuppisch followed, three ships left the convoy for Reykjavik, and three destroyers, three corvettes and three ASW trawlers of 3rd Escort Group arrived in company with auxiliary cruiser HMS *Ranpura* and four freighters from Iceland to relieve 7th Escort Group running low on fuel. As Kuppisch attacked, OB318 had 16 warships in company. Firing a full submerged bow salvo, he claimed four ships hit and sunk, though he only sank two, followed by severe and accurate depth charging after HMS *Rochester* sighted the periscope in light cast by burning ships. Eighty-nine charges shook the boat and caused severe damage before *U94* slipped away to effect repairs.[*]

That evening, Lemp in *U110* contacted OB318 and brought Adalbert 'Adi' Schnee's *U201* into the fray. Schnee, formerly First Watch Officer for Otto Kretschmer aboard *U23*, was on his maiden patrol as captain of the new Type VIIC, and the two commanders discussed tactics via megaphone the following morning. With a clear sky and bright moon expected that night, they elected to launch submerged daylight attacks, Lemp leading with Schnee following 30 minutes later. Both commanders expected escorts to have departed OB318, and Lemp was apparently surprised to see warships of 3rd Escort Group through his periscope as he approached, nonetheless deciding to continue despite Third Watch Officer Albert Krumbügel urging delay, as he was certain the escorts would soon depart. Lemp prepared a full bow-salvo on four

---

[*] Kuppisch learned by radio on 14 May that he had been awarded the Knight's Cross for successful mining operations and credited sinking of a destroyer and 17 merchant ships totaling 90,260 tons (in reality HMS *Astronomer*, a Boom Defence Vessel, and 16 merchants totaling 73,707 tons). To celebrate the award, the crew fashioned a large cross out of lead and hard rubber which they fastened around their captain's neck. Kuppisch had become increasingly nervous during the last of his 13 war patrols as captain of *U58* and *U94*, noticeably anxious to his crew when departing and returning from a cruise, though once at sea his anxiety lessened. During his final patrol in *U94*, Kuppisch mounted only a single failed attack and was subsequently transferred ashore to BdU staff and later OKM before returning to sea in 1943. He was killed in action as captain of Type IXD-2 *U847* on 27 August 1943.

separate ships, and two torpedoes struck home and sank a pair of steamers while the third missed. The final torpedo misfired and Lemp ordered it readjusted for a shot against a tanker as the convoy made a dramatic turn to port.

As Schnee attacked and sank another pair of ships, the escort group's flagship HMS *Bulldog* as well as HMS *Aubretia* and *Broadway* (one of the 50 'four-stack' ex-American destroyers) made firm ASDIC contact with *U110*, lookouts aboard *Aubretia* sighting Lemp's periscope moving from port to starboard dead ahead despite *U110* travelling in the wake of *Broadway*, conforming to *Broadway*'s zig-zag patterns. Only at the last moment did Lemp turn his periscope to starboard and see *Aubretia*'s bow wave bearing down on him, *U110* crash diving as depth charges exploded around the shallow boat.

Survivors recalled heavy damage – gauges and instruments smashed, electric motors inoperative, an aft fuel tank ruptured and leaking diesel oil – as *U110* sank rapidly stern first to at least 95 metres. Lemp, a thin trickle of blood visible on his forehead as he had been knocked off his feet by the blast and struck the metal decking with his head, ordered his Chief Engineer Hans-Joachim Eichelborn to prepare to blow ballast tanks, but before he could give the order *U110* surfaced on its own accord, perhaps a ruptured high-pressure air line already having blown the ballast tanks.

We are enveloped in a whole series of accurately placed depth charges. The boat is terribly shaken and it seems as though all the instruments are out of action. Chlorine gas is escaping and then the Captain gives the order to blow the tanks. But the blower has been smashed, the batteries are out of action and there seems scarcely any possibility of reaching the surface. A very bitter end. We are slowly sinking and then suddenly the boat begins to roll. For some inexplicable reason the boat reached the surface, the Captain opens the conning tower hatch and gives the order 'Abandon Ship'.*

---

* Diary written by *Obersteuermann* Albert Krumbügel after his capture (*U110: Interrogation of Survivors*, May 1941, Naval Intelligence Division, Admiralty, NID 08409/43).

As was customary, Lemp led the way on to the conning tower, greeted by the sight of all three British ships firing upon the crippled U-boat with weapons of every calibre. He ordered everybody out as fast as possible and vents opened – the fastest way to scuttle a U-boat as there appeared no time to connect fuses to the scuttling charges. As a 3-inch shell struck the conning tower and British gunners began seeing men leap overboard, fire from heavy weapons was ceased, machine guns continuing to hasten the Germans' departure.

Broadway attempted to ram *U110*, but Lieutenant Commander Thomas Taylor realized that the U-boat was not sinking and swung away at the last moment, grazing *U110* whose hydroplane holed the destroyer's port forward fuel tank. A single shallow depth charge was dropped close to the U-boat's bow to hasten evacuation as *Bulldog's* captain, Lieutenant Commander Joe Baker-Cresswell, ordered armed men to board *U110*.

Twenty-year-old Sub-Lieutenant David Balme led a boarding party comprising six seamen, one telegraphist and a stoker to *U110* without apparently being seen by the panicked Germans in the water.* What exactly happened to Lemp remains a matter of some debate to this day. He was seen definitely abandoning ship and swimming away, some German survivors later claiming that they were shot at in the water and he may have been hit, though Balme later denied that anybody was deliberately targeting swimming men. Others recalled Lemp shouting that he was returning to the boat, while still others speculated that, suffering from concussion, he may well have drowned either accidentally in his heavy leather gear and sea boots, or deliberately when he realized the scope of the unfolding disaster. Erich Topp remained convinced that explosives had been set on the torpedo tubes and electric motors but had failed to detonate, with Lemp shot as he attempted to swim back to *U110*.[3] Regardless, though waves were breaking over the U-boat's deck in the moderate sea, *U110* was not sinking and Balme's party rowed swiftly across, running

---

* A.B.S. Pearce, C. Dolley, R. Roe, K. Wilemen, Ordinary Seaman A. Hargreaves and J. Trotter, Telegraphist A. Long and Stoker C. Lee.

the whaler hard on board, a wave carrying it on to the deck, where it was wedged between guard rails and conning tower, later smashed by the rising sea.

To Balme's surprise, considering that the aim had been to scuttle the U-boat, the outer conning tower hatch was closed, and on unscrewing the handwheel the hatch sprung open as soon as securing latches released.

> I went down the ladder to the lower Conning Tower where there was a similar closed hatch. On opening this hatch, I found the Control Room deserted! Hatches leading forward and aft were open and all lighting on. On the deck there was a large splinter from the conning tower. There was a slight escape of air in the control room but no sign of Chlorine so gasmasks which had been taken were now discarded. So, also, were revolvers which now seemed more of a danger than an asset.
>
> The U-boat had obviously been abandoned in great haste as books and gear were strewn about the place. A chain of men was formed to pass up all books, charts etc. As speed was essential owing to possibility of U boat sinking (although dry throughout) I gave orders to send up ALL books, except obviously reading books, so consequently a number of comparatively useless navigational books etc. were recovered. All charts were in drawers under the chart table in the Control Room; there were also some signal books, logbooks etc. here. The metal sheet diagrams were secured overhead.
>
> Meanwhile the telegraphist went to the W/T office, just forward of the control room on starboard side. This was in perfect condition, apparently no attempt having been made to destroy any books or apparatus. Here were found Code Books, Signal Logs, Pay Books, and general correspondence, looking as if this room had been used as ship's office. Also, the coding machine was found here, plugged in and as though it was in actual use when abandoned. The general appearance of this machine being that of a typewriter, the telegraphist pressed the keys and finding results peculiar sent it up the hatch.[4]

Fifteen men, including Lemp, were lost from *U110*, the remaining 32 survivors rescued and hustled below decks, unaware that their boat had been boarded. In total two journeys were made between *U110* and *Broadway*, which had lowered its boat to assist. Despite German recollections, the U-boat appeared in reasonable shape, the port motor running slow ahead and wheel to starboard. As more British sailors arrived, attempts to either shut down the motor or start the starboard one came to nought as nobody could understand how it worked. In total, the Royal Navy men were aboard for nearly five hours, *U110* was then abandoned and taken in tow by *Bulldog* until it finally swamped and sank stern first in worsening weather the following morning.

By that stage, possession of the actual U-boat was largely unimportant. The true value of the capture of *U110* was recovery of code books for the *Heimisch* code, keys to the double-encyphered *Offizier* ('Officers Only') code, the *Kurzsignale* ('Short Signal') code, Kriegsmarine grid charts, technical plans and manuals for the Type IXB, charts of the latest German minefields in the North Sea and Biscay and a complete working Enigma machine with all rotors intact. A second weather ship captured in June gave *Heimisch* settings for July, and with diligent processing of previously established 'cribs' into the Enigma code, *Heimisch* (Dolphin) was finally broken completely in August until the end of the war.

The full extent of the disaster facing Dönitz's U-boats would unfold slowly. Halifax convoys were skilfully diverted away from the 'West' patrol line, although in order not to betray their penetration of the *Heimisch* code, the Admiralty chose not to immediately attack U-boats whose positions were now known through daily location reports. Dönitz had intended to use tankers positioned to support *Bismarck* and merchant raiders to replenish his combat boats at sea, thereby lengthening their patrols, and it was these that the British now targeted. First was *Belchen*, 80 miles southwest of Greenland at the southern entrance to the Davis Strait. Already having refuelled *U111* and *U557*, the tanker was ambushed on 3 June by cruisers HMS *Aurora* and *Kenya* while in the act of refuelling Claus Korth's *U93*, *Kenya* opening fire with its main armament and setting *Belchen* ablaze as hoses were cut and *U93* dived to safety. Listing badly, *Belchen* was finished by a torpedo from *Aurora*.

Korth, awarded the Knight's Cross during this patrol for his accumulated successes, had already requested resupply but failed to find *Belchen* at the specified coordinates. Continuing on one engine, Korth was denied permission to head for France and two days later Korth met *Belchen*, only 34 tons of fuel transferred before British shells began falling. Following the British withdrawal from the scene, Korth rescued 49 of the tanker's crew, five others including the captain having drowned. Ordered to rendezvous with a second supply ship, *Friedrich Breme*, Korth refused as his fuel level was critical and, should the second rendezvous fail, he would be unable to reach France. Ironically, during his slow return in radio silence, Korth sighted a southbound convoy but, his boat badly overloaded, opted not to transmit a sighting report or attack. His deviation from Dönitz's standard radio contact requirements unwittingly prevented British intelligence from tracking *U93*, bringing him into contact with convoy traffic routed around U-boats hunting in vain. For its part in the unfolding drama, *Friedrich Breme* was caught by cruiser HMS *Sheffield* on 12 June and forced to scuttle, the crew captured.

Coordinated attacks took a heavy toll among the tanker supply chain. On 4 June, in the North Atlantic *Gonzenheim* was similarly attacked and forced to scuttle, as was *Esso Hamburg* in the mid-Atlantic west of Freetown. *Egerland* was scuttled as *U38* approached to replenish after interception by HMS *London* and *Brilliant*, and the ship due to relieve *Egerland* off West Africa – 8,923-ton *Gedania* carrying 48 torpedoes bound for the West African boats – was intercepted by the ocean-boarding vessel HMS *Marsdale* and, following a two-hour chase and unsuccessful scuttling attempt, boarded and captured. On 15 June, *Lothringen* was captured by HMS *Dunedin*, eliminating the last of the ships planned to resupply African U-boats. A major setback for Dönitz, it provided fresh impetus for the building of dedicated supply U-boats.

The idea of a supply and workshop U-boat had been suggested during the early days of German rearmament, though capture of French Atlantic ports appeared to render the concept less urgent.

Nonetheless, the 1,688-ton dedicated supply Type XIV design had been finalized and the first four (*U459–U462*) ordered from Deutsche Werke on 14 May 1940, an order for the additional *U464* laid at the same office on 15 August. Construction, which only commenced in November, was delayed by priority given to combat boats. But following the most recent setbacks, supply U-boats were back on the agenda, and on 17 July 1941 Germaniawerft received an order for another four (*U487–U490*). Deutsche Werke's *U459* was the first to be launched on 13 September 1941, though it was not operational until April 1942.

By the end of June, the gradual relocation of Dönitz's main combat flotillas from Germany to France had been completed, though the presence of *Scharnhorst, Gneisenau* and *Prinz Eugen* in Brest harbour had attracted major RAF bombing raids, confirming the need for extensive concrete U-boat shelters. These would provide safe wet and dry docks and protected points of repair for U-boats, and in Brest the Organization Todt commenced construction on the seafront of Lanninon at the beginning of 1941. This single huge structure would eventually measure 333m long, 192m wide, and 17m high – a combination of 'wet pens' that could hold two U-boats and single boat dry docks. Carved within the granite ridge to the bunker's rear were subterranean stores for artillery and torpedo storage and maintenance; the first portions of the U-boat bunker were operational by the end of 1941.

Similar constructions were taking place at all Atlantic U-boat bases, the most ambitious project reserved for Lorient. As in Brest, U-boats were initially serviced in docks protected only by netting and tarpaulins; early air raids sharply highlighting the vulnerability of this practice. During November 1940, Fritz Todt had toured Lorient with both Raeder and Dönitz, the three planning an expansive project to construct three separate submarine bunkers at the foreshore of Keroman. Two huge, arched bunkers (known as *Dombunkers*) were first built at Lorient's fishing port, functioning as dry docks for Type II U-boats and served by an existing slipway and turntable. A small tidal shelter was also constructed on the southern bank of the Scorff River near Gueydon Bridge, capable of holding a pair of Type VII or IX U-boats, but only a temporary solution. Work began in January 1941 on the Keroman project and was completed in stages: bunkers Keroman I, II and III were finished in September 1941, December 1941 and January 1943 respectively.

Keroman I provided sufficient room for five dry-dock pens and a protected slipway for lifting submarines from the water, Keroman II on dry land immediately behind Keroman I. The final bunker, Keroman III, was truly massive and lay on the river, having two repair pens, each capable of accepting two U-boats side by side and five mooring docks again capable of handling two U-boats apiece. Imposing steel doors 3 feet thick could be swung closed across each pen, and two ships were moored immediately before the bunkers with tethered barrage balloons. As this massive task was still under way, the first operational U-boat bunker was inaugurated at Saint Nazaire on 30 June in a ceremony conducted by Dönitz.

That same month, the 2nd U-Flotilla was officially established in Lorient and 7th U-Flotilla in Saint Nazaire. By October, 3rd U-Flotilla would also officially operate from La Rochelle/La Pallice, and in Brest the 9th U-Flotilla was established in the incomplete Morvan Hospital complex. Training establishments were also transformed during 1941; in Danzig, Wilhelm Schulz's 6th Flotilla resurrected during July, occupying the role of training flotilla for its first few months until transfer in February 1942 to Saint Nazaire and conversion to combat. Coordinating the logistical train for the French Atlantic flotillas, the office of FdU West would be reinstated in July 1942 with Hans Rudolf Rösing in command.

During July, Dönitz moved boats within the North Atlantic south, partially due to Hitler's explicit restrictions surrounding *Barbarossa*, partly due to a lack of convoy location. During the entire month, not one ship of the Halifax convoys was lost to U-boats, and only a small number of empty ships outbound. Instead, Dönitz concentrated on Gibraltar shipping, though, bedevilled by persistent fog and with Admiralty rerouting convoys and reinforcing escorts, nothing was intercepted that month.

Off Freetown the situation was little better. Numerous American ships were sighted entering and leaving the port by Reinhard Hardegen in *U123*, despatched to Sierra Leone in mid-June alongside *U66*. With visibly increased ASW patrolling and no independently sailing ships sighted, both boats were moved to the area of the Cape Verde Islands, Dönitz denying requests to allow operations west of 30° longitude against suspected convoy traffic using the Pan-American Security Zone, both in deference to the USA but also to protect prizes that had been taken by Kriegsmarine auxiliary cruisers and traversed that route back to France.

With the loss of South Atlantic tankers, OKM attempted to persuade Vichy French authorities to allow supply ships *Kota Pinang* and *Python* to station at Dakar. Negotiations at first appeared promising, and in anticipation that Dakar would soon be a functioning resupply point, Dönitz despatched a fresh wave of four U-boats to the south at the beginning of July: *U93*, *U94*, *U109* and *U124*. Heinrich Bleichrodt's *U109* was forced to divert to Cadiz to obtain spare parts for its broken freshwater distilling machinery, resupplying from the covert tanker *Thalia* (codenamed *Moro*) under cover of darkness. The remaining three proceeded in a rake formation, making a broad sweep in search of any merchant targets.

Meanwhile, though Vichy Admiral François Darlan had approved Dakar for German use, these 'Paris Protocols' were never ratified and negotiations with Vichy authorities broke down shortly thereafter. This was partially a result of pressure applied on Marshal Pétain by the United States government, who feared expansion of German influence in West Africa could spread across the Atlantic to Brazil, a key territory in the American principle of Western Hemisphere defence. A U-boat support station in Dakar was no longer viable, but fortunately for Vichy, Hitler's attention remained on the east and he ignored the French snub, perhaps mollified by Pétain's timely radio broadcast confirming ongoing Vichy collaboration with Germany. More U-boat supply problems struck during July, when intense British diplomatic pressure on Spain closed covert refuelling in the Canary Islands, now an open secret. Refuelling from *Corrientes* during June, Hardegen had reported civilians observing as *U123*

The Type IIB *U23* before the war. Numbers on the conning tower and small bow plaques were removed before the outbreak of hostilities.

Type VII *U33*, with the external stern torpedo tube clearly visible; the tube was integrated internally from the VIIB onwards.

U33 in Wilhelmshaven on 28 September 1939, with souvenirs from
the British steamer *Olivegrove*.

This illustration by Guy Griffiths shows his Skua attack on *U30*.

Günther Prien (with binoculars), his ears wadded with cotton wool as crewmen prepare to test fire an MG34.

Fritz-Julius Lemp with Karl Dönitz aboard *U30* in Kiel, 30 August 1940.

Otto Kretschmer (in leather jacket), the highest-scoring U-boat 'Ace' of the Second World War.

Schnurzl photographed aboard *U30* by Georg Högel.

Lemp's *U110* and Schepke's *U100*, Kiel, 9 March 1941.

The Type IID *U139* being commissioned by Robert Bartels in Kiel on 24 July 1940.

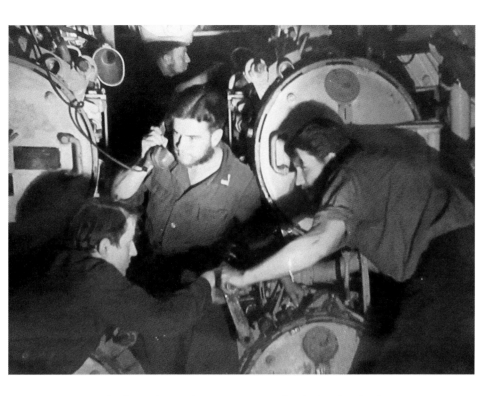

The forward torpedo compartment of *U43*. (Paul Milner)

Victor Oehrn celebrates the award of his Knight's Cross following *U37*'s return to
Lorient in October 1940.

Joachim Schepke speaking at the
Berlin Sportspalast in a state-sponsored
recruitment drive.

Horst Degen, Engelbert Endrass
and Erich Topp.

Victor Oehrn (left) and Eberhard Godt (centre); the latter headed BdU Ops.

Karl Dönitz (seated in car) with Hans-Rudolf Rösing (centre) at the latter's Angers FdU West headquarters.

Size comparison of a Type VIIC and a Type XB minelaying U-boat, moored in Kiel.

The cook aboard *U43* in his cramped galley. (Paul Milner)

Hans-Heinz Linder's *U202* docks in the Penfeld River, Brest, used for mooring before the construction of U-boat pens. (Paul Milner)

The forward gun of *U111* during severe winter conditions near Newfoundland. (Paul Milner)

Jost Metzler, commander of *U69*, the first Type VIIC to be launched.

'Adi' Schnee and men aboard *U201* taking advantage of the mid-Atlantic 'air gap' for coffee, cake and music.

Trainee captains of the 21st U-Training Flotilla aboard *U141*.

Dönitz inspects a crew of the 7th U-Flotilla at La Baule, 30 November 1942.

The time-consuming task of moving a torpedo from its under-deck storage to inside the forward torpedo room.

Certificate for the award of the U-boat Badge to Edmund Prochnow.

U203 enters the first completed U-boat bunker pens at Saint Nazaire, 30 June 1941.

Helmut Rosenbaum in La Spezia, 5 September 1942, after being awarded the Knight's Cross for sinking HMS *Eagle*.

Hitler awards the Oak Leaves to Rolf Mützelburg (*U203*) and Adalbert Schnee (*U201*), 15 July 1942.

Wolfgang Lüth was one of the two most highly decorated men of the U-boat service.

The stern of the Type VIIC *U737* in the North Atlantic. (Paul Milner)

departed in early morning light, *U103* shadowed from Las Palmas by fishing boats following resupply during early July. Bleichrodt's would be the last to use the resupply point, and with *U93*, *U94* and *U124* finding nothing, BdU ended southern operations, all four of his southern group ordered instead to head towards Gibraltar.

Condor aircraft provided several sightings for BdU, though to little effect as their own fortunes declined. Although during the first seven months of 1941 Condors had taken part in sinking 56 ships, during the rest of the year only four were either sunk or damaged. Low-level attacks were abandoned for high-altitude bombing, further decreasing effectiveness. The Allied introduction of Fighter Catapult Ships (FCS) and Catapult Aircraft Merchant (CAM) ships to convoys, able to launch – but not recover – a single fighter posed a new deterrent to shadowing Condors, though only one was actually brought down by a CAM ship Hurricane on 1 November 1942 when Flying Officer Norman Taylor shot down an aircraft of 7./KG40, killing all seven crewmen.* The September introduction of British escort carrier HMS *Audacity* – an emergency means of providing convoy air protection, built from captured and converted German merchant *Hannover* – was another watershed moment. Carrying eight Fleet Air Arm Martlets of 802 Squadron, *Audacity* took part in only four Gibraltar convoys between September and December 1941 but shot down six Condors before being torpedoed and sunk by *U751* on 21 December.

While U-boats achieved little, Italian submarine *Barbarigo* sighted convoy traffic west of Gibraltar on 22 July, sinking two ships – though neither travelling in convoy – and summoning *Bagnolini* to unsuccessfully join the attack as Dönitz raced his four returning Freetown boats to intercept. With *U109* unable to reach the area in time, Mützelburg's *U203* was brought in, having chased a solo sailing merchant ship far to the south of his intended patrol line position, bringing him within potential range. The effort failed, however, as the Italian's position report had been too brief and vague and, at any rate, the Admiralty changed the convoy's course to evade German detection.

---

* The '7.' indicates 7th Staffel (Squadron).

Finally, on 25 July, acting on B-Dienst intelligence, the first of repeated Condor sightings of OG69 brought about its successful interception the following day, despite Dönitz nearly calling off the hurriedly organized chase due to inaccurate Luftwaffe fixes. It was Karl-Friedrich Merten's *U68* on its maiden patrol that stumbled upon OG69 late that afternoon, shadowing until joined by *U79*, *U126* and *U203* and authorized to open fire. Merten's attack was disrupted by an escorting corvette, but in total eight U-boats – all relatively inexperienced on their first or second war patrols – were vectored towards OG69. Between the nights of 27 and 28 July, they claimed to sink 19 merchant ships totalling 108,000 tons and two escort vessels in what Dönitz recorded as a 'great convoy battle'. It was unhelpful for German radio broadcasters to subsequently inflate this figure yet further to 24 ships when the U-boats had, with 25 fired torpedoes, destroyed only seven ships amounting to 11,303 tons.

Elated, Dönitz tempered his report with the fact that, though the relatively new captains had acquitted themselves well, they required continual instruction on maintaining and reporting contact, on transmitting beacon signals and, occasionally, even on tactical matters. It was an acknowledgement that commander tactical training now occupied only three weeks of Baltic exercises, torpedo firing practice itself dramatically reduced due to a lack of torpedo recovery vessels and the urgency of getting U-boats to the front as soon as possible.

Such overclaiming was particularly bad against the Gibraltar convoys. After OG71 was also attacked by a group of eight U-boats in August, the combined tally of ships claimed sunk numbered 15 merchants (amounting to 90,129 tons), and two destroyers as well as damage inflicted on another five steamers. The corvette HMS *Zinnia* and Norwegian four-stacker destroyer HMNoS *Bath* had indeed been sunk, but only eight merchants accruing 13,225 tons. Goebbels' propaganda network added their own extravagant flourish, leading the Admiralty to release a press counterclaim, as 'total tonnage of convoy was less than 30 per cent of sinkings claimed by the Germans'.[5]

Using OG71 as an example, although most of the U-boat commanders involved were still relatively new to their own command, they had all served as Watch Officers beneath experienced skippers who had become 'Aces' during the early war. For instance, the extremely capable and respected 'Adi' Schnee had learned his craft as First Watch Officer to Otto Kretschmer aboard *U23* and later captained *U60* in which he claimed to have destroyed 40,000 tons of shipping (actually 18,622 tons). From OG71 Schnee claimed the destruction of six ships totalling 37,000 tons. Though the number of claimed sinkings was only two above the reality, the tonnage was wildly inaccurate. His confirmed total was 7,825 tons; Schnee's average ship size claimed, estimated at over 6,000 tons, was, in reality, less than 2,000.

Similarly, Reinhard 'Teddy' Suhren had been First Watch Officer aboard *U48*, the highest-scoring U-boat of the war albeit under three different commanders. As such he had been responsible for all surface firing and was unusually decorated while First Watch Officer with the Knight's Cross on the insistence of his captain Heinrich Bleichrodt.* During the battle, as well as *Zinnia*, Suhren torpedoed two merchant vessels – *Clonlara* (1,203 tons) and steam tug *Empire Oak* (484 tons) – but claimed four merchants sunk for an aggregate tonnage of 20,000 tons.

Both U-boats belonged to the 1st U-Flotilla, and within the flotilla War Diary, Cohausz appears to contradict Dönitz's entire modus operandi of a tonnage war when he recorded that the effectiveness had been proved of 'the boats' tactic of punching into the convoy at a weak point and just as quickly retire after emptying all tubes in fan or individual shots aimed at a wider target group. The number of ships sunk is important, less so the exact tonnage.'

Such zealous assertions of success can be seen on the face of it to be purely dishonest and did, in April 1942, receive a gentle admonishment from Dönitz when he reportedly reminded his

---

* Suhren's torpedo record aboard *U48* illustrates the propensity for surfaced attacks by early war U-boats. As First Watch Officer he was generally responsible for the actual firing of torpedoes. Suhren fired 65 torpedo shots as First Watch Officer of *U48* – 30 hits and 35 misses. By comparison, Schultze fired a total of 27 (ten hits), Rösing eight (three hits) and Bleichrodt two (both hits).

commanders that 'wish should not be father to the thought… we are a solid firm.' However, it was frequently the result of an already chaotic situation, viewed through the periscope or 'observed' only audibly as attacks were increasingly mounted by night because of the escalating strength of Allied escort and ASW power. Suhren later wrote of this in his autobiography *Nasses Eichenlaub*:

> It was no longer possible to achieve the quick successes of the first year of the war. The situation had gotten much more difficult, with greater risk involved. That was especially true of the Gibraltar route where the aircraft kept us down and tried to separate us from the convoys. Before we could surface again the convoy was up and away… We didn't actually see many of the hits, we simply heard them. It went down in the log as, for example: '… Heard 4 separate explosions, saw three separate bursts of flame, followed by lifeboats.'

During the first half of August, the returning Freetown U-boats took part in the disastrous attempt to attack convoy HG70, its 25 ships reported leaving Gibraltar either in ballast or carrying trade goods on the 9th by an agent ashore. The convoy was found and shadowed by *U79*; ten U-boats were brought into contact. However, not a single U-boat obtained firing position, several severely depth charged and forced to abort to France. Dönitz went so far as to issue an order to attack the escorts first, speculating they were equipped with a new 'surface location apparatus', but to no avail. The strong Royal Navy escort was indeed equipped with HF/DF (High Frequency Direction Finding) and located the gathering U-boats by tracking their location reports to BdU.

To complicate matters, as the battle developed, *U501* outbound to its patrol area as part of the *'Grönland'* group in the north, sighted a northbound convoy (ON4) south of Iceland, *U129* another northwest of Rockall Bank and *U209* yet another further west. Ironically, for once, convoy location had not been the problem, as recorded by BdU:

Thus, four convoys were being attacked at the same time by U-boats, although at times only one U-boat was operating against three of them. At the end of the second year of war conditions while shadowing convoys have become more difficult, a situation not improved by the inexperience of many young captains where there seems little chance of maintaining contact long enough to make an attack possible. We now need three to four times the number of U-boats available a year ago owing to the far stronger air and surface escorts.

The location of four convoys at one time in different areas on the same day, illustrates the volume of English traffic and proves the necessity of the greatest possible concentration of forces. Despite the large number of U-boats there are today, there are too few to scatter around, and one is liable not to be able to maintain more contacts made than such weak forces can cope with.[6]

Results from all four separate encounters were disappointing. Nothing was achieved against HG70, four U-boats suffering heavy damage, and three of the Knight's Cross-holding skippers of the Freetown group subsequently moved ashore: Claus Korth (*U93*) appeared run down during his post-patrol interview with Dönitz, as did Herbert Kuppisch who had apparently developed a severe case of nerves after being in action since the war's beginning. Both were posted to BdU staff to rest and recuperate off the front line. Georg-Wilhelm Schulz (*U124*) took command of the 6th U-Training Flotilla. Of the four Freetown commanders, only Bleichrodt remained in action, as commander of *U109*, until January 1943.

From ON4 only Joachim Preuss in *U568* (also of the 'Grönland' group) sank a ship, the corvette HMS *Picotee* of the 4th Escort Group mistakenly hit by a torpedo aimed at a tanker, struck beneath the bridge and sinking swiftly. There were no survivors. *Picotee* had begun sweeping astern of the convoy after reports of an unidentified submarine. Two officers aboard Danish freighter *Delaware* then reported a large cloud of smoke and the hiss of escaping steam from the direction of the corvette, its bow observed as the smoke cleared, rising to a 45° angle before sliding backwards into the sea. No flash or blast was heard, and it was initially believed that an internal explosion had claimed the warship, though a U-boat was seen approaching surfaced from the same direction 15 minutes later, rockets fired from a merchant ship sending it away at high speed.

The destruction of the corvette was the only convoy success of the sprawling 'Grönland' group which Dönitz kept in action for most of August. Three other ships were hit: unescorted 1,700-ton *Longtaker*, sunk by *U38* on 18 August; minelayer HMS *Southern Prince*, torpedoed by *U652* on 26 August but towed to Belfast and repaired; and 230-ton steam trawler *Ladylove*, sunk with a single G7e by *U202* on 27 August, the fishing vessel going under in 16 seconds and leaving none of the 14-member crew alive.

Dönitz's complicated reshuffling of U-boats south of Iceland during August failed to find HX144, SC40 and HX145; all diverted south thanks to Ultra and the work of former barrister Rodger Winn in the Admiralty's U-boat tracking room. Dönitz's war was failing as imports to the United Kingdom continued to arrive at a steady rate of nearly 1 million tons a week, and whereas 57 merchant ships had been lost in May, after Ultra success, only 22 were sunk during August.

Churchill and Roosevelt also held their first face-to-face summit meeting between 9 and 12 August, Churchill travelling aboard HMS *Prince of Wales* to the Canadian harbour of Argentia which American forces had occupied as a military base. The 'Atlantic Charter' resulting from this meeting presented a vision of post-war Europe, and during the conference Roosevelt agreed to implement 'Western Hemisphere Defence Plan Number 4'. Under these terms, the US Navy would assume responsibility for escorting North Atlantic convoys as far as 26° West longitude, releasing approximately 50 British destroyers and corvettes for duty in the Eastern and Southern Atlantic. Roosevelt hesitated to announce this new initiative to a nation still mired in isolationism, preferring to wait for the opportune moment in which to inform the American public. This moment would be provided by USS *Greer* in September.

The disappointing trend for BdU was crowned by Hans-Joachim Rahmlow when he surrendered *U570* to a Coastal Command

Hudson aircraft of 269 Squadron. The inexperienced captain had served in surface craft and artillery before transferring to the U-boat service, assuming command of the new Type VIIC *U570* and taking it for its maiden patrol from Trondheim on 23 August. Most of the crew were similarly inexperienced and suffered prolonged periods of seasickness as the boat headed to sea, and *U570* ran submerged for extended periods to provide some respite from the heavy seas for the wretched crewmen.

Following one such cycle Rahmlow surfaced from a depth of 30 metres, neglecting to check the sky periscope for potential threats. Hudson 'S' was almost directly overhead when the *U570* broke surface and the bomber swiftly dropped four 250-pound depth charges which narrowly missed. Again, inexperience showed as damage inflicted was relatively negligible and would not have prevented an experienced crew from diving once more, the aircraft having no more depth charges to drop. However, in this case, the appearance of gas (thought incorrectly to be deadly chlorine gas from cracked battery cells), smashed instruments, and the ingress of a small amount of water proved too much; with his panicked crew racing to the bow, Rahmlow ordered them to prepare to abandon ship, transmitting in clear language to BdU (and Allied listening stations), 'Am not able to dive. Being attacked by aircraft.'

Dönitz immediately ordered nearby U-boats to assist, *U82* attempting to close and rescue the crew but prevented by the growing number of aircraft to which Rahmlow surrendered his U-boat. Although the Enigma machine and most cypher and secret material was thrown overboard, *U570* was captured intact and provided a bonanza of information regarding the Type VIIC's capabilities. Among the items recovered were the lid of the Enigma machine – an extra slot providing clues of a new four-rotor variant being prepared for introduction – plain text messages, and some Enigma key setting information as well as a large array of personal papers, photos and diaries carelessly kept by the crew. The boat itself was later tested thoroughly under its new title HMS *Graph* and showed the Admiralty that it was capable of much greater depths than previously thought; depth-charge settings were adjusted accordingly. A subsequent Royal

Navy interrogation report provides an interesting snapshot of the crew that highlights the rapid degradation of elements of the U-boat service since the early days of war:

> The inexperience of this crew was most striking, the Engineer Officer, one or two petty officers and one rating being the only men to have taken part in a war cruise prior to *U570*'s first and last cruise. The chief petty officers were men who had been in the Navy for a number of years, the Chief Quartermaster [*Obersteuermann* Otto Grotum, who had served aboard Schepke's *U19*] having joined in about 1926; the average length of service of the petty officers was three and a half years while only one rating had more than 18 months' service; about half of the ratings, all very young, joined the Navy in April 1940, and the other half more recently than that date. Most of the technical ratings had done three to six months' U-Boat training, the seamen even less.
>
> The chief petty officers, and to a lesser extent, some of the petty officers, expressed great concern at the inadequacy of the training and the lack of U-boat experience, not only of the men, but also of the officers and petty officers; no attempt was made to disguise the incompetence of the crew and the officers were severely criticised by all the men.[7]

Following their capture, the crew of *U570* were held in London and interrogated before being separated and sent to various POW camps. The officers, excluding Rahmlow, were sent to No. 1 Camp (Officers) at Grizedale Hall, where news of their impending arrival generated much unrest among the prisoners. The capture of a virtually undamaged U-boat had been widely reported in the British press, and the camp's senior German officer, Otto Kretschmer, and his fellow prisoners were incensed by what they considered to be cowardice in the face of the enemy. *U570*'s First Watch Officer Bernhard Berndt, Second Watch Officer Walter Christiansen and Chief Engineer Erich Menzel arrived at Grizedale Hall in September and faced an illegal 'Council of Honour' that placed them on trial along with Rahmlow *in abstentia*. In due course both Christiansen and Menzel were found not guilty. Berndt, on the other hand, accepted full responsibility for his part in the capture of *U570* and was found guilty, as was Rahmlow. Convinced of the imminence of the German invasion of Great Britain, Kretschmer ordered Berndt ostracized by all prisoners to be later handed over to German authorities, tried by court martial and likely executed.

Using code that Dönitz had established for his men in the event of capture, Kretschmer communicated his decision to BdU, hidden among seemingly innocuous messages to his family in letters delivered by the international Red Cross. British newspapers, freely available to the prisoners, soon reported *U570* held in Barrow-in-Furness undergoing examination by the Royal Navy, and Berndt proposed an ambitious escape plan by which to regain his honour he would reach the boat and scuttle it. On the evening of 18 October, Berndt successfully escaped but was later found by British soldiers sheltering beneath a tarpaulin stretched across a sheep pen, and shot while making a sudden break for freedom, dying of his wound. Rahmlow, briefly arriving in Grizedale Hall, was moved elsewhere after British authorities learned of Kretschmer's trial.

With several U-boats damaged by aircraft attacks south of Iceland and no convoy traffic intercepted, Dönitz again moved his boats further west towards Greenland and out of range of Iceland-based aircraft. A dual blow was then dealt to Dönitz in his North Atlantic struggle. As well as reinforcing Arctic U-boats, despite repeated objections from both Raeder and Dönitz, Hitler on 22 August ordered the despatch of six U-boats to the Mediterranean to assist the Afrika Korps.

Chapter Six

Sun and Snow

'Yes, the Germans are in the Mediterranean!'
Hans Cohausz, 1st U-Flotilla War Diary,
15 November 1941

The redirection of even negligible Atlantic U-boat strength was a strategic blunder on behalf of OKW, but it was not unexpected. Since before the invasion of Greece in May 1941, repeated enquiries had been made by OKW for U-boats to support ground operations around the Mediterranean basin. During October 1940, Mussolini had launched an ill-considered war against Greece, the offensive a disastrous fiasco as Greek forces defeated the invading Italians and pushed them back beyond their starting points. Worse, the attack settled any question of Greece's obscure political alignment, and it joined the Allies, providing a Balkan staging post for British and Commonwealth forces. Winston Churchill's preoccupation with the Balkan region had been established during the previous war, and Greece's accession to the Allied cause allowed him to transport forces from North Africa almost immediately, occupying Crete and Lemnos, much to the consternation of his overstretched commanders in Egypt.

The Royal Air Force now lay within striking distance of Romania's Ploiești oilfields, and while bolstering Romanian defences, Hitler ordered the invasion of Greece and Crete. German objectives soon linked potential operations in North Africa, Gibraltar and Greece to take control of the Mediterranean basin, but failure to convince

Franco to render Spanish aid for Operation *Felix* and the seizure of Gibraltar restricted the original plan to the invasion of Greece, codenamed *Marita* and scheduled for optimal weather conditions in May 1941. As preparations began, Italy suffered further calamity in North Africa when British troops drove Italian forces in Libya west in disarray, complete Italian defeat appearing almost inevitable by January 1941. To prevent disaster, Luftwaffe units transferred to Sicily and the lead elements of the Afrika Korps were despatched to Tripoli during February, marking the beginning of Erwin Rommel's fabled career in the desert.

The war in North Africa centred on logistics, and British depredation of predominantly Italian supply shipping by air and sea forces mostly based on Malta was extremely problematic. Despite Italy possessing the largest Mediterranean fleet, they apparently lacked the energy and will to challenge the Royal Navy, and Rommel was forced to plead directly with OKW for German aid. The issue of U-boats being included in that aid had been raised and deflected multiple times by both Raeder and Dönitz. Dönitz reasoned that, given the nature of the Mediterranean Sea – relatively constricted sea room, clear waters, and more easily patrolled by air – only the most experienced commanders could be considered and that at least ten U-boats would be required, significantly reducing the weight of his Atlantic force. Furthermore, he argued correctly that a major part of the supply convoys' losses had been inflicted by British submarines, for which U-boats were no answer. Instead, he advocated the despatch of small surface units and the withdrawal of all but 11 large Italian submarines from BETASOM to the Mediterranean. Regarded as a decision of some psychological importance between 'allies', Hitler handled this request himself, in conference with Mussolini, at the Brenner Pass and still issued a final demand for the six-strong *'Goeben'* group to transfer into the Mediterranean Sea.

This marks the most direct use of U-boats in support of a land campaign since the invasion of Norway. Tasked with immediate interception of British supply traffic running from Alexandria to Tobruk, the first *'Goeben'* boat, *U371*, passed through the Strait of Gibraltar on 21 September. Within a week, *U559* and *U97* had followed, and by 5 October the last three boats – *U75*, *U79* and *U331* – all signalled their presence within the Mediterranean to BdU. Their initial actions did not augur well for the new venture. During the early hours of 10 October, Hans-Diedrich Freiherr von Tiesenhausen fired a torpedo at a small convoy of three 'A' lighters (Landing Craft Tank Mk 1) carrying tanks and motor transport from Mersa Matruh to Tobruk under tow by a British tugboat. The torpedo passed harmlessly under the shallow draught vessels and *U331* surfaced to open fire with its 88mm deck weapon. In the skirmish that followed, HMS *TLC-18* (*A18*) suffered some damage from gunfire and later returned to Mersa Matruh with one wounded man. In return, defensive fire from 40mm cannon hit *U331* and wounded two men of the gun crew as well as causing damage to the conning tower. After hurriedly retreating below decks, *U331* dived to safety though *Bootsmann* Hans Gerstenich later died of his wounds.

Von Tiesenhausen brought *U331* into its new Greek base of Salamis on 23 October as the first boat of the newly formed 23rd U-Flotilla. The port lay on the eastern side of the island, previously a major base of the Royal Hellenic Navy, and only 16 kilometres west of central Athens. Flotilla commander was Fritz Frauenheim, Knight's Cross holder and former captain of *U101*. Initially, all U-boat operations within the western Mediterranean as far as the Strait of Messina remained under BdU control, Frauenheim exercising regional control for everything east of that demarcation line under the direction of Admiral Aegean, Vizeadmiral Erich Förste; an unusual role for flotilla commander. This situation changed during November when the regional FdU Italy was created (briefly known as FdU Mediterranean). The first to occupy this office was Dönitz's trusted subordinate Victor Oehrn although, despite his proven ability, OKM deemed the post required an officer of minimum *Kapitän zur See* rank, and subsequently Leo Kreisch, former cruiser captain, arrived to supersede Oehrn on 27 January 1942, the latter relegated to Kreisch's senior staff officer.

Although administratively still ruled by BdU, from 8 December 1941 Kreisch's office became responsible for operational control of all U-boats in the western Mediterranean, directly subordinate to Vizeadmiral Eberhard Weichold, senior officer of *Marinekommando Italien* responsible for German naval assets within the Mediterranean. Both offices occupied space within Rome's sprawling Italian Naval Ministry next to the Tiber River. Within the eastern Mediterranean, with communications not yet in place to allow direct contact with Rome, 23rd U-Flotilla remained in operational control. One month later, the 29th U-Flotilla was created under the command of Franz Becker, previously a staff officer from FdU West, in the Ligurian port of La Spezia with a subsidiary centre in Pola within the Adriatic Sea.

'*Goeben*' boats achieved only moderate success, despite several unconfirmed claims. Two days after von Tiesenhausen's attack on Tobruk supply traffic, Helmuth Ringelmann's *U75* attacked a similar convoy of three 'A' lighters under tow on their return from Tobruk, torpedoing HMS *TLC-2* (*A2*) and then shelling both it and HMS *TLC-7* (*A7*), sinking both despite return cannon fire. Both British commanding officers, 26 ratings, an officer in the Royal Engineers, four Australian soldiers, and two Italian prisoners of war were lost; only Leading Seaman William Alfred Henley from *A7*, surviving the attack and rescued by *U75*, eventually transferred to Germany as a prisoner of war.* Later that day, Ringelmann's boat was sighted and unsuccessfully attacked by British aircraft 70 miles north of Tobruk.

That day the British opened Operation *Cultivate* – the resupply and the relief by sea of Australian troops holding Tobruk and replacement with men of the British 3rd Division from Syria. Against this Udo Heilmann's *U97* achieved the greatest success of these opening patrols when he torpedoed both steamers of a small *Cultivate* convoy – 1,208-ton Greek *Samos* and 758-ton British *Pass of Balmaha* – 50 miles west of Alexandria on 17 October. Both merchants were under escort by anti-submarine whaler HMS

---

* Henley was awarded the Distinguished Service Medal on 11 November 1941.

Cocker, which failed to locate *U97*, *Samos* going under leaving only three survivors and the British tanker exploding as its cargo of aviation fuel ignited, killing all 20 men aboard.

Local Royal Navy light forces were employed either in shore bombardments, Operation *Cultivate* or anti-submarine sweeps, and *'Goeben's'* final success was the severe damaging of 625-ton First World War vintage gunboat HMS *Gnat*, torpedoed by Wolfgang Kaufmann's *U79* on 21 October providing fire support off Tobruk for the besieged garrison. *Gnat* had its bow blown off by the explosion as far as the 6-inch gun, was towed to Alexandria by HMS *Griffin* and beached, later declared a total constructive loss and converted to a stationary anti-aircraft platform. It was to be the last of four ships torpedoed by Kaufmann during his career; *U79* was sunk on 23 December 1941 north of Sollum by depth charges from British destroyers HMS *Hasty* and *Hotspur* escorting convoy AT5, and the entire crew captured.

Cultivate was concluded by 26 October; 7,138 troops transported to Tobruk, while 7,234, including 727 wounded, returned to Alexandria. They had suffered more at the hands of Junkers Ju 87 dive bombers than the gathered U-boats. In total, the *'Goeben'* boats had destroyed 3,707 tons of shipping with the expenditure of nearly all torpedoes and weeks at sea.

Reports regarding the difficulties of destroying shallow-draught vessels resupplying Tobruk were relayed to Dönitz, who questioned the wisdom of employing U-boats against them, urging instead their redeployment east against Alexandria and Beirut. In Salamis, the port facilities were found to be inadequately equipped, as all six U-boats returned to refit. Hundreds of skilled workers were transferred from French and German shipyards to Greece, further exacerbating problems for Atlantic U-boats and those already logjammed in overworked German shipyards and harbours. La Spezia, the principal Italian naval dockyard alongside Taranto in the south and Venice in the Adriatic, was hastily prepared for German use, though it was already operating at high capacity with Italian naval casualties. Subsidiary harbours at Palermo and Maddalena were investigated for emergency use.

Dönitz remained perpetually frustrated with the loss of Atlantic boats to the 'mousetrap' of the Mediterranean, from which none would ever exit. The diversion of technicians and workers complicated an already difficult logistical train. As early as July, a report by the U-Boat Division of the Naval War Staff on U-boat construction revealed that the number of U-boats to be constructed per month had dropped from the planned 29, first to 25, and then 22. This reduction was due simply to a lack of workers; the Russian campaign had led to a severe personnel drain, and now there were further shortfalls as men were transported to Italy and Greece. Redirected from the centre of operations within the Atlantic, the report starkly warned that the 'U-boat weapon would fail in its task of destroying British shipping.' It was estimated that 2,400 workers were needed to produce one U-boat per month. Therefore, to produce the 25 boats per month demanded by Hitler required 60,000 workers. The total number of men needed to produce only 15 new boats per month but also to keep 190 U-boats repaired and refitted was estimated to be 76,150 workers, as each U-boat under repair required 85 workers. Predictions for the end of 1941 numbered monthly U-boat output from shipyards at only 14 boats unless at least 25,000 skilled workers were found. Hitler's promise that with the 'end of the war in the east' the Kriegsmarine would have its workers was little reassurance.

During September BdU tightened radio security with a number of measures. First, all U-boats were now to be addressed in communication not by number but by the commander's surname; therefore, *U109* became 'U-Bleichrodt'. Grid references were also double encyphered as of 9 September by use of a complicated system using a double-letter code table which seemed to baffle as many U-boat commanders as it did Allied intelligence eavesdroppers. Most importantly, a four-rotor Enigma machine was slated for introduction during late September. This machine would use a new Enigma net, codenamed *Triton*, separate from the *Heimisch* net and used only by eight naval commands and the six Atlantic U-boat flotillas. Known to cryptographers at Bletchley Park as 'Shark', it was scheduled to reach full use by February 1942 and would cause an Ultra 'blackout' that lasted for most of the year.

Dönitz recognized the need for new methods of locating convoys, initially opting simply to push further west rather than any fundamental tactical change, hoping to take the fight into the so-called 'Greenland air gap'. He began a period of continuous and faster-paced patrol line movements, intended to cover greater sea area. Against them, Allied convoys no longer sailed without escort and, using extended routes, escort ships carried out the first experiments at refuelling at sea to increase the endurance of smaller warships.

Dönitz's first large-scale movement positioned 'Markgraf' group between Iceland and the southeast coast of Greenland. Joining 'Markgraf' was Georg-Werner Fraatz's U652 sailing from Trondheim, spotted on 4 September by British Coastal Command Hudson 'M' of 269 Squadron but completing an emergency dive before any attack could be made. On the distant horizon, the approaching silhouette of destroyer USS Greer delivering mail, passengers and freight to Iceland was visible, and the Hudson warned the American that a U-boat lay within its path. Aboard Greer Lieutenant Commander Laurence Frost brought his crew to General Quarters and began a sonar search for the submerged U-boat, located at 0920hrs directly ahead. Greer then trailed U652, broadcasting Fraatz's position as the Hudson circled above. Low on fuel, a little over an hour later the Hudson was forced to leave, dropping four depth charges in U652's vicinity. For over three hours Greer had manoeuvred to keep U652 on its bow, and at 1245hrs an exasperated Fraatz fired two torpedoes, one of which was observed by the American crew crossing the wake of the ship from starboard to port 100 metres astern. At that point Greer lost sonar contact, initiating a search and reacquiring U652 at 1512hrs, attacking immediately with depth charges.

Although U652 suffered no damage and eluded Greer, which soon abandoned the hunt and resumed its passage to Iceland, this marked the first direct confrontation between U-boat and US Navy and provided the perfect platform for Roosevelt to justify enaction of 'Western Hemisphere Defence Plan Number 4'. On 11 September, Roosevelt made it a central topic during his 'Fireside Chat', condemning U652's attack as part of 'a policy of indiscriminate violence against any vessel sailing the seas, belligerent or non-belligerent' and describing it as 'piracy; legally and morally'. He then explained that 'active defence' was now in operation, a shoot on sight order against any German and Italian vessels of war. 'From now on,' he stated, 'if German or Italian vessels of war enter these waters [Iceland and similar areas under American protection] they do so at their own peril.'

As a result, both Dönitz and Raeder strongly urged Hitler to rescind restrictions on U-boats to inhibit accidental clashes with American ships, though Hitler remained intractable and requested such limitations remain in place until the middle of October as fighting on the Eastern Front began to bog down. The U-boats' operational zone was instead extended to the equator in the south and as far west as the 300-mile American zone.

Fraatz proceeded to join '*Markgraf*', 14 boats hunting in a loose patrol line southeast of Greenland. At 0655hrs on 9 September, *U81* found unescorted 5,591-ton *Empire Springbuck* and, while submerged, fired two torpedoes which hit the British steamer on the port side, engulfing it in flames before exploding as its cargo of phosphates ignited, all 39 men aboard killed. *Empire Springbuck* was a straggler from SC42 of 62 merchant ships escorted by RCN Escort Group 24 of destroyer HMCS *Skeena* and corvettes HMCS *Alberni*, *Kenogami* and *Orillia*. The '*Markgraf*' deployment had been betrayed by Ultra decryption, allowing five convoys to reroute before Dönitz ordered the patrol line loosened to cover a greater area. With exact U-boat positions suddenly unknown to Ultra, SC42 was unable to divert due to stormy weather and the ice barrier fringing Greenland. Eberhard Greger in *U85* made contact with the convoy body later that afternoon, an initial torpedo shot missing as the boat began to shadow.

Though the entire '*Markgraf*' group was ordered to home in on Greger's beacon signals, only five U-boats opened the attack during the early hours of the following morning. Between then and early afternoon on 11 September, 14 merchant ships totalling 60,457 tons were sunk. Five days later, *U98* fired four single torpedoes at the convoy northwest of St Kilda and sank *Jedmoor* with its cargo of 7,400 tons of iron ore. Abandoned *Baron Pentland* that had suffered heavy damage after being hit by *U652* during the initial attack was also found and sunk by *U98* on 19 September southeast of Greenland. In total 16 ships, totalling 68,259 tons, had been destroyed and two others damaged in what was the second most successful North Atlantic convoy attack of the Second World War.

In return, Fritz Meyer's brand new *U207* was sunk with all hands on 11 September by depth charges from the British destroyers HMS *Leamington* and *Veteran*, reinforcing the Canadian escorts, and Hugo Förster's *U501* sunk the previous night by depth charges and ramming from Canadian corvettes HMCS *Chambly* and *Moosejaw* also urgently despatched as reinforcements, interrupting their training cruise.

Förster and 36 of his men were captured from *U501* – the first U-boat sunk by Canadian forces – as Canadian boarders very nearly managed to penetrate the U-boat's interior. *Chambly* had obtained ASDIC contact first, dropping four depth charges which caused considerable damage inside *U501* and disabled the stern hydroplane. Shortly thereafter *U501* surfaced between *Chambly* and *Moosejaw*, the latter opening fire until the main gun jammed after the first round, and instead swinging around to ram. Apparently unwilling to attempt to run for it surfaced, as crewmen emerged from the conning tower *U501* changed course slightly, and the two vessels ended up alongside one another at which point the 36-year-old Förster inexplicably jumped aboard *Moosejaw*. Fearing that the corvette was being boarded, Lieutenant Frederick Ernest Grubb ordered his ship away from *U501*, which then appeared to cross the corvette's bow, Grubb increasing speed and ramming as fire was opened once again. Abandoned by his captain, First Watch Officer Werner Albring ordered the boat scuttled and all crew to abandon ship.

As the two Canadian ships began pulling German survivors from the sea, *Chambly* quickly despatched a boarding party of nine armed men led by the ship's First Lieutenant Edward Simmons. Reaching the U-boat, which was still moving slowly ahead, Simmons found 11 Germans still on deck and attempted to force two of them below to identify potential secret documents. However, the boat was settling rapidly by the stern, Simmons opening the stern torpedo hatch to find the compartment below fully flooded and making a brave attempt to descend the conning tower ladder as the control room lights suddenly extinguished and water rushed upward to meet them. Stoker William Brown, first man aboard of the boarding party, was trapped in the conning tower and killed as the U-boat went under; Simmons was also sucked underwater as *U501* sank but was able to reach the surface and was rescued.

Förster, formerly a torpedo boat commander and officer aboard the cruiser *Blücher*, had only transferred to U-boats recently, undergoing abbreviated training before taking command of the new type IXC *U501*. His and his crew's subsequent interrogation makes for intriguing reading:

[Förster's] lack of experience, his cowardice and other defects were bitterly criticised by his officers and men, some of whom went so far as to threaten to take vengeance into their own hands should Förster not be adequately punished by Court Martial after the war. According to his crew, Förster not only surrendered without a fight, but subsequently thought solely of his own skin, and not of the fate of his ship, nor of the lives of his men, eleven of whom were drowned. He was the first to desert his U-Boat and the only man to jump from her to the British corvette without even getting wet, let alone having to swim for some time before being rescued. Later, when visiting his men, he offered his hand to his Chief Quartermaster [*Stabsobersteuermann* Robert Lemke], a man of fourteen years service in the German Navy, who refused to shake hands with him... [Förster] explained his precipitate leap from his U-Boat by stating that he felt impelled to get aboard *Moosejaw* at once in order to insist the British rescue his men; otherwise, he added, the German crew might have been left to drown. His explanation, while failing to convince the British, succeeded in infuriating his own men into a state of high blood pressure.[1]

Förster arrived at the prison camp Grizedale Hall at around the same time as Rahmlow and faced the same Council of Honour convened by Otto Kretschmer. Apparently accepting his likely fate, the camp commander had once more gotten wind of what was happening and intervened; Förster was immediately transferred that afternoon to a different camp where his military record was not known. Later, in January 1945, he was repatriated to Germany in a prisoner of war exchange and arrested to face court martial for cowardice in the face of the enemy. Using a pistol smuggled into his cell, he committed suicide on 27 February 1945, unable to live with his public disgrace.

With many U-boats returning from action against SC42, Dönitz thinned the patrol line now slanted in a southeasterly direction from the tip of Greenland, forming the *Brandenburg* group of nine U-boats, its new commander Otto Ites' *U94* chancing upon straggling ships from ON14 on 15 September and sinking three steamers in well-constructed torpedo attacks. Three days later, Eitel-Friedrich Kentrat's *U74* found the slow convoy SC44, sending shadowing reports which BdU did not receive due to atmospheric interference. Though nearby *Brandenburg* boats arrived, in drifting patches of heavy fog and mist, only *U74* sank two ships and recently promoted Erich Topp's *U552* another three.

During this difficult engagement, the faster convoy HX150 passed to the south beyond the U-boat patrol line. Composed of 50 merchant ships – including the 16,090-ton troopship *Empress of Asia* carrying approximately 2,000 Canadian troops to Britain – this was the first Halifax convoy to be escorted entirely by the US Navy as far as the 'Mid-Ocean Meeting Point' south of Iceland, where the five US Navy destroyers handed over to British escorts.

During October, *Brandenburg* was dissolved and a new patrol line created to occupy the Greenland air gap once more. With Ultra providing this new concentration's location, convoys were rerouted to the south until a two-day blackout from Enigma left the Admiralty groping in the dark again estimating positions. Despite recovering Ultra on 14 October, the following day Karl Thurmann's *U533* at the line's southern end ran straight into SC48. At 0830hrs Thurmann reported contact: *U568* nearby, *U502* to the north and *U432* and *U558* to the south. All of these were ordered to immediately close on this convoy within 24 hours. Other boats – *U77*, *U101*, *U751* and *U73* – were ordered to join at high speed.

With only *U573*, *U374*, *U208* and *U109* remaining off the southern tip of Greenland, far too few for the expanse of ocean, Dönitz ordered them west to reconnoitre the Belle Isle Strait and ascertain whether convoys were slipping between Labrador and Newfoundland, following the Great Circle route to Britain. Nucleus of the *'Mordbrenner'* group, these were the first U-boats within American waters given permission to open fire on convoy traffic. However, their movements were also disclosed by Enigma decryption and they found nothing, beset by storms, driving snow and ice.

Thurmann in *U553* continued shadowing SC48, launching a daring surface attack on the morning of 15 October. Approaching head-on, Thurmann took *U553* between columns 7 and 8 and fired all four torpedoes. Two steamers were hit and sunk but, unfortunately for Thurmann, incorrect settings in the torpedo data computer wasted the remaining shots. Thurmann's surfaced boat was seen by at least three of the convoy's merchant ships, *Silverelm* in station number 83 unsuccessfully attempting to ram as *U533* passed across its bow, though none could operate their defensive weapons for fear of hitting other convoy members. At no point did the corvette escort see *U553*.

Naval reinforcements and Catalinas from Iceland raced towards the scene as battle developed over the next three days, U-boats destroying nine merchant ships and two escort vessels with damage to a third. This latter proved slightly problematic, as it was destroyer USS *Kearny* of Task Unit 4.1.4 which was detached from convoy ON24 to reinforce SC48. In early morning darkness, Joachim Preuss in *U568* had been unable to distinguish the warship's flag and fired four torpedoes, one of which hit *Kearny*, causing significant damage and killing 11 men.

Diplomatic protests and American sabre-rattling followed, amplified to its extreme at the end of October, when Topp in *U552*, as part of the new *'Stoßtrupp'* group southeast of Greenland, encountered HX156.

AK 9982, Sea 1-2, cloudy, bright moonlit night
0510: Convoy sighted in the moonlit night at about 5 nm range.
Large ships…
0700: Initiated the attack after the moon has set. Although
visibility is still too great due to aurora borealis and stars. Escorts
are positioned far from the convoy but are so numerous that in
the short time available before it gets light no way through is
found…
0834: At 1,000 metres a destroyer silhouette attacked and
sunk with a two-fan. Both hit. High tongue of flame. Wreck is
disintegrated by enormous detonation own depth charges.[2]

His destruction of USS *Reuben James* from US Escort Group 4.1.3
was the sole success against HX156. The destroyer broke in two, the
forward section sinking immediately with all hands while the stern
remained afloat for five minutes before it too sank, unsecured depth
charges exploding and killing some survivors in the water. In total
there were only 45 men rescued from the crew of 160. The de facto
state of war that existed between American and German forces in
the Atlantic had never been more obvious, and on 13 November
the United States Congress voted to repeal the provisions of the
Neutrality Act of 1939 that prohibited arming American merchant
ships and their entry into combat zones.

The North Atlantic was lashed by increasingly fierce gales
during the last three months of 1941, and in October only 12
merchant ships were sunk by U-boats. This weather also caused
havoc with convoys, many scattered and forced to heave to,
while ships were forced to abort journeys with storm damage.
During November, the unprecedented act of an entire convoy
aborting its transit occurred when SC52 was off Cape Race,
targeted by the 14 U-boats of the *'Raubritter'* group. In drifting
fog and atmospheric disturbances that incessantly disrupted
communication with BdU, Hans-Heinz Linder's *U202* and Rolf
Mützelburg's *U203* sank two freighters apiece northeast of Notre
Dame Bay. Though driven off by Canadian depth charges, in
the fog and confusion two ships ran aground while evading and,

as panic took hold, the Admiralty ordered SC52 returned to Sydney, Nova Scotia.

Bad weather also thwarted U-boats west of Ireland despite sporadic assistance by aircraft of KG40. Exasperated, Dönitz initiated a move to the south to search near the Azores for HG76, reported to have left Gibraltar on 1 November. Over the week that followed, U-boats of the *'Störtebecker'* group unsuccessfully hunted for HG (Gibraltar to UK) and OG (UK to Gibraltar) convoy traffic as well as SL91 (Freetown, Sierra Leone, to UK), its presence reported by B-Dienst. Intelligence reports from Italy also indicated likely British landings in Vichy Algeria and, with the war in North Africa already delicately balanced, OKM ordered more U-boats to the Mediterranean and the waters immediately west of Gibraltar. Despite resolute arguments from Dönitz that Allied supply convoys for the Mediterranean passed via Cape Town and West African waters, Raeder insisted on the relocation of U-boats to southern Biscay, heavily patrolled by British air and sea forces. On 22 November Dönitz recorded his frustrations:

> U-boat warfare in the Atlantic has practically ceased owing to the concentrations in the Mediterranean; the only boats from which any result may be expected are the boats of *Steuben* group which are to operate off Newfoundland. Although this fact is regrettable, it is nevertheless necessary of course to put every effort into dealing with the dangerous situation in the Mediterranean.

Wolfgang Lüth's *U43* – the oldest Type IXB still on operational duties – had been part of the six-strong *'Steuben'* group that scoured the area off Newfoundland in atrocious weather conditions. Brought east towards Gibraltar, their journey began on 23 November and signified complete cessation of offensive U-boat operations within the North Atlantic. After five days, *U43* reached the Azores where lookouts sighted OS12 (UK to Freetown), which had become dislocated by bad weather. In a surfaced night attack, Lüth torpedoed 5,569-ton British ammunition ship *Thornliebank*, which exploded, killing all 80 men aboard and raining debris on the unsuspecting *U43*, slightly injuring the boat's *Obersteurmann*. The following day, an unexploded 100mm shell was found wedged in the diesel exhaust where it had fallen from the merchant's far-flung cargo. Lüth accounted for one other ship from OS12 during the following night, sinking *Ashby* with one of two G7e torpedoes as it straggled behind the convoy body.

Following extension of the southern operational area to the equator and as far west as the American 300-mile zone, *U111*, *U108* and *U125* became a first wave of a renewed southern offensive. Combing the seas between 30° and 35°W, passing either side of St Paul's Rocks, they found none of the expected heavy traffic. Wilhelm Kleinschmidt's Type IXB *U111* sank two unescorted sailing ships ten days apart northeast of Natal, each time closing the lifeboats and offering brandy, food and a course for the nearest land while asking for ship name and cargo.

Nevertheless, more U-boats followed. To discover whether merchant traffic was using the Pan-American safety zone as cover, *U66* was ordered to reconnoitre as far as the Brazilian coast, and Richard Zapp's U-boat became the first to cross the equator on 21 September. Two days later, two separate steamers were sighted, Zapp manoeuvring ahead at 14 knots to overhaul the first:

> Tanker has strong side and steamer lights additionally illuminated stern and side of the hull. Due to the strong illumination the name and nationality could not be determined at night. <u>Decision</u>: Determine the flag by day submerged, as soon as it is certain, the steamer does not turn for South America, while not losing position ahead for the time being.[3]

The second steamer appeared on the horizon, forcing *U66* to dive, but the tanker passed within 500 metres of Zapp's periscope:

> Tanker is very suspicious, because
> 1. small dirty Panama flag,
> 2. missing the ship's name,

3. tanker is not noted in the Handbook of Merchant Fleets.

4. everything unscrupulous sails under this shoddy flag.[4]

The following day he remained undecided, keeping position on the target, radioing BdU that he suspected a British tanker disguised by the Panamanian flag and requesting instructions. With no special dispensation, BdU approved the attack and Zapp trailed for another day as the ship headed for Cape Town before making a submerged night attack with two torpedoes, one hitting the starboard side and bringing the ship to a brief stop, underway again within 15 minutes. Zapp hit the ship with two more torpedoes which broke the hull in the middle as it began to burn.

> 0404: Crew goes into the lifeboats. Steamer constantly turns in circles to port because the rudder is obviously hard over. Tanker settled lower and lower in the middle, stern and bow were always steeper, but still doesn't sink.
> 0530: Coup de grâce from about 1,500 metres, because the lifeboats are still in the vicinity. Shot goes past the continually turning steamer. Remained in the vicinity, to observe the sinking.
> 0740: [Quadrant] FK6745. Tanker sinks.[5]

Zapp had destroyed 7,052-ton American-crewed but Panamanian-registered *I.C. White* destined for Cape Town with 62,390 barrels of crude oil. Three men were killed, the remaining 34 survivors picked up from two lifeboats six days later after sailing nearly 500 miles towards the Brazilian coastline. It was *U66*'s sole success from a patrol that lasted 74 days.

Meanwhile, U-boats headed south sighted SL87 southwest of the Canary Islands on 21 September, Merten's *U68* opening the attack in the early hours of the following morning, hitting 5,302-ton *Silverbelle*. The heavily damaged ship was taken under tow but sank a week later. Contact boat *U107* suffered four torpedo failures and malfunctioning diesels, forcing Günter Hessler to break away for repairs, but SL87 suffered seven ships sunk by *U68*, *U103*, *U67* and

U107, leaving only four in SL87. Warships of the 40th Escort Group were ineffective, posing no problems for the attacking U-boats, and the group's senior officer, Commander (retired) Ronald Keymer, aboard HMS *Gorleston*, was criticized for his handling of the attack and would lead no more escort groups. Admiralty critique was levelled at escort ships' lack of radio discipline as well as the breaking of radio embargo by listening to BBC broadcasts aboard merchant ship *Ashby*, thought to have betrayed the convoy position to German intelligence.

The four boats that had savaged SL87 travelled independently onwards to join *U108* and *U125* off Freetown. B-Dienst reported that merchant ships capable of over 11 knots were being ordered to proceed independently between Cape Verde and St Paul's Rocks, while slower ships were to make for Freetown for onward convoying. Kleinschmidt's *U111* possessed only sufficient fuel for return to France and BdU ordered it back to Lorient, meeting inbound *U67* and *U68* first. While Merten, notorious for hoarding supplies, suggested that he take aboard spare torpedoes from *U111*, Günther-Müller Stockheim's *U67* carried a man suffering from gonorrhoea who would benefit either from the attention of medical officer Gernot Ziemke aboard *U68* or from possible transfer to Kleinschmidt's boat and return to France.*

The isolated site chosen was Tarrafal Bay on Santo Antão of the Cape Verde archipelago, Merten first to arrive during the morning of 27 September. Kleinschmidt was sighted a little after noon and both boats came to hailing distance to confirm plans for anchor location and the transfer of supplies. That night, they entered the bay, a heavy swell forcing them to approach the shore closer than anticipated. Anchoring in 30 metres of water, they lay only 180 metres from the shoreline beyond which a white cottage and church gate were visible.

People began gathering ashore, including brown-uniformed Portuguese Coast Guard observers. Deeming internal torpedo

---

* Several Type IX U-boats engaged on long-distance missions began receiving medical officers as part of the crew. Previously, and aboard smaller boats, it was the domain of the radio crew as they were considered likely to have the cleanest hands.

transfer too difficult and wanting to retain some ammunition for the return journey, *U111*'s external canisters were emptied, and torpedo transfer began. During this arduous task, a small boat approached carrying uniformed men apparently to determine the submarines' nationality; the local Coast Guard likely expecting American occupation. The German crews were forbidden to talk with the Portuguese, a letter that probably contained an ultimatum to depart was not accepted, *U68*'s First Watch Officer chasing them away and Merten recording that the remark 'nationality American' was clearly heard from the Portuguese.

Just over four hours later, the difficult transfer of four G7a torpedoes was complete; anchors were lifted and both boats retreated to open sea to await *U67*. Running surfaced, *U111* led the way with Kleinschmidt, First Watch Officer Friedrich Wilhelm Rösing (Hans-Rudolf Rösing's younger brother), and *Bootsmannsmaat* Hermann Gedrat on the bridge when they observed a shadow at first taken to be a Portuguese destroyer but solidifying into the unmistakeable silhouette of a large 'snow white' British submarine: River-class HMS *Clyde* under the command of Lieutenant Commander David Ingram.

Clyde had been headed for the Canary Islands to await the expected departure of a German tanker when Ingram received instructions to divert to Tarrafal Bay, Admiralty planners having been made aware of the meeting planned by the three U-boats by Enigma decrypts. Although the danger of tipping Ultra's hand to the Germans was great, the opportunity to destroy three U-boats was deemed worth the risk and *Clyde* despatched immediately. Ingram planned to approach submerged during daylight, surfacing 7 miles offshore west of Tarrafal Bay. Despite bright moonlight, a thick haze made visibility towards land exceptionally poor, whereas *Clyde* would be obvious from shore against the light horizon, and Ingram patrolled between West and South Points until moonset before heading further inshore.

Clyde stopped 3 miles to seaward of the bay, bow pointed inshore and hydrophone watch detecting the two U-boats drawing out to sea, *U68* sighted on the starboard bow clearing South Point. Ingram prepared a full bow salvo as he turned the boat towards Merten until, only about one minute later, *U111* was seen approaching almost nose on and close on the port beam. Abruptly breaking off his attack, Ingram ordered full speed and hard to port, preparing to ram while the gun crew prepared for action.

At that moment, according to members of his crew, Kleinschmidt appeared to momentarily lose his head, and instead of increasing speed to ram the submarine which could not prevent it, he elected to crash dive instead, disappearing before the British gun could be cleared for action, *Clyde*'s bow passing over the wash of the descending conning tower, missing the U-boat by mere inches.

Ingram returned his attention to *U68* to the west, firing a full bow salvo which was spotted by Merten's lookouts, allowing *U68* to dive while combing the tracks, two torpedoes exploding, possibly after having sunk into the depths or hitting submerged obstacles near the shoreline. Ingram now faced two submerged enemies and elected to dive, reloading tubes as he made a hydrophone search.

As the two submerged U-boats slipped away, *Clyde* resurfaced to charge batteries just as *U67* entered the area. Alarmed by distant explosions, Müller-Stockheim had dived, his hydrophone operator detecting propellors. Sighting nothing through the periscope, *U67* surfaced once more to assess the situation, the sky overcast and now pitch dark with a heavy wind developing. Lookouts sighted *Clyde*'s shadow at about the same time that the British crew saw the white streak of foam left by the U-boat's bow, Ingram ordering *Clyde* full ahead and hard to starboard to ram and the gun crew to open fire. As *Clyde* swung towards *U67*, Müller-Stockheim threw his diesels into reverse and put the rudder hard over. Though he avoided being rammed, the U-boat's bow hit *Clyde*'s stern No. 7 torpedo tube, riding up on to the submarine's decking before sliding back into the water and both boats breaking away to dive. Ingram had quickly ordered his men below, unable to open fire with main or Lewis guns as *U67* disappeared. Despite momentary panic from two crewmen at the unexpected ingress of water into *Clyde*'s stern compartment, the damage was slight and quickly repaired. Though Ingram searched for another eight hours, contact was lost as *U67* slipped away, having suffered greater damage than *Clyde*.

Müller-Stockheim finally radioed Kernéval at 1256hrs reporting the U-boat nose buckled and bow caps 1–3 out of action and unable to be repaired with equipment aboard. Both *U111* and *U67* were ordered back to France, Müller-Stockheim rendezvousing with Merten 14 nautical miles from the coast of Mauretania, south of Cape Timris. Lying submerged by day on the bottom in 50 metres, the two boats surfaced with nightfall, and over subsequent nights transferred 55m³ diesel, 1.5m³ lubricating oil, 75 litres distilled water, three E-torpedoes, four Air torpedoes and 2 tons of provisions. With that, *U67* departed for home.

The odds of a British submarine being at the precise spot and time of such a remote U-boat rendezvous were infinitesimally small; a fact not lost on Dönitz: 'The most likely explanation is that our cypher material is compromised or that there has been a breach of security. It appears improbable that an English submarine would be in such an isolated area by accident.'[6]

An emergency modification to U-boat Enigma was enacted at the beginning of October, briefly shutting out Bletchley Park, though they had cracked it once more within a week. In Berlin, *Vizeadmiral* Erhard Maertens, Director of Naval Signals, mounted an immediate investigation into cypher security, the second he had undertaken since examining the possibility that code material had been captured from *U570*.

Unfortunately for BdU, Maerten's current investigation was slipshod as he not only underestimated British codebreaking but overestimated Enigma security. Despite acknowledging that Kleinschmidt had rather carelessly mentioned the location of the meeting in a radio transmission to Kernéval, he reasoned that, had the British Admiralty really known of the rendezvous, they would have sent more than one submarine and achieved more results. Convinced of the impenetrability of Enigma, Maertens concluded that the submarine had been engaged on a lucky routine patrol. The fact that convoys continued to elude gathered U-boats and vital supply ships were being sunk in remote locations seems not to have been considered. Furthermore, with the expected introduction of the new *Triton* code net, security was due to be upgraded anyway. Instead, Maertens attributed British success to efficient direction finding and sighting reports by neutral shipping. On 24 October, in a letter to Dönitz, Maertens assured him, 'The acute disquiet about the compromise of our Secret Operation cannot be justified. Our cipher does not appear to have been broken.'[7]

In the meantime, as Kleinschmidt brought *U111* towards France, he opted to expend some of his remaining torpedoes destroying abandoned *Silverbelle* reported west of Las Palmas and to which a British tug had apparently been sent, neither German nor British authorities aware that it had already sunk of its own accord. On 4 October, ASW trawler HMT *Lady Shirley* was 220 miles west southwest of Tenerife when the masthead lookout sighted an object bearing 30° to starboard, identified initially as a merchant ship's funnel and then probable submarine conning tower at 10 miles' distance. *Lady Shirley*'s captain, the tall, blue-eyed and bearded Australian Arthur Calloway, had specialized in anti-submarine warfare while in the Royal Australian Navy before transferring to the Royal Navy in November 1940.

Aboard *U111* the approaching vessel had been seen and the U-boat dived as Kleinschmidt studied the ship through his pericope. He inexplicably made a grievous error, deducing that the ship was a large freighter at a more considerable distance than his lookouts had reported, estimating a merchant at 5,000 metres. *Lady Shirley* made ASDIC contact with *U111* at only a third of that distance, approaching propellors becoming plainly audible aboard *U111* and both hydrophone operator and Rösing loudly questioning Kleinschmidt's estimation, arguing more forcefully by the moment as Kleinschmidt irritably remained adamant. As he turned to berate the two, Callaway dropped a pattern of three depth charges set to explode between 150 and 350 feet, a fourth jamming in its rails and not dropping.

At only 13 metres' periscope depth, *U111* suffered little damage but Kleinschmidt's surprise appeared absolute, causing him to make his second grave error of judgement and order the boat surfaced for gun action. The British crew were surprised to see *U111* surface in their wake, Calloway immediately turning his ship to port to bring the 4-inch gun to bear and, if necessary, to ram the U-boat as Hotchkiss machine guns opened fire.

Aboard *U111*, the small amount of water that had entered the boat caused the diesel to misfire and then fail completely, filling the engine room with dense white smoke. Kleinschmidt hurriedly ordered the boat dived once more but, coming under shellfire, valuable seconds were lost in order and counter-order. Kleinschmidt threw open the conning tower hatch and climbed on to the bridge followed by Rösing and gun crews while mechanics struggled to revive the diesels.

The two vessels blazed away with all weapons at each other, the gun layer aboard *Lady Shirley*, Leading Seaman Leslie Pizzey, hit in the stomach by a 20mm cannon round and killed, his place taken by Sub-Lieutenant Frederick French and the rate of fire barely faltering. Both Hotchkiss machine gunners were also hit and wounded but remained at their posts and maintained a continuous stream of fire. As Third Watch Officer Helmut Fuchs ordered both gun crews hurriedly on deck, a 4-inch shell hit *U111*'s conning tower but did not penetrate the pressure hull. Although the stern gun crew never attempted to reach their 37mm cannon, the first shell put into the breach of the boat's 105mm forward gun could not be rammed home and two of the gun crew were then hit, one having his leg severed and later dying from blood loss, the other lightly injured, but all racing back towards the shelter of the tower when a second shell hit the base of the periscope and exploded, killing Rösing, Fuchs and Kleinschmidt, whose body fell down the open hatchway to land on the internal conning tower floor, blood pouring onto the control room deck below.

With the recalcitrant diesels still billowing smoke, Hans-Joachim Heinecke, aboard as an officer under instruction before taking his own command, ordered *U111* abandoned and Günther Wulf opened vents to scuttle. The battle had lasted 19 minutes since the first depth charges were dropped.

Forty-four prisoners were pulled from the sea as *U111* sank stern first. During the return to Gibraltar, *Oberbootsmannsmaat* Gerhard Hartig attempted to redeem his failure to man the aft gun by hatching a plan to overpower the 28 British crewmen and steal the trawler, but with only one willing accomplice, the scheme was abandoned. They were the first prisoners captured from a U-boat operating in the South Atlantic, and British interrogators made much of their performance.

The crew of *U111* put up a poor fight and surrendered speedily to their much less powerful adversary. This fact, taken into consideration in conjunction with the circumstances of the capture of *U570* and the sinking of *U501*, shows that all three crews gave in quickly when real and obvious determination was encountered. The previous high morale was, in each case, apparently artificial morale based on propaganda assurances and not on real confidence in the reliability of the men themselves. This inability to surmount a crisis is an encouraging fact and of psychological interest in the examination of Nazi education and naval training.*

The southern U-boats received a further crippling setback that underlined Dönitz's contention that U-boats were unsuitable escort vessels. With *U129* ordered to escort supply ship *Kota Pinang*, Nicolai Clausen arrived on 4 October just as HMS *Kenya* was shelling the tanker as part of the coordinated Ultra-led offensive. Unable to intervene, once *Kenya* had retreated Clausen surfaced and took 119 survivors on board, severely limiting the boat's diving capability. Dönitz, aware of what peril the boat could face crossing Biscay surfaced, ordered *U129* to unload survivors at El Ferrol, and two days later Clausen transferred them to a Spanish tugboat before returning to Lorient.

---

* Lieutenant Commander Arthur Calloway was awarded the DSO for this action. He was killed in action on 11 December after HMT *Lady Shirley* was torpedoed by *U374* and sunk with all hands (C.B. 4051 (32), 'U111', Interrogation of Survivors, November 1941, Naval Intelligence Division, Admiralty).

The loss of *Kota Pinang* complicated West African operations which by mid-October comprised *U66, U103, U107, U125* and *U126*, with *U68* reconnoitring the waters off St Helena. During his time off Freetown, Ernst Bauer's *U126* sank American steamer *Lehigh*, despite the ship carrying a clearly painted American flag on the hull. Bauer mistook the zigzagging ship for a Greek vessel during his submerged attack, only recognizing its markings after he had fired the torpedo, and sinking the second American merchant ship destroyed by U-boat.

U66, U103, U107 and *U125* all possessed roughly the same fuel reserves and were ordered back to France in a rough patrol line for potential opportunities. Due to his squirreling away of stores, only Merten's *U68* possessed sufficient reserves to remain off West Africa while incoming reinforcements *U126* and *U129* were ordered by BdU to resupply from returning raider *Atlantis, UA* and *U124* shortly to join them and resupply from the tanker *Python*.

Agents associated with Germany's Abwehr had reported significant numbers of ships passing Cape Town and within the harbour itself, and, faced with impoverished returns off West Africa, Dönitz pushed four of these long-distance boats towards the South African harbour city. The route of shipping bound for Freetown passed the Cape of Good Hope, ensuring that key South African ports were invariably used as stop-over points, Saldanha, Walvis Bay, Cape Town, East London, Port Elizabeth or Durban the primary harbours. In response to the seizure of five Vichy merchant ships bound from Madagascar to Europe by South African forces, two Vichy French submarines had begun operating off Cape Town during November 1941, sinking Norwegian freighter *Thode Fagelund* carrying scrap iron, jute and tea to Britain – the first submarine sinking off South Africa. Following occupation of Madagascar by Allied forces by early November 1942, South African threat assessment concluded that the greatest danger for South African ports stemmed from Japanese or Italian submarines (from the Red Sea). Instead, *UA, U124, U126* and *U129* were to open an entirely new arena of combat for Dönitz, though completely reliant on successful resupply at sea.

However, *Schiff 16 'Atlantis'*, a successful raider that had been at sea since March 1940 and sunk 16 ships, capturing another five, was the first such supply vessel to be sunk. German merchant raiders had escaped Ultra intelligence because they used the 'Distant waters' Enigma cypher, which Bletchley Park had never penetrated. However, on 18 October, *Atlantis* was ordered to rendezvous with *U68* 500 miles south of St Helena and refuel Merten's boat before proceeding north to refuel *U126* north of Ascension Island. The initial rendezvous passed uneventfully, but Bauer's radioed instructions for meeting *Atlantis* were transmitted in the *Heimisch* key, deciphered by Bletchley Park and passed to the Admiralty. Ironically, Bauer's resupply was now deemed less imperative, as the boat had developed engine problems and been granted permission to return to France. Heavy cruisers HMS *Devonshire* and *Dorsetshire* and the light cruiser HMS *Dunedin* were immediately sent to hunt *Atlantis* in another direct operational use of Ultra.

On the morning of 22 November, *U126* contacted *Atlantis*, Bauer and his senior officers going aboard to confer with the captain, Bernhard Rogge, and take a bath before provisioning began. As Bauer relaxed, the mastheads of HMS *Devonshire* were spotted heading straight for *Atlantis*, whose attempt at bluffing its identity was futile. While *U126* dived under the command of its Second Watch Officer, *Devonshire* opened fire at a considerable distance, beyond the range of the raider's guns or U-boat torpedoes. Hit by two salvos, seven men were killed and the ship irreparably damaged; Rogge ordered it abandoned and scuttled, and he was the last to leave.

As *Devonshire* retreated, *U126* surfaced to recover its skipper and officers and Bauer appraised BdU of the sinking, the other three U-boats of the Cape Town group all ordered to assist Bauer who took aboard 107 survivors – 55 below deck, 52 above decks – while the remaining 198 men were distributed between six towed lifeboats. *U126* was ordered to proceed to *Python*'s location and transfer survivors aboard, estimated to be two days' sailing: 'The sinking of "Ship 16" proves once more what difficulties and dangers are entailed in conducting surface warfare and the refuelling of U-boats. The construction of U-boat tankers started at the beginning of the war and the conversion of Dutch boats to torpedo transport boats will shortly probably constitute the sole refuelling facilities.'[8]

With *U126*'s diesels still unreliable, Bauer was to refuel from *Python* for return passage to France, while *U68* took his place in the Cape Town assault, Merten ordered to make yet another refuelling stop, this time with *Python*. Clausen's *U129*, Joachim 'Jochen' Mohr's *U124* with its distinctive Edelweiss emblem, Karl-Friedrich Merten's *U68* and Hans Eckermann's *UA* were all to take supply from *Python* and head south, strictly forbidden to attack shipping between the equator and South African waters.

On 24 November, *Python* homed on beacon signals from *U126* and successfully met Bauer, taking aboard the 305 survivors from *Atlantis* while refuelling *U126*, after which a single officer from *Atlantis* was taken aboard and course laid for France, finally docking in Lorient on 13 December. Meanwhile, *Python* sailed nearly 2,000 miles to the south to resupply the Cape Town boats, U-boat radio traffic again betraying the meeting point and HMS *Dorsetshire* and *Dunedin* headed to the area. As Mohr approached the rendezvous, he sighted *Dunedin* zigzagging at high speed, and made an optimistic three-torpedo fan shot at 4,000 metres' range, hitting the light cruiser under the bridge and after mast, tearing up the quarterdeck, dislodging the No. 6 6-inch gun and blowing off the port propeller. Mohr noted wreckage flying into the air as *Dunedin* listed to starboard and made a lazy circle to port, capsizing and sinking within half an hour. Only four officers and 63 men survived.

Despite this disaster, on 1 December HMS *Dorsetshire* found *Python* in the act of refuelling *UA* and preparing torpedo transfer to *U68*. Within minutes the tanker was under attack, scuttled in the face of accurate artillery fire as the U-boats dived, *U68* losing momentary control and unable to attack, *UA* underestimating the cruiser's speed at long range and missing with five torpedoes. After *Dorsetshire* had departed the scene, hundreds of survivors were scattered between lifeboats and the pair of U-boats.

Went to the [life]boats. The people on the rubber rafts were taken on board on deck. There are now 104 men on each U-boat, in the cutters still about 200 men. The cutters (5 each) are taken in tow by both U-boats.

2350hrs: Redistribution is completed... Came to course 330°, speed 5 knots. Intention is, to run towards the boats *U124* and *U129* and get as much distance from the sinking point as possible. Crew is stowed away in the boat, initially up to 24 men must remain on deck in rubber boats. In case of a crash dive the rubber rafts will be put off and remain with the released cutters. In the boat, room for all must be created slowly at first. Artillery ammunition is thrown overboard to empty the magazine, torpedoes were reloaded, provisions stowed. There is a huge rummaging in the boat.[9]

Dönitz ordered *U124* and *U129* to aid in the return of survivors and all plans for the Cape Town assault abandoned, not to be revisited until August 1942. As Mohr raced to assist, he chanced upon American steamer *Sagadhoc* and sank it after seeing no visible neutrality markings – the third American steamer sunk before declared war. The Cape Town U-boats eventually carried about 104 survivors each northwards, meeting and transferring men aboard Italian submarines *Torelli*, *Calvii*, *Finzi* and *Tazzoli* that had sailed from Bordeaux at Dönitz's request. The last of the U-boats carrying survivors, *U124*, arrived in Saint Nazaire on 29 December. The possibility of supplying southern U-boat operations had been eliminated.

Once again, such precise operational use of Ultra intelligence by the Royal Navy should have rung alarm bells in Berlin, but another lazy investigation by Maertens concluded Enigma remained secure. Despite the loss of these two crucial ships and previous supply vessels with almost surgical Royal Navy precision, admission of potential cypher compromise was prevented by the arrogant acceptance of Enigma's superiority and woeful underestimation of Allied cryptanalysts. Successful arrivals and departures of other blockade-breaking ships from France were used as proof of Enigma's security, the assumption made that, if broken, such intelligence would be used every time a target presented itself.

By 10 November, BdU counted 220 U-boats of all types in service, though only 84 operational. A further 55 were school boats and 79 still undergoing trials, hampered by a lack of torpedo recovery vessels. U-boats now entered service four months after commissioning, rather than the previous average of three. The loss of boats to the Mediterranean was not Dönitz's only malaise; he had been ordered to provide six U-boats for escort duties during November as well as reinforcing the Arctic on direct instructions from the Führer.

Towards the end of August, *U571*, *U451*, *U566* and *U752* all patrolled independently off the Kola Coast, sinking a Soviet minesweeper and severely damaging large steamer *Marija Uljanova*, though by the month's end, the first British convoy to the Soviet Union arrived undetected by German forces in Archangelsk.

The value of these Russian convoys was both military and political. In terms of total wartime tonnage received by the Soviet Union, approximately 23 per cent arrived via the Arctic convoys, 27 per cent via the United States through the Persian Gulf, from mid-1942, and 50 per cent through the Pacific to Vladivostok, also from mid-1942. However, in 1941 the Arctic convoy route was the only practicable method of assisting the Soviet Union, and both symbolism and military value compelled establishment of the 'PQ' convoys, empty ships comprising 'QP' convoys headed back to Britain.

Dönitz elected to use new combat U-boats from Germany for Arctic patrols, Kurt Vogelsang's *U132* mounting the longest Arctic mission thus far – 45 days beginning in September – and proving also the most successful. On 18 October, Vogelsang sighted unescorted 3,487-ton steamer *Argun* 5 miles off the Gorodetzkij lighthouse and hit it with a single torpedo, two more required before the ship broke it in two. Just over an hour later, Vogelsang missed hydrographic ship *Mgla* with a single G7a torpedo that struck the shallow seafloor and detonated, *Mgla* going on to rescue *Argun* survivors from their lifeboats. Later that evening, Vogelsang fired a close-range G7a at 608-ton trawler *RT8 'Seld'*, the ship sinking with all hands within 30 seconds.

However, Dönitz's tonnage war was not to be decided by Arctic patrols and nor, for that matter, was the grinding war of attrition developing on the Eastern Front. Regardless, BdU remained under pressure to place at least nine U-boats within the Arctic area, which under Dönitz's rule of thirds would allow three to patrol at any given time. Furthermore, Commanding Admiral Norway, Hermann Boehm, objected to the assignment of only new, inexperienced U-boats, arguing that veteran U-boat commanders were required in such a challenging environment. Though persuaded to allow U-boats to remain with Boehm for more than one patrol, Dönitz steadfastly refused to remove veterans from the Atlantic. By November, four U-boats were on Arctic patrol and the post of *Admiral Nordmeer* (Admiral Northern Waters) had been established, Hubert Schmundt occupying the position until August 1942 and responsible for U-boat deployment within a central band of the Arctic Ocean from his headquarters in Kirkenes, the remainder remaining under Boehm's control, in a confusing arrangement.

Meanwhile the cypher war continued. During September, BdU began benefitting from B-Dienst decoding of the main Royal Navy cypher (Naval Cypher No. 2) with ever greater speed, and within three months they also began penetrating Naval Cypher No. 3, used to encrypt all communications for North Atlantic convoys. Between February 1942 and June 1943, B-Dienst could provide reliable decrypts of up to 80 per cent of Cypher No. 3 signal traffic.

A new coding system was introduced by BdU in December whereby standard Kriegsmarine grid chart references were frequently changed according to a set of tables identifying the Christian name, surname and address of an imaginary person, set forth within an 'Address Book' issued to U-boats. This extra layer of security remained problematic for Allied cryptanalysts until June 1944.

At sea, however, demands being placed on combat U-boats were many and varied. From May, several surface ships were escorted to and from European waters. *U106* had been tied to *Lech* in the South Atlantic, Oesten then tasked with accompanying inbound *Annelise Essberger* carrying crude rubber from Kobe to Bordeaux. During August, the raider *Schiff 36 'Orion'* was escorted to France by *U46* and *U205*, and in late September *U204* was designated escort for outgoing blockade breaker *Rio Grande*. *U129* escorted tanker

Kota Pinang and during November *U109* was released from the
'*Mordbrenner*' group to escort inbound prize *Silvaplana*, while *U561*
and *U652* were attached to inbound raider *Schiff 45* '*Komet*'. It was
a task heavy on fuel consumption, thereafter largely disallowing
U-boats to resume operations once escort was complete. It was also
a task for which they were patently unsuited as radioman Wolfgang
Hirschfeld remembered in his autobiography:

> On 7 November the Commander announced the mission to
> the men: *U109* was to meet the *Silvaplana* at a point close
> to the Anton Corridor, an internationally agreed sea lane for
> neutral ships, and there protect her against attacks from both
> sea and air.
>
> Otto Peters scratched his head. 'Did you hear that? Protect
> her against attack from the air? What do they think we are, a
> flak cruiser?' Cdr Hoffmann, who heard this as he was passing,
> laughed. 'Yes, that wording was definitely dreamed up in
> Berlin.'[10]

From Dönitz's slender forces, four U-boats had been detailed
for 'special purpose reconnaissance' in the North – scouting ice
and enemy warship dispositions in preparation for the planned
breakout of cruiser *Admiral Scheer* into the North Atlantic – though
cancellation of *Scheer*'s mission at least released them for North
Atlantic operations. Six more were also earmarked for immediate
transfer to the Mediterranean: *U81*, *U205*, *U433* and *U565* were
already at sea when reassigned and *U95* and *U431* in harbour
and ready to sail. Named '*Arnauld*' group, the bulk of them were
directed to Tobruk to intercept seaborne supplies in support of
Rommel's planned attack on the besieged British garrison holding
the Libyan port.

Passing undetected through the Strait of Gibraltar on the night of
11/12 November, *U81* and *U205* separately encountered the Royal
Navy's 'Force H', comprising aircraft carriers HMS *Ark Royal* and
Argus, battleship HMS *Malaya*, light cruiser HMS *Hermione* and
seven escorting destroyers. The force was returning from delivering

Hurricane and Blenheim aircraft to embattled Malta when Franz Reschke in *U205* sighted them and fired three torpedoes, claiming a hit on *Ark Royal* after observing a flash through his periscope. In fact, he had hit nothing, one torpedo exploding in the wake of HMS *Legion*.

Later that afternoon, Force H steamed directly at submerged *U81*, and Friedrich Guggenberger carefully manoeuvred for a full bow salvo, primarily targeting HMS *Malaya*. A little over six minutes later a single explosion was heard, followed by a second, Guggenberger leaving the scene and assuming a hit on *Malaya* and a second possibly on an aircraft carrier beyond the battleship. Detected by ASDIC, a five-hour depth-charge attack caused no significant damage as *U81* went deep. HMS *Ark Royal* had been hit and, despite valiant attempts to save the stricken carrier, rolled over and sank the following morning. Miraculously, only a single man was lost, though the only Mediterranean fleet carrier and a source of great British prestige was gone. Its nine ASV Mk II radar-equipped Swordfish aircraft of 812 Squadron had been able to fly off for Gibraltar where they proved invaluable for anti-U-boat patrols.

Forewarned of Rommel's imminent offensive against Tobruk by decryptions of Luftwaffe Enigma messages, the British Eighth Army launched Operation *Crusader* on 18 November which, despite fierce resistance from German and Italian forces, steadily pushed its way forward, a linkup between Tobruk's defenders and a small force of the advancing 2nd New Zealand Division achieved nine days later.

Berlin declared an emergency, compounded by fears of phantom Anglo-French amphibious landings to Rommel's rear, and on 22 November under SKL orders U-boats either in or headed to the mid-Atlantic were redirected to Gibraltar, some to operate west of the Strait, some to enter the Mediterranean. Ten U-boats were to be placed on constant operations within the eastern Mediterranean and the number committed to action within the Mediterranean ordered not to fall below 18. By the end of the month, ten U-boats were headed for the Strait and five safely penetrated the Mediterranean, though two subsequently sunk.

Gerd Schreiber's *U95* had slipped past the Rock surfaced on the night of 24 November; searchlights swept the sea, but none found *U95*. After days of fruitless searching near Gibraltar, *U95* sighted an unidentified submarine at 2300hrs on 27 November. Schreiber opted to tail the potential target, needing firm identification, though its end-on profile prevented this. Shortly before 0020hrs, three men manned the 20mm flak weapon and a pocket torch was used to flash a challenge to the submarine. *Oberbootsmannsmaat* Fritz Kober later related what followed:

I put on my leather jacket and quickly put my cigarette case in my pocket, folded back the seat, and went up into the conning tower. Then No. 1 said: 'Take your life jacket, we're in for something.' At that moment I had no idea where mine was; under my pillow, perhaps… In the meantime, we got the order: 'Close the caps', then again: 'Open the caps', and then another order to close them. The men forward were starting to curse… The order was given again: 'Open the caps.' As we were about to make our fourth approach, they spotted us before we came too close. It was a beautiful moonlight night, just three days before full moon. You could see your way about better than by day, when it is often a bit misty down there at that time of year… When we were seen we were in an unfavourable position with the moon behind us. They could see us in the moonlight better than we could see them. While we still held our fire, they drew away and showed their stern; so we challenged them two or three times in Morse. The Captain ordered: 'Gun crew, clear away!' As a matter of fact, we always had the guns ready, and the ammunition lay ready below in the control room; it always lies there. So, the first thing was to get the gun loaded and sights on the target… While they were getting the gun ready, we went ahead at slow speed. Then the Captain said: 'Now try some gunfire', and we went full speed ahead. At that moment the Dutch fired their torpedoes, but we couldn't see them easily on account of the moonlight. Luckily, the Junior Officer saw it; he has good eyes trained in flying. He shouted: 'Torpedo track

to port!' The Quartermaster, who was standing forward at the
port lookout, pushed him out of the way, leapt to the bridge
rail, had a look over the side and put the helm hard over to
starboard. Suddenly I heard a hissing noise – if that one had hit
us amidships or forward, I shouldn't have been able to get out;
it was a very nasty feeling! I heard a bang aft and we supposed
that the first torpedo had just grazed along our side. The second
one came a bit further over to port, so we turned to starboard
and turned, so to speak, right into the course of the torpedo.
The torpedo must have exploded right on the screw. There was a
loud report, and I thought my head would split. I looked down
and saw a red flame and a fearful cloud of smoke. I pulled myself
up and at that moment water began to come in. I was outside.
I looked round and there were a few men aft and a few to our
right. The Captain shouted: 'Keep together!' Then he began to
count us all and call our names to see who was there. He asked
me: 'Has anybody else come out?' And I said: 'No, I'm the last.'
Then we began swimming... All at once I saw the black bow of a
ship in front of me. My greatest fear as I swam towards the ship,
was that they might open fire with machine-guns. Then the first
of us got on board and I heard them speaking German. Three
men pulled me up on the deck.[11]

The submarine was Dutch *O21* returning to Gibraltar, and only
Schreiber and 11 men survived the sinking of *U95*.

The destruction of the second new Mediterranean boat lost was
perhaps less dramatic but more deadly. Veteran Ottokar Pauhlsen's
U557 had passed through the Strait two nights after *U95* and sunk
six merchant ships totalling almost 32,000 tons as well as British light
cruiser HMS *Galatea*. Misidentified as British, *U557* was rammed on
16 December south of Crete by Italian destroyer *Orione* escorting
fuel transport to North Africa and sunk with all 43 crew.

The remaining six U-boats attempting to break into the
Mediterranean during November failed. Hans Ey's *U433* had been
sunk in Biscay on 16 November 1941 by depth charges and gunfire
from corvette HMS *Marigold* with six men killed and 38 survivors

taken prisoner.* *U96* was bombed by a radar-equipped Swordfish formerly from *Ark Royal* and forced to submerge, where it was hunted for five hours by surface forces before repairs were made and the boat crept back to France.† Klaus Bargsten's *U563* was bombed by a 502 Squadron Whitley bomber in Biscay on 30 November and badly damaged, Bargsten wounded in the shoulder by strafing. Unable to dive, Bargsten radioed for help and Dönitz ordered two other Mediterranean-bound boats to assist: *U71* and *U206*. Unbeknownst to BdU, *U206* had already been sunk, probably by a mine west of Saint Nazaire. Escorted by minesweepers and KG40 aircraft, *U563* returned to France, the boat later forced to sail to Germany and almost completely rebuilt. Walter Flachsenberg's *U71*, plagued by engine trouble, returned to Saint Nazaire, while Günther Krech's *U558* was heavily damaged by warships vectored to the boat as it attempted to slip past Gibraltar by radar-equipped aircraft. Depth charged by HMS *Stork* and *Samphire*, Krech aborted back to Brest for repairs.

However, those that made it into the Mediterranean announced their presence felt. *U331* had sailed from Salamis on 12 November with eight Brandenburger commandos aboard who were landed on the night of the 17th between the Capes Ras Gibeisa and Ras el Schaqiq. The Brandenburgers were mounting Operation *Hai*, intended to cut the new Allied coastal supply railway, and landed as planned by rubber dinghy, a single U-boat crewman helping row them ashore. *U331* then stood off to sea before a scheduled return the following night inshore to pick up the raiding party. However, despite laying their explosive charges, the Brandenburgers were captured without a fight, and subsequent interrogation revealed the pressure-fused charges, which were soon disarmed. Radioing headquarters in Salamis that the troops had failed to return, *U331* was ordered away from the coast to a waiting position north of Mersa Matruh.

---

* Ey, who had previously been First Watch Officer aboard Kuppisch's *U94*, made a briefly successful escape attempt with Schreiber of *U95* from Gibraltar to reach Spain. Both officers were, however, recaptured and moved onward to England.

† The event was heavily dramatized by the on-board propaganda reporter Lothar-Günther Buchheim who drew upon the experience for his novel *Das Boot*.

Von Tiesenhausen had been lying submerged by day and surfaced at night, searching for traffic headed to Tobruk as artillery fire lit the horizon ashore. Destroyers were occasionally seen headed west at high speed, but no targets presented themselves. The sound of distant propellors detected by hydrophone during daylight hours of 25 November brought *U331* to the surface, destroyer mastheads sighted at 1441 hrs.

Admiral Sir Andrew Cunningham – Mediterranean Fleet Commander – was badgered by Churchill to disrupt Italian supply traffic to Benghazi as *Crusader* troops became bogged down before Tobruk with heavy armour losses. An acrimonious exchange of messages followed as Cunningham spelt out fuel shortages and the existing danger posed by Italian torpedo aircraft, Cunningham stating that he was fully aware of the importance of intercepting Benghazi convoys, two already either destroyed or forced to return to Italy that month. However, firm Ultra intelligence revealed another attempted transport, this time the German merchant ships *Maritza* and *Procida* under Italian escort, carrying vehicles and fuel for the Luftwaffe. Cunningham embarked upon his flagship HMS *Queen Elizabeth* as it and HMS *Barham* and *Valiant* of Force H covered the lighter groups of Force K and Force B in case Italian heavy ships appeared. In due course, the two German merchants were sunk by Force K's HMS *Penelope*, the Italian escort ineffectual in defence. The three battleships sailed echeloned to port, *Queen Elizabeth* leading followed by *Barham* and then *Valiant*, with destroyer screens on either flank and Cunningham sipping tea in his bridge cabin as *U331* prepared to attack.

1547: To Action Stations! Now or never – opportunity has come. Two of the destroyers move forward to take position ahead of and just to port of the battleships. Apparently, the destroyer formation is a screen against torpedo planes. I succeed in passing unseen between these two [destroyers] at periscope depth. Distance to each 250 meters. I can no longer reach shooting position on the first battleship due to the difficult target angle (too broad/too far aft). Therefore, on the second. Type not recognized. I must turn

towards, hard. Shot despite the difficult target angle (too broad).
I have the sun at my back.

1619: 4-fan on battleship, range 375 meters, running time 24
seconds, depths: tube I – 3 meters, tube III – 4 meters, tube II – 5
meters, tube IV – 4 meters. Target angle 70°, torpedo course 295°.
After 24 seconds running time, 3 bright detonations, somewhat
later one more. By sound bearings the torpedoes ran together
with the battleship sounds. After the detonations cracking sounds
which suggest bulkheads are breaking. The three detonations
themselves were not very heavy. The effect of the shot cannot be
observed because due to the hard turn while shooting there is
danger of broaching. At depth 9.5 meters the boat was brought
down. Because the 3rd battleship closely followed the one shot at,
there was danger of ramming. I evacuated the conning tower and
closed the hatch. Fortunately, the boat gets under at AK. And yet
despite all measures remains hanging at depth 80 meters. I have
the forward depth gauge read and by this it turns out that the deep
control room depth gauge and at the same time the pressure gauges
of the ballast tanks and bunkers are turned off, at the hull valves.
In the rush, of four awkwardly located valves, the wrong one was
turned off. In any case, when the supply lines are opened to the
large depth gauge and the ballast tank pressure gauges the pointers
register at full scale. From their position the boat is at 130 meters.
Blew immediately and pumped and finally – the pointer is steady,
the pointer trembles – the boat comes up. It holds tight well except
slight leak at the rear construction hatch (6 places), both periscopes
leak heavily. Main ballast tank 3 leaks at three places on the weld
seam. The port hull valve of the E-motor leaks a bit. Due to the
pressure and high-speed setting the clutch grinds at the packing
sealing ring. The heat was reduced with fire extinguishers. The
boat holds well. A good testimonial for the North Sea Shipyard,
Emden.[12]

Despite the conning tower of *U331* alarmingly breaking surface
only 130 metres or so from *Barham* and hanging there for nearly 30
seconds as compensatory flooding misfired, it escaped depth charges

that were tardily thrown at some distance and later surfaced by night, observing a fiery glow to the south and battleship torpedoed. Von Tiesenhausen had sunk HMS *Barham*, the battleship turning over on its beam ends within minutes. Survivors were seen on the hull sides until the magazine erupted, a drama caught on newsreel film by Gaumont British News cameraman John Turner aboard *Valiant* and soon becoming a defining image of the naval war in the Mediterranean. It was, however, an image not seen until after the war had ended; impounded by British authorities to avoid a detrimental effect to national morale.

Lieutenant Ian Hunter McDonald, Royal Australian Navy, serving as flag lieutenant to the second in command of the Mediterranean Fleet, Vice Admiral Sir H.D. Pridham-Wippell, embarked on *Barham*, and Squadron Signal Officer of the 1st Battle Squadron later described the sinking:

> When I scrambled over the barbette and onto the heavily barnacle encrusted ship's bottom and over the bilge keel, it was probably only about four minutes since the ship had been hit. I estimate she then had a list of about sixty degrees. Those of us who were scrambling over the barnacles, which were pretty sharp, were close to the swirling sea when there was a tremendous shudder throughout the ship which turned out to be a major explosion in one of the fifteen inch magazines aft. One sailor near me said 'Christ, another torpedo', and another said 'Nah, the bastard's blowin' up'. That was enough for me to hurl myself at the sea and hope for the best.[13]

Pridham-Wippell and 450 other men were later rescued, but 55 officers, including the ship's captain Geoffrey Cooke, and 806 men were killed. For von Tiesenhausen would come the Knight's Cross, awarded on 27 January when *Bahram's* sinking was finally confirmed.

Nor was that the end of ruin visited upon Cunningham's Mediterranean fleet. The following day Australian sloop HMAS *Parramatta* escorting heavily laden ammunition ship *Hanne* to

Tobruk was torpedoed northeast of the port by Hans Heidtmann's *U559* with 138 men, including all officers, killed. On 14 December light cruiser HMS *Galatea* of Force K had been sunk by *U557* off Alexandria with Captain Edward Sim, 22 officers and 447 ratings killed. Four days later, the three cruisers and four destroyers of Force K ran into an Italian minefield; cruiser HMS *Neptune* was sunk with only one survivor, destroyer HMS *Kandahar* sunk with 73 men killed, cruisers HMS *Aurora* severely damaged and *Penelope* lightly damaged. The following day, six Italian frogmen using *Maiale* 'human torpedoes' disabled battleships HMS *Queen Elizabeth* and *Valiant* and destroyer HMS *Jervis* as well as blowing the stern off 7,554-ton Norwegian tanker *Sagona* in Alexandria harbour. By this stage Cunningham's Mediterranean fleet had been reduced to three light cruisers and a few destroyers.

Further U-boats were transferred into the Mediterranean during December, *U374* passing along the African side of the Strait on 11 December and sinking HMT *Lady Shirley* and 515-ton patrol yacht HMS *Rosabelle* during a difficult though successful passage.

U-boat losses had been heavy both within the Mediterranean and in the relatively confined space west of Gibraltar. Convoy HG76 of 32 ships under escort by Commander Frederic 'Johnnie' Walker's 36th Escort Group – two Bittern-class sloops, HMS *Stork* and *Deptford*, and seven corvettes, HMS *Convolvulus*, *Gardenia*, *Marigold*, *Pentstemon*, *Rhododendron*, *Samphire* and *Vetch* – sailed from Gibraltar on 14 December into the hastily convened *'Seeräuber'* group. The escort was heavily reinforced, including escort carrier HMS *Audacity* and her three-destroyer screen, until 17 warships covered HG76, while a separate group of Force H destroyers sailed as an independent U-boat hunting force.

Eitel-Friedrich Kentrat's *U74* contacted HG76 late on 14 December, joined during the early morning hours by Heinrich Schonder in *U77*, both boats headed to the Strait of Gibraltar but instructed to attack before dawn before resuming their journey to the Mediterranean. With a heavy presence of radar-equipped Swordfish from Gibraltar, both U-boats were harried relentlessly and only Schonder successfully torpedoed an independently sailing ship before both passed successfully into the Mediterranean Sea.

While 'Seeräuber' formed a patrol line south of Cape St Vincent, HG76 passed without being observed. Bruno Hansmann's *U127*, positioned at the line's southern end, was seen by a Sunderland flying boat which reported its position to the 'hunter-killer' group from Force H. The force located the surfaced boat and opened fire, all shots falling wide. As *U127* was forced to dive, HMS *Foxhound* and HMAS *Nestor* made strong ASDIC contact with the U-boat, depth charges producing a strong underwater explosion and splintered debris that included human remains.

The convoy was not detected until noon on 16 December by a patrolling Condor that guided *U108* to the ships as the 'Seeräuber' group was ordered to close on HG76. By the morning of 17 December, the convoy had passed beyond the range of Gibraltar-based aircraft, their place taken by Martlets launched from HMS *Audacity*. That night Arend Baumann in Type IXC *U131* found himself at periscope depth in the middle of the convoy – a miscalculation later attributed to imperfectly functioning hydrophones, badly repaired after *U131* had collided with anti-torpedo nets in the Baltic. Recovering from his surprise, Baumann submerged quietly and allowed the convoy to pass over his head before following at a more discreet distance. *U131* was sighted to starboard of the convoy by a Martlet early the following morning, the aircraft circling above as Walker raced several ships to the location and dropped depth charges. Considerable damage was caused, water entering aft and the U-boat tilting downward and beginning to sink. Several control room gauges were smashed and the electric motors damaged, oil from a leaking tank beginning to pour into the diesel room. The uncooperative hydrophones had also been rendered completely dead, and as hull plates groaned and paint blistered off the contorted walls trim was gradually achieved before Baumann ordered tanks blown with their last compressed air. When *U131* broke surface and began to run, HMS *Stanley* summoned five other warships to the chase, while *Audacity*'s relief fighter dived to attack, shot down by the U-boat's flak gun.

However, unable to outpace pursuit or turn and fire with his main deck weapon, Baumann signalled BdU, reporting the circumstances. The reply dashed his hopes as no aid was available; *U131* should instead scuttle if no other alternative was available and, with shellfire straddling the boat, Baumann ordered vents opened and the crew overboard, all 47 men rescued as prisoners.

Reinforcements rushed to 'Seeräuber' as the battle around HG76 deteriorated for the U-boats. Despite HMS *Stanley* being sunk by *U574*, HMS *Audacity* by *U751* and the loss of two merchant ships, the contest ended in German disaster; *U127*, *U131*, *U434*, *U574* and *U567* were lost, the latter captained by the acclaimed Engelbert Endrass who had served as Günther Prien's First Watch Officer, lost with his entire crew to depth charges from HMS *Deptford*. BdU broke off the attack on 22 December as Dönitz despondently lamented commitment of all Atlantic U-boats to the Gibraltar area. Assuming British knowledge of the shift, he reasoned that HG escorts had been heavily reinforced and sent *U653*, a new boat from Germany, into the North Atlantic to act as a radio transmitting decoy. During December he also ruled that inexperienced U-boat commanders would not be committed against the formidable defences around Gibraltar, instead their U-boats to be refuelled in France and sent to the Newfoundland Bank. Furthermore, large, heavy Type IX U-boats were obviously patently unsuited to operations around Gibraltar or within the Mediterranean and would not be used there. Slower to dive than the Type VIIC, larger and more conspicuous and more difficult to trim underwater, their greatest asset of long-range capability was completely wasted.

Portending further ill, Eberhard Hoffmann's *U451* became the first to be sunk by aircraft at night on 21 December. Hoffmann, who had patrolled aboard Bleichrodt's *U109* as part of his commander-in-training course, had been transferred from the Arctic to the Mediterranean, opting to slip through the Strait surfaced in early morning darkness. The U-boat's First Watch Officer, Walter Köhler, was on the bridge with three lookouts and *U451* was proceeding at full speed when an aircraft roared overhead, its approach drowned out by the noise from diesel exhausts. It was a Swordfish of *Ark*

Royal's 812 Squadron, whose radar had detected the U-boat at 3½ miles, dropping three depth charges, the centre depth charge set shallow and exploding immediately beneath *U451*. Calling for an alarm dive, the three ratings disappeared through the conning tower hatch as water poured through it, but Köhler was unable to follow before the hatch was closed, the U-boat going down sharply by the bow, leaving two large oil patches behind. Instead, he dived into the water and swam for an hour and a half before being picked up by corvette HMS *Myosotis*. Although under interrogation Köhler later reasoned the boat's chance of survival as '50/50', he was the only survivor as *U451* never resurfaced.

Dönitz remained displeased about transferring veteran U-boats to the Mediterranean. By the year's end he recorded that to simultaneously operate ten U-boats in the eastern Mediterranean and 15 divided either side of the Strait of Gibraltar, required about 34 U-boats within the Mediterranean. By the year's end, 22 U-boats were already there, meaning that another 11 at least would be required. Between the sinking of *Ark Royal* and the end of December, passage through the Strait of Gibraltar had incurred 33 per cent losses: of 24 U-boats, four had been lost in the Strait, four turned back owing to bomb damage and only 16 got through, some of which were also soon casualties. From this he extrapolated that to transfer 11 further boats successfully would require 17 to be sent, since five must be expected lost or damaged during the passage. Furthermore, keeping seven U-boats west of the Strait entailed about ten U-boats on station since, even in the new moon period, loss must be expected in this heavily patrolled area. With enemy traffic slight and escort and ASW forces heavy, prospects for U-boats were bleak and he questioned his superiors whether potential success outweighed inevitable losses.

He did, however, admit that operations within the eastern Mediterranean had been justified by destruction of Royal Navy assets and potential relief of pressure on Axis supply convoys. Hitherto, ASW activity had been weak, and traffic relatively heavy. On land, Operation *Crusader* came to a halt by the year's end, Rommel's depleted forces pushed back to a defensive line between

Ajedabia and El Haseia. However, relative stalemate settled over the North African battlefield, Axis supply lines now considerably shorter while the Eighth Army's trailed over hundreds of miles of desert. Rommel had not been comprehensively beaten, and the race for logistics assumed paramount importance once more as both sides stockpiled for 1942. In Berlin, OKM still believed U-boats could prove decisive.

As the year 1941 ended it did so with some despondency in Kernéval. At the beginning of January Germany had successfully occupied the French Atlantic bases and, though few, U-boats sailed into the Atlantic in the age of the 'Aces'. Significant damage had been inflicted on some convoys, which, combined with Luftwaffe attacks, caused Britain some shortages in consumer goods and food. However, this had been countered with effective rationing and there had been no real oil or fuel crisis as, through the leasing of foreign tanker tonnage, Britain's tanker fleet had increased in size. In return, 35 U-boats had been sunk during 1941, bringing the total lost thus far in the war to 67 U-boats, with 1,734 men killed in action. The North Atlantic battleground had been abandoned, the South Atlantic theatre no longer feasible, and heavy losses inflicted while failing to disrupt Gibraltar convoys.

The end of the year also saw the Wehrmacht engaged in desperate defensive fighting on the Eastern Front against extreme winter conditions and a seemingly inexhaustible enemy, defensive positions in North Africa as both sides restocked and reinforced, and manning an occupied coastline that stretched from the Arctic to Spain. On 7 December Japan attacked Pearl Harbor and initiated the war in the Pacific. Four days later Adolf Hitler declared war on the United States. While resources remained critically balanced for U-boat construction and preparation – as for all Wehrmacht branches – Germany was now to pit itself against the world's greatest industrial power.

Chapter Seven

Drumbeat in the New World

'The New Moon night is black as ink; off Hatteras the tankers sink...'

Joachim Mohr, *U124*[1]

The Germans had received no advance notice of the Japanese intention to attack the United States and were perhaps as stunned as everybody at what had unfolded at Pearl Harbor. The de facto undeclared war with the US Navy was now over, and on 9 December all restrictions placed on U-boat operations against American shipping and within the American neutrality zone were removed on Hitler's direct orders. That day Dönitz requested to OKM that 12 long-range Type IX U-boats be released for an attack along the eastern American seaboard. Those stationed near Gibraltar were denied and he received a total of six: 'It is only regrettable that there are not sufficient boats available to strike a truly spectacular blow.'[2]

On the first day of 1942, BdU mustered a complete force of 249 U-boats; 100 on test and 58 relegated to training, leaving 91 operational U-boats, 71 of them Type VIIB and C, 19 Type IXB and C plus the oddity, *UA*. From these, 54 were undergoing repairs at base, a process considerably lengthened by a lack of skilled workers. Of the remaining 37, 15 were sailing to their operational areas and five returning, leaving the grand total of U-boats active within operational areas on 1 January as 17: three in the Arctic, eight within the Mediterranean and six in the North Atlantic.

Yet, Dönitz's memorandums regarding Mediterranean commitment had at last penetrated SKL who belatedly backed his intention to transfer only two more U-boats, bringing the number to its maximum of 25. Losses were not to be replaced, as BdU was once again freed to return to the Atlantic where U-boat operations had practically ceased. Within the Mediterranean, only two or three boats were to patrol the west, the bulk moving east, concentrating around Alexandria.

The six U-boats that spearheaded the attack on America were all from Lorient's 2nd U-Flotilla: *U66*, *U109*, *U123*, *U125*, *U130* and *U502*, though the latter aborted to Lorient after two days at sea due to a ruptured fuel tank, reducing the initial wave to five.

The story of Operation *Paukenschlag* (literally 'a roll on the kettle drums', more colloquially known as 'drumbeat') has been repeatedly told and in great depth. U-boats arrived on station to find a nation behaving as if in peace time. Lessons in convoying had apparently been forgotten, and merchant traffic plied a coastline illuminated by lights as authorities were loath to interfere with coastal holiday trade. Each of the *Paukenschlag* boats operated independently, spread along the top half of the eastern seaboard lest the few available U-boats be stretched too thinly. In the north, veteran Heinrich Bleichrodt in *U109* and the less experienced Ernst Kals in *U130* were to patrol around Newfoundland and Nova Scotia, reinforced by a group of ten Type VIIs operating at extreme range but the only extra boats on hand until a fresh wave of Type IXs could be readied. Richard Zapp in *U66*, Reinhard Hardegen's *U123*, Ulrich Folkers' *U125* and Jürgen von Rosentiel in the tardy *U502* ranged between New York and Cape Hatteras, North Carolina, all commanders encouraged to attack the largest possible targets, using two-torpedo fan shots and the deck gun if circumstances permitted.

The Type VIIs assigned patrol areas off the Canadian coast were a mixture of new and experienced U-boats: *U84*, *U86*, *U203*, *U552* and *U553* all having seen action already, while *U87*, *U135*, *U333*, *U701* and *U754* were undertaking their first patrols with skippers new to command. Dönitz hoped that their addition would not only increase torpedoes in the area, but also pin escort vessels in the north away from the United States. The Type VIIs needed extra fuel shipped aboard within ballast and freshwater tanks to extend their range by nearly 1,000 extra nautical miles. Navigating using the Great Circle Route – the shortest route between two points on a sphere – U-boats travelled at their most economical speed to the Americas. By the end of December, they had all sailed west and ran headlong into terrible weather, Second Watch Officer Bernhard Weinitschke, aboard Horst Degen's *U701*, washed overboard after failing to secure his safety harness to hard points within the conning tower. He was the U-boat service's final casualty of the year.

While *U125* encountered convoy HG76 but was instructed to ignore the developing battle and remain on course, *U701*, *U333* and *U87* attacked ships sighted during their voyages, *U701* wasting 11 torpedoes in missed or failed attacks before sinking 3,657-ton *Baron Erskine* straggling from SC62 with a paired shot.* Thirty-four survivors in a single lifeboat were questioned by Degen, after which they were never seen again as gale force winds developed within hours of the U-boat departing.

Hardegen in *U123* was the first of the *Paukenschlag* boats to open fire when he sank 9,075-ton British steamer *Cyclops* on 12 January while still travelling south to his patrol area through Canadian waters. By the end of the following day, all *Paukenschlag* boats were in position and at 0118hrs that morning Kals in *U130* had made what he called an 'attack on the first drumbeat' when he torpedoed unescorted 1,582-ton Norwegian *Frisco* off Nova Scotia – hit with a single torpedo and finished off with a coup-de-grâce. The following morning, Hardegen sank another when he hit unescorted Panamanian 9,577-ton *Norness* with one of two stern torpedoes 60 miles from Montauk Point, Long Island: the first ship to be sunk off the eastern coast of the United States. The tanker was sunk with a third torpedo, taking 12,222 tons of

---

* While Horst Degen's wartime record of tonnage sunk was not particularly impressive, he was noted for his bold and vigorous attacks, a style that he had learned while commander-under-instruction aboard Erich Topp's *U552*. Like Topp, Degen inspired great devotion in his crew, which would ultimately save his life after *U701* was sunk in July 1942.

Admiralty fuel oil to the shallow seabed. The following day, the *New York Times* headlines screamed of the developing U-boat attack: 'Tanker Torpedoed 60 Miles Off Long Island'. The United States Navy's Eastern Sea Frontier War Diary recorded the opening of *Paukenschlag*:

> The sinking of the *Norness* was the signal for the opening of an unprecedented submarine attack upon the merchant shipping in the coastal waters. In the remaining seventeen days of the month, thirteen vessels were lost through enemy action. The worst day of all was the 19th when three ships went down off Cape Hatteras. This area, where the land reaches out almost to the 100 fathom curve, proved to be a favourite hunting ground for the U-Boats. The [naval] losses in these waters during the month were six vessels, almost half the total for the whole Frontier.[3]

Open season was declared against North America, and *Paukenschlag* and its supporting Type VII U-boats harvested a grim tally of shipping from the unprepared coastal traffic. On 22 January, the merchant sea lanes were moved 60 miles out to sea around Cape Hatteras in an effort to reduce casualties, but to no effect; they were moved back inshore by the month's end. Towards the end of the month, as intense cold created problems for U-boat drive mechanisms off Canada, captains were granted freedom to use their own initiative whether or not to move south to warmer areas.

While Canadian defences were considerably more dangerous and bad weather plagued the northern U-boats, those off the United States benefitted from good weather and were aided by coastal illuminations and ships often still blazing navigation lights. In general, the *Paukenschlag* U-boats lay submerged by day and attacked at night, frequently operating in dangerously shallow waters which, if there had been any effective countermeasures, would have placed them in extreme jeopardy. However, American response was uncoordinated and inexperienced, possibly not helped by the fact that Commander-in-Chief, United States Fleet

(COMINCH) Admiral Ernest King was perceptibly Anglophobic with a natural antipathy towards British advice. Yet, although King has been frequently criticized for the dismal American response to *Paukenschlag*, it cannot be laid entirely at his feet, as commercial pressures kept ports and seaside towns ignoring the war. Nor is it unreasonable that he appeared preoccupied with war in the Pacific, where his fleet was in direct peril. Admiral King's much-noted aversion to all things British proved no hindrance to face-to-face advice from the commander of the Admiralty's U-boat tracking room, Rodger Winn, after the latter flew to Washington. This resulted in the establishment of an American equivalent of the U-boat tracking room as part of the Office of Naval Intelligence – the 'Atlantic Section', known as F-21, under the control of Commander Kenneth A. Knowles.

King initially refused to accept the transfer of several British escort vessels but was unwilling to implement coastal convoying, predominantly for the lack of American escorts. Ignoring lessons already learned, he maintained that safety lay in individual sailings, convoys merely providing inadequately protected grouped targets for U-boats. The so-called 'Bucket Brigade' of assorted US Navy and Coast Guard ships, aircraft and blimps was established, which shepherded ships by daylight as close inshore as possible, sheltering in mined anchorages by night protected by torpedo nets. This was, however, no satisfactory solution. Nor was the emergency fitting out of five Q-ships (Project LQ), none achieving success and one, USS *Atik*, sunk by *U123* on its maiden patrol though not before engaging Hardegen's boat with gunfire and mortally wounding *Fähnrich zur See* Rudi Holzer.

> Like a raw recruit I fell for a heavily armed U-boat trap. With the first burst of gunfire *Fähnrich zur See* (FzS) Holzer was wounded and it was difficult to get him through the conning tower hatch... A 20mm round detonated in his right thigh, ripped open the flesh from the hip joint to the knee and partially removed it. One could not see if the bone had been shattered. The leg was only hanging on small flaps of skin.

We bound off the leg. We could only wrap a towel around the big wound because we had not enough dressing material for such injuries. It was immediately clear that such an injury could not be treated even by a doctor under the circumstances aboard a U-boat. We were many days from the next neutral harbour, so I took the decision to make it as easy as possible for him and injected a substantial dose of morphine. Holzer acted bravely in an exemplary manner. For one hour he was conscious, without a single word of complaint despite being in unbearable pain as he told us after being asked. About 0400hrs he lost consciousness.[4]

Holzer died of his injuries as *U123* submerged and a coup de grâce torpedo sank USS *Atik*, buried at sea later that morning.

By February, as well as changing the Weather Code Book, the four-rotor *Triton* Enigma net was in full use throughout the U-boat service and Bletchley Park effectively 'blacked out' from its priceless Ultra intelligence source. Rodger Winn's U-boat tracking room still provided crucial information on U-boats sailing and returning thanks to their continued use of the inshore *Heimisch* communications net (later renamed '*Hydra*') for boats travelling in and out of harbour – the four-rotor *Triton* only for use within the Atlantic – as well as formulating educated predictions of likely U-boat deployments. Furthermore, the timing of the Enigma blackout was, ironically, fortuitous for the Allies. With no real Atlantic U-boat groups, sudden Allied inability to reroute convoys *could* have been discerned by astute German observations, potentially highlighting compromise of the Enigma codes. With the change of operational method to individual U-boats against the Americas and other distant targets, no such trend was revealed.

German submariners initially triumphed in American waters, though there were numerous reports of unexplained torpedo failures, particularly among the northern Type VIIs, which, combined with snow storms, fog and heavy seas, left them each only sinking two or three ships. Furthermore, thanks to the failure of the magnetic firing pistols and continued use of only contact pistols, the number of hits it often took to sink merchants spent precious ammunition on single targets. The failure of the magnetic pistol robbed U-boats of their 'one torpedo for one ship' philosophy, and it was in operations such as this, so far from resupply, that it was felt most keenly.

Nonetheless, the three U-boats that attacked the United States left a trail of burning ships, leading Hardegen to crow in his War Diary, 'These are some pretty buoys we are leaving for the Yankees in the harbour approaches as replacement for the lightships.'[5] But despite the dramatic impact and the loss to the Allies of a number of valuable tankers, *Paukenschlag* boats destroyed only a confirmed total of eleven ships within United States waters – *U123* five (excluding *Cyclops*), totalling 28,070 tons and damaged another; *U66* five, totalling 36,114 tons; and *U125* only 5,666-ton *West Ivis* off Cape Hatteras – far from the triumphant hammer blow of legend. Hardegen also destroyed two ships dispersed from convoys during his return voyage, sinking both with artillery fire. By contrast, in the north the remaining two *Paukenschlag* Type IXs – *U109* and *U130* – and the Type VIIs sank 21 ships in Canadian coastal waters, excluding Hardegen's destruction of *Cyclops*. Bleichrodt's *U109* claimed only one near Seal Island, before sinking three on his return journey. Kals sank two off Canada's coast before exercising BdU's newly granted freedom to manoeuvre and doglegging out to sea and then south to Maryland, sinking three more during the transit before beginning his return to France.

Endurance demonstrated by the medium Type VIICs had surpassed BdU expectations, although conditions aboard the boats were gruelling, as every available space was used for supplies and fuel. The return of the first wave and its supporting Type VIIs was also tinged with tragedy when Peter 'Ali' Cremer in *U333* mistakenly sank returning 5,083-ton German blockade runner *Spreewald*. After a successful maiden patrol in which Cremer had sunk three ships, he used his last two torpedoes against a zig-zagging darkened freighter which transmitted a clear language SOS as it sank, identifying itself as British merchant *Brittany*, no doubt assuming it to have been an Allied torpedo attack.

Spreewald carried a cargo of 3,365 tons of rubber and 230 tons of tin, crewed by 35 men, with 25 repatriates and 86 prisoners of war from *Schiff 41* carried aboard. The ship had been scheduled to rendezvous with Günther Heydemann's *U575*. He and his crew were briefed on its likely appearance, as its survival relied on disguise; notably, laundry would be prominently displayed airing on the vessel's poop deck, and an anchor ball hoisted before the front stack. However, *Spreewald* was ahead of schedule, though still within the edge of the Anton Corridor for neutral shipping (and used by German merchant ships) when torpedoed. Upon his return to La Pallice, Cremer faced immediate court-martial for the disaster.

> My 45-day patrol was at an end, but there were no flowers, none of the usual pleasant reception. Just as I was, dirty and unshaven, logbook and radio book under my arm, I had to get into an official car which rushed me to Dönitz's command post. The duty staff officer greeted me briefly and coolly: 'The court martial is waiting for you.' The charge read: 'Disobedience in action, manslaughter and damage to military property.'[6]

Ultimately, with the assistance of a defending argument by Günter Hessler, who pointed out that *Spreewald* was nowhere near its expected location, Cremer was acquitted, all personnel aware of the incident sworn to secrecy. U-boats assisted by KG40 Condors searched for shipwrecked survivors; *U105* recovered 25 Germans and 55 British prisoners, one German survivor badly injured. Dönitz requested a Red Cross Dornier Do 24 flying boat sent to recover the man for urgent treatment, the aircraft crashing during landing near *U105*, and all seven crewmen also taken aboard the boat.

Nevertheless, *Paukenschlag* struck a psychological blow to North American residents. As well as the screaming headlines within the United States, Canadian newspapers recalled lurid details of an artillery attack on a Greek freighter in which survivors in lifeboats alleged that they had been deliberately fired upon. Though baseless, such stories cemented the image of fanatical and merciless U-boat men which persisted long after the war had ended.

Reinforcing Type IX U-boats sailed for North America during January, Schuch's *U105* chancing upon convoy SL98 450 miles west-southwest of Cape Clear late at night on 31 January and firing a salvo of four torpedoes. Two hits and a large explosion were clearly sighted, leading Schuch to believe he had hit an ammunition ship. The ship headed to the bottom was sloop HMS *Culver*, the first escort vessel to be equipped with a prototype improved FH4 HF/DF set that used a cathode ray tube display. Almost immediately upon reporting the destruction of his 'steamer', Schuch was redirected to search for *Spreewald* survivors, and subsequently returned to France.

The remaining six Type IXs that sailed for North America during January – *U103*, *U106*, *U107*, *U108*, *U128* and *U504* – found conditions unchanged, the latter pair ranging south into Florida waters. Between them they destroyed 23 ships, including 11 tankers. A corresponding wave of 14 Type VIICs also sailing in January added to the destruction, predominantly in Canadian waters, though both Heinrich Lehmann-Willenbrock's *U96* and Heydemann's *U575* demonstrated the unexpectedly extreme range of unassisted Type VIIC operations when they reached New York, Suhren's *U564* and Feiler's *U653* sailing as far as North Carolina. Reinhard Suhren later wrote of his part in the operation:

I first crossed the pond with the second wave. The LI had filled every available crevice – indeed just about every toothmug – with diesel oil… I started by managing to sink the Canadian tanker *Victolite*, a juicy morsel of 1,500. But then, just off the Cape, the crew reported to me on 13 February, 'German U-boat approaching!' It turned out to be *U107* under the command of my old crewmate Harald Gelhaus. Visibility wasn't good. Dusk had already set in and the warm waters of the Gulf were giving off a mist in the wintry air. I had just had a nap, and was still rubbing my eyes, when the boat appeared through the gloom. It was hard to estimate its distance away from us and on this occasion I was way out in my estimation. The IWO alerted us at the last minute of the need to turn hard away from her, but it was too late... There was the noise of a dreadful crash and when I looked at the damage, I had managed to slice into my friend Gelhaus' fuel tank.[7]

Both boats were compelled to abort, the angry Gelhaus now forced to husband his fuel and Suhren's *U564* having had all four forward torpedo doors bent by the impact and inoperable. Despite sinking British tanker *Opalia* with gunfire during his return, it was a dejected Suhren that docked in Brest harbour: 'When I reported back, it must have been obvious that I was unusually subdued. Dönitz just looked down at me and said: "You muttonhead!"'

Among the second Type VIIC wave was Siegfried Rollmann's *U82*, which attacked convoy ON56 en route, sinking two ships and later a single escorting destroyer from troop convoy NA2 departing Halifax. After no further successes, Rollmann was returning to France when he chanced upon OS18 east of the Azores and shadowed, unable to attack through a lack of serviceable torpedoes. The British escorts were equipped with radar, and on 6 February HMS *Rochester* and *Tamarisk* hounded *U82* underwater where it was destroyed with all hands by depth charges. Rollmann's was the first boat lost among those that had sailed to America. The following month *U656* and *U503* were also lost headed for Canadian waters, two of the seven U-boats destroyed during March.

Within the US Navy the reformatting of spheres of responsibility had been completed on 6 February. American command regions that had been known as 'Naval Coastal Frontiers' were reorganized into more expansive 'Sea Frontiers'. The North Atlantic Naval Coastal Frontier, spanning from the Canadian border to the southern extreme of Hatteras Inlet under Vice Admiral Adolphus Andrews, was merged into the Eastern Sea Frontier, and Andrews became commander of all coastal waters from Canada to Jacksonville, Florida. The Gulf Sea Frontier, headquartered originally at Key West before moving to Miami, was responsible for the waters of the remainder of Florida and the Bahamas as well as the Gulf of

Mexico, Yucatán Channel and Cuba. Captain Russell S. Crenshaw was acting commander until the arrival of Rear Admiral James L. Kauffman in June 1942. The Panama Sea Frontier was established under Rear Admiral Frank H. Sadler, responsible for the coastal areas from the Mexico–British Honduras boundary on the Yucatán Peninsula to Punta Gallinas in northern Colombia. Continuing south, the Caribbean Sea Frontier was under the command of Vice Admiral John H. Hoover and not only covered its namesake area but also the Atlantic coast of South America. It was Hoover's sphere that was soon to reel under a fresh U-boat initiative, though one not wholly unexpected.

While reinforcing U-boats had sailed for North America, a separate group of long-distance Type IXCs had been recalled from action and designated *Neuland*, destined to open Operation *Westindien* with an attack within the Caribbean. Dönitz had taken advice from two ex-merchant navy captains of the Hamburg-Amerika Line who provided valuable local knowledge, and the boats intended to interdict the major flow of oil and raw materials from South to North America by mounting a coordinated surprise attack in the Aruba-Curaçao-Trinidad area. Trinidad possessed its own oil refineries and hosted a major terminus for small ships carrying raw bauxite from South America before transhipping to larger vessels for onwards movement to Mobile, Alabama, for use in the manufacture of aluminium. Both Aruba and Curaçao processed huge storage facilities for oil from Venezuela's Lake Maracaibo fields before it too was shipped to the United States for refining. The busy Lago Pan American Petroleum facility on Aruba unloaded crude oil from small shallow-draught lake tankers into storage tanks before being pumped aboard larger tankers for transport to the United States. Additionally, immediately next to this storage facility was a refinery that produced 100-octane aviation fuel bound for Britain. On Curaçao, Royal Oil/Shell had established a large refinery on the Isla Peninsula in Willemstad harbour as well as hosting the Bullenbaai Company petroleum storage facility for transporting oil onwards. As a measure of the importance of the refineries located on these two small Dutch islands, during 1939 they supplied 43 per cent of British and French oil requirements and about 80 per cent of that required by the Royal Air Force, mainly high-octane petrol. Later, the American forces involved in Operation *Torch* were 100 per cent fuelled by these plants, and in the Pacific the fighting between 1944 and 1945 relied on 75 per cent of its oil from the Antilles.

The new moon period of 16 February was chosen for *U67*, *U129*, *U156*, *U161* and *U502* to make their initial attacks, though opinion differed between Raeder and Dönitz as to how best to achieve the greatest effect. Raeder advocated U-boats open the assault by shelling the major refineries, setting them ablaze, while Dönitz considered this an unpalatable risk, putting his few boats at the mercy of defensive shore batteries. Instead, he pushed for interception of tanker traffic by torpedo, with attacks on refineries and harbour installations *if* circumstances permitted. Dönitz prevailed. By the end of January, the *Neuland* boats crawled across the Atlantic on single diesels to conserve fuel. Aboard Werner Hartenstein's *U156* was the new FuMO 29 radar, its fixed array mounted on the front of the upper conning tower. With a range of just under 5 miles and a field of view only 30° either side of the forward centreline, this would be its first operational test.

By the night of 15 February, after ignoring several sighted ships as per operational orders, three of the five *Neuland* boats were positioned. *U156* lay submerged off Aruba, *U67* outside Curaçao's Willemstad harbour and *U502* off the uninhabited islands of Los Morjie, preparing to move into the Gulf of Venezuela and attack shallow-draught tankers, known as the 'Mosquito Fleet'. These ships would be difficult to replace, yet crucial to the shipment of oil from shallow Lake Maracaibo. The final pair approached their allocated areas, *U129* heading for the merchant lanes between Trinidad and Guiana and *U161* the north coast of Trinidad. The problem of convoy location that had so bedevilled Atlantic operations was removed by Caribbean geography, with obvious choke points for tanker traffic, particularly those from Maracaibo.

Hartenstein opened the attack, heading towards Oranjestad a little after midnight, illuminated American tanker *Arkansas* observed at the sea pier of the Eagle refinery at Oranjestad before *U156* swung towards San Nicolaas harbour where another two anchored tankers were visible. At 0301hrs local time, the first surfaced torpedo shot was aimed at 4,317-ton British tanker *Pedernales*, which was hit amidships and immediately began to burn. Two minutes later, tanker *Oranjestad* was also hit amidships and burst into flames, sinking an hour later as burning oil covered the placid sea surface. Hartenstein swung his boat to 300° and ordered the main 105mm gun cleared for an artillery attack on the refinery and storage tanks, and, only ten minutes after the first torpedo, Second Watch Officer Dietrich von dem Bourne ordered the first artillery round fired. Unfortunately, the watertight tampion had not been removed and the shell exploded in the barrel, severely wounding gun layer Heinrich Büssinger, his stomach ripped open and both legs shattered, as well as von dem Bourne, whose leg had been sliced open by red hot metal fragments.

As the two men were carried below, Hartenstein ordered the stern 37mm gun fired, 16 shots arcing in the general direction of the storage tanks, causing slight dents and damaging the Bernhard School in San Nicolaas before fire was ceased as no effect could be seen from the U-boat. Hartenstein headed to Oranjestad at ¾ speed, passing a guard vessel searching vainly with a weak searchlight, and tried three surfaced shots against the empty *Arkansas*, two shots inexplicably missing – one of which ran up on to the beach where it was found by Dutch troops – and the third hitting the starboard hull, blowing a large hole and causing severe structural damage.[*] Then *U156* headed once more to sea, to a holding position off Martinique. Below decks, Büssinger had lived for one agonizing hour before succumbing to his injuries, while the bleeding from von dem Bourne's leg was finally stopped. Büssinger was buried at sea after a short funeral service, and, aware that the extent of the Second Watch Officer's injuries were beyond the capabilities of care aboard the U-boat, Hartenstein requested and was granted

---

[*] The grounded torpedo was later examined by Dutch troops, exploding after they attempted to move and defuse it, killing four marines.

permission to land the wounded officer on Vichy Martinique. French officials were aware that they were under heavy American surveillance but reluctantly accepted his transfer aboard a French guard vessel on the night of 21 February at Fort de France.[*]

Hartenstein ordered about 38cm of the wrecked 105mm gun barrel removed with a steel saw during the following day and later test fired, noting that 'cannon appears useful; rifling unaltered; recoil from the firing table moderate; heavy overbalance of the breech end (approximately 40kg) therefore very difficult to aim'.[8] The weapon did indeed prove useful, and, by 27 February, all 105mm and 37mm ammunition had been exhausted, with only 1,300 20mm rounds remaining.

Off Curaçao, Günther Müller-Stockheim had been forced to submerge repeatedly by shore searchlights and approaching steamers that passed overhead. The fiery glow of burning tankers at Aruba was visible on the horizon, and at 0452hrs (local time) *U67* opened fire with two torpedoes at heavily laden 3,177-ton Dutch tanker *Rafaela*, both missing for unexplainable reasons. The tanker picked up speed in the direction of Willemstad, and a third torpedo also missed as *U67* fired at a range of only 500 metres. Finally, a single stern G7a torpedo hist *Rafaela* just aft of centre, breaking the ship's back. An attempted coup de grâce also failed, and Müller-Stockheim judged the ship as good as sunk and retreated, unwilling to waste more valuable torpedoes. It was his sole success of the night, frustrated in several attempted pursuits by aircraft and one tanker target disappearing into a tropical squall. Once again, one of the unexploded torpedoes was found ashore, washed up on the coastal reef with visible scratches on its warhead where it had grounded on the coral, missing the fuse whiskers. The last of the three to open attacks that night, Jürgen von Rosenstiel's *U502*

---

[*] A French surgeon later amputated von dem Bourne's leg and he was eventually repatriated to Germany. American authorities did indeed learn of his arrival via *U156* and Vichy authorities were soon accused of actively assisting U-boats. Roosevelt insisted that the Vichy naval units in Martinique were effectively immobilized lest they face an American bombing raid. The Vichy naval contingent complied.

sank three shallow-draught tankers headed away from Maracaibo, though he too suffered unexplained torpedo failures.

Albrecht Achilles opened *U161*'s attack in the Trinidadian harbour of Port of Spain. Despite having been detected after passing over magnetic detector loops trailing across the Bocas del Dragón, the indication was dismissed as a routine patrol vessel out of station. Achilles' bold foray yielded two tankers heavily damaged after torpedoes were fired with only 12 metres of water under the U-boat's keel, before Achilles retreated to deeper water. He would repeat this type of attack in March when he torpedoed two ships in Castries harbour, Saint Lucia, firing from a surfaced position north of the entrance channel only 200 metres from Vigie Peninsula and in water only 9 metres deep. After the explosions, machine-gun fire from shore followed *U161* as Achilles once more raced for open water.

The last of the *Neuland* boats, Nicolai Clausen's *U129*, sank its first ship north of Trinidad on 20 February, hitting 2,400-ton Norwegian *Nordvagen* in the stern with a single torpedo, the freighter going down in under a minute with all 24 crewmen killed. It was the first of seven ships that Clausen would sink during *Neuland*.

The Caribbean offensive had opened spectacularly for the five U-boats whose captains found Allied defences quicker to adapt to their presence, but still outmatched. Submarine warnings and radioed instructions for merchant traffic were either broadcast in plain language or decoded by B-Dienst and swiftly passed on to the boats in time for operational use. They attacked with what Winston Churchill later called 'a freedom and insolence which were hard to bear' and accumulated a total of 41 ships sunk, 18 of them tankers.[9] A further 11 ships were severely damaged, seven of them tankers. These numbers would have been even more destructive had the U-boats not all experienced repeated torpedo failures and if some ships sunk had not been in harbour waters shallow enough to facilitate successful salvage. The toll among the shallow-draught Mosquito Fleet was particularly high, prompting a brief mutiny from their predominantly Chinese crews to not sail without Allied escort. As well as throwing the crucial Venezuelan oil transport into some measure of confusion, *Neuland* had sunk 222,651 tons of Allied shipping; over 70,000 more tons than *Paukenschlag*. During January and February, in all areas, U-boats had sunk 144 ships accounting for 800,000 tons of shipping. The sole immediate reinforcement for the Caribbean was Ernst Bauer's *U126* that sailed in February and returned alongside the other *Neuland* boats after operating off Cuba and Haiti, sinking seven ships and damaging two others.

Numerous valuable observations were also presented to Dönitz by the returning *Neuland* captains, particularly Hartenstein. He explained that the tropical water was so clear that while proceeding surfaced, the forward diving planes were visible from the conning tower, and at periscope depth he could see his own foredeck and stern as a 'terrifying shadow'. He also urged increased upper deck torpedo storage as none of the five U-boats had returned due to lack of fuel, but all because they were out of torpedoes. Though artillery had indeed proved useful for the destruction of merchant shipping, artillery attacks against shore targets as advocated by Raeder had consistently failed. Under pressure from OKM, both *U502* and *U67* had received detailed instructions from BdU to attempt fresh bombardment of shore installations, and both commanders demurred as defences had increased and, in their judgement, conditions did not allow such action. Although some have argued that the reluctance of both Dönitz and his commanders to bombard the refineries and storage tanks was a major strategic blunder, the likelihood of successful hindrance of these installations by U-boat shelling was slight, particularly once the offensive had begun.

As the *Neuland* U-boats had been in action, five Italian submarines had been stationed by BETASOM east of the Windward Isles, and between them delivered the most successful Italian group operation of the war, sinking 15 ships – six of them tankers – totalling 93,000 tons.

With such success, Hitler ordered operations against the Americas extended and intensified, as Raeder vociferously complained to Dönitz about the lack of reinforcement for the Caribbean offensive and resultant inability to maintain there a constant U-boat pressure. However, they were simply not available given the lack of long-range cruiser U-boats and the number of medium boats in the Arctic or Mediterranean. At any rate, the latter's independent range was insufficient for Caribbean operations, although this would dramatically change in April when *U459* departed for its first operational mission from Helgoland to a rendezvous area south of the Newfoundland Banks on 29 March. This was the first of ten Type XIV U-tankers commissioned – famously known as the *Milchkuh* – under the command of the oldest active U-boat skipper, veteran of the Imperial Navy 48-year-old Georg von Wilamowitz-Möllendorf.

The deployment of the Type XIV had become a matter of increased urgency following destruction of the German Atlantic surface supply network. *U459* had been found difficult to hold steady on a straight course during trials, though enlarging the lower stern design had helped. Capable of carrying 650 tons of fuel – 200 for itself and the remainder for those U-boats it would supply – the tanker also carried 13 tons of lubricating oil and fresh provisions stored within refrigerators as well as loaves produced by an on-board bakery: 13,100kg of provisions and approximately 800 loaves of rye bread distributed to various U-boats, 250 more loaves consumed by *U459*'s 53-man crew. The Type XIV also carried a doctor and small medical facility for the treatment of injured or sick men. Large iron davits were provided for hoisting provisions through deck hatches whereupon they were intended to be loaded aboard a 6-metre rubber dinghy for transfer. However, generally, with decks slightly awash, only the conning tower hatch could be utilized, and the rubber dinghy was lost during the first attempted resupply. A more satisfactory rope transfer method, slung between U-boats, was used instead. Unfortunately, only four torpedoes were carried in canisters under the external decking; therefore, the *Milchkuh* could not provide much by way of ammunition replenishment. These were generally wrapped in lifejackets and pushed into the sea from the tanker with its deck slightly awash, then manoeuvred to the receiving boat who would likewise lower its deck into the sea to receive the torpedo on its deck.

For its inaugural mission, *U459* took along the Chief Naval Construction Adviser to assess and recommend improvements. His report, submitted after the boat's return during May, contained much useful information for BdU, including the fact that out of 15 U-boats supplied – of which only *U571*, *U572* and *U582* were on their return voyage from operations – only five crews appeared to have been fully briefed on efficient refuelling at sea and that a high level of seamanship was required to successfully complete the task even in relatively calm conditions.

The War Diary of *U103*'s veteran commander Werner Winter describes the difficulties of their first resupply from a Type XIV on 2 May while outbound from Lorient bound for the Caribbean:

Taking over the tow connection and hose was difficult due to the Sea State [4]. The empty tanker yaws strongly while on my loaded boat work on the upper deck can only be done roped in... I had to sail so that the hose was always loose. [Between] 1340hrs and 1500hrs, 30m³ diesel taken over. The tow connection is very weak and broke despite the utmost caution without any particular rush.

While releasing the connection the hose line went under the forepart of the pitching boat and caught under the diving plane. All attempts to free the hose failed. The last attempt by me to free the line by slowly reversing, failed, the hose with the line tore. Later, it was possible to get the hanging down hose off the diving plane. However, it was still hung under the boat. Despite the bad experiences with free diving on the previous trip, I wanted to send the First Watch Officer with *Tauchretter* to determine the hooked location under water so as not to leave anything undone to save the hose. While preparing for this, the hose jumped off where it had been caught and sank because the end cap loosened and air escaped. It is unlikely under the prevailing sea conditions the diving rescue plan would have been successful. In my opinion, it was too rough for the two unmanoeuvrable boats, especially since this was being carried

out by us for the first time. Seamen working on deck went
overboard twice. However, I had left the decision to carry out
the supply to the more experienced tanker *Kommandanten*...
I declined the transfer of provisions, because we would have to
sail close alongside where, with the Sea State and low speed,
there is danger of ramming. Left the tanker with mutual good
wishes.*

To bolster the appearance of the first Type XIV, *UA* was temporarily
used as an auxiliary tanker, later augmented by the first Type XB
minelayer *U116*, which first sailed operationally during April.
The largest U-boat produced by the Kriegsmarine, the Type XB
was designed to lay 66 SMA anchor mines from 30 mine shafts,
12 located on each flank and six in the bow. These 'wet-shafts'
were covered at the top by slatted metal sheeting to allow
ventilation and eradicate issues related to trapped air should they
have been 'dry shafts', initial technological difficulties regarding
the adjustment of mine setting within 'wet shafts' having been
overcome. However, an embargo had been placed on the weapon
after they were discovered to have a design fault that caused
premature detonation requiring months of modification and it
was not ready for service until March 1943. In the meantime,
the 2,177-ton U-boats served as tankers, freight containers held
within the mine shafts, although, unlike the Type XIV, they did
carry offensive torpedo armament – 15 torpedoes that could be
launched via two stern tubes.

Work had also begun on a medium U-boat capable of carrying
the SMA shaft mine, resulting in the Type VIID – a standard Type
VIIC elongated by an additional compartment aft of the control
room where five vertical shafts were installed, each capable of
holding three SMAs. This enlargement also had a commensurate
effect on fuel bunkerage, an extra 50 tons extending the vessel's
endurance. *U213* was the first commissioned Type VIID, on

---

* This was to be Winter's final combat patrol before taking command of the 1st
U-Flotilla in Brest. He was captured after the ferocious battle with American troops for
the city in September 1944 (*U103* KTB 2 May 1942).

30 August 1941, making its baptismal war patrol during January as a traditional torpedo carrier, one of six U-boats stationed west of the Hebrides and Faeroes on Hitler's direct orders.[*]

Dönitz had envisioned a concerted minelaying effort against the United States using these new tools at his disposal, but with the SMA proving faulty, the first such attempt would not be made until May and then only by one Type VIIB (*U87*) and two Type VIICs (*U373* and *U701*) carrying TMB mines. Aboard Joachim Berger's *U87* original plans to foul New York harbour were changed while at sea to Boston, though no special chart of the harbour was on board and instead one drawn based on regional Sailing Instructions and Navigational Light List. Though in shallow, heavily travelled water and harassed by small boats on apparent anti-submarine patrols, *U87*, helped by the lights of Boston and its coastal lighthouses, laid four mines in the northeastern harbour entrance and another two within the eastern approach on the night of 12 June. Later, after hauling out to sea and reloading with torpedoes, *U87* encountered convoy XB25 from Halifax to Boston northeast of Cape Cod. In a submerged attack Berger sank two large freighters before surfacing in heavy rain and escaping retribution. Over the days that followed, *U87* encountered frequent destroyers engaged on 'wild searches' like a 'startled wasp's nest' and repeated aircraft alarms but was not caught out until 23 June, by three well-placed bombs that exploded below the stern of the boat as it crash dived away from a Lockheed Hudson dropping out of the sun. Heavily damaged, *U87* limped back to Saint Nazaire. Despite *U87*'s audacious effort and incorrectly perceived success at BdU, the mines claimed no victims.

Paul Loeser's *U373* laid 15 TMB mines in Delaware Bay, which later sank a small steam tug, while subsequent torpedo attacks

---

[*] Commanded by Amelung von Varendorff, former Second Watch Officer aboard Günther Prien's *U47*, *U213* was never used for its intended minelaying task. Its second patrol landed an Abwehr agent named Langbein in the Bay of Fundy, New Brunswick, before unsuccessful hunting as part of *'Pfadfinder'* group. Eight days into its third patrol, the boat was depth charged and sunk southeast of the Azores on 31 July 1942, all 50 crewmen killed. Meanwhile, Langbein, who clearly had no intention of fulfilling his mission, adopted the name 'Alfred Haskins' in Canada and lived quietly in Ottawa until his Abwehr-supplied funds ran out in 1944 whereupon he surrendered to authorities.

were foiled by misses and repeated failure of the starboard diesel engine. Horst Degen's *U701* laid 15 TMB mines near Chesapeake Bay, which later sank ASW trawler HMT *Knigston Ceylonite* and heavily damaged destroyer USS *Bainbridge* and two tankers from convoy KN109 from Key West. Rearming with torpedoes and heading to Cape Hatteras, *U701* shelled American ASW trawler USS *YP-389* for 1½ hours until it sank and then patrolled the area for the next week, attacking three more ships, damaging two and sinking the third. On 7 July, *U701* was surprised while surfaced by a USAAF A-29 Hudson of 369th Bomber Squadron. Degen, along with all three of his Watch Officers, was on the bridge as extra aircraft lookouts in such dangerous waters. Degen had previously admonished his First Watch Officer, Konrad Junker, for not paying enough attention to the skies, and it was from his quarter that the bomber was spotted too late to escape, *U701* suffering two direct hits while just below the surface. Within two minutes, the control room was filled with water, most of the crew escaping the sunken boat but only seven of them rescued by American Coast Guard PH-2 flying boat after surviving for 49 hours at sea under a blazing sun. Degen was among them, thanks to the support of his companions, as he spent the majority of the time unconscious.

Away from the western battlefield, although Dönitz had prevailed regarding further Mediterranean transfers, an unnecessarily large number of U-boats had been reassigned to Norway despite his strongest objections. Intensifying paranoia radiated from Hitler that Norway, his proclaimed 'zone of destiny' of Germany's war, faced imminent Allied invasion with collusion from Swedish authorities. Demanding 'unconditional obedience' from all commands, he ordered every available vessel held in defence of the occupied country, and it was only the early results of *Paukenschlag* that caused him to relent from including all U-boats within those demands.[10] Nevertheless, plans had been drawn up by SKL for the commitment of 20 U-boats to cover Norway; eight in the Iceland-Faeroes-Scotland area, six within the Arctic, two in Narvik, two in Trondheim and two in Bergen. Those on Arctic Sea operations would be directed by Group North, those with stationary assignments by the Commanding Admiral, Norway, and those near the Faeroes remaining under BdU control. In Norway itself, Kristiansand, Bergen, Trondheim, Tromsø and Kirkenes had been selected as suitable U-boat bases, each port to host two operational U-boats by the middle of February. Shortly thereafter Narvik was added and, in January 1943, Hammerfest.

Immediate results were dismal, and at least four medium U-boats that were earmarked for March departure for North America were instead diverted to Norway, their combined achievement the sinking of 1,180-ton steam trawler *RT-19 Komintern* and three patrol boats. The greatest immediate contribution to the U-boat service was at least the discovery by Otto Ites aboard *U94* near the Faeroes of the increased pressure build up within torpedo balance chambers during torpedo ventilation on 30 January. *U94* had been bedevilled by mechanical problems during this brief patrol as a result of negligent maintenance at the Oderwerke in Stettin: a missing part allowing water to stream into the submerged boat, wiring for the diesels cross connected, some batteries and associated equipment damaged, control room indicators for 'Ahead' and 'Astern' inverted, and the main bilge pump non-operational. Aborting to Saint Nazaire, Ites' boat underwent overhaul before its next mission to American waters, though the final mystery regarding erratic torpedo running had finally been revealed.

Within the Arctic during March, PQ12 successfully evaded U-boat group '*Umhang*', four boats next forming the '*Zeithen*' group to lie in wait for PQ13 or outbound QP9, and *U655* rammed and sunk by one of the latter's escorts – minesweeper HMS *Sharpshooter*, southeast of Bear Island. Hastily regrouped into '*Eiswolf*', U-boats torpedoed two ships from PQ13 which had already suffered casualties to Luftwaffe and German destroyer attack. Both *U378* and *U585* suffered depth charging, the latter heavily damaged and forced to abort, striking a German mine that had broken loose from its anchor and sunk with all hands. This rate of exchange was disastrous, with destroyer *Z26* and two U-boats destroyed for the sinking of five of PQ13's 19 merchants: two by the Luftwaffe, one by destroyer and two by U-boats.

Conditions were horrendous inside the Arctic boats, icing posing a severe problem that required frequent submergence in the warmer seawater to melt lest the boat become top-heavy and potentially unstable. Oil thickened and lost lubricant qualities; nuts and bolts froze and were shorn off, creating myriad mechanical problems; crewmen were exposed to the worst possible conditions while on watch, while heaters provided for the crew within their frigid steel home frequently drew too much electrical current and could not be continuously run.

Results remained disappointing, and lengthening hours of daylight robbed U-boats of covering darkness. In March they at least finally received their own dedicated commands on BdU's recommendation. Veteran skipper and former commander of Brest's 9th U-Flotilla, Jürgen Oesten began serving as U-boat staff officer to *Admiral Nordmeer* in Kirkenes. He remained at the post until January 1943 when FdU Norway was finally established. To the south, handling the same duties for MGK Nord, Herbert Schultze, veteran skipper and erstwhile commander of La Rochelle's 3rd U-Flotilla, was assigned as Boehm's U-boat staff officer.

During March, BdU despatched six Type IX and 20 Type VIIs to American waters to maintain pressure on this new hunting ground. Thanks to tankers *U459* and *UA* (which supplied three Type VIIs after being released from supply duty in defence of Norway), the Type VIIs were able to fully operate off the United States, though their endurance only extended by about a week. Three of the Type IXs – *U66*, *U130* and *U154* – were directed to enter the Caribbean, between them sinking 13 ships, including eight tankers, and damaging another. Richard Zapp in *U66* was particularly successful, destroying six ships between Trinidad and Aruba (four of them tankers), totalling an impressive 43,956 tons of shipping sunk. Awarded the Knight's Cross, he transferred ashore upon his return to Lorient to take command of 3rd U-Flotilla in La Rochelle.*

---

* Zapp remained in this position until the war's end, leading 'Marine Regiment Zapp' during the siege of the port long after the U-boats had departed, holding La Rochelle until the last day of the war.

Ernst Kals in *U130* – who only sank two ships during his return voyage – had also carried out Raeder's cherished artillery attack on Curaçao on 19 April. After firing a total of 12 105mm rounds at the Bullenbaai storage depot during the early hours, defending coastal gunners opened fire and Kals retreated and submerged. His attack had hit nothing, and the temporary suspension of much tanker traffic caused by *Neuland*'s initial impact left him bereft of targets until leaving the Caribbean.

The integration of the Type XIV tankers into the U-boat fleet was of enormous benefit to extending operations by combat U-boats. At this stage of the war there still existed the air gap within the mid-Atlantic, in which U-boats were safe from all but carrier aircraft. Mindful of the minimal torpedo-carrying capacity of the Type XIV, a torpedo transporter was ordered along the lines of the extended Type VIID minelayer, yielding the Type VIIF. This boat was similarly elongated by an extra compartment immediately abaft the control room, this time capable of holding 21 stored torpedoes, while maintaining the normal Type VII armaments. Widened saddle tanks increased the beam by over a metre to 7.3 metres, and it was 70cm longer than the Type VIID. Four were placed under contract with Germaniawerft in August 1941 but were secondary to traditional combat boats and not expected to be in service until 1943, the first – *U1059* – operational by May of that year, by which time the air gap had been closed. Given the resultant impossibility of time-consuming resupply of torpedoes at sea, the four Type VIIFs were either used for torpedo supply missions to Norwegian harbours or intended for the Far East, carrying ammunition for the U-boats that had begun operating from Malaya and Singapore. In the interim, two Dutch submarines captured in dockyards in 1940 and rechristened *UD3* and *UD5* were converted to torpedo supply vessels, though neither was ready in time to make any appreciable difference.

Type VIIs operating off the United States destroyed a significant amount of merchant shipping, yielding the award of more Knight's Crosses and the Oak Leaves for Erich Topp in his 'Red Devil' boat *U552*. However, by mid-April a discernible toughening of defensive measures was noted by BdU and the waters off Cape Hatteras – which had achieved the unwelcome sobriquet of 'Torpedo Junction' – became particularly difficult and unproductive. The first U-boat sunk in American waters had been destroyed a little after midnight on 14 April, when the aged four-stack destroyer USS *Roper* detected Eberhard Greger's *U85* by radar near Bodie Island, South Carolina, and ran down the contact. Unaware his enemy was radar-equipped, and trapped in only 30 metres of water, Greger attempted to run surfaced, firing a stern torpedo as the faster ship gained on him. At point-blank range Lieutenant Commander Hamilton W. Howe ordered *Roper*'s searchlight trained on *U85* and opened fire. Believing the destroyer was intending to ram, Greger prepared the boat for scuttling and the crew abandoned ship. As *U85* sank by the stern 'about forty' of the German crew were seen on deck and in the water but, believing it too risky to mount a rescue operation at night lest a second U-boat be nearby, Howe ran *Roper* straight through the struggling survivors and dropped 11 depth charges on the sunken *U85*, killing most survivors. Twice during the night *Roper* passed men calling from the water, but the entire German crew was dead by dawn.[11] Long after daylight and further depth charges, 29 bodies were recovered (two further bodies found badly mutilated were stripped and dumped back in the sea), including several with *Tauchretter* and mouthpieces clenched between their teeth, indicating they had attempted to escape *U85* after it went down. In such shallow water they were likely to have survived the ascent. They were all buried with military honours at Hampton National Cemetery, Virginia, on the evening of 15 April.

The 20 Type VIIs that had sailed for American during March sank a confirmed 46 ships for about 242,000 tons – Topp alone sinking seven for 45,731 tons, while Hans Oestermann in his second patrol as captain of *U752* sank another seven, totalling 31,578 tons. The six Type IXs destroyed 29 ships (164,100 tons), not including those later salvaged and returned to service.

Though this was a spectacular result for the U-boats, it did reveal some disquieting indications that the tide was already turning in this fresh war zone. The number of ships sunk was on a par with those destroyed by *Paukenschlag* and the supporting Type VIIs. However, the U-boats of March and April sailed with refuelling support, better weather, a greater number of experienced captains and against American defences that were notably weaker than Canadian ones. Yet the result had been the same. Mindful of this, Dönitz intended next to concentrate on the Caribbean and the as-yet-untested tanker routes within the Gulf of Mexico. Furthermore, with OKM estimating that Britain and the United States were between them committed to building 7,000,000 tons of shipping in 1942, German, Italian and Japanese sinkings in all theatres would need to maintain a monthly total of at least 600,000 tons to offset this increase. Unfortunately for BdU, rampant overclaiming by many commanders had disguised somewhat the degree to which U-boats were falling short of their ambition.

During March, Dönitz had himself undergone two unexpected changes. The first was announced to U-boats at sea by radio message on 14 March: 'At suggestion of the Supreme Commander in Chief, the Führer has promoted me to Admiral. In this promotion I see thanks and appreciation for you, my U-boat men.' The promotion reflected U-boat achievement against the United States and Canada as well as his ascending star within the military hierarchy of the Third Reich. Where Raeder was respected by Hitler, Dönitz was swiftly developing a closer relationship to the German leader, perhaps as much through deference as ability, unconstrained by Raeder's natural Prussian formality. The second change was, however, less palatable to Dönitz, when BdU was ordered relocated from Kernéval to Paris:

The Führer decree that all U-boat control stations must occupy positions from which they will be able to direct forces under their control under any circumstances, means that our own control station will have to move. Removal to station being prepared in Paris will be arranged.

This is a regrettable backwards step as far as administration is concerned, since the direct contact with the front, that is, the personal touch between Commanding Officer and his operational boats and crews, will not be possible to anything like the same extent from Paris.

I intend to find out immediately which area can be considered sufficiently secure and as soon as possible fit up and occupy a control station as far forward as possible; at the moment I am considering area around Angers.[12]

Synchronicity then reared its head, as two days later Operation *Chariot* struck Saint Nazaire – the audacious British commando raid to disable the only dry dock on western France capable of handling the *Tirpitz*. The move to Paris was hastened accordingly, as BdU's location at Kernéval was considered dangerously exposed to any such attack; by 29 March, *Fregattenkapitän* Eberhard Godt as BdU (Ops.) and two staff officers were ensconced within their new headquarters on the Avenue Maréchal Maunoury. Transfer of control from Kernéval took place at 1000hrs the following morning, Dönitz arriving that night after inspecting the damage at Saint Nazaire. The shift was seamless, BdU's control W/T station remaining at Kernéval and a delay of only ten minutes caused to radio messages by teleprinter transmission to Paris – reduced once a more effective order transmission system was integrated. The location near Angers, within the luxurious grounds of the Château de Pignerolles, would later be used as the headquarters of Hans Rösing's FdU West office from the beginning of 1943.

On 30 April Harro Schacht's *U507* became the first U-boat to penetrate the Gulf of Mexico. Sailing earlier that month, Schacht had originally been instructed to operate between the Florida Strait north of Cuba to the Windward Passage, until on 20 April BdU instructed both *U507* and Erich Würdemann's *U506* to steer instead for grid square DA90 south of New Orleans.

While moving a torpedo under cover of darkness from its external canister to the torpedo room, a winch shackle broke and the torpedo slipped on its chute into the boat, crushing a radio operator's left forearm and inflicting an excruciating compound open forearm fracture. Ordered to his bunk with the splinted arm raised, sterile dressings and cod liver oil ointment was applied and cognac given to drink as the only form of pain relief available. Schacht and Würdemann were ordered to meet on 6 May for morphine stored aboard *U506* to be transferred across on radioed instructions from medical officers of the 2nd U-Flotilla, and three times their attempted rendezvous failed as both U-boats were harassed by aircraft.

Fortunately, the patient improved to a degree no longer requiring morphine and ultimately both boats exhausted their torpedoes, suffering multiple failures while doing so. The last of Schacht's victims was stopped by 37mm cannon and machine-gun fire and then missed after the crew had abandoned ship by his last G7a, which became a 'circle runner'. Instead, the boat's Second Watch Officer and the control room mate swam across to the steamer to open its hull valves. As the two men were engaged on their task, *U507* was forced to dive by an American aircraft that dropped five ineffectual bombs nearby. After dark and the aircraft's departure, Schacht resurfaced to retrieve his two men.

> Surfaced before the bow of the steamer, where the sea lay completely in the shadow and ran into the lee of the steamer. There after a short search found the sinking commandos drifting on a raft and took them on board again. The sinking commandos brought the papers of the steamer, among them the zig zag plan. It was the 4,148-ton steamer *Amapala* of the Standard Fruit and Steam Ship Company, proceeding under the Honduras flag.
>
> The Captain, who had been sitting in a boat alongside at about 0030 hours, told me he did not know that Germany was at war with Honduras or why his ship was to be sunk. I pointed out to him that he had requested U.S. aircraft against me. He said he had orders to do it. I then said that I had orders to sink his ship.[13]

The ship was still afloat but badly awash when survivors were rescued by USCGC *Boutwell* the following day, taken in tow but foundering soon thereafter.

The first foray into the Gulf of Mexico had proved successful: *U507* sinking nine ships, four of them tankers (44,782 tons) and damaging another; *U506* sinking eight, including four tankers, (39,906 tons) and damaging three more. Dönitz despatched *U106*, *U763* and *U103* to strengthen the attack on the Gulf, and by the end of May 19 more ships had been sunk. This was one of the most successful months of the war, U-boats sinking a total of three warships and 123 merchants aggregating 596,706 tons of merchant shipping, over three-quarters of it within the Gulf and Caribbean theatres. Not until June was the first U-boat sunk within the Gulf when *U157*, intending to patrol the Mississippi Delta, was destroyed by depth charges from UCGC *Thetis* after being sighted by a Pan American commercial aircraft north of Havana.

Long-distance operations had become predominant, and *U68* and *U505* were sent to Freetown during March, the first U-boats to haunt the Eastern Atlantic since the end of 1941. Both sank two ships apiece shortly after arriving on station, though British authorities reacted swiftly and held independent sailing ships in port until escorted convoys could be formed, neither U-boat reporting any further traffic. Both commanders requested permission to cross the Atlantic to Brazil but were denied by BdU: Axel-Olaf Loewe's *U505* was ordered to remain off Freetown while Merten's *U68* was moved onward to Nigeria. While southbound, Merten ran into multiple independents off Liberia and sank four freighters with torpedoes and artillery fire. Finding nothing near Nigeria, he headed home at the end of March and chanced upon convoy ST18 off Monrovia and sank his final ship, bringing his patrol total to seven, totalling 39,350 tons.

Following Merten's report of Liberian shipping, *U505* was directed to the seas off Cape Palmas, but now found traffic heavily escorted. Not until the beginning of April did he sink two ships off the Ivory Coast, the last of his 86-day patrol.

The decision not to allow them to cross to Brazil was made so as not to inflame tensions with the country already teetering on the brink of joining the Allied cause. Even though *U162* hunted bauxite transport from Brazil off the coast of British Guyana during April

Helmut Möhlmann, here as commander of *U571* returning to La Pallice.

The bridge watch aboard *U737*, which mounted nine war patrols as part of the Norwegian 13th U-Flotilla. (Paul Milner)

Reinhard Reche's *U255* returns to Narvik victorious after the attack on PQ17.

Werner Hartenstein, commander of *U156,* which opened the *Neuland* attack on
Caribbean oil traffic and installations.

Christmas 1942 aboard *U604*.

An unexploded torpedo from *U67* ashore in Curaçao, with the badly damaged Dutch tanker *Rafaela* being towed into St. Anna Bay.

The Metox 'Biscay Cross' is mounted at the front of this Type IX conning tower.

U20 (left) and *U19* of the 30th U-Flotilla in Constanta harbour.

Reichsminister Josef Goebbels visits 6th U-Training Flotilla in Danzig during 1942, signing the flotilla guest book. On the right is flotilla commander *Kapitänleutnant* Georg-Wilhelm Schulz.

U43 refuelling from the Type XIV *U461*, July 1942.

The Type3 XIV *U462* photographed from *U604* during resupply near the Azores on 27 February 1943.

One of nine Type VIIC U-boats handed over for commissioning into the Italian Navy during 1943.

U43's *Oberleutnant zur See* Hans-Joachim Schwantke bringing a bottle aboard *U109*
during a mid-Atlantic meeting. (Paul Milner)

U511 arrives off the Japanese-occupied harbour of Penang, July 1943.

U271 was sunk with all hands by depth charges during this attack by a USAAF Liberator bomber on 28 January 1944.

The lower extended *Wintergarten* of a Type VIIC with 37mm flak weapon.

Looking from the conning tower hatch at crewman manning the FuMB-26 Tunis radar detector aboard *U861* in the Indian Ocean.

Oberleutnant zur See Helmut Herglotz bringing *U290* into Bergen, 16 June 1944.

U441 showing the fearsome array of weaponry for this original 'flak boat'.

U290 showing the round dipole antennae of the FuG 350 Naxos radar detector.

U43 making a surfaced torpedo attack. Hans-Joachim Schwantke stands at right and maintains overall control. (Paul Milner)

The Brest U-boat pens after the fall of the city to Allied troops, September 1944.

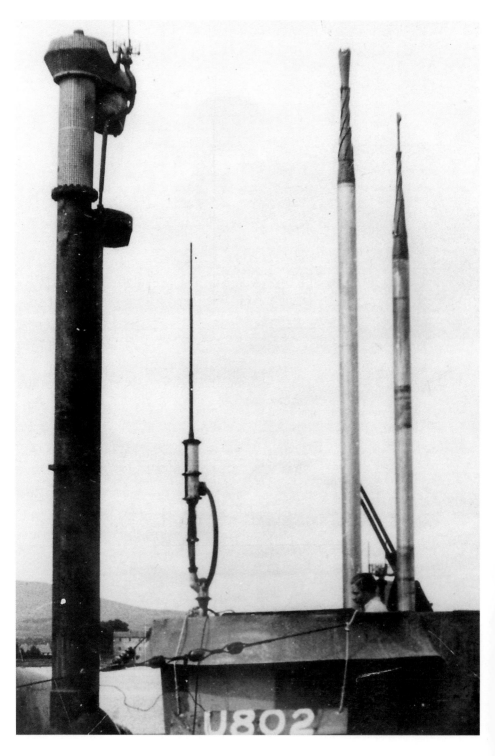

U802 after its surrender showing (from left) the snorkel, radio DF loop, observation periscope, and attack periscope.

The Type XXIII *U4709* leaving Kiel. It was commissioned on 3 March 1945 and scuttled on 4 May.

The Type XXI *U2519*, captained by Peter 'Ali' Cremer, formerly of *U333*. (Paul Milner)

Kapitänleutnant Heinrich-Andreas Schroeteler of *U1023* was one of the last U-boat skippers to sink an enemy ship on 7 May 1945. (Paul Milner)

and May and three more U-boats – *U126*, *U128* and *U161* – were travelling in company with secret instructions to attack shipping in a tightly constrained strip of water near Fernando de Noronha Island, Dönitz had resisted an instinctive full attack on Brazil.

Following the declaration of war on the United States by Germany, trade between Brazil and Europe became difficult, and Brazil's government aligned closer to the Allies by curbing activities by all Axis nations through such measures as freezing credits, closing news agencies, and suspending the German-controlled Condor airline. American staff had begun 'assisting' at Brazilian airfields, an increasing number of American troops landed to enhance defensive forces. Transport aircraft of the USAAF were beginning regular operations through Brazil to destinations such as Freetown, and German fears of fully fledged USAAF bomber bases being established had become very real. Between February and April, seven Brazilian ships had been sunk by U-boats within the Western Atlantic. As tensions increased, on 16 May SKL decreed that attacks without warning were permitted against all visibly armed merchant vessels of the South American nations and Mexico, which had broken off diplomatic relations with the Axis powers. Only Argentina and Chile were exempt from this order. The sinking of Mexican tanker *Protero de Llano* by Reinhard Suhren's *U564* near Miami led the Mexican government to threaten war on 17 May; the destruction of tanker *Faja de Oro* northwest of Cuba by Hermann Rasch's *U106* four days later sealed the issue. On that day, Mexico declared war on Germany – ratified on 31 May – and 'friendly' diplomatic pressure increased on Brazil's president to follow suit.

Raeder requested Dönitz investigate likely results of a sudden surprise attack by up to 15 U-boats against Brazil. He concluded that such an operation was wholly dependent on the presence of a U-tanker in the South Atlantic and the unlikely ability to be able to despatch the requisite number of U-boats sailing at approximately the same time. At that moment, the sole operational U-tanker was *U459*, already scheduled to sail on 6 June with 80 per cent of its stocks allocated to boats in action – many Type VIIs who would be unable to return unless supplied. The second Type XIV,

U460, would be leaving Kiel on 7 June and reach Biscay about 11 days later. Not until the second week of July could it be expected to reach equatorial waters. Furthermore, BdU recorded that in western France, ready to sail during the period 6–16 June were 11 Type VIICs, three Type IXCs and one Type IXB. These could not be considered for the operation because of uncertainty that *U460* could reach its operations area. However, between 22 June and 4 July, two Type IX and eight Type VIICs would be ready to sail, able to be considered for such an operation as soon *U460* had reached the open Atlantic.

Despite this possibility, such a concerted effort at such long range would have a seriously debilitating effect on the remainder of Atlantic warfare. The diversion of those ten U-boats would result in only eight to ten Type VIICs and five to seven Type IXC boats maintaining the offensives against the North American eastern seaboard, the Caribbean, the Gulf of Mexico and West Africa for the bulk of July, those reinforcements sailing from Germany no longer able to operate against long-distance targets due to the proposed reassignment of *U460*. Dönitz's final recommendation was that, if deemed 'politically possible', a major attack on Brazil would be better postponed until *U461* became operational at the tail end of June and 'a constant flow of new boats from home' could bolster his front-line numbers.

The three U-boats despatched to hunt off Fernando de Noronha Island found nothing within the strip of waters which had been opened for U-boat operations and were quickly relocated to the Caribbean lest they pointlessly waste fuel, each subsequently successful though to a lesser extent than previous experience predicted. Interestingly – and perhaps best illustrating Dönitz's original contention that convoy attack presented the surest path to victory over Allied forces – *U161*'s final victim of its patrol was freighter *Fairport* from convoy AS4 sighted south of Bermuda. The convoy comprised nine cargo ships under American escort, and 6,165-ton *Fairport* carried 8,000 tons of material bound for Suez, including a deck cargo of armoured vehicles and holds carrying 300 Sherman engines, the new American tanks bound for British forces in North Africa. There, Rommel appeared on the verge of winning the protracted war of manoeuvre, Tobruk having fallen and 33,000 men surrendering to an inferior Axis force. With the sinking of *Fairport*, Albrecht Achilles unknowingly struck a heavy blow to British chances of holding Egypt, *U161* savagely depth charged but successfully returning to Lorient.

As events transpired, the desperate need for the Sherman engines brought renewed appeals from Whitehall for replacement of the destroyed cargo and a second ship was hurriedly loaded and despatched, reaching Suez before the remainder of AS4. American industry was clearly reaching high gear.

By early June the Kriegsmarine considered a latent state of war to exist with Brazil, and SKL requested Hitler declare war to coincide with an attack by the ten U-boats Dönitz believed possible to use. Despite regretting the deviation of U-boats from existing Atlantic theatres, he believed a quick operation off major Brazilian ports stood a good chance of success given expected heavy traffic and minor ASW presence. Brazilian claims that their aircraft had attacked U-boats off their coast (Italian) and intelligence sources reporting routine arming of Brazilian merchants poured fuel on the flames. Berlin considered the optimal moment to strike being five to eight days before a new moon, leaving three windows of opportunity: 13 June (unfeasible due to lack of U-tanker), 11 July and 9 August. Following proposals submitted to Hitler, the group of ten U-boats was ordered to attack principal Brazilian harbours, sailing by 20 June under Operations Order No. 53. Then, as abruptly as the attack had been ordered, it was cancelled on direct instructions from Hitler following strong objections from Foreign Minister Joachim von Ribbentrop that neutral shipping was likely to be affected by any such attacks on Brazilian ports. A suggested operation by 2nd U-Flotilla Type IX U-boats against refrigerator ships sailing from the River Plate was also vetoed for the same reason. Dönitz and the BdU staff were no doubt relieved by cancellation of the unnecessary burden on already overstretched U-boat numbers, though, regardless of the plan's cancellation, on 22 August Brazil declared war on Germany, its airfields quickly occupied by American ASW squadrons.

In American waters, the tide had already turned. Conferences held between US Navy senior officers and the Port Director of New York had begun on 9 March to discuss convoying, initially between Aruba, Key West and New York, later extended to Trinidad. This convoy network commenced operation between Norfolk and Key West during mid-May, after U-boats had cumulatively sunk 85 merchant vessels on the American Eastern Sea Frontier since the year began. With opposition stiffening, U-boats changed their point of concentration to the Caribbean, the Gulf of Mexico and the sea area near Panama, sinking 73, 98 and 15 vessels respectively, before convoying was extended and fully operational as far as Trinidad by early July. To that point, U-boats had destroyed 325 merchant ships along the coastline from Canada to Brazil, *U533* even opening what became known as the 'Battle of the St Lawrence River' by penetrating the Canadian river to sink two ships in May.* During August, tightly interlocking convoys were further extended into the Gulf of Mexico to Galveston, Texas – approximately 33 per cent of all ships in the coastal convoy system tankers – and though losses within the Caribbean continued until the end of 1942, they dramatically decreased.

> During 1942, of the 1,556 merchant vessels (excluding escorts) lost worldwide by all types of enemy action 512 ships or 33 per cent, were sunk by U-boats in our four Sea Frontiers, Canadian Coastal Zone and Brazilian Area. As these ships averaged 5,164 gross tons each, there were over 2,600,000 gross tons of coastal shipping sunk in one year; 11 per cent of all the losses from enemy action, worldwide, for the entire war. During 1943, however, while comparable worldwide losses dropped sharply to 562 merchant vessels, only 65, or 12 per cent, were sunk by U-boat in these same coastal areas, primarily because of convoying and effective attacks on the enemy.[14]

---

* This sporadic 'battle' ended on 25 November 1944 when corvette HMCS *Shawinigan* was sunk by *U1128* with no survivors in the Cabot Strait.

The initial relative ease of U-boat operations within the Caribbean sharply diminished. As an example, Werner Hartenstein's second patrol with *U156* to the area during May and June appears on the surface to have been wildly successful, with 11 ships sunk totalling 44,385 tons and another two damaged. However, only two of the destroyed ships were fully within the Caribbean, and a third on the border between the Caribbean and Atlantic south of Barbados – an 80-ton Venezuelan schooner carrying rum to Trinidad and shelled into oblivion. The remainder were all encountered sailing independently within the Atlantic on Hartenstein's approach and retreat from the area. *U156*, and several other boats, had chanced upon a new shipping route that stopped after the period of the full moon as convoying was swiftly instigated.

Anti-submarine operations within the Caribbean were rapidly gaining traction. *U156* was ordered to attack American warships maintaining a watching guard over Vichy Martinique, damaging aged destroyer USS *Blakely* with a torpedo that blew the ship's bow off and killed six men. However, hounded constantly by aircraft during this full moon period, Hartenstein reported to BdU on 30 May that 'during seven tropical days, 121 hours dived. Limit of efficiency. Request freedom to manoeuvre.' The ambient water temperature turned the unventilated U-boat interior into an unbearable sweatbox, reducing the crew to a stuporous state, and *U156* was granted free movement, heading initially west but only spending three more days within the Caribbean Sea.

The same traffic choke points that had helped U-boats find merchant targets now worked against the Germans as heavy air patrols saturated these likely hunting grounds. Though naval anti-submarine vessels were still thinly spread, aircraft became a dominant factor.

On 13 July, the first U-boat was lost within the Caribbean when recently promoted Wilfried Reichmann's Type IXC *U153* was depth charged and sunk by destroyer USS *Landsdowne* after an intensive hunt by combined forces of the US Navy's Panama Sea Frontier, following an abortive attack by Reichmann on net-tender USS *Mimosa* off Almirante. By the year's end, Ludwig Forster's *U654* was sunk with all hands north of Colón, Otto Ites' *U94* sunk east of Jamaica with 26 survivors (including a wounded Ites who had recently been awarded the Knight's Cross) and Jürgen Wattenberg's *U162* sunk northeast of Trinidad with two men killed. Within the Gulf of Mexico, Hans-Günther Kuhlmann's *U166* was lost with all hands to aerial depth charges southeast of New Orleans on 30 July after laying nine TMC mines off Port Eades in the Mississippi Delta. The wreck of *U166* was identified in 2001 by a remotely operated vehicle; it was found less than a mile from the last of its four torpedo victims, *Robert E. Lee,* having been depth charged and sunk with all hands in water over 1½ kilometres deep by escorting patrol craft USS *PC-566.*

Contrarily, within the Arctic, U-boats finally appeared to have vindicated their presence. During May, the first Arctic Ocean flotilla had been created under command of Hans Cohausz. Previously, Arctic boats had remained administratively on the strength of combat flotillas in Germany and France, but with the creation of the 11th U-Flotilla, logistical matters transferred to Bergen, Cohausz no stranger to the requirements of a combat flotilla, having previously commanded Brest's 1st U-Flotilla.

On 28 June, the German summer offensive opened on the southern Russian steppes, and with Soviet forces in chaotic retreat, Stalin demanded greater supply by the western Allies. PQ17 was assembled with 35 merchants under Royal Navy escort, and as it departed Iceland's mid-point stop Oesten ordered four boats of the 'Eisteufel' group to locate and shadow while six others formed a patrol line across its expected path. Outbound QP13 was located but ignored in favour of the incoming laden merchants, *U255* shadowing PQ17 and others given freedom to attack but thwarted by escorts and poor marksmanship.

The Kriegsmarine had determined to throw everything at PQ17 and organized Operation *Rösselsprung,* activating *Tirpitz* and *Admiral Hipper,* which departed Trondheim to move north in preparation, their movement detected by Allied intelligence as they joined *Admiral Scheer* awaiting orders to sail against PQ17. On 4 July, the convoy suffered its first casualties to Luftwaffe attack, with the American freighter *Christopher Newport* damaged and abandoned, located by Karl Brandenburg's *U457* and sunk with a single torpedo. Liberty ship *William Hooper* was similarly damaged and abandoned, subsequently sunk by Hilmar Siemon's *U334*; the number of vessels damaged by Luftwaffe torpedoes but later sunk by U-boat was quite high as airborne torpedoes and warheads were smaller, only 45 cm diameter compared with the 53.34cm U-boat torpedoes.*

While the Kriegsmarine refused to order the heavy ships of *Rösselsprung* into action until the whereabouts of enemy carriers could be ascertained, Oesten's U-boats were thrown against PQ17. In Altafjord, *Admiral* Otto Schniewind aboard *Tirpitz* seethed at his inability to put to sea and join battle until 1500hrs on 5 July, when he was granted permission to sail and *Tirpitz, Admiral Hipper, Admiral Scheer*, seven destroyers and two torpedo boats departed port. It was a brief journey. The ships were sighted by British Catalinas and submarines. Messages intercepted by B-Dienst caused consternation in Berlin, and after only six hours at sea, Raeder ordered the ships recalled. Unbeknown to them, in Britain news that *Tirpitz* had sailed caused virtual panic within the Admiralty and a series of escalating messages withdrawing the escorts culminated in tragedy at 2136hrs: 'Most immediate. My 2123/4. Convoy is to scatter.'

Despite the convoy having successfully driven off repeated air attacks, albeit at the loss of four merchants, they were now ordered to disperse and lose the collective defence at the heart of the convoying principle. To make matters worse, the weather had cleared. The result was devastating. As the first PQ17 survivor made landfall in Arkhangelsk on 13 July, thick fog at the entrance to the White Sea brought operations against PQ17 to an end, though Oesten directed U-boats to find whatever scattered merchants remained, five boats combing the area and sinking the

---

* The 'Liberty ship' was an American standardized design cargo ship created for mass, low-cost wartime production, with 2,710 built between 1941 and 1945. See Chapter 9 for further details.

final U-boat casualty from PQ17 that day, the 7,168-ton *Paulus Potter*.

> It was *U255*, Reche, who found an abandoned Liberty Ship with a Dutch crew called *Paulus Potter*. The crew had left the ship in a hurry; the ship was damaged by bombs from the Luftwaffe. The crew had left the ship in such a hurry that they didn't even decode the last messages received. So Reche sent three men aboard, including his Chief Engineer, to find whether the ship could be saved and taken to Norway, but it was too badly damaged so he took whatever intelligence they could find; convoy orders and details such as sailing instructions and port approach routes as well as the convoy composition, decoding material and so forth. And, among the things they found were these sort-of instructions for British merchant seamen. I guess that cartoons were easy to remember. Reche then torpedoed the ship once everything had been taken off. It was one of the most successful convoy attacks of the war. You didn't think about the men involved – we were at war and Russia needed those supplies. Reche then sank the ship with torpedoes.[15]

Of the 34 ships that had departed Iceland, 24 had been sunk – 16 by U-boats and the remainder by the Luftwaffe – killing 153 merchant seamen. Of the ten '*Eisteufel*' boats, only *U408* and *U657* failed to successfully score a torpedo hit on target, and statistically, in terms of tonnage sunk, it was the most successful U-boat convoy attack of the war, accruing 102,311 tons. Five Luftwaffe aircraft had been lost, while the U-boats suffered no casualties. The defeat of PQ17 reached far beyond burning ships and dead bodies in the Arctic. Soviet authorities accused the Royal Navy of cowardice and dishonesty about the number of ships lost, while in Washington Admiral King was enraged at the destruction of 14 American ships and refused to cooperate with the Royal Navy any further within the region, moving his forces to the Pacific.

Determined to inflict a second serious defeat upon the presumed imminent arrival of PQ18, Oesten formed the group '*Nebelkönig*' for the end of July between Iceland and Jan Mayen. By the early part of August, the group comprised ten boats, but PQ18 had been postponed until September as the Royal Navy focussed instead upon the Mediterranean crisis. Though three PQ18 ships would later be sunk by U-boats and another ten by the Luftwaffe, the price was heavy. Three U-boats and 49 aircraft were destroyed. Of the Luftwaffe's entire complement of trained torpedo bomber crews, 42 per cent of them had been lost in action against PQ18, and the Luftwaffe was never again able to mount such strong attacks on Russian convoys. Nonetheless, the severe losses accrued by both PQ17 and PQ18, coupled with Allied naval demands of Operation *Torch*, led to the suspension of the Arctic convoys until December 1942.

At the other end of the Eastern Front a new U-boat operational sphere had also opened within the Black Sea. U-boats stationed there could support troops fighting in the Crimea, by intercepting Soviet warships threatening supply lines and engaged in shore bombardment. Initial ideas to exchange some Mediterranean Type VIIs for Turkish submarines within the Black Sea were soon dismissed as were ideas for the sale and resale of U-boats, as a thin deception displaying Turkish disregard for her obligations as a neutral power. A separate proposal to simply purchase existing Turkish submarines was also refused by OKM, as they would require considerable conversion and upgrade to reach the standards required by the Kriegsmarine. Instead, on 15 April three Type IIB boats – *U9* and *U24* of Pillau's 21st U-Training Flotilla and *U19* of Gotenhafen's 22nd – were chosen for transfer by river, canal and overland route to Constanta, Romania.

The entire transfer was expected to take 26 weeks, though if the schedule was met, they could be operational in the Black Sea before the Danube froze for winter. In Kiel they were stripped of as much as possible, the conning tower, diesel engines, electrical motors, batteries, decking and other smaller items lifted out to reduce hull weight. The hulls were then placed aboard shallow-draught rafts which, beginning with *U24*, were moved through the Kiel Canal to Hamburg and from there upstream along the Elbe River to Dresden. In the suburb of Übigau, the pontoons were lifted by slipway from the water and the U-boats craned aboard low-bed transport trailers pulled by heavy Kuhlemeyer trucks. From the slipway the autobahn that stretched to Ingolstadt was easily accessible, and travelling at a maximum of 8km/h the transport occupied 600 men and took 56 hours of constant movement, drivers changed without halting the convoy. Once in Ingolstadt the boats were returned to the pontoons, which had been shipped by rail from Dresden and towed via the Danube to Galati, Romania. There they were reassembled over one and a half months, ready for operations.

Before the transfer was complete, it was already planned to strengthen the U-boat Black Sea presence, considered an ideal training ground for future crews once Russia was beaten and exerting a 'favourable political influence' on pro-Axis Turkey. Three more Type IIBs from the 21st and 22nd U-Training Flotillas were chosen for transfer, while the original trio was still in transit, *U18*, *U20* and *U23* leaving Kiel in September. The U-boats in Galati were recommissioned into the Kriegsmarine once complete, continuing along the Danube and on through the Black Sea to the Romanian naval base at Constanta, where the 30th U-Flotilla was established under the command of veteran U-boat skipper Helmut Rosenbaum, former captain of *U73*. Like control of Arctic U-boats, Rosenbaum was not directed by BdU but rather formed his own operational staff within the Kriegsmarine's regional 'Admiral Black Sea' command.

Chapter Eight

Losing the Race

'He was sorry he had to blow up our ship, sorry we had to meet
in such circumstances. I liked the man. I liked his approach.'
David Cledwyn, SS *Quebec City*, talking about Werner
Hartenstein, *U156*[1]

As the Luftwaffe declined, Allied air forces reciprocally improved
and aircraft became the bane of Caribbean U-boats, a small number
of British and Canadian warships also appearing within the region.
Corvette HMCS *Oakville* took part in the destruction of *U94*
with an American Catalina aircraft, the only Canadian U-boat
kill within the Caribbean Sea and one in which a boarding party
entered *U94* before forced to evacuate without finding anything of
value as the boat went down.

Allied aircraft also intensified attacks on U-boats in transit to and
from their Biscay bases; once again, obvious traffic choke points
worked against the Kriegsmarine as well as coastal use of the broken
Heimisch code. Almost inexplicably, the RAF had failed to attack
the U-boat bases while bunker construction was under way and at
its most vulnerable. Though Brest became one of the most heavily
bombed cities in Europe, raids were aimed at capital ships within its
docks which returned to Germany during the fabled 'Channel Dash'
of February 1942, withdrawn to Germany for use in the 'defence' of
Norway. A tactical victory for Germany, the ships' movement and
removal of their Atlantic threat was a major strategic reversal.

Allied radar remained underestimated by the Kriegsmarine and insufficient effort was devoted to developing countermeasures. British airborne search radar (ASV, or 'Air to Surface Vessel') had been developed pre-war, the improved and more reliable ASV Mk II entering service towards the end of 1940. By early 1942, all anti-U-boat aircraft carried radar and, incredibly, it was not until June of that year that the Director of Kriegsmarine Signals Intelligence visited Dönitz in Paris and admitted that, despite previous departmental assurances that airborne radar was incapable of detecting such a small target as a surfaced U-boat, the Allies probably *were* able to after all.*

A major shortcoming of the ASV II was a minimum range of approximately 1 kilometre, whereupon any target trace disappeared from the radar screen. By daylight this posed no problem, but by night the U-boat became invisible during an attacking aircraft's final approach. Through the first half of 1942, no U-boats were sunk by radar-equipped aircraft within Biscay, although in return six bombers had been shot down by defending Luftwaffe aircraft. A Royal Air Force personnel officer, Wing Commander Humphrey de Verd Leigh independently created a prototype solution to this problem with the installation of a powerful (22 million candela) 24-inch carbon arc searchlight aboard an aircraft, designed to be ignited once the radar trace disappeared. Receiving official sanction, the 'Leigh Light' was refined and mounted in two differing configurations aboard Wellington and Liberator bombers as well as some Catalina flying boats deployed to Biscay.

On 5 July American Pilot Officer Wiley B. Howell, flying Wellington 'H' of RAF 172 Squadron, was on Biscay anti-U-boat patrol when radar contact was made in early morning darkness at a range of 7 miles. The aircraft's Leigh Light was switched on a mile from target, illuminating Jürgen von Rosenstiel's *U502* running surfaced for Lorient at the end of a successful Caribbean patrol. Four

* Ludwig Stummel, a devout Catholic and National Socialist, was chief of staff to Erhard Maertens, and it was he who had carried out the initial investigations into Enigma security at Maertens' behest following Dönitz's fears of its compromise. Eventually, he replaced Maertens who was fired by Dönitz in 1943.

depth charges were dropped from a height of only 50 feet, straddling the U-boat's bows from starboard to port just as it began to crash dive. As the Wellington passed overhead, the rear gunner fired 400 rounds into the spray of detonation, Howell returning to drop a flame float on a swirling mass of water 'darker than the rest of the sea', the oil patch marking the end of *U502* and its 52-man crew.

The following night, the returning Hartenstein in *U156* reported a similar attack: 'An aircraft approaching from 10°T. Searches with searchlight at 50–80 metres altitude. This is not directable side to side. Fired with 2 cm. Failed at the 3rd shot. Aircraft flies over the boat and illuminates it. Crash dive! No bombs.'[2] The tardy official admission that Allied aircraft probably carried effective radar led to a scramble for countermeasures. During June, three U-boats were so severely damaged by aircraft in Biscay that they were forced to abort their missions, and on 24 June BdU ordered all crossings made submerged by day and night, surfacing only to charge batteries, dramatically increasing Biscay passage times. Flak weaponry was to be increased, with Dönitz requesting design of a twin-mounted 37mm cannon installation, though necessary structural alterations would require time to design and complete, eventually leading to the extended U-boat *Wintergarten*. In the interim, two double mounts for MG151 machine guns to be attached to conning tower railings were provided, though their low stopping power made them next to useless.

The air war over Biscay escalated rapidly during 1942, directly impacting U-boat operations. Dönitz had protested vociferously to Göring that the RAF were operating with 'absolutely no opposition', bomber patrols augmented by heavily armed Bristol Type 156 Beaufighters – a twin-engined, two-seater aircraft of superb performance, fractionally faster than a Junkers Ju 88 and carrying four 20mm nose cannon and six .303 Browning machine guns in the wings. On 4 March, BdU and *Fliegerführer Atlantik* had entered into an agreement for air cover to be provided for U-boats in Biscay, dependent on sufficient Arado Ar 196 floatplanes and suitable weather conditions. Though the nimble Arado aircraft were effective scouts, and capable of self-defence and limited attack capabilities – shooting down 12 Sunderland, Wellington and Whitley bombers between April and September 1942 – they were no match for the Beaufighter, and Focke-Wulf Fw 190 fighters were soon required to escort the Arados.

The antidote to the Beaufighter was found in a heavy-fighter (*Zerstörer*) version of the ubiquitous Junkers Ju 88 (Ju 88C-6) that boasted a solid metal nose housing a single 20mm MG FF/M cannon and three 7.92mm MG 17 machine guns. Two further MG FF/M cannons could be mounted in the ventral gondola, and a pair of defensive 7.92mm MG 81 machine guns faced astern from the glazed canopy.

During June, four of these Ju 88 *Zerstörer* aircraft arrived at Bordeaux, allocated to *Luftflotte* 3 exclusively for protection of damaged U-boats arriving from the Atlantic and escort of blockade-runners. They swung into action on 24 June, when returning U-boat *U753* was badly damaged approaching La Pallice, receiving a chain of Junkers as escort. Four days later, the larger Type IX *U105* left El Ferrol, Spain, at dawn and was picked up by the escorting Ju 88C-6s at 0745hrs. While outbound from France, Heinrich Schuch's *U105* had been attacked by an Australian Sunderland flying boat and damaged, seeking shelter in El Ferrol and requesting fighter protection. Schuch reached the safety of the neutral port, beginning repairs and awaiting developments. Within the pages of his War Diary, Dönitz vented his despair at the inability to protect U-boats from the growing aerial threat:

> The attack on *U105* has shown once more the great dangers to which U-boats are exposed on their passage through Biscay. As there is no defence against Sunderlands and heavy bombers, Biscay has become the playground of English aircraft, where, according to *Fliegerführer Atlantik*, even the most ancient types of Sunderland can be used. As the English aircraft radar set is developed further, the boats will be more and more endangered, damage will be on a larger scale and the result will be total losses of boats. It is sad and very depressing for the U-boat crews that there are no forces whatever available to protect a U-boat unable to dive

as a result of aircraft bombs. Therefore a few long-range *Zerstörer* or modern bombers would be sufficient to drive off the [enemy] maritime aircraft, which at present fly right up to the French Biscay coast without fighter escort. Or at least these aircraft could escort a damaged U-boat until she has reached the area covered by our minesweepers and patrol vessels.[3]

Fliegerführer Atlantik had long requested Dönitz's support in lobbying for additional aircraft and, with express permission from OKM, Dönitz flew first to Luftwaffe Headquarters and then to Göring's Rominten East Prussian hunting lodge on 2 July to personally plead for enhanced fighter protection. Despite their often-frosty personal relationship, he secured the *Reichsmarschall*'s pledge of 24 more Ju 88C-6s.

The initial drive to develop a radar detector resulted in the VHF heterodyne receiver FuMB 1 'Metox' 600A, named after its French manufacturer Metox-Grandin and Sadir. An aerial wrapped around a flimsy wooden cross was connected to a receiver below decks, becoming known as the 'Biscay Cross' to crews. Tuned to detect the 1.5m waveband (200MHz) used by the ASV II radar, Metox received the transmitted radar pulses and rendered them as audible beeps to its operator. The U-boat captain was therefore able to dive his boat as a precautionary measure, knowing there was a radar-equipped aircraft in the vicinity, a primitive direction-finding aid for the searching radar provided by hand-turning the aerial in its mounting. If the U-boat was detected, the pulse rate and subsequent beeps doubled in speed. Rudimentary, flimsy, connected by a lead trailing through open hatches and having to be dismounted upon submergence, Metox was nonetheless successful and was issued to combat boats during August.

Technologically, Germany was already losing the naval war. While design work on acoustic torpedoes and an improved magnetic firing pistol progressed painfully slowly at the TVA, Dönitz harboured strong hopes for an advanced U-boat type under development by Professor Hellmuth Walter. Walter had patented the idea of hydrogen peroxide (H_2O_2) as an oxygen-rich fuel source that could power a submerged turbine engine and therefore create an extremely efficient 'closed cycle' source of underwater propulsion. Encouraged by Dönitz, his first prototype test vessel recorded underwater speed in the Baltic of 28.1 knots during 1940. Kriegsmarine decision makers ordered the immediate construction of six coastal vessels, until opposition arose from an unexpected direction. With a shortfall of operational U-boats and amid the initial torpedo crisis, Dönitz needed U-boats at sea now, not later. In a Paris conference with Walter he learned that the craft was nowhere near service-ready, having been side-lined by hard-pressed construction yards. The vessels required difficult construction techniques to extremely high tolerances and would demand complex maintenance once built. Pragmatically, Dönitz therefore requested that production be reserved for conventional Types VII and IX, of which he felt a more immediate need. However, this same conference provided impetus for development of a U-boat utilizing Walter's streamlined hull-form with vastly increased battery capacity, thereby going some way to satisfying the demand for a '100 per cent underwater vehicle'. This idea would later yield the advanced 'electro-boats' Type XXI and Type XXIII. Furthermore, Walter suggested creation of a retractable ventilation apparatus that could allow diesel engines to run, thereby recharging batteries, while remaining submerged. Dovetailing with technology captured from the Dutch Navy, from this would emerge the *Schnorchel* (snorkel) which prolonged the operational life of Type VII and Type IXs.

While it is true that the *Schnorchel* allowed diesel running while submerged, they were relatively primitive, with valves that unexpectedly closed if the *Schnorchel* head cut under due to swell or imperfect trim. In this case, as diesels continued to draw air, it would instead be taken from the boat interior, causing painful debilitating eardrum and sinus squeezes. Dangerous leakage of exhaust carbon monoxide into the boat was not uncommon. Travelling at speed submerged also negated periscope use due to vibration, and hydrophone reception due to engine noise rendering the U-boat deaf and blind. With extended periods beneath the waves, there was also no opportunity to jettison rubbish and waste generated by

50 men, normally thrown overboard. Instead, it was stored aboard until such time as the boat could surface long enough to get rid of it, the resultant stench doing nothing to enhance the already grim life aboard a combat U-boat. Furthermore, navigation became difficult without surfacing; potentially noisy machinery such as the gyro compass frequently turned off while attempting to run shallow and silent. *U763* proved this during early July 1944 when it drifted into Spithead and surfaced, miraculously undetected, near destroyers lying anchored in the bright moonlight before sneaking back into deeper water.

By January 1942, the U-boat war's character had changed, and after further meetings with Dönitz, contracts were signed for four of Walter's Type XVIIA vessels to be built, two keels laid in Hamburg's Blohm & Voss in December 1942, and the rest at Kiel's Germaniawerft in February 1943. The first to undergo water tests would be *U792*, launched on 28 September 1943, joined by *U794* in October. Both were used as experimental and training units and during test runs in 1944 reached a submerged speed of 25 knots. In late 1942, Walter proposed a project for a 1,475-ton U-boat – the Type XVIII – capable of carrying 23 torpedoes. Contracts were issued on 4 January 1943 for two examples to be built, designated *U796* and *U797*; however, nearing completion in December 1943, they were both cancelled the following March in favour of the Type XXI, considered an improvement of existing technologies and presenting a lower technological risk.

Away from the technical battles, by May 1942 mid-Atlantic convoy operations had been suspended for six months, any convoy action coming about by accident during voyages to and from the western battlegrounds. Most notable was ONS67 during February, attacked by an eventual total of six U-boats vectored individually to the convoy and losing eight ships, six of them tankers. Among the casualties was tanker *Empire Celt*, which streamed the newly developed Admiralty Net Defence – steel mesh anti-torpedo nets trailed from booms on either hull side. Imperfect though it was, covering only 75 per cent of the vessel and reducing the ship's speed, a total of 768 merchant ships were subsequently fitted with the nets. Of these, 21 were attacked with torpedoes, five damaged and six sunk, including *Empire Celt*.

Dönitz decided to form a group from westbound U-boats, to sweep south-westwards along the Great Circle from the North Channel to the Newfoundland Bank. B-Dienst intelligence deduced this the most likely convoy routing, and BdU ordered *U94*, *U96*, *U124*, *U404*, *U406*, *U569*, *U578* and *U590* to form 'Hecht' group. If nothing was sighted, they were to continue onwards to American operating areas. On 11 May, *U569* detected the 41 merchant ships of ON92, escorted by American Ocean Escort Group A3. Comprised of destroyer USS *Gleaves*, a USCGC cutter and four Canadian corvettes, none carried HF/DF gear and only HMCS *Bittersweet* carried Type 271 radar, though its operators were inexperienced. The only ship carrying HF/DF was merchant *Bury*, the equipment used for locating lost or damaged ships, but detecting a radio burst from *U569* and reporting it to *Gleaves*. The US Navy ship failed to act. A possible surfaced U-boat sighting later that day led *Gleaves* and USCGC *Spencer* to begin a protracted and unsuccessful chase which separated them from the convoy, while *U124* became the first of the approaching boats to open fire. That night, between Mohr's *U124* and Ites' *U94*, seven ships were sunk before ON92 disappeared in heavy rain and poor visibility.

Refuelled by *U116* about 600 miles south of Cape Race, 'Hecht' failed to maintain contact with ON96, *U124* finding ON100 during the night of 8 June, from which five ships were sunk, including French corvette *Mimosa*. On 17 June, *U94* contacted ON102, bringing *U590*, *U406*, *U96* and *U124* into action, the U-boats repeatedly forced to submerge and both *U94* and *U590* depth charged for hours, returning with damage and casualties. Only one freighter was sunk by *U124* in a highly phosphorescent sea. Aboard *U590*, Heinrich Müller-Edzards related suspicions that escort forces were using radar, prompting BdU to ask Mohr's opinion, the young captain disagreeing, stating that he avoided pursuit through rapid evasive manoeuvres. He was wrong.

'Hecht' had been relatively successful and Dönitz next formed 'Endrass', this time with the specific intention of tying down Allied forces within the East Atlantic and preventing reinforcements being sent to the United States where conditions for U-boats were rapidly deteriorating. 'Endrass' would target HG convoy traffic though, if nothing was found, refuel from either U459 or U460 and sail west.

Following agents' reports of ships departing Gibraltar, Condors found HG84 on 11 June and 'Endrass' directed towards it. Four nights later, Topp's U552 alone attacked the convoy in spectacular fashion, sinking five ships. The remaining U-boats faced escort forces stronger than expected and supported during daylight by land-based bombers. While U552 returned to France alongside U71 which had suffered depth-charge damage, the remainder refuelled as planned and sailed for the United States.

Both experiences were considered instructive at BdU who judged the convoy situation unchanged within the Atlantic, deciding to renew convoy offensives. To the south, five Type VIICs of 'Hai' group were assembled southeast of the Azores to sweep to the south, refuelling from U116 and carrying on to Freetown. As well as two independently sailing merchant ships and the small patrol boat HMNZS ML-1090, six ships from dispersed OS33 were sunk.

Group 'Wolf' was assembled from nine U-boats 500 miles west of the North Channel on 13 July, returning U-boats to the Mid-Atlantic air gap, supported by U-tanker U461. Bad weather camouflaged one convoy's passage, also weakening strikes against ON113; three merchant ships were sunk over five difficult nights and U90 was lost with all hands to depth charges from Canadian destroyer HMCS St Croix. 'Wolf' then morphed into the expanded group 'Pirat' positioned ahead of ON115's anticipated track, initially sighted by U164 inbound for the Caribbean before U210 of 'Pirat' group began shadowing.

Although Canadian escort group C3 possessed neither Type 271 radar nor HF/DF gear, U-boat transmissions were intercepted, and aboard destroyer HMCS Saguenay the escort commander Dickson Wallace aggressively manoeuvred convoy and escort, complicating U-boat pursuit, U588 sunk with all hands by corvette HMCS Wetaskiwin and destroyer HMCS Skeena. Only one merchant ship was sunk – 9,419-ton Lochkatrine torpedoed by U552 – and two damaged before ON115 reached fogbanks off Newfoundland. With reinforced escorts that actively hunted pursuing U-boats, damaging two, BdU broke off the attack.*

While some 'Pirat' U-boats moved onward to American and Caribbean patrols, those that remained re-formed once more into 'Steinbrinck', which vainly chased strongly defended convoys in thick fog. On 5 August, U593 latched on to SC94 and sank a single ship before being driven off. Reinforced by six more outbound U-boats, 'Steinbrinck' maintained intermittent contact, although constantly recurring fog rendered continuous shadowing or attack almost impossible as U-boats suddenly chanced upon the enemy in poor visibility and were usually immediately spotted and driven off by HF/DF-equipped escorts with liberal depth-charge use. U210, captained by Rudolf Lemcke, who appears not to have been highly regarded by his relatively inexperienced crew, blundered into Canadian destroyer HMCS *Assiniboine* as most of the crew had just sat down to a supper of ham, pickles, bread and butter, and tea with lemon. At point-blank range, the destroyer began shooting, Third Watch Officer Otto Holst returning fire with the 20mm flak weapon and starting a small blaze on the Canadian's forecastle. Holst was then shot through the neck by machine-gun fire and killed outright, his loader Willi Krumm wounded, moments before a 4.7-inch shell hit the conning tower, reducing it to a twisted shambles and literally blowing Lemcke to pieces; Krumm was virtually decapitated. As U210 attempted to dive, it was rammed behind the conning tower and began flooding, Chief Engineer Heinz Sorber ordering the crew to abandon ship; 37 men were rescued.

Night attacks were impossible, and attempted torpedo attacks by five different U-boats suffered torpedo failure or misses, until almost simultaneous attacks by U176 and U379 sank five

---

* Erich Topp's *U552* was among them, hit by shellfire from HMCS *Sackville* and narrowly escaping ramming after being surprised in the fog. Crossing Biscay, *U552* was bombed by a Coastal Command aircraft but only slightly damaged. After his return to Saint Nazaire and travelling to Berlin, Topp was decorated by Hitler with Swords to his Oak Leaves and Knight's Cross, the second U-boat man after Kretschmer to receive the award. He was transferred ashore to command the 27th U-Training Flotilla in Gotenhafen.

ships between them. Some merchant crews began to panic and three ships were abandoned without reason, one of them 3,701-ton *Radchuch* found drifting by *U176* and destroyed. In return, *U379* was located between rain squalls by HMS *Dianthus*. Depth charged and forced to surface, the U-boat was rammed and hammered by further depth charges. Although most of the crew escaped, with other U-boats nearby *Dianthus* retrieved only six before reluctantly moving on, leaving a float with rations behind. *U379*'s captain, Paul-Hugo Kettner, was last seen swimming in the Atlantic, asking who had his lifejacket. In total SC94 lost 11 ships, for the destruction of two attacking U-boats before '*Steinbrinck*' was dissolved on 11 August, those still operational forming '*Lohs*' for a renewed convoy hunt.

This pattern repeated itself with groups formed and dissolved along the North Atlantic convoy routes. To the southeast, groups also intercepted Sierra Leone traffic; '*Hai*' was succeeded by '*Blücher*', supported by U-tanker *U461* and sinking four ships from SL118 and two from subsequent SL119. Orders had been issued by BdU during June for the capture of merchant skippers and chief engineers to deprive the Allies of experienced seamen who, if recovered, were reassigned and back in service as soon as possible; their sea pay callously stopped at the moment of sinking. Hitler had enquired as to the possibility of killing survivors in the hope of denying the enemy such 'recycled' merchant crews and been firmly rebuffed by both Dönitz and Raeder. This policy of capture was Dönitz's compromise suggestion, provided that stopping to do so did not endanger the U-boat. He had also pointedly remarked to his Führer that a functioning magnetic torpedo fuse, still under laborious development, would largely achieve the desired effect by the very swift nature in which ships sank following the power of detonation beneath the keel.

With Caribbean and American operations in steady decline as the US Navy swiftly learned the ASW trade, a long-distance operation ordered by OKM to 'maintain strategic pressure' on the enemy planned a fresh attempt against Cape Town – a traffic hot-spot and also of direct consequence to military supplies bound for Allied forces in North Africa. Dönitz selected five experienced U-boats in a group designated *'Eisbär'*: Hartenstein's *U156*, Merten's *U68*, Fritz Poeske's *U504* and Carl Emmermann's *U172*, supported by Wilamowitz-Möllendorf's U-tanker *U459*. Despite their 'group' nomenclature, the attack boats were instructed to operate independently beyond coordination of the initial assault. Following this first wave would come four larger U-cruisers – *U177*, *U178*, *U179* and *U181* – to reinforce the attack and round the cape, crossing for the first time the 20° East meridian that bisects Cape Agulhas and separates the Indian Ocean from the wild expanse of the Atlantic.

Impetus had been provided by Japanese submarine *I30*, which had arrived in Lorient on 5 August as a part of the *Yanagi* supply missions, its commander, Shinobu Endo, bringing news of easy successes against Indian Ocean merchant shipping. The *Yanagi* missions were an Imperial Japanese Navy initiative to bring supplies and technology to Europe by submarine, a reciprocal arrangement with Germany expected to follow. *I30* had carried 1,500 kilograms of mica and 660 kilograms of shellac and would return carrying technological goods: a torpedo data computer, newly developed sonar decoy know as '*Bold*', 'Seetakt' radar, Metox, Enigma machines, and G7a and G7e torpedoes. *I30* began its return journey on 22 August, reaching Singapore in October but sunk after resailing for Japan and straying into a Japanese defensive minefield.

With complete surprise a perquisite, for *'Eisbär'* SKL issued 'Operations Order 52' forbidding engagements once past the equator, excepting battleships and aircraft carriers, providing firing data was 'certain'. Dönitz reminded his four commanders of their freedom to attack *before* the equator was reached, this 'free-fire' area later expanded to reach 5° South, an extension that would prove of great consequence to Hartenstein.

The first *'Eisbär'* pair to sail, *U156* and *U172*, were tasked with reconnoitring the Cape Town roadstead, their attacks then acting as a signal for the remaining boats to open fire; *U68* to operate southwest, south and southeast of areas earlier mined by the German raider *Doggerbank*, while *U504* was to cover to the north, northeast and northwest of Cape Town.

On 12 September, the *'Eisbär'* mission appeared in dire jeopardy after all four boats were diverted to join the hunt by *'Blücher'* group for SL119 east of the Azores, *U156* sinking a single straggling freighter. Ordered to sweep south in a loose patrol line, *U156* was approaching the new cease-fire latitude of 5° South when Hartenstein torpedoed *Laconia*, Captain Rudolph Sharp going down with his ship, which sank after an hour. However, *Laconia* carried with its 200 tons of general cargo, 366 passengers and 1,809 Italian prisoners: 97 crew members, 133 passengers, 33 Polish guards and 1,394 prisoners were ultimately lost. As *U156* surfaced, Italian voices were heard, and Hartenstein realized the scope of the unfolding disaster. His crew began pulling people from the water as a radio message was transmitted to Paris requesting instructions.

Dönitz faced a dilemma. Despite wanting to maintain the operational integrity of *'Eisbär'*, abandoning a rescue attempt already under way was unthinkable. After brief deliberation he directed remaining *'Eisbär'* boats, nearby *U506* and *U507* and BETASOM boat *Capellini* to make for Hartenstein's position and assist, redistributing the hundreds of survivors crammed aboard *U156* and in scattered lifeboats or floating in the ocean. Vichy authorities were requested to help, and the ships *Gloire*, *Annamite* and *Dumont d'Urville* sailed from Dakar with permission from blockading British ships. British authorities in Freetown also despatched merchant ships *Empire Haven* to assist after receiving a message sent in plain language on the 25-metre waveband: 'If any ship will assist the ship-wrecked *Laconia* crew, I will not attack her, providing I am not attacked by ship or air force. I have picked up 193 men. 4° 52' S, 11° 26' W. German submarine.'

In Berlin, Hitler was furious at Hartenstein's actions. Through Raeder he demanded the *'Eisbär'* boats resume their mission, refusing a 'diplomatic neutralization' of the area suggested to BdU by Hartenstein. Complying with orders, the remaining *'Eisbär'* boats resumed course, *U156* replaced by Helmut Witt's *U159* already at sea; incredibly, an intelligence report by the Royal Navy's Commander-in-Chief South Atlantic, Vice Admiral William Tait, did not note the movement of the southbound U-boats.

The same Freetown naval authority that despatched *Empire Haven* requested 'air cover' for it from the USAAF airfield on Ascension Island, and after *U506* had rendezvoused with *U156* and begun taking survivors aboard, a USAAF B24 Liberator flown by James D. Harden overflew the strange assemblage. Not responding to Morse signals from *U156*, which displayed a 2-metre-square improvised Red Cross banner, the aircraft requested instructions. From Ascension's commander of 1st Composite Squadron, Richard C. Richardson, the reply was soon received: 'Sink sub.'

Harden began the first of four attack runs, his bombs landing close to *U156* and amid lifeboats, capsizing some and killing people in the water. The last delay-fused bomb detonated beneath the control room and water was incorrectly reported to be entering the boat. As his crew donned *Tauchretter* escape gear, and amid fears of chlorine gas, all passengers were ordered overboard. *U156* and *U506* both dived away, Hartenstein reporting the attack to BdU as his crew began what he recorded in his War Diary as a 'first class repair job'.

Dönitz ordered all remaining U-boat assistance cancelled; *U506* was also bombed the following day but escaped virtually unscathed, Würdemann later transferring his rescued passengers to the Vichy sloop *Annamite*. Schacht's *U507* also met with the Vichy ship and placed its survivors and towed lifeboats in their charge, keeping *Laconia*'s Third Officer and an RAF Flying Officer aboard for return to France, judging they had observed the operation of Metox aboard the U-boat and could not be repatriated. Hartenstein remained off Freetown, though *U156*, unlikely to withstand serious depth charging and after sinking one more ship, returned to France. On 17 September he was awarded the Knight's Cross for his accumulated tally of ships sunk.

Dönitz was infuriated at what he considered to be the bombing of an obviously humanitarian gesture and appended his usual comment to the boat's War Diary:

The *Kommandant* was in a difficult position during the rescue operation of the *Laconia* shipwrecked. It was wrong to believe in an 'implied armistice'. It almost led to the loss of the boat.

Because leadership refrained from transmitting the status and refusal of the neutralization, he acted in his best belief. The incident is renewed proof of the harmful effect of humanitarian feelings with such an enemy.

From this near disaster came the infamous 'Laconia Order' to U-boat officers, later used against Dönitz during the Nuremberg trials.

1. All efforts to save survivors of sunken ships, such as the fishing out of swimming men and putting them on board lifeboats, the righting of overturned lifeboats, or the handing over of food and water, must stop. Rescue contradicts the most basic demands of the war: the destruction of enemy ships and their crews.
2. Orders concerning the bringing-in of captains and chief engineers stay in effect.
3. Survivors are to be saved only if their statements are important for the boat.
4. Be harsh. Remember that the enemy has no regard for women and children when bombing German cities!

After a final refuelling from *U459* south of St Helena, the *'Eisbär'* boats took up their positions. However, instead of dozens of enemy ships lying vulnerable at anchor in the roadstead to the South African port, Emmermann reported them empty, while Merten noted a heavy searchlight barrage before Table Bay and thick patrol craft traffic between Robben Island and Fort Wynard. With no targets, it appeared an inauspicious start to an assault against South Africa. Dönitz responded by radio that same night, granting *'Eisbär'* freedom of action as of 8 October, guessing that previous Japanese submarine operations off Madagascar may have highlighted Cape Town's potential vulnerability. A lack of practical cooperation between Germany and Japan had directly forestalled U-boat operations, the Kriegsmarine also incorrectly assuming Japanese naval forces would maintain pressure on the African coast throughout 1942.

Although 'Eisbär' appeared less than promising, matters rapidly improved. Emmermann opened fire before the agreed hour, sinking two ships and blaming 'garbled reception' of BdU instructions. Regardless, 'Eisbär' sank 13 more merchant ships within three days, Merten destroying six in less than 27 hours. The first of the reinforcing Type IXD2 U-cruisers from the 10th U-Flotilla to arrive was Ernst Sobe's *U179*, sinking 6,558-ton *City of Athens*. However, destroyer HMS *Active* – engaged in rescuing 98 survivors and the ship's cat – detected the surfaced U-boat by radar and illuminated *U179* with star shells, shelling and forcing *U179* to dive where depth charges destroyed it and all 61 men aboard.

By mid-October, weather off South Africa deteriorated and achieved what relatively lacklustre ASW forces couldn't, as 'Eisbär' boats were forced away from Cape Town in search of milder meteorological conditions. By 1 November they had destroyed 22 ships in total, many laden with valuable war materiel and including three huge troop transports. The three brand-new Type IXD-2 U-boats continued applying pressure as 'Eisbär' returned to France, Merten and Emmermann departing first, both sinking one further ship each as they headed north. Merten thought his target to be a freighter, but he sank 8,034-ton liner *City of Cairo*, carrying 150 passengers, mainly women and children. Unable to rescue survivors due to both the impracticality of taking people aboard a crowded U-boat engaged in a lengthy patrol and the 'Laconia Order', Merten sailed *U68* among the lifeboats, directing the rescue of people in the water through a megaphone. Eleven days later he was awarded the Knight's Cross by radio for claimed sinking of over 200,000 tons, not far from a confirmed total of 27 ships adding up to 170,248 tons.

The Type IXD-2s that had arrived were the largest of the Type IX series of ocean-going cruiser submarines, built in substitute for the abandoned Type XI artillery U-boat design. The tried and tested Type IXC provided the basis for this expanded version, an initial Type IXD-1 using experimental propulsion from six combined 1,500hp Daimler-Benz *Schnellboot* engines, the total 9,000hp, 20-cylinder power-plant providing an exceptional surface speed. Only two – *U180* and *U195* – were completed, the engine a failure, removed and replaced with more conventional diesels as the boats were converted to transports.

The Type IXD-2 was provided the same diesels as the IXC, but with an additional diesel-electric drive. Living and stowage spaces and the outer hull on the IXDs were enlarged, and the bow and stern drawn out, providing a boat nearly 11 metres longer and with 400 tons more surface displacement than the IXC due to an additional accommodation compartment forward of the conning tower. This was counterbalanced with extra engines within another additional section towards the stern. Its true strength lay in the Type IXD-2's fuel capacity: 442 tons compared with the 214 of the Type IXC, giving a potential surfaced cruising range of 23,700 nautical miles at 12 knots. In operational use they were even more impressive, capable of 32,000 miles at 9 knots if five of the eight diving cells were used as fuel bunkers from the outset. Double-hulled, the fuel tanks wrapped around the pressure hull and comprised a massive diesel storage space. However, these capabilities came at a price, as the Type IXD-2 was even slower to dive and harder to control than its predecessors. This issue was belatedly addressed when the upper forward deck was reshaped into an hourglass to negate the effect of the large flat plane's interaction with the plane of the sea surface, holding the boat pinned for priceless seconds as sheer weight gradually dragged it through and below the waves.

The three Type IXD-2s cruised in atrocious conditions off Cape Town and added few victims to the tally of 'Eisbär' before granted freedom of action by BdU and proceeding into calmer waters, sailing northeast towards Lourenço Marques, the capital of Portuguese East Africa (now Mozambique). An important deep-water harbour for Allied shipping near to the Rand – South Africa's industrial and mining heartland – there were few ASW defences and they suffered accordingly. Among the casualties, on 28 November Robert Gysae's *U177* torpedoed *Nova Scotia* southwest of Lourenço Marques, carrying 769 Italian civilian internees and POWs after misidentifying the ship as an armed merchant cruiser. Gysae radioed BdU, urging contact with Portuguese authorities to coordinate rescue efforts. Two Italians were taken on board, relating tales of panic as fire instantly spread through crowded holds and cabins, well over 200 people killed during the sinking. Mindful of the recent *Laconia* debacle, Gysae distributed what water and medical supplies he could and reluctantly departed. Forty-eight hours later, Portuguese destroyer *Alfonso de Albuquerque* arrived and rescued 117 Italians and 64 South African and British soldiers. In total, only 181 of the estimated 1,200 people aboard *Nova Scotia* were saved.

By the time that the three Type IXD-2s disengaged and began returning to France, they had destroyed 25 ships, accumulating 134,780 tons, the original *'Eisbär'* boats entering port having destroyed 28 ships amounting to 182,174 tons. Statistically one of the single most successful U-boat operations of the war, and certainly responsible for temporary dislocation of South African shipping, it had taken the four *'Eisbär'* boats nearly four months to achieve. Dönitz had been unhappy at OKM's 'strategic pressure' justification for such a long-range endeavour, reasoning that the same effect could have been realized between the equator and 15° South latitude, rather than *'Eisbär'* being forbidden to attack below 5° and compelled to journey so far south. The boats and their crews would take considerable rehabilitation before fit for sea once more, essentially occupying them for half of a year.

Up to eight U-boats hunted off Freetown during the beginning of October, but results were poor, with heavily covered convoying robbing the Germans of opportunity. By November, the last two U-boats – *U128* and *U552* – were moved towards the Cape Verde Islands, and Freetown was abandoned until April 1943. German intelligence had highlighted central African harbours being used by high concentrations of shipping, Britain and American transportation of heavy military materiel running through Massabi and Pointe Noire, Congo, up towards Leopoldville and Brazzaville and then following the Nile to North Africa. Dönitz sent *U161* and *U126* to the Congo Delta. Bauer's *U126* was damaged by depth charges while attempting to attack a small convoy south of Liberia after sighted by USAAF aircraft from newly established Liberian airbase Robertsfield, which effectively covered the 'waist' of the Atlantic.

Neither U-boat found anything off the Congo, though *U161* damaged cruiser HMS *Phoebe* before they were moved to the Gulf of Guinea for a similarly frustrating patrol near Lagos and Takoradi, glittering phosphorescence betraying their presence and leading to repeated depth charging. Between them they sank four ships in heavy seas and strong currents, before granted permission to head for Brazil where they achieved little. It was a dismal return for nearly four months at sea.

Within the North Atlantic, U-boat groups continued hunting convoy traffic with varying success. In late October SC107 and SL125 suffered particularly heavy losses to the 'Veilchen' and 'Streitaxt' groups off Greenland and West Africa respectively, though the latter battle would have unforeseen consequences for the North African land war. This five-day battle pitted 'Streitaxt' against a convoy with reduced corvette escort, destroying 12 merchant ships totalling 80,005 tons, but drawing U-boats stationed off Morocco gradually south until aircraft forced the action broken off on the last day of October.

Within the Mediterranean, U-boats had achieved some measure of success during 1942, beginning the year by sinking two British destroyers through intensified patrolling around Alexandria. The accidental torpedoing on 7 April of hospital ship *Somersetshire* by *U453* led to official German denials, and, as in the case of *Athenia*, the U-boat's War Diary altered accordingly. Minelaying and the shelling of shore targets within the eastern Mediterranean dominated the months that followed.

Incoming U-boat commanders found that tactics normally applied within the Atlantic could not be used in the Mediterranean. Wide-ranging patrols were narrowed to an allocated restricted operational area, U-boats acting at the commanding officer's discretion, frequently waiting submerged and listening with hydrophones for any approaching target. While surfaced, the large bow wave created on frequently calm water rendered them easily detectable, as did clear water and generally lighter nights.

During May, the Mediterranean boats were amalgamated and 23rd U-Flotilla dissolved, everything now controlled by 29th

U-Flotilla under new commander Fritz Frauenheim. Victor Oehrn transferred from Rome to Libya as Axis forces concentrated on what they perceived to be their final push to the Suez Canal, assigned to Kesselring's staff and effectively replaced by Georg Schewe as FdU after his departure from *U105*.* Malta was being relentlessly bombarded, though cancellation of its invasion was a serious German strategic error. On 20 June, Tobruk fell to the Afrika Korps and Rommel captured huge amounts of fuel and supplies as FdU Italy ordered attacks on Allied troopships and supply traffic from Syria and Palestine destined for Egypt. Thirteen ships were sunk during that month, and on land Rommel appeared on the brink of victory as the British constructed their last defence at El Alamein only 40 miles from the British bastion at Alexandria. Admiral Harwood ordered the Royal Navy to temporarily evacuate the Alexandrian naval base, ships retreating to Beirut, Haifa and Port Said, losing 14,650-ton submarine depot ship HMS *Medway*, stocked with spare parts and torpedoes, to *U372* on 30 June. Many small freighters and sailing vessels used as supply transports were sunk by artillery and torpedo within the eastern Mediterranean.

As the land war fought itself to a standstill at El Alamein, an all-out effort to resupply Malta via Operation *Pedestal* was mounted by the Admiralty, and 14 heavily escorted merchants carrying fuel, ammunition and food battered their way through air attack and 21 Axis submarines, three of them German. Helmut Rosenbaum's *U73* sighted escorting 'Force Z' and attacked on 11 August, sinking carrier HMS *Eagle* with a full bow salvo at only 500 metres' range. Two officers, 158 ratings and 16 Hurricanes bound for Malta were lost, but despite this and heavy casualties elsewhere, five of *Pedestal's* merchant ships reached Malta and the island revived once more.

A 'decoy' convoy simultaneously sailing from Alexandria as Operation *Drover* suffered troopships *Princess Marguerite* lost to *U83* with 55 British soldiers and five crew killed. In return, *U372* was sunk and *U97* and *U83* severely damaged by depth charges

---

* Oehrn was badly wounded and captured after Australian troops attacked his vehicle as he travelled towards Rommel's headquarters. He was repatriated to Germany by the Red Cross in November 1943.

and aerial bombing. Within the Aegean, *U565* was also severely damaged by aircraft attack.

On the night of 30 August, Rommel launched his offensive against Alam Halfa. Facing him were extensive minefields and a reshaped British Eighth Army now under the command of General Bernard Montgomery. More damning than all, his enemies knew intimate details of his plan, as the Luftwaffe Enigma network through which Rommel reported to his commander Kesselring had long been compromised. After intense fighting, by 3 September Rommel was forced to withdraw, his last grasp for victory now over and the long retreat to Tunisia soon to begin. Despite U-boats within the eastern Mediterranean given freedom to act at will, they achieved little and had no direct influence on the fighting ashore.

By the beginning of October, seven U-boats had been lost within the Mediterranean during 1942 and reinforcements were requested; group *'Tümmler'* was formed of *U438, U660, U605, U89, U593* and *U458* to pass through the Strait during the mid-October new moon period. Both *U89* and *U438* were prevented from making their attempt after failure of their Metox gear, the remainder passing through without difficulty and headed for La Spezia.

On the last day of October, the U-boat service suffered one of its most catastrophic losses when Hans Heidtmann's *U559* was sunk northeast of Port Said. Detected while surfaced in early morning darkness by radar-equipped Sunderland 'W' from 201 Squadron, Heidtmann dived while the Sunderland directed HMS *Hero* to the scene. Destroyers HMS *Petard, Pakenham, Dulverton* and *Hurworth* sailed from Port Said, as Wellesley 'F' from 47 Squadron spotted *U559*'s periscope and the shadow of a submerged U-boat. The Wellesley dropped flares and three depth charges before destroyers took over and hunted *U559* for ten hours, inflicting such severe damage that Heidtmann was forced to surface and attempt to run under cover of the night.

As soon as the conning tower emerged, it was raked with 20mm and 40mm anti-aircraft guns, too close for HMS *Hurworth* and *Petard* to depress their main weapons. Several bodies were seen to pitch over the side, probably including Heidtmann, and the crew opened seacocks to scuttle and began to abandon ship. In panicked confusion, the radiomen neglected to destroy the Enigma or codebooks, and *Petard*'s captain Mark Thornton, who obsessed over capturing a U-boat and its code books, immediately saw the potential to board, bringing his destroyer alongside as men jumped on to *U559*, attempting to secure lines to the stricken U-boat. Whalers being lowered for boarding parties became enmeshed in struggling German survivors, and *Petard*'s executive officer Lieutenant Tony Fasson leapt aboard *U559*, followed by Able Seaman Colin Grazier and NAAFI Canteen Assistant Thomas Brown.* The three entered the flooding boat and began ransacking Heidtmann's 'cabin' and the radio room, passing secret documents written in water soluble ink to Brown who in turn passed them to waiting hands outside as ASDIC operator Ken Lacroix joined them. With *U559* rapidly sinking, Brown and Lacroix narrowly escaped as the boat suddenly disappeared underwater, both Grazier and Fasson last seen trying to climb the control room ladder.†

As 41 of the 48-man crew were captured, the haul of material was soon found to include the new short signal code book for sending weather reports and another for reporting tactical information to FdU Italy. Though the short signal code book did not immediately help break the *Triton* Enigma cypher, it did provide 'cribs' – a part of the plain text which is known to correspond with a part of the code – by which Bletchley Park cryptographers began to decipher messages. On 13 December, their breakthrough arrived when they discovered that short signals were sent using only three of the new Enigma's four rotors, and therefore were able to be broken with existing knowledge. By extension, the fourth rotor settings for other messages could be deduced, leading to penetration of *Triton*

---

* The 'Navy, Army and Air Force Institutes' (NAAFI) was a company formed by the British government in 1920 to service recreational needs and sell goods to British service personnel.

† The two were posthumously awarded the George Cross, although the significance of their actions would remain secret for decades. Fifteen-year-old Brown was awarded the George Medal for his part in the action, discharged from the service after having lied about his age.

and the end of the Ultra blackout that had lasted for most of 1942. Although patchy in their ability to read *Triton* in a timely and effective manner – it would take until August 1943 for *Triton* to be completely mastered by the combined powers of Bletchley Park and US Navy cryptanalysts – a corner had been definitively turned.

On 24 October, Montgomery opened his El Alamein battle with a thunderous artillery barrage. Able to build up overwhelming material superiority – facing Rommel's last 32 operational panzers – the British launched Operation *Supercharge* on 2 November and surged out of the Alamein line. Two days later, OKM ordered more U-boats sent to the Mediterranean and a hurriedly created '*Delphin*' group of seven boats passed Gibraltar between 8 and 10 November, bringing Mediterranean strength up to 25. Envisioning clashes against major surface warships and troop transports, Dönitz also ordered the first of the new magnetic firing pistols, the Pi39H (Pi2), despatched directly to La Spezia and Pola from Germany. Also effective as a contact detonator, it was finally declared operational in connection with an improved G7e torpedo (TIII). Between January and June 1942, Dönitz recorded that it had taken 816 contact-fused torpedoes to sink 404 ships. By reintroducing a magnetic detonator capable of sinking a ship with a single explosion, he reasoned, it would equate to doubling a U-boat's torpedo load.

Furthermore, a newly developed pattern-running steering unit – the *Feldapparat*, or FAT – for the G7a was also shipped as priority over Atlantic ports. This device permitted the torpedo to make a programmable left or right turn after an adjustable-length straight run from the firing-boat. Theoretically, the G7a FAT stood a greater chance of hitting another ship if fired at a convoy and missing the intended target. Due to the slight bubble wake left by the steam torpedo, it was intended only for use at night and required minor modification to torpedo tubes.

Further torpedo developments continued slowly via the understaffed and overtasked TVA. The desire for an acoustic homing torpedo had resulted in the G7es *Falke* (TIV) for use against merchant ships. Unsuitable for tropical use due to battery degradation, the *Falke* carried a sound-detection receiver mounted in the nose, reducing the warhead to 274kg of explosive. Suitable against deep-draught merchants ideally moving between 7 and 13 knots, the *Falke* was contact fused and had a range of 7 kilometres at the relatively low speed of 20 knots. While produced during 1942, it would not see operational test use until February 1943.

The issue of battling escorts had become a major point of concern to Dönitz, expressed on 28 September in conference with Hitler and naval leaders at the Reich Chancellery. Convoy protection was now extremely strong and ranged from an inner screen held closely around the convoy and a distant screen which complicated U-boat approach, these warships capable of undertaking protracted hunts on contacts. The Type 271 radar had become widely distributed and ASW weaponry improved, including the forward-throwing spigot mortar 'Hedgehog', though crews seemed reluctant to use it.

The spigot mortar mounted the propellant charge as part of the main weapon rather than the projectile, the force of the explosive working against a spigot, which fitted inside a tubular tail of the bomb. Hedgehog's 24 bombs, armed with a 16kg Torpex warhead, were fired in a staggered series of six, each in an arc that was designed to land all 24 projectiles simultaneously in an elliptical area approximately 30 metres in diameter at a fixed range before the ship's bow. It possessed several advantages over depth charges: first, the target could be held by ASDIC throughout the attack; second, target depth was irrelevant; third, one direct hit by a Hedgehog bomb could rupture a U-boat's hull; lastly, there was no warning of it being deployed.

Hedgehog use was actively pushed by the Admiralty during November as 'it is vital that more U-boats should be destroyed as opposed to damaged... present ammunition should give 50 per cent probability of killing per attack... compared with 18 per cent for a full 14-depth charge pattern.'[4] Commanders were then specifically warned that they would have to explain why, if the Hedgehog was not used at the outset of engaging a submarine contact.

However, the weapon was not without limitations, and in the same year that it had been issued, the improved 'Squid' was rushed into service. This was a three-barrelled 12-inch mortar, the barrels mounted in a laterally staggered series to spread projectiles, the frame mount rotatable through 90 degrees for loading. Most 'Squids' were mounted in pairs aboard ship, all six bombs fired in salvo with settings directly transmitted from the ASDIC range recorder. Fired at the moment calculated to achieve optimal success, the weapon fulfilled the true potential of sonar as a U-boat killer as ASDIC 'programmed' a clockwork fuse to detonate the explosive at the correct depth. Three projectiles could form a destructive triangle at a range of 250 metres before the ship, and with two weapons firing, the opposing triangular spreads set to detonate above and below the target could create a pressure wave capable of crushing a U-boat's hull.

Dönitz desired creation of an anti-escort weapon and initially favoured a remotely controlled rocket, though Hitler warned against optimism with such projectiles given relatively unsuccessful army and Luftwaffe experiments in that field. Instead, the acoustic-homing G7es *Zaunkönig* (TV) torpedo would be used; tuned to home on the higher pitched propellor cavitation created by warships, it was not ready for operational use until the tail end of 1943. Even then, it possessed certain flaws that would both inflate reported successes and render it a danger to the firing U-boat as well as its target.

Furthermore, Allied intelligence were already aware of *Zaunkönig* and a relatively simple decoy being developed. The 'Foxer' comprised one or more hollow metal pipes with holes cut along their length. Dragged 200 metres or so behind the ship, the water rushing through the holes – plus the pipes themselves banging together – created noise akin to propeller cavitation, at least 20 decibels higher than the towing ship and frequently likened by U-boat crews to the noise of a circular saw.

This was still in the distant future when the Allied armada of Operation *Torch* began unloading troops in northwest Africa on the morning of 8 November, amphibious landings near Casablanca, Oran and Algiers intending to advance east into the Afrika Korps' rear. In a dramatic German intelligence failure, the massed shipping was believed yet another attempt at supplying Malta. Somewhat ironically, the five-day battle by U-boat group *'Streitaxt'* against SL125 drew the U-boats covering Morocco into concentrated action and away to the south, leaving the coastal approach unguarded. Suspicion remains to this day that SL125 was intended to lure 'Streitaxt' away from Gibraltar; the group was formed in response to agent reports of massed Gibraltar shipping, and SL125 sailing while other south Atlantic convoys were suspended due to escorts re-tasked with *Torch*. This point of view was somewhat reinforced by the post-war recollection of Convoy Commodore Sir Cecil Reyne that it was the 'only time I have been congratulated for losing ships'. Similarly, the fast convoy RB1 – codenamed 'Maniac' – comprised of Great Lakes steamers that sailed for Britain in late September, is frequently cited as a decoy from shipping carrying men and materiel for the *Torch* build up; RB1 was intercepted by U-boats in the North Atlantic and lost three steamers and one of the escorting destroyers, HMS *Veteran*. The high superstructures of the steamers led to misidentification as troopships, U-boats claiming four times their actual tonnage sunk in the action.

On the morning that *Torch* began, Dönitz ordered all boats between Biscay and the Cape Verde Islands to head at speed for the Moroccan coast, soon extended to include all U-boats west of Ireland possessing sufficient fuel. The landings were unopposed by U-boat, *U572* arriving on 9 November but failing to penetrate protective destroyer screens.[*] Not until two nights later did Hans-Adolf Schweichel's *U173* fire torpedoes towards ships near Casablanca, damaging a tanker and destroyer and sinking troop transport USS *Joseph Hewes*, completely unloaded and just having taken aboard 30 wounded men, destroyed with the loss of 100 lives. Schweichel attempted a fresh attack in the same area on 15 November and damaged freighter USS *Electra* before being detected by American destroyers and sunk with all hands by depth charges. Ernst Kals in *U130* achieved the greatest success against this anchorage in the Fedala roadstead when he crept inshore in extremely shallow water to launch five torpedoes, sinking three troop transports, the

---

[*] *U572*'s commander, Heinz Hirsacker, was later denounced by his officers and court martialed for cowardice, shooting himself using a pistol smuggled to him in prison on 24 April 1943.

Allies moving their ships to more easily defended ports. In total, 25 U-boats had been rushed to the area, sinking 11 ships and losing three of their own, with six more U-boats heavily damaged.

Within the Western Mediterranean, nine U-boats were immediately available to the regional FdU Italy command, which deployed them in consecutive defensive lines. Pressure on BdU to send further reinforcements after 'Delphin' was successfully resisted, and the U-boats were spread between Algiers and Oran, sinking in total eight ships, two of them destroyers and two troopships. Italian submarines had accounted for only four ships sunk or damaged. Among the Mediterranean U-boats, Albrecht Brandi aboard *U617* proved to be the most 'optimistic' commander, claiming to have sunk two steamers, one destroyer, a cruiser and a battleship, when in fact he had hit nothing at all. He would later become one of the two most highly decorated Kriegsmarine officers of the war.* In return, six Mediterranean U-boats were forced to abort with heavy damage, another lightly damaged; *U77* was incorrectly claimed as the first Hedgehog kill achieved by the Royal Navy after corvettes HMS *Lotus* and *Poppy* hunted Otto Hartmann's boat northeast of Algiers. *Lotus* launched its Hedgehog barrage following five depth-charge attacks, observing underwater explosions after which the contact disappeared, Hartmann successfully creeping away. Five U-boats were sunk, the last of them being von Tiesenhausen's *U331*, the captain and 16 survivors captured. The invasion was not impeded at all. Despite Dönitz's continuing objections, four further reinforcements would be sent during December, with one aborting and one damaged, the remaining two passing safely past Gibraltar.

Wasting their time and extremely vulnerable to enemy air and sea forces, U-boats near the Moroccan Atlantic coast were withdrawn west of the Azores to lie in wait for UGS supply convoys (from

---

* At his award of the Diamonds, to his Swords and Oak Leaves to the Knight's Cross, he was officially credited with having sunk 20 ships of 115,000 tons as well as three cruisers and 12 destroyers. Mediterranean sinkings were effectively 'doubled' for award purposes, and extra credit for warships put him over a theoretical 200,000 tons for this prestigious honour. In reality, he sank eight merchant ships, totaling 25,879 tons, a steam tug, cruiser minelayer and two destroyers.

the United States to Gibraltar) carrying equipment bound for North Africa. There they formed the *'Westwall'* group strung in a north-south patrol line. Five refuelled from the Type XB *U118*, but although U-tankers vastly improved Atlantic U-boat capabilities, the practicalities of refuelling in increasingly bad weather had barely figured in BdU estimations. Awaiting conditions enabling refuelling, several U-boats were forced to ride out storms with engines shut down and electric current conserved, leaving men shivering within icy hulls without heating or the ability to cook hot food.

A scattering of ships were sunk both approaching and leaving Gibraltar, including the carrier HMS *Avenger* by *U155*, going under in less than two minutes with 514 of its 526 crew killed. *U98* was lost to destroyer HMS *Wrestler* before *'Westwall'* was pulled further back into the North Atlantic during early December, encountering dispersed ships from ON149 and sinking four in atrocious weather; a total of 892 people were killed and only two survivors from all four ships taken aboard the attacking U-boats. With no further convoy traffic found and B-Dienst revealing shipping routes beyond available fuel range, SKL ordered a reluctant Dönitz to draw *'Westwall'* back towards Spain where further fruitless patrolling finally ended with the group's dissolution.

Somewhat ironically, given the predictably poor results against *Torch*, November 1942 yielded the highest sinking figures of the year, thanks in equal parts to the resumption of Atlantic convoy hunting and, particularly, long-distance operations off Canada, South Africa, Freetown, Brazil and Trinidad. As well as ten enemy warships, U-boats sank 113 merchants for 732,884 tons (only 30 per cent of which was from protected convoys) – the highest cumulative tonnage total of the war – leading Dönitz to wonder what could have been achieved within the North Atlantic if U-boats had been allowed to remain rather than despatched on a futile race to support the North African front.[5] Despite Hitler's exhortation to U-boat men that 'the fate of the Afrika Korps rests in your hands, I expect a completely victorious operation', the catastrophe in North Africa was beyond Kriegsmarine help.

Tonnage sunk fell dramatically during December to less than half that of the previous month, due to the cessation of many long-distance patrols and return for long periods of rest and refit; even those that had refuelled from tankers were reaching the end of their endurance. Regardless, convoy ONS154 still suffered heavy casualties when attacked by a total of 19 U-boats. The Canadian escorts of one destroyer and five corvettes were swamped by the massed assault and sank only *U356* in return. Although equipped with Type 271 centimetric radar, most of the operators were inexperienced at handling the equipment and the escort group had not trained as a unit or achieved any real cohesion. Nevertheless, a major technological step forward, centimetric radar enabled detection of small objects and used smaller antennas than earlier lower frequency radars, perfect for use aboard aircraft once a suitable receiver had been designed.

There is a caveat to the U-boats' seemingly victorious months of November and December. If we study in isolation Dönitz's pivotal point of his tonnage war – the North Atlantic – we find that during this period, the Allies sailed 1,218 merchant ships in 31 convoys headed both east and west. From these, 627 ships were fully loaded and heading for Great Britain, and only three of these were sunk by U-boats. Of the 591 ships sailing west empty, 31 were sunk. In return, though Allied forces recorded a particularly low number of U-boats sunk in the North Atlantic – only five out of 18 lost in all theatres – from those five, only ten men survived to be captured, the remaining 357 lost in action.

At the outset of war, BdU had estimated that 300,000 tons of British shipping needed to be sunk monthly to overwhelm Britain's merchant shipping fleet, a number achieved only four times: June and October 1940 and May and June 1941. With America's entry into the war, this number rose to a 700,000-ton target that was met only once in November 1942. As time passed and the United States' prodigious shipping output became apparent, BdU's estimation rose to 900,000 tons per month. Dönitz had lost the race.

Chapter Nine

Tipping Point

*'The U-boat was firing away merrily… the CO asked: "How do
I attack this thing?"'*
  Flight Lieutenant Jim Paine, 500 Squadron, RAF, attacking
U595[1]

January 1943 opened with Britain facing a perceived shipping
crisis. Cumulatively, North Atlantic merchant ship losses during
1942 amounted to 5,471,222 tons, nearly three-quarters of the
total from every theatre. The number of available ocean escort ships
remained in deficit, and demands worldwide on British shipping
ran at an all-time high. However, thanks to intense building
programmes, particularly within the United States, when newly
built tonnage was considered, the net loss to the Allies was reduced
to 700,000 tons and during the second half of 1942 became net
gains to merchant tonnage. Despite perception of a developing
oil crisis within Great Britain caused by tanker losses, the country
maintained healthy reserves, and Dönitz had yet to once reach his
stated monthly tonnage destroyed – 900,000-tons – to strike a
mortal blow.

Among the ambitious building programmes, United States
shipyards were churning out a new class of freighter known
as a 'Liberty ship' that had originated from British requests but
harmonized with American production methods. A standardized
design, each ship displaced in the order of 14,474 tons, constructed

in sections then welded together. In total 2,710 Liberty ships were built between 1941 and 1945, averaging three new ships every two days, although a publicity stunt in a California shipyard saw the *Robert E. Peary* built (though not 'finished') in four days, 15½ hours.

In the North Atlantic the few U-boats in action repeatedly failed to find convoy traffic in appalling weather and dogged by bad radio reception near Greenland. Refuelling was frequently delayed, and diesel consumption rose battling the heavy seas. Isolated vessels were chanced upon and sunk as Dönitz blamed the lack of experience aboard many boats for their inability to fully interpret hydrophone information – illustrated when *U201*, under new commander Günther Rosenberg, chased a school of whales for several hours.*

Further south within the Central Atlantic, TM1 of nine tankers bound from Trinidad to North Africa with the thin protection of one destroyer and three corvettes (British Escort Group B5) was sighted by Hans-Jürgen Auffermann's *U514* on 3 January. Approximately 900 miles east, a group of six Type VIICs (*'Delphin'*) travelling to Brazil to operate inshore along the coast, supported by refuelling from *U463*, was ordered to close on TM1 as *U514* shadowed. That night Auffermann torpedoed and damaged 8,093-ton *British Vigilance*, which was set aflame and abandoned, the drifting wreck sunk by *U105* three weeks later. With *'Delphin'* reinforced by every U-boat available, the Admiralty U-boat tracking room provided diversion information for TM1 which was ignored, and the convoy ran headlong into the approaching U-boat line on 8 January. During a struggle that lasted for the next two nights, six of the remaining eight tankers were sunk: *Generaloberst* Hans-Jürgen von Arnim, commander of the 5th Panzer Army in Tunisia, sent his personal congratulations to Dönitz for their contribution to the Tunisian front.

The battle was a resounding German victory, though the faster TMF1 and TMF2 oil convoys reached Gibraltar intact. The

---

* Adi Schnee, *U201*'s previous captain, had gone ashore in August 1942 after the award of his Oak Leaves, joining BdU Staff until taking command of the Type XXI *U2511* in September 1944.

unexpected action had also altered planned U-boat dispositions, Brazil cancelled for the expanded *'Delphin'* group, instead hunting further traffic to North Africa, with two U-boats bound for the West Indies folded into its strength. Furthermore, *U511*, most recently involved in a renewed attack on Cape Town, was forced to return through fuel shortage.

Following the success of *'Eisbär'*, Dönitz planned another foray in the same vein to South Africa using Type IXCs. The only available IXD-2 cruisers were already engaged within the Indian Ocean, and by refuelling within the South Atlantic, the new group, *'Seehund'*, would arrive as winter storms subsided. A single Type IXD-2, *U182*, did become operational in time to join *'Seehund'* and was in fact the first to depart port, leaving Horten, Norway, on 9 December before becoming embroiled in the *'Delphin'* group battle. Staggered over the following three weeks, *U506*, *U509*, *U511* and *U516* departed for Cape Town, supported by U-tanker *U459* positioned 600 miles south of St Helena. Following *U511*'s departure, veteran Georg Lassen's *U160* was added to *'Seehund'*, receiving orders while refuelling from *U459* on 4 February, later joined by Clausen's *U182*.

However, the situation around the Cape had changed dramatically. Instead of independently sailing merchants, there were tightly knit and heavily defended convoys, often hugging the coastline, benefiting from land-based radar and direction-finding posts, and shadowed by highly effective RAF and SAAF air patrols. With *Triton* now compromised and *'Seehund'* revealed, successes were slim, the most dramatic made by *U160* when it attacked DN21 and sank four ships and damaged another two; the first convoy to be hit by U-boat directly south of Durban. Despite this, the results of *'Seehund'* were relatively meagre for the distance covered and time taken. Seventeen ships were confirmed sunk, totalling 100,577 tons, with a further three damaged. Moreover, both *U506* and *U509* each sank only two ships during nearly five months at sea.

'Seehund' began returning during April. Clausen's *U182* had sunk four ships before setting course for France, torpedoing another on 1 May and taking its captain prisoner. Two weeks later, *U182* was bombed west of Madeira by a USAAF B24, four depth charges

straddling the diving boat and an oil slick observed in the water. During early morning darkness of the following day, destroyer USS *MacKenzie*, escorting LSTs of UGS8 from the United States to Gibraltar, made radar contact at a range of 7,330 yards. The suspected U-boat dived and *MacKenzie* obtained a solid trace on a submerged U-boat. During two attacks, eight Mk VII depth charges were dropped; an underwater explosion was detected but no other hint of *U182*, which went to the bottom with all 61 men aboard.

Between January and the time of Clausen's death, the nature of the U-boat war, and indeed that of the Wehrmacht in all theatres, had changed completely. On land, disaster had overtaken the Wehrmacht when the surrounded Sixth Army surrendered at Stalingrad on 2 February and the battered remains of North African Axis forces in Tunisia on 13 May. Already during March, with the strategic situation on the Eastern Front much changed and the Middle East secure, the Admiralty had suspended Arctic convoys as long days of summer approached, plentiful supplies flowing into southern Russia via the Persian Gulf.

A disastrous Operation *Regenbogen* of Kriegsmarine surface ships failing to attack convoy JW51B of the resumed Arctic route resulted in a fit of apoplectic rage from Adolf Hitler and demands that Germany's surface fleet be scrapped and the guns used ashore. Within days, *Grossadmiral* Raeder resigned in protest, and Dönitz was promoted to fill the vacant position of naval commander-in-chief on 30 January. There was a certain irony regarding Dönitz's accession of the throne of command, as just the previous December, Viktor Schütze, former *U103* commander then senior officer of the 2nd U-Flotilla, had confided in Albert Speer that serious dissension between BdU and OKM portended the likelihood of Dönitz being relieved of his command. Indeed, Speer had also discovered from State Secretary Werner Naumann of Goebbels' Propaganda Ministry that the navy censor had stricken Dönitz's name from all captions given to photographs of a recent inspection tour undertaken by Dönitz and Raeder.

Retaining the post of BdU, once again headquarters was relocated, now within a combined building and bunker complex near

Bernau, named *Koralle*, staff officers occupying the nearby Hotel am Steinplatz and the new headquarters operational by 31 March. On the other side of the hill, during January 1943 Churchill and Roosevelt convened the SYMBOL conference at Casablanca to plan the conduct of the war during 1943. They agreed several key principles, prioritizing 'defeat of the U-boat must remain a first charge on the resources of the united nations.'[2] The most salient points agreed were that escorting North Atlantic convoys would become the sole responsibility of British and Canadian navies, the middle Atlantic bound to and from Gibraltar would become the American domain, and modified USAAF B24 very long range (VLR) aircraft would be added to those forces already used to patrol the North Atlantic, thereby plugging the Greenland air gap until escort carriers became available, with British B24s from Ireland and Iceland covering the eastern portion of the gap.

A brief skirmish with convoy HX224 by five U-boats not yet formed into a tactical group resulted in three ships sunk, Hans Karpf taking the sole survivor, Chief Engineer I.C. Bingham, from his heavily laden victim *Cordelia* aboard as a prisoner. Unfortunately, Bingham revealed a large convoy following close behind, and 20 U-boats were hastily grouped to intercept the 61 merchant ships of SC118 escorted by British escort group B2, later reinforced by land-based aircraft and American warships. The convoy was confirmed in Berlin, where B-Dienst had again penetrated Naval Cypher No. 3 and a steady flow of signals intelligence regarding Atlantic shipping was operationally available to BdU until May.

After passing through days of gale force winds and still riding a Force 5 on the night of 4 February, the bridge watch aboard *U187* were startled to see a burst of 'Very lights' to port, the result of the carelessly discharged Snowflake rocket by a seaman aboard Norwegian freighter *Annik*. Closing rapidly, mastheads and smoke from SC118 were sighted and three radioed contact reports despatched as *U187* positioned itself ahead of the convoy track. Aboard the convoy's rescue ship *Toward*, HF/DF operators reported the signals and triangulated them with USS *Bibb*, allowing destroyers HMS *Vimy* and *Beverley* to attack at speeds high enough to surprise the surfaced U-boat, a brief attempt to run cancelled by diving and subsequent destruction by depth charges.

They were the opening salvoes of what Dönitz later described as 'perhaps the hardest convoy battle of the whole war'.³ The first straggling ship sunk was 5,376-ton American *West Portal*, torpedoed by *U413* on 5 February; the last was 9,2762-ton Norwegian *Daghild* in early morning darkness of 8 February, torpedoed by *U608* after already being damaged and abandoned.* Twelve ships were sunk, seven of them by Siegfried Freiherr von Forstner's *U402*, among them the rescue ship *Toward* and troop transport *Henry R. Mallory*, with 272 men killed. In return *U187*, *U609* and *U624* were destroyed (*U624* by a British B17 aircraft) and four other U-boats heavily damaged. The interrogation of the 45 survivors from 26-year-old Ralph Münnich's *U187* – on its first patrol and sunk by depth charges from destroyers HMS *Vimy* and *Beverley* – makes for harrowing reading:

In *U187* a second series of explosions was heard rather nearer than the first. Prisoners said that no appreciable damage was done, but *U187* was trimming badly and that whenever she lay on an even keel she tended to rise. Because of all this all the crew who could be spared from action stations were sent forward to the bow compartment. Here they appear to have become alarmed, for *Leutnant zur See* Rudolf Strait stated that he was sent forward to calm the men. One of his actions was apparently to disconnect the depth gauge in this compartment... a third depth-charge pattern fell fairly near the U-Boat and caused the first major damage. Lights failed in the listening room and in the conning-tower... The *Funkmaat* [telegraphist] prisoner stated that throughout these attacks he had been on duty in the listening room. Each time he had reported; 'Run in beginning. Alter course'; Münnich had said, 'Yes', but had kept the U-Boat

---

* This ship carried 13,000 tons of diesel and a deck cargo of aircraft, barges and the British landing craft HMS *LCT-2335*, the latter generally added to shipping casualties from this convoy.

on the same course, except for a slight alteration after the second attack.

Prior to the fourth and last depth-charge attack the noise of two destroyers was picked up on the hydrophones, one bearing 000° and the other 180°. The *Funkmaat* prisoner said that he realized at once that their position was desperate. He reported: 'Run is beginning'; and commented, 'If we don't alter course now it's all up.' This time his anxiety was shared by the Junior Officer who suddenly flung down his earphones and dashed out of the listening room white in the face. A prisoner described the explosion of this series as 'like the roar of an avalanche.' It was believed by many survivors that some depth-charges actually exploded on the outer casing. Lights failed in all compartments forward of the control room, but not aft. The gyro-compass was wrecked. A fracture 4ft long and ½in wide was caused in the pressure hull aft, and the U-Boat becoming stern heavy, inclined at an angle of at least 45°. In addition, the port side of the control room was stove in and oil from a port fuel tank cascaded into the boat, swamping the batteries generating dense fumes. At this moment Meyer, the Engineering Officer, told Münnich that their position was hopeless and they must surface at once if anyone was to escape alive. The U-Boat laboured slowly upwards, while the calmer members of the ship's company convinced that their end was near, solemnly shook hands in farewell. Prisoners estimated that *U187* took five minutes to surface and, they added, that when she finally emerged most of their air was exhausted. No order to abandon ship reached the bow compartment but Strait led the men there through the galley hatch. Simultaneously, the remainder were leaving through the control room hatch. Once on the upper deck a number of ratings clustered round the 105mm gun for support, others misguidedly attempting to clear the gun away. This caused fire to be opened upon them from the destroyers then about 600 yards distant. Confusion reigned for some seconds until a wave swept those on deck into the water. No clear account as to the fate of Münnich or Meyer has been forthcoming. According to one prisoner he last saw Meyer hustling men up the conning-tower hatch and he believed that he stayed within the U-Boat. Münnich has been variously described as shooting himself, and as standing on the conning-tower as the U-Boat went down for the last time.[4]

As U-boat groups, supported by refuelling from U-tankers, formed and dissolved, ONS165 was located in gales by *U69*, which engaged alongside *U201* before both veteran boats were sunk with all hands by escorting destroyers. The Luftwaffe Signals Regiment in Paris next detected DF bearings on escorting aircraft for ON166, and the groups *'Neptun'* and *'Ritter'* deployed to cover the convoy track. Their movements betrayed by Ultra, ON166 was rerouted, these radioed instructions in turn decoded by B-Dienst; ten U-boats of *'Ritter'*, four from *'Knappen'* to the southeast and five more arriving on station, counter-moved to lie in wait, *U604* making contact at midday, 20 February. The sprawling battle over 1,100 miles of ocean lasted for five days and claimed 14 merchant ships sunk – the largest number of 1943 – totalling 88,001 tons destroyed for the loss of *U606*, depth charged by USCGC *Campbell* and the Polish destroyer *Burza*. Simultaneously, Adolf Graef's outbound *U664* found ONS167 150 miles to the east, unable to summon other boats but sinking two merchants before losing contact; group *'Wildfang'* quickly formed to relocate the convoy but failed to do so.

Operations against Mediterranean-bound convoys had failed to achieve significant results. As six long-distance Type IXC boats were assembled near the Azores, initially bound for the United States, they were formed into the *'Unverzagt'* group to lie in wait for UGS6 – 43 laden merchants under escort by several brand new US Navy Fleet destroyers. *U130*, under new commander Siegfried Keller after Ernst Kals had moved ashore to take charge of Lorient's 2nd U-Flotilla, sighted the oncoming merchants on 12 March and began shadowing, transmitting the required beacon signals. All the American destroyers possessed new centimetric radar impervious to Metox detection, which operated only on the 1.5-metre waveband, centimetric radar capable of showing something as small as a periscope. Surfaced *U130* was detected by USS *Champlin* in the darkness and surprised, crash diving and depth charged, going to the bottom with all 53 men aboard. As Dönitz despatched reinforcements, the American escort aggressively repulsed attacks, though two steamers were lost to Emmermann's *U172* and another damaged before the U-boats called off.

Remote patrols to Freetown, America, the Gulf of Mexico and the Caribbean achieved only minor successes during this period. Three U-boats patrolled east of the Lesser Antilles, including Caribbean veteran Werner Hartenstein's *U156*, which was hounded by aircraft. He radioed disquieting news for BdU during the night of 5 March: 'Off the Port of Spain as far as Grenada very strong continuous air activity with a new type of location which cannot be picked up by Metox – precise attacks without search lights. Convoys sail to and from Testigos. Operations there impossible.'[5] His transmission triangulated by American shore stations, *U156* was detected surfaced by a radar-equipped Catalina of Trinidad's VP-53 on the afternoon of 7 March, dropping out of cloud cover and machine-gunning what appears to have been a considerable number of men on deck, probably effecting repairs. Four depth charges sank *U156*, Lieutenant John Dryden circling his Catalina to drop a life raft to 11 men, including 'an officer in a white shirt' and radioing their position to his home airfield. They were never found.

Operations against America were becoming 'hopeless' in the face of Allied air superiority, in the words of Albrecht Achilles after *U161* returned from an 87-day patrol in which it had sunk only one small Canadian yacht. Several veteran U-boats were despatched to the region during March, achieving little. Joachim Mohr's *U124* chanced upon convoy OS45 headed to Sierra Leone while outbound, independently attacking as the only U-boat within range and sinking two heavily loaded freighters. Detected by centimetric radar aboard HMS *Black Swan*, *U124* was surprised while surfaced and depth charged into oblivion with all hands after a hasty crash dive. The fourth most successful U-boat of the war was gone.

Nevertheless, despite intensifying Allied bombing of Germany, U-boat production figures actually rose under the guidance of Albert Speer as Armaments Minister and with Dönitz as commander-in-chief of the navy. An increasing number of operational U-boats within the North Atlantic finally enabled Dönitz to deploy more expansive patrol lines in search of the enemy. Distribution of operational U-boats on 1 March saw 193 deployed in the Atlantic theatre, 19 within the Mediterranean, 14 in northern waters and three in the Black Sea. It was this strength that brought the North Atlantic U-boat war to fever pitch during March: SC121 was intercepted by two groups totalling 26 U-boats and lost 14 ships, sinking only *U633* from the attackers, HX228 another six merchants, albeit with *U432* and *U444* destroyed. With fortuitous synchronicity for Dönitz and disaster for the Allies, on 10 March, U-boats changed their short weather codebooks, blacking out Ultra penetration of *Triton* once again for a period of nine days. Into this potential maelstrom came slow convoy SC122 steadily being overhauled by HX229, which had departed New York three days behind. The slow convoy was approaching two separate groups – '*Dränger*' and '*Stürmer*' – and shadowed behind by a third, '*Raubgraf*', with four more independent U-boats headed towards it. Forty-three U-boats were arrayed against a cumulative total of nearly 90 merchant ships.

HX229 had managed to slip past '*Raubgraf*' during storms but was located by homeward-bound *U653* searching for a U-tanker and which possessed only a single defective torpedo. As the boat shadowed, the two eastern groups were moved to block the convoy's path, presumed by intelligence reports to be the scheduled SC122. By dawn the following morning, eight merchants had been sunk. Later that day, the two U-boat groups approaching from the east found a 'slow section' of the convoy ahead of the main body, and it dawned on BdU that the initial contact had been HX229 and only now had SC122 been found. As the faster convoy already under attack was poised to overtake SC122 within the mid-Atlantic air gap, the distance between the two narrowed to only a few miles, presenting the gathering U-boats with a single common objective, given freedom to operate by BdU. In freshening seas, the battle was properly joined as extra escort ships raced from Iceland to the scene.

Only five U-boats managed attacks during daylight of the second day due to strong air activity from Coastal Command VLR B24s; their presence and depth-charge harassment resulted in no U-boat kills, but drove them repeatedly to dive, frustrating attempts to shadow or reach effective torpedo range. The following night was particularly bright, making it difficult for U-boats to attack, and the next day wind strengthened and drifting snowstorms produced visibility varying between 500 and 5,000 metres. At 0900hrs, *U610* regained contact with SC122 but could only maintain touch by hydrophone bearings in prevailing conditions. Nine more U-boats approached, many detected by destroyers and depth charged while daylight air cover frustrated U-boat attempts to draw ahead and lie in wait. On the battle's final day, the weather calmed and the largest commitment of air cover yet saturated the area with VLR B24s reinforced by long-range Coastal Command B17s and Sunderland flying boats. Hans-Achim von Rosenberg-Gruszcynski's *U384*, on its second patrol, was sunk with all hands by four depth charges from 206 Squadron B17 'E', straddled as it attempted to crash dive and disappearing, a spreading pool of oil marking its end.

By the time BdU broke off operations on 19 March, 22 Allied ships had been sunk, totalling 146,596 tons, for the loss of only *U384*. Taken as a single action, it remains the biggest convoy battle of the Second World War and one majorly influenced by aircraft, significantly, newly introduced VLR Liberator bombers.

Loudly trumpeted by German propaganda as an unparalleled success, the statistics of this great battle bear closer scrutiny, particularly in a broader context. Of 43 U-boats involved, only 20 fired torpedoes, of which 16 scored definite hits. From ships sunk, five had already been hit and damaged. For the Allies, in terms of tonnage sunk, HX229 was the second greatest loss of any single convoy, and only developing winds near hurricane force prevented any other North Atlantic convoys from being attacked during March. However, the story does not end with this battle.

Overlooking the terrifying fate of the men lost at sea, during the entire month of March, 16 convoys passed through the North Atlantic and U-boats managed attacks against four, sinking (in cold statistics) less than 10 per cent of merchant ships involved. A second part of HX229 – 39 merchants grouped together as HX229A that sailed one day after the main body – successfully reached Britain without mishap. Although authorities in Britain claimed March to have been a major crisis in terms of shipping and imports, the figures simply do not seem to fully support this. Sinkings in all theatres of war by *all* Axis submarines, as compiled by German historian Professor Jürgen Rohwer, amount to 110 ships totalling 635,609 tons. For Dönitz's U-boats their cumulative losses during the month were 15 (including U_5 in a training accident) from which only 49 men survived. Thus far in 1943, BdU had lost 40 U-boats.

The operational introduction of centimetric radar inflicted severe U-boat casualties. Equipping of Coastal Command aircraft was delayed due to arguments with Bomber Command over radar resources – initially planned for ground-mapping target location – but at the beginning of March a Wellington bomber of 172 Squadron flew the first day patrol equipped with the ASV Mk III over Biscay. In the United States, the centimetric ASV set designated DMS-1000 had been developed and installed on B24 Liberators, the first of them posted to Britain arriving during March 1942, though, lacking a Leigh Light, the ASV could not be fully exploited over Biscay.

The Bay of Biscay had become the focal point of much Allied anti-U-boat effort. KG40's heavy Ju 88C-6 fighters had been countered by heavily armed and manoeuvrable Beaufighters and de Havilland Mosquitoes, and Dönitz was informed by *Fliegerführer Atlantik* on 2 March that the situation had deteriorated over Biscay; effective protection for incoming and outgoing U-boats could no longer be guaranteed. For Dönitz this news could not have come at a worse time as he and his staff began to realize that Metox was incapable of detecting all enemy radar. BdU was even led to believe that radiation from Metox was being used by enemy aircraft to locate

U-boats by night, after a captured British bomber pilot planted this misinformation in his interrogators at Oberursel transit camp. Once German technicians confirmed that this was indeed a slight possibility, Metox was incorrectly viewed as the potential source of Allied success against surfaced U-boats at night and its use banned from 14 August.

On 20 March, Coastal Command's No. 19 Group launched the eight-day Operation *Enclose* in which 115 aircraft – many equipped with centimetric radar and Leigh Light – flew anti-U-boat patrols in a box area of Biscay between 7° and 10° West. Of the 41 U-boats that crossed this area, 26 were sighted and 15 attacked, with *U665* sunk and *U332* damaged. Operation *Enclose II* followed in April, with *U376* sunk and *U465* damaged, in turn followed by the expanded Operation *Derange* covering a wider search area.

Darkness no longer sheltered U-boats, and from 1 May Dönitz ordered cessation of night transit through eastern Biscay. Instead, perhaps encouraged by *U333* shooting down a Wellington during a Leigh Light attack and *U338* a Halifax aircraft in the bay during March, he ordered U-boat flak armaments reinforced and the boats to travel submerged by night and surfaced by day with anti-aircraft guns manned. By daylight, any attacker should be visible, and U-boats already equipped with suitable flak weapons would 'fight it out' as per new standing orders which came into force on 1 May 1943. Additional flak installations of the *Vierling* quad 20mm and Skoda rapid-fire 37mm cannon were rushed into production to be fitted on expanded *Wintergartens*. Deck guns, all but useless by this stage, were ordered removed from 27 April to compensate for the weight increase; only remote operating U-boats and those in the Arctic and Mediterranean were allowed to retain deck weapons if requested.

Furthermore, seven Type VIIC U-boats were to be converted into 'flak boats', designed to lure enemy aircraft into battle so as to destroy them with exceptional firepower: the so-called *Unterseebootflugzeugfalle* (submarine aircraft-trap). *U441* of Brest's 1st U-Flotilla was the first such flak boat, designated 'U-Flak 1', and as well as the usual anti-aircraft stations of the rear kiosk and *Wintergarten*, the conning tower was extended forward, providing a third weapon position. In the stern-facing *Wintergarten* was a single-barrelled 3.7cm weapon, itself positioned beneath the four barrels of a shielded 2cm quad *Flakvierling*. The forward extension carried another fearsome *Vierling*, the heavily armed U-boat sacrificing some fuel storage capacity for the increased weaponry and intended to either sail independently as a 'trap' or to escort other U-boats through Biscay.

Coastal Command's Operation *Derange* hammered U-boats crossing Biscay between 13 April and 6 June. While Leigh Light and centimetric radar-equipped aircraft ensured U-boats travelled submerged by night, by day greater numbers of aircraft could operate without such equipment, and four U-boats and Italian *Enrico Tazzoli* were sunk during May – including veteran U-tanker *U463* – and seven so badly damaged they were forced to abort, spending considerable time under repair.

U441's initial anti-aircraft sortie departed Brest at 1000hrs on 22 May under command of new captain Götz von Hartmann, late of *U563*, the previous commander, Klaus Hartmann, incapacitated in hospital wrestling with a severe case of pneumonia. With 67 men aboard, including a doctor, two engineers to test newly installed radar detection equipment, and an additional team of specialist gunners, the U-boat's four days at sea resulted in the shooting down of Sunderland 'L' of RAF 228 Squadron two days later. Despite one of the U-boat's *Vierling* weapons not being fired (poor welding at the weapon's base had weakened under exposure to seawater, making the weapon unstable), the sudden flak barrage brought the Sunderland down into the sea only 300 metres from *U441* with all crewmen killed.

Although successful, there were injured among the U-boat crew, and *U441* had received moderate damage to her bow from depth charges released immediately before the Sunderland crashed. The fact that the U-boat itself did not emerge unscathed from the skirmish appears to have escaped BdU's notice and conversion work on the remaining six 'flak-boats' continued.

The balance of power within the North Atlantic had tilted undeniably in the Allies' favour. A running battle between what became three groups totalling a massive 53 U-boats and convoy ONS5 of 42 heavily escorted merchants developed at the beginning of May during a temporary Ultra 'blackout'. Twelve ships were sunk (not including one several days earlier) but at the loss of six U-boats. It was a ruinous exchange rate. The initial attack proceeded well, Dönitz's exhortations to his commanders keeping torpedoes firing into the next day; the last steamer was sunk that evening, with only *U638* lost. However, during the night thick fog developed and U-boats lost cohesive contact. All escorts carried Type 271M centimetric radar against which Metox was no defence, and combined with HF/DF, five more U-boats were surprised and sunk by depth charges, Hedgehog attacks and ramming. Seven others were so severely damaged that they were forced to head home. The high casualty rate among cumbersome Type IX U-boats finally convinced Dönitz of their unsuitability in fast-moving convoy actions, and their use was exclusively reserved for remote operations thereafter, excepting those on their first transit patrols to France from Germany. It was to be the last major tally claimed by U-boats against a North Atlantic convoy, opening the most disastrous month of the war for Dönitz.

Heavy losses had caused a profound slump in U-boat morale during April and into May. German reaction to improving Allied ASW technologies was often borderline makeshift and involved modifications to variants of the same model U-boats with which war had begun. In Britain, Admiral Max Horton had replaced Dudley Pound as C-in-C Western Approaches at the same time as American shipyards hummed with productivity and *Torch's* demands placed upon the Royal Navy slackened. Improved depth charges, with Torpex replacing weaker Amatol explosive deeper settings, centimetric radar in naval vessels and aircraft, HF/DF, Hedgehog, VLR aircraft and the introduction of escort carriers USS *Bogue*, HMS *Biter* and HMS *Archer* to the North Atlantic convoy routes crushed U-boat operations during May. The initiation of support groups whose entire purpose was to hunt a U-boat to exhaustion, rather than break away after a maximum of 90 minutes to resume convoy escort, increased U-boat kills near convoys by almost half.

The Americans had also developed the Mark 24 Mine – known more commonly as 'Fido' – a homing air-dropped torpedo that would perform a circular search and lock onto U-boat propellor cavitation. Relatively slow, it could still outpace a submerged U-boat and, issued during March, the first successful use was by a US Navy Catalina of VP-84 that sank *U640* southwest of Iceland on 14 May as the *'Iller'* group attempted to intercept ONS7.

May reached its climax with attacks on SC130 by 21 U-boats ranged in three patrol lines: *'Iller'*, *'Donau'* and *'Oder'*. Not one ship was sunk, while one U-boat was heavily damaged and three destroyed, including *U954* in which Peter Dönitz – the *Grossadmiral's* son – was serving as Watch Officer. All three boats were lost with all hands. Twenty-two U-boats were then arrayed to attack HX239, betrayed by B-Dienst codebreaking, as was the Ultra-based attempt to reroute the convoy. On the eve of the battle, BdU transmitted encouragement to the North Atlantic boats including the somewhat desperate lines, 'If there is anyone who thinks that combatting convoys is no longer possible, he is a weakling and no true U-boat Captain. The battle of the Atlantic is getting harder, but it is the determining element in the waging of the war.'[6]

Decoded by Ultra, it must have been heartening to the British. The following day, 22 May, *U305* sighted escorting destroyers of HX239 but was promptly bombed and damaged by an Avenger aircraft from USS *Bogue*, one of two escort carriers attached to the convoy. Surfacing after repairs around noon, the boat was bombed again and forced to abort. *Bogue's* aircraft subsequently sank *U569* while Swordfish from HMS *Archer*, equipped with new air-to-sea rockets, sank *U752*. With several other U-boats reporting serious damage to aircraft attack, the U-boats were withdrawn from the action. On 24 May, Dönitz summarized the present situation in a message transmitted to all U-boats:

… the situation in the North Atlantic now forces a temporary shifting of operations to areas less endangered by aircraft. The following areas come into consideration: the Caribbean Sea, the area off Trinidad, the area off the Brazilian and West African coasts.

It is, therefore, intended to operate primarily with VIIC boats in these areas, as far as permitted by the supply situation. If necessary, operational boats must also be sent in to supply other boats. With the boats at present in the North Atlantic, operations will be made against the traffic between USA and Gibraltar – as far as these boats are able to do this with their fuel. The North Atlantic cannot, however, be entirely denuded of boats. It is necessary, by means of single boats, to leave the enemy in ignorance as long as possible regarding alterations in tactics. For this operation in the North Atlantic boats are available now which cannot be sent elsewhere in view of their fuel supplies, and boats coming from home waters for their first operations, which must be assigned the stay in the North Atlantic despite difficult conditions. It is intended to attempt attacks on a convoy only under particularly favourable conditions, i.e. in the time of the new moon. The new moon period at the end of June is the first to come into consideration since the boats at present in the North Atlantic are no longer operational enough. It will be necessary to assign several veteran boats for this as a support for the newer boats in the North Atlantic.

These decisions comprise a temporary deviation from the former principles for the conduct of U-boat warfare. This is necessary in order not to allow the U-boats to be beaten at a time when their weapons are inferior, by unnecessary losses while achieving very slight success. It is, however, clearly understood that the main operational area of U-boats is, as it always was, in the North Atlantic and that operations must be resumed there with every determination as soon as the U-boats are given the necessary weapons for this. Equipment with 2cm quadruples, which will begin from June to an increasing degree will be the first step in this direction, equipment with *Zaunkönig* torpedoes the second step, while improvement of location devices at the moment is still to be considered. It is, however, anticipated that after equipment with *Vierling*, i.e. from the autumn, the battle of the North Atlantic will be completely resumed once more.[7]

This did not apply to middle Atlantic operations, and with firm intelligence of the incoming GUS7A convoy, BdU disposed 17 Type VIICs as group '*Trutz*', supported by refuelling from *U488*, beyond the range of land-based aircraft in the first attempt on a Gibraltar convoy from the United States since March. The initial BdU transmission of 24 May forming '*Trutz*' was read immediately by the Allies and passed onwards, US Navy Task Group 21.12 of escort carrier USS *Bogue* with a four-destroyer screen, informed of the location of '*Trutz*' by COMINCH intelligence.

Three U-boats were sighted and attacked by Avenger aircraft on 4 June, *U217* sunk the following day in the first instance of Enigma decryption directly resulting in a U-boat kill by the US Navy. On 8 June, *U758* fought with its new *Vierling* when it was also attacked by *Bogue*'s Avengers, putting up a fierce defence that damaged one attacker, wounding its radioman. Despite some damage from depth-charge near misses, *U758* successfully repulsed its attackers and escaped, with seven men from the gun crews wounded and the boat forced to return to France. This, and other actions, briefly convinced Dönitz of the validity of his 'fight back' order.

Having missed GUS7A, the 15 remaining U-boats of '*Trutz*' refuelled from *U488* and moved east towards Spain in three separate lines (*Geier* 1–3), which proved disastrous. With not one merchant ship sighted, four more U-boats were sunk by aircraft attack, including auxiliary U-tanker *U118*. While three remained operational west of Spain, the remaining U-boat survivors returned to France with damage. US Navy tactical methods had successfully transformed, as close-support escort groups, centred on carriers, became roving convoy support and then finally independently operating hunter-killer groups.

Allied strategic and tactical improvements had finally prevailed. Although combat U-boats were at their peak operational strength, casualties for the month amounted to 34 destroyed in the Atlantic – one for every merchant ship sunk within the same area – and nine elsewhere. Though he did not yet know it, Dönitz was never to regain initiative within the North Atlantic. The B-Dienst intelligence flow also rapidly ebbed after the British Admiralty introduced Naval Cypher No. 5 on 10 June, additional cyphering added in January 1944 rendering it completely secure.

On 5 June, Dönitz met with Hitler at the Berghof to explain his decision to withdraw from the North Atlantic and outline requirements for a successful resumption of his U-boat campaign: efficient ship location radar, enemy radar countermeasures, acoustic torpedoes and powerful U-boat flak. Originally planning to resume in July, he was forced to abandon this decision because none of the required improvements would be ready. He also retrospectively complained that suitable maritime aircraft should have been built concurrent with the expansion of the U-boat service as a means of countering the omnipotent aerial threat, Hitler agreeing without appearing to remember Raeder's doomed struggle against Göring for a naval air arm. Hitler also pledged to push for the completion of Messerschmitt's 'Amerika Bomber' to fulfil long-range U-boat reconnaissance requirements.

Dönitz was fighting a war with antiquated weapons, and complete Kriegsmarine failure to establish a dedicated technological development branch is difficult to understand. Early hopes pinned on Hellmuth Walter's pioneering submarine proved misplaced, but the design utilizing Walter's streamlined hull-form with vastly increased battery capacity in place of a hydrogen-peroxide engine had been embraced in the Types XXI and XXIII, though not likely to be available before the end of 1944. Walter's suggested *Schnorchel* was to be retrofitted to existing Type VII and Type IX U-boats in a belated answer to dominant Allied air power.

Further improvements, such as the FAT II G7e torpedo, capable of looping and running a circle, enhanced search radar derived from the Luftwaffe *Hohentwiel*, radar decoys fitted with aluminium strips – *Thetis* a buoy with a long spar to which the strips were affixed and *Aphrodite* with the foil suspended from a balloon – were all hastily added to the U-boat inventory. To combat ASDIC, already during 1942 U-boats had been fitted with the *Bold* anti-sonar device, comprising a small cylindrical mesh container filled with calcium hydride. When ejected from a submerged U-boat the compound reacted with seawater, generating hydrogen bubbles and a false echo to ASDIC operators. Moderately effective, it boosted the morale of crewmen if nothing else. Less successful had been experiments with *Alberich*, consisting of 4mm-thick sheets of synthetic rubber secured to the outer hull with adhesive, claiming a 15 per cent reduction in sonar echo reflection as well as acting as sound insulation for the internal machinery of a U-boat. Tested on *U11* as far back as 1940, results had been encouraging, though trials in 1941 with recently commissioned Type IXC *U67* encountered problems with adhesion, and as panels came loose, they caused hydrodynamic resistance and created water eddies that generated excess noise and therefore the direct opposite of what was desired.

Not until the dawn of the 'Schnorchel war' in 1944 was *Alberich* used on patrol, *U480* the first U-boat to enter successful combat clad in the rubber sheeting affixed with an improved adhesive compound. Later planned to be applied to 'electro-boats', none that saw action received it, only Type VIICs *U480*, *U247*, *U999*, *U485*, *U486* and *U1105* on active patrol with it applied. Material of a similar nature more commonly used was *Tarnmatte*, a compound synthetic rubber and iron oxide powder that coated the head of a U-boat's *Schnorchel*, claimed to reduce by 90 per cent waves emitted by the British ASV Mk III airborne radar.

From 14 June, no U-boat was permitted into action without at least a double 20mm flak upgrade and from August not without 'Bridge Conversion IV' of two twin 20mm flak weapons side-by-side on the bridge platform, and either a 20mm *Vierling* or single 37mm flak on a lowered *Wintergarten* aft of the bridge.

The end of June marked the opening of two new Coastal Command offensives in two Biscay areas not far from Spain's northwest coast. The first, *Musketry*, utilized aircraft of 15 and 19 Groups with Royal Navy's Support Group 2, while the second, *Seaslug*, was further west and remained the domain of 15 Group VLR Liberators and other long-range aircraft. Five British and five American B24 Squadrons formed a heavy backbone to this new onslaught as Air Marshal Sir John Slessor (AOC-in-C of Coastal Command) determined to capitalize on the apparent U-boat policy of remaining surfaced and fighting back. The *Musketry* zone was to be constantly swept by seven aircraft at a time, flying parallel tracks three times a day, while Johnnie Walker's new command Support Group 2 patrolled the western edge, ready to join the hunt for and opening their part of the offensive by sinking *U119* and *U449* within six hours of each other, the former Type XB returning from minelaying off Halifax.* Leigh Light aircraft would continue to patrol the area at night. Although it was known that Dönitz had ordered his U-boats to submerge during darkness, it was considered that at the very least Leigh Light aircraft would provide nuisance value and keep U-boats pinned underwater where their batteries would be slowly drained.

The critical danger posed by aircraft is reflected in the fact that of 63 U-boats lost in all areas during July and August, 46 were sunk by aircraft, two by a combination of aircraft and surface warship, one by a port air raid in Norway and only nine by warships alone. Among the most devastating losses to Dönitz during July and August were five of the seven remaining Type XIV U-tankers and the Type XB *U117*. The slow and unwieldy *Milchkuh* submarines had been high on the Allied hit list, though most were sunk incidentally, falling easily to aircraft of the *Derange*, *Musketry* and *Seaslug* operations, rather than because of the Enigma-led offensive against them that had been repeatedly urged by Admiral King.

The U-boat 'flak traps' had fared no better than others during this period. On 8 July, the original flak boat *U441* slipped from Brest, four days later attacked by three nimble and powerful 248 Squadron Beaufighters and suffering severe damage. During early afternoon, the three aircraft attacked as Götz von Hartmann directed fire from the fearsome array of flak weaponry. The weather was clear with a moderate breeze that rocked *U441* in a softly rolling swell, making it virtually impossible to target the fast Beaufighters, which raked the exposed crew with cannon and machine-gun fire. Ten men were killed and 13 wounded, including Hartmann and all three Watch

---

* Walker, a veteran of the First World War, was the most successful U-boat hunter of the war, credited with sinking 17. A charismatic leader and workaholic, Walker never saw the war's end. He died of a cerebral thrombosis on 7 July 1944 at the age of 48, his death attributed to 'overwork and exhaustion'.

Officers. It took prompt action by the on-board medical officer Paul Pfaffinger, 'a keen amateur yachtsman', to order the boat dived and brought back to Brest. Though obviously a poor gun platform, this did not mark the final attempt to use the 'flak traps'.

The idea of group sailings for collective anti-aircraft defence had been proved a fallacy by the loss of so many U-boats in Biscay, and on 2 August departures from Atlantic bases were suspended. Those U-boats already in transit were ordered to disperse, incoming boats to take the 'Piening Route' close inshore to the Spanish coast – disregarding territorial limits if need be – submerged by day and surfaced by night. The situation had deteriorated so markedly that on 5 August as part of an 'Officers Only' message from BdU it was suggested, 'Do not report too much bad news, so as not to depress the other boats; every radio message goes the rounds of the crew in every boat. If necessary, report matters which ratings do not need to know by officer's cipher.'[8] Still oblivious to centimetric radar, BdU replaced the banned Metox with new device *Wanze*, developed by German electronics company Hagenuk. This automatically scanned radar frequencies in the range between 120 to 180cm and therefore, despite some initially recorded successes, was useless against centimetric radar; following several undetected surprise attacks, it too would be banned on 5 November.

Centimetric radar remained a mystery to the Kriegsmarine until information was belatedly passed on by the Luftwaffe after recovery of a 10cm HS2 radar from wreckage of an RAF Stirling bomber shot down over Rotterdam in February. From this the FuMB-7 Naxos was developed by Telefunken to detect ASV Mk III radar, and as it covered wavelengths between 8cm and 12cm, it also detected the RAF's H2S radar. The device consisted of a parabolic reflector, commonly referred to by its nickname *Fliege* and, like Metox, was not watertight and had to be dismounted before diving. Although reliable, it nevertheless possessed a short detection range of only 5,000 metres, providing about one minute's warning.

With convoy operations within the North and Central Atlantic having failed, emphasis returned to distant theatres. U-boats that had been despatched to the West African, Caribbean and Brazilian

areas encountered nothing during their outbound voyages but
began to bite once more while on station. Their numbers peaked on
20 July, when two were between the Bahamas and Cape Hatteras,
seven within the Caribbean, seven between Trinidad and the mouth
of the Amazon, five sailing from the northeastern Brazilian coast to
Rio and nine off the African coast between Dakar and the Niger
estuary.

Within the Gulf of Mexico there had been nothing sunk since
March, and only *U527* appeared unsuccessfully there from June,
sunk while returning to France on 23 July by depth charges from
a USS *Bogue* Avenger. Only two more U-boats would venture
to the Gulf, *U518* achieving nothing during four months at sea
between August and November, and *U193*, which sank 10,172-ton
turbine tanker *Touchet* on 3 December 1943. It was the last ship
sunk within those waters after armed convoys became the norm
and the opening of the 'Big Inch' pipeline from Texas to New
Jersey dramatically reduced seaborne crude oil shipments within
the United States.

Chapter Ten

Reinforcing Failure

'I was annoyed... because of this senseless enterprise. Nothing has been proved.'

Günther Reiffenstuhl, First Watch Officer, *U862*[1]

On 3 July, Werner Musenberg entered Bordeaux harbour at the end of a 145-day voyage with the experimental Type IXD-1 *U180* that had marked something of a watershed moment. While a Japanese *Yanagi* submarine had already reached France, his was the first transfer by U-boat of 'cargo' to the Far East, albeit by rendezvous with *I29* within the Indian Ocean.

Additional to the exchange of goods and technology between Japan and Germany, key personnel were required to travel between the two, the Japanese steadfastly refusing proposals for the establishment of an air link. With surface blockade-runners in crisis during 1943, transport by U-boat remained the last option. On 10 February, *U180* slipped from Kiel, meeting a small boat off Laboe from which two passengers came aboard: Indian nationalist Subhas Chandra Bose and his adjutant, Arab nationalist Dr Habid Hassan. Cambridge-educated Bose presided over the Indian National Congress Party, imprisoned during 1940 by the Raj for anti-war activities before paroled and fleeing to Berlin in 1941. There, Hitler somewhat begrudgingly supported his suggestion of the creation of an Indian Legion that could fight alongside German troops and eventually help free India of British rule.

Unable to match Type IXD-2 endurance, Musenberg could not reach Japanese-occupied territory; he was instructed to rendezvous with Japanese *I29* to transfer passengers and technical samples and blueprints along with mail for the Tokyo German embassy. In return, he would take aboard 11 tons of cargo, including three torpedoes for German scrutiny and 146 crates of gold bound for the Japanese embassy in Berlin as well as two Japanese officers bound for Germany.

After refuelling from *U462*, Musenberg entered the Indian Ocean, by which time the experimental diesels had shown numerous technical problems. Not only did they 'smoke like an old coal burning tramp' when changing from low to high revolutions but they generated a temperature of 60° Celsius within the submarine's pressure hull, an almost unbearable heat particularly debilitating within tropical latitudes. On 18 April, Musenberg sank unescorted 8,132-ton British tanker *Corbis* carrying 11,310 tons of diesel oil and 50 tons of highly volatile aviation spirit; a second attack two days later was foiled by poor depth keeping and badly smoking engines.

U180 met *I29* in rough seas on 26 April, suggestions they proceed to Sabang awaiting better conditions declining due to *U180*'s fuel levels. Despite difficulties, transfer of men and materiel was achieved and Musenberg began the laborious return to France, encountering aircraft near South Africa and sinking 5,166-ton Greek *Boris* on 3 June. *U530* refuelled *U180* west of the Canary Islands; Musenberg had initially been ordered to take diesel from *U463*, but the latter had been sunk with all hands, the news resonating aboard *U180* as a diesel room engineer's brother had been serving aboard the tanker. After arriving in France, the Type IXD-1 was immediately placed into dock for engine replacement and would only sail once more as a transport boat before posted missing in August 1944.

While U-boats had been used for transportation periodically since 1940, incentive to construct transport U-boats began with Hitler's request in November 1942 for such vessels to support an invasion of American-occupied Iceland for establishment of a

Luftwaffe base. Such 'inspiration' unlocked production possibilities amid fierce inter-service competition for raw materials.

In the interim, unwilling to divert fighting boats to transport missions, Dönitz strongly recommended that nine unwieldy BETASOM submarines be converted into transports, unsuitable as they were for convoy actions. Theoretically, these large submarines could reach Indonesia without refuelling, and although Hitler at first rejected the idea, Dönitz flew to Rome and secured agreement directly from Mussolini, Hitler relenting, agreeing to an exchange of the Italian boats for ten upgraded Type VIIC/41s.*

This updated design was capable of diving deeper, reducing depth charge effectiveness. With various power and electrical systems replaced by more compact versions, a total of 11.5 tons of hull weight was saved, converted to an increase in pressure hull thickness from 18.5mm to 21mm, extending test diving limits from 150 metres to 180 metres and theoretical hull failure depth from 250 metres to 300. With a slightly widened forecastle and 13cm tapered extension to the bow to decrease water resistance, this became the Type VIIC/41, the first, U293, launched on 30 July 1943.

With surface blockade running from the Far East increasingly disrupted, the Kriegsmarine toyed with U-boat-towed freight containers, shipyards in Kiel, Bremen and Hamburg also contracted to build a new ocean-going transport U-boat, designated Type XX. These would have displaced 2,708 tons surfaced and a colossal 2,962 tons submerged and, armed only with flak weapons, could carry 800 tons of freight. With a scheduled finish of spring 1944 at the earliest, production clashed with Type XXI and XXIII electro-boats and was suspended.

During January and February 1942, the Italian boats began refitting as transports; attack periscopes, deck guns and torpedo tubes were removed, and ammunition storage areas converted to fuel bunkers. Capable of carrying between 100 and 240 tons of

---

* U428–U430, U746–U750 and U1161–U1162 scheduled to be renamed by the Italians as S1 to S10. The last of these, U1162 (S10), was never actually handed over before the Italian armistice.

freight, the group was codenamed 'Aquila' ('Eagle') I to IX, a base being established for them in Singapore with logistical and liaison support from officers and crew of Italian sloop *Eritrea*, which had arrived in Japan from the Red Sea during March 1941. The first conversions were completed so quickly that *Aquila I* (*Tazzoli*) departed Bordeaux in May, followed immediately by *Aquila II* and *III* (*Giuliani* and *Cappellini*). *Aquila V* and *VI* (*Barbarigo* and *Torelli*) followed during June, although ultimately only three would reach Singapore between July and September 1943.

Even before the major North Atlantic debacle of May, Dönitz had committed seven U-cruisers to another major penetration of the Indian Ocean. Six were Type IXD-2s, the seventh the yet-untried Type IXD-1 *U195*. The experienced commanders were all older than average, some, such as Werner Hartmann, returning to active service after time ashore. Hartmann's *U198* departed on 9 March, followed at regular intervals by *U196*, *U195*, *U181*, *U178*, *U177* and *U197*.

As they sailed towards South Africa, Italian submarines *Da Vinci* and *Cagni* were already there in action, two of five ordered to patrol either the Brazilian or South African coasts in what became cumulatively the most successful Italian voyages of the war. *Da Vinci* attacked and sank six ships during its voyage, earning its commander the Knight's Cross from Dönitz and the Italian Gold Medal. Aboard *U195* Heinz Buchholz was forced by his recalcitrant diesels to radio BdU in late March that he would have to return, his scheduled patrol south of Madagascar cancelled and the troublesome Type IXD-1 later reconfigured like *U180* as a transport boat with ordinary diesels. Buchholz had sunk two ships outbound (including one straggling from UGS-7) and damaged another during its 126 days at sea.

The voyages that the U-boats were undertaking would be the longest and most punishing of the entire war, testimony to the discipline and spirit of the crews and leadership abilities of these commanders. All seven U-boats independently patrolled southeast of the Cape of Good Hope, achieving only slight success until mid-June, with 18 ships sunk and another damaged. Rendezvous with the tanker *Charlotte Schliemann* 600 miles south of Mauritius was made between 22 and 27 June, U-boats not immediately being supplied fuel providing anti-aircraft cover for the meeting. Following British diplomatic insistence to Spain, *Charlotte Schliemann* had broken out of Las Palmas in February 1942 and sailed into the South Atlantic, supplying two surface raiders before laying course for Japan. In Yokohama *Charlotte Schliemann* was reprovisioned and armed with six flak weapons, to become one of two key German tankers within the Indian Ocean.

The difficulty of long U-boat voyages included constant struggle against boredom and its corollary, complacency. Captains organized sporting endeavours when possible, as well as competitions, musical events, and on-board newspapers. Beards grew thick and long, and hygiene became problematic in high humidity. With little on-board refrigeration, non-preserved foodstuffs rotted, and crews were limited to tinned or salted produce augmented by occasional fresh fish. Health issues, generally minor, became commonplace, although *U178*'s captain Wilhelm Dommes suffered from severe stomach cramps, probably stemming from battle fatigue after years of Mediterranean combat. He frequently lay in deep depression, mumbling to himself that he would never return from this voyage, provoking heated rebuke from both Chief Engineer Karl-Heinz Wiebe and First Watch Officer Wilhelm Spahr who gradually assumed greater command responsibilities.

Few successes against enemy ships punctuated the boredom. An attack on 3 August by Kentrat's *U196* against convoy CB1 northeast of Memba Bay, Tanganyika, sank 7,323-ton British *City of Oran* (one of only two ships sunk by *U196* in 225 days at sea) and resulted in sudden heavy air patrols. Forced to repeatedly crash dive, Kentrat recorded in his War Diary: 'There has never been so much air traffic in the Indian Ocean. The convoy attack must have upset the people very much.'[2]

The Type IXD-2 was confirmed as a difficult boat to handle. Large and clumsy on the surface, its relatively slow diving time increased vulnerability to air attack. Conversely, while proceeding at periscope depth in any seas above a Force 4, the boat would yaw and pitch wildly, often unexpectedly broaching. Torpedoes also suffered from the humid environment once past the Tropic of Cancer. Mostly equipped with electric G7e torpedoes, maintenance became difficult and batteries within the 'eels' deteriorated rapidly, designed for use within European climates. Torpedo performance was correspondingly erratic, frequently travelling slower than normal and rendering all but the most secure firing solutions void. Nonetheless the presence of U-boats within the Indian Ocean threatened thinly spread Royal Navy forces in what the Admiralty considered a strategic backwater.

Among the arsenal of the Type IXD-2 was the Focke-Achgelis Fa330 – an unpowered towed gyrocopter, commonly known as *Bachstelze* (water wagtail). Designed to extend surveillance capability by a higher horizon, the lightweight Fa330 was quick to assemble, launch and recover. Tethered to the U-boat, wind movement through rotor blades generated lift, the pilot using a small control stick hanging from the blade hub for accurate pitch and roll control. Foot pedals moved the large rudder, controlling yaw, and a simple altimeter, airspeed indicator and tachometer were the only instruments. Impractical for use within the Atlantic, due to its large radar signature, the Indian Ocean was considered ideal. Stored when not in use within two watertight metal canisters built into the lower *Wintergarten* platform, one housed the blades and tail, the other the fuselage; a third horizontal container contained the 300-metre tethering cable and winch. Once aloft the pilot communicated with the U-boat via an interphone system, its wire wrapped around the tow cable. To land, the crew simply winched him back aboard. However, if the U-boat came under threat and needed to dive, a large red lever above the seat was pulled, activating a quick release coupling which simultaneously jettisoned towline and rotor blades, deploying a parachute for the pilot who in turn ditched his seat and harness before falling into the sea. In theory, the U-boat could later surface and recover the pilot.

As the six U-boats separated after refuelling, *U178* and *U196* occupied the Mozambique Channel, *U181* near Mauritius, *U197* and *U198* between Lourenço Marques and Durban and *U177* south of Madagascar, where *Bachstelze* observation aided in the sinking of Greek steamer *Efthalia Mari* on 5 August. This post-refuelling period proved more successful for all, Lüth's *U181* achieving most, with six ships sunk around Reunion Island.

Meanwhile, the first German U-boat to reach Malaya had already docked in Penang. Hitler had partially acceded to Japanese requests for an evaluation pair of Type IXC U-boats, a single example granted in partial payment for some of Germany's imported raw materials already arrived by surface blockade runner. Despite Dönitz asserting that the Japanese would be unable to build such boats on a scale sufficient to influence the war, *U511* was made ready for the journey to Japan, codenamed *Marco Polo I*. Fritz Schneewind, born in Padang, Sumatra in 1917, departed Lorient on 10 May 1943 carrying bottles of mercury, a 3,000hp Daimler Benz engine, blueprints for Type IX U-boats, three Kriegsmarine engineers for technical missions in Japan, and several dignitaries.

U511 refuelled from *U460* during late May before Schneewind rounded the Cape of Good Hope and entered the Indian Ocean, sinking two American freighters and mistakenly attacked by Japanese ASW patrol boats, despite running surfaced with huge Swastika and Rising Sun ensigns attached to the conning tower. Finally convincing the Japanese of their error, 'Marco Polo I' entered Penang harbour on 15 July, later moving on to Kobe, where the Kriegsmarine ensign was replaced by the Rising Sun and *U511* became *RO500* of the Imperial Japanese Navy. Schneewind and his men were given ten days of supervised leave at Mount Fujiyama before being transferred to Singapore, planning to travel onward to Penang and form a small reserve pool of U-boat crewmen, bolstering a core of men from various German military and merchant ships already forming a logistical hierarchy and personnel reserve.

With much merchant shipping reported sailing independently within the Indian Ocean, despite meagre return thus far, Dönitz accepted proposals by the Imperial Japanese Navy to base U-boats in Malaya or Indonesia. Since November 1942, German Naval Attaché, *Admiral* Paul Wennecker, had promoted establishment of German installations within Japanese ports, though protracted negotiations requiring guarantees limiting European claims within Asia proved obstructive and it was not until 1943 that any agreement was reached. Ports in Java, Jakarta, Surabaya and Singapore were made ready for clearing transport submarines, while Georgetown, Penang, was chosen for combat U-boats.

Plans for the six Type IXD-2s already within the Indian Ocean to continue to Malaya were soon discarded, nearly all low on torpedoes and unable to launch the concerted attack into the Arabian Sea with which Dönitz wanted to begin his new offensive. Malayan logistical stocks were not yet sufficient to resupply six combat U-boats, and Penang still required an experienced U-boat administrator.

Dommes' *U178* sank the last of its six ships on 16 July, torpedoing *City of Canton* northwest of Madagascar, although plagued by erratic torpedo performance during the submerged attack. Left with a single torpedo, Dommes expected to return to France but instead received a query from BdU whether *U178* remained capable of reaching Penang. They had already endured nearly four months at sea, and Dommes was uncertain whether his men would be capable of recovering in Penang where unknown facilities awaited them; the majority were in good shape, but several ill men, himself included, required hospital care. Assured of necessary support by BdU, *U178* turned east and headed in company with inbound *Aquila VI* to Malaya, docking on 29 August at Swettenham Pier.

The Italian crew of *Aquila VI* were joined by those aboard *Aquila II* and *III*, between them transporting nearly 300 tons of valuable cargo. The remaining '*Aquila*' boats that had departed Bordeaux disappeared to unknown causes in the Gulf of Gascogne. Though news of Mussolini's fall reached them in Singapore, the announcement of the Italian armistice on 9 September caught them unprepared while loading for return to Europe. Despite most professing allegiance to Germany, they were imprisoned by Japanese authorities. In Bordeaux, the two remaining '*Aquila*' boats not yet departed were also seized by the Kriegsmarine, becoming *UIT22* and *UIT23*, the codename '*Aquila*' changed to '*Merkator*'.

Confusion reigned within Italian ranks both in Europe and Malaya. BETASOM commander Enzo Grossi pledged allegiance to Mussolini and his German allies, before absconding towards Spain with 3,400,000 francs and being arrested on the international bridge in Irun. Mussolini announced his new *Repubblica Sociale Italiana* (RSI) on 23 September, maintaining control over BETASOM where many elected loyalty to the RSI while others immediately surrendered. *Cagni*, the last BETASOM boat still in action and unaccounted for within the Indian Ocean, chose the latter, setting course for Durban, South Africa. Likewise, the sloop *Eritrea* received official notice from Reuters on 8 September, evading Japanese ships and surrendering to the British at Colombo, Ceylon.

Japanese authorities suddenly found themselves owners of three large Italian submarines, turning them over to German authorities as *U511*'s crew arrived in Singapore en route to Malaya. The three boats were swiftly redesignated and armed with deck and flak guns, becoming *UIT23*, *UIT24* and *UIT25*. Italian volunteers willing to continue fighting for the RSI were retained aboard ship, with a sprinkling of Kriegsmarine personnel filling their ranks.

Plans continued for a U-boat strike deep into the Indian Ocean to the Arabian Sea. Codenamed *Monsun*, 11 combat boats – Type IXCs *U188*, *U532*, *U168*, *U509*, *U183*, *U514*, *U506*, *U533* and *U516* and Type IXD-2s *U200* and *U847* – supported by a Type XIV U-tanker were scheduled to reach the target area in September 1943 as the intense rainy season diminished.

The first *Monsun* boat, Heinrich Schonder's new *U200*, slipped from Kiel on 13 June carrying an additional five men of the Brandenburger Regiment's *Küstenjäger* battalion, all either of German colonial South West and East African descent or having lived and worked there. Tasked with landing the troops to sabotage Durban's dry docks, Schonder hoped to make good speed into the Atlantic, but was surprised fully surfaced by an RAF 120 Squadron B24 bomber escorting ONS11 and depth charged; oil, debris and 15 swimming men were observed behind the sunken U-boat, but never found.

The Type IXCs were dependent on tanker refuelling; Type XIV *U462* was forced to abort its support mission twice through air attack and forcing a complicated alternative refuelling schedule. Helmut Metz's Type XIV *U487* was already active southwest of the Azores, though low on fuel stock after already having supplied ten U-boats. Dönitz ordered outbound *U160* to rendezvous and refuel the tanker which in turn could supply the *Monsun* Type IXCs with 40 tons of diesel each. However, *U487* was attacked by an Avenger/Wildcat team from USS *Core* and sunk, with 33 survivors rescued by destroyer USS *Barker* as Dönitz's rendezvous area was in proximity of four US Navy aircraft carriers – USS *Core*, *Santee*, *Bogue*, and *Card* – all engaged on ASW missions.

The tanker's fate remained uncertain for some time before its presumed loss led to BdU appointing two other U-boats and *U160* as de facto tankers, though the latter had also been sunk with all hands the day after *U487* by a 'Fido' homing torpedo from aircraft of USS *Santee*. The *Monsun* group suffered severe attrition to aircraft within the Atlantic; *U514* lost on 8 July, followed four days later by *U506*, and *U509* on 15 July. Emergency measures led to Adolph Piening's *U155* bound for the Central Atlantic diverted to refuel *U168*, *U183* and *U188* west of the Cape Verde Islands, *U516* then scrubbing its own mission to the Indian Ocean and passing fuel and provisions to *U532* and *U533*.

The departure of *U847* was delayed by iceberg collision, and by the time Knight's Cross holder Herbert Kuppisch sailed from Bergen, he had been designated emergency tanker for the *Monsun* boats and others coming back from West Africa and the Americas. The first to rendezvous with Kuppisch within the Sargasso Sea was Carl Emmermann's *U172* returning from South America and alarmed at the apparent nonchalance aboard *U847* regarding the aerial threat. Though Kuppisch was a combat veteran, he had last been to sea at a time when aircraft were far from a dominant factor. As Emmermann refuelled, an Avenger/Wildcat team from USS *Core* sank *U185* nearby, though Kuppisch successfully supplied five homebound Type VIICs and *U508*. Aboard *U230*, First Watch Officer Herbert Werner later wrote of meeting *U847*:

Knowing that we were helpless while taking the heavy oil into our tanks, our boys manned the guns and stood ready to cut the hoses instantly. Not so the crew of the supply boat; they simply stood around the large superstructure like street corner idlers. In disgust I yelled to the Exec of *U847* through the megaphone, 'What's the matter with you people, don't you have any respect for aircraft?'

'We haven't seen any since we passed Greenland,' he shouted back.

Two hours after our departure the supply boat broke radio silence and reported that she had completed the refuelling of all four [sic] boats. By sending that message, *U847* not only jeopardised the four boats she had supplied but also sealed her own fate.[3]

The transmission fixed by Allied HF/DF, *U847* was located by an Avenger and two escorting Wildcats from USS *Card*, forced to dive and destroyed with all hands by a 'Fido' homing torpedo.

Replenished once more in early September by German tanker *Brake* despatched from Penang, *Monsun* was ready to begin its main attack. BdU recorded on 7 September:

> *U533* – Gulf of Aden, *U188* – Gulf of Oman, *U168* – Gulf of Cambay, *U532* – Southern tip of Peninsular India, *U183* off Mombasa.
>
> Boats have a free hand in this area according to the defenses and shipping. *U533* may penetrate as far West as the entrance to the Red Sea at her own discretion. Surprisingly large successes may be possible there.[4]

Ottoheinrich Junker's *U532* made the first successful attack of the reduced *Monsun* group, when on 19 September he sank British steamer *Fort Longueuil* southwest of the Chago Archipelago. Two days later, Siegfried Lüdden's *U188* added its own weight to combat in the Gulf of Oman where, east of Mogadishu, Lüdden torpedoed and sank American Liberty ship *Cornelia P. Spencer*.

However, *Monsun* experienced repeated failure despite frequent small convoys and inexperienced ASW forces. Hazy mist often obscured the horizon, making it difficult for lookouts to distinguish sea from sky while, by night, bright phosphorescence within the dead calm sea frequently left sparkling silver trails behind U-boats and torpedoes. Heat played havoc with the crew and machinery, overworked diesels suffering from excessive exhaust temperatures that required large quantities of lubricating oil to counteract. Constant attention by the engine room crew in temperatures that soared almost above endurance was required to nurse the engines during the voyage. Finally, and crucially, the now familiar problems of battery degradation caused torpedoes to run erratically.

Helmut Hennig's Type IXC/40 *U533* achieved nothing and was surprised on 16 October by a twin-engine Mark 5 Blenheim light bomber while surfaced off the coast of Oman, bombed and sunk with only mechanic Günther Schmidt surviving, swimming for 28 hours and washing ashore at Khor-Fakkam on Somalia's Muscat coast before found by local Arabs and passed over to the British.

By the end of October, *Monsun* had been reduced to four U-boats which had managed to sink an aggregated six ships and six small sailing vessels; on the penultimate day of the month, *U183*, *U188* and *U532* arrived in Penang escorted by Japanese patrol boats. Despite high expectations, Heinrich Schäfer's *U183* had sunk nothing during 17 weeks at sea, *U188* two ships, while Junker's *U532* had sunk four. The final arrival, Helmut Pich's *U168*, had sunk a single confirmed 2,183-ton British freighter by torpedo near Bombay, and six sailing cargo boats with artillery in the same region before docking in Penang on 11 November.* Remarkable voyages of endurance, they had little effect on British trade to and from India or Egypt.

With North Africa securely in Allied hands and the successful subjugation of pro-Axis hotspots within the Middle East, the expected amphibious assault on Sicily followed on 10 July. By this stage, U-boats of 29th U-Flotilla had also established a presence

---

* *U168* was an improved Type IXC/40 with a slightly enlarged outer hull allowing 6 extra tons of fuel, giving an extra 400 miles range. Internal machinery was also upgraded.

in Toulon and Marseilles after Vichy France had been occupied by German troops because of Operation *Torch*, though planned bunker construction never fully began. With uncertainty over Italian commitment to the Axis cause, flotilla headquarters was moved to Toulon during July, FdU Italy relocating to Aix-en-Provence from Rome, soon redesignated FdU Mediterranean and supplied their own Enigma net codename 'Medusa', which was swiftly broken by Ultra during June. Losses remained constant; successes low.

The invasion of Sicily – Operation *Husky* – blindsided German intelligence once more, and U-boats rushing to intervene were successfully fended off by stifling naval forces, only the dwindling Luftwaffe managing some measure of success. *U409*, *U561* and *U375* were all sunk by the end of July, and OKM demanded three more U-boats pass Gibraltar as reinforcement; *U614*, *U454* and *U706* were destroyed by aircraft in Biscay as they obeyed instructions to fight it out. By 17 August, Sicily was in Allied hands. Just over two days later, British forces landed on the toe of Italy and were inching forward, followed by Operation *Avalanche* and the major landing at Salerno.

The strength of 29th U-Flotilla had been whittled to 13 serviceable boats by this stage, under intense bombing pressure while berthed in Toulon and suffering further losses at sea, including the overclaiming 'Ace' Albrecht Brandi when *U617* was depth charged by a Leigh Light Wellington attack. Brandi limped towards Spain and scuttled his boat, he and his crew briefly interned before repatriated, and Brandi taking command of *U380*. Once again, reinforcements were despatched; seven more U-boats were ordered through the Strait, the first group of four running into the devastating *Musketry* offensive in Biscay and only *U223* reaching the Mediterranean before the attempt was cancelled by Dönitz.

While new T5 *Zaunkönig* torpedoes sank USS *Bristol*, HMS *Hythe* and *Quail* alongside Liberty ship *James Russell Lowell*, damaged beyond repair, reinforcements were once again ordered, and five Atlantic U-boats attempted to pass Gibraltar at the end of October equipped with new Naxos radar detectors. Only two survived the voyage.

A smattering of successes during November included destroyer HMS *Quail*, minesweeper HMS *Hebe* and Dutch sailing ship *Jela*, sunk after activating mines laid by *U453* off Bari. The following month Gerd Kelbling's *U593* and Karl Wächter's *U223* attacked convoy KMS34, Kelbling hitting HMS *Tynedale* with a *Zaunkönig*, while Wächter damaged HMS *Cuckmere* so badly it was later written off. Royal Navy escorts hunted the U-boats, and Kelbling sank pursuing destroyer HMS *Holcombe* with another T5. However, after a 32-hour chase, USS *Wainwright* gained a firm sonar trace on *U593* and, with HMS *Calpe*, depth charged and damaged the boat, which then surfaced and scuttled, all 51 hands rescued.

By the end of 1943, the Mediterranean boats had been reduced to 13, and after activation of USAAF Fifteenth Air Force in Tunisia, La Spezia and Toulon came under heavy bombardment, inflicting damage on unprotected U-boats in harbour despite reinforcing naval flak and smoke screen units. Desperate hopes remained pinned on the expected introduction of the Type XXIII and dawn of a revolutionary age of submarine warfare.

While Type XXI and XXIII production suffered constant delay by Allied bombing of German component factories, availability of T5 *Zaunkönig* escort-killer torpedoes restarted the North Atlantic battle. By the beginning of August, 80 had been delivered to French bases and BdU planned a group operation by U-boats equipped with four *Zaunkönig* each as well as FAT II and conventional G7e torpedoes. With improved flak weapons, new torpedoes and new radar detectors, Dönitz believed that he could once again regain the North Atlantic initiative.

Ordered to radio silence – excepting distress signals and tactically important messages – the group was assembled roughly midway between France and Newfoundland in what had been the 'air gap'. Once refuelled from *U460*, the 21 U-boats would sweep north and form a patrol line, each boat 17 miles distant from the next and instructed, once battle began, to operate at full speed and surfaced for collective flak defence. The group gathered as planned, named 'Leuthen', and began their hunt with a message from Dönitz transmitted on 13 September:

After an interval lasting for months you will once again wage submarine war in the North Atlantic, the most important theatre. You have been provided with new weapons and gear for this task. Events in Biscay have shown that in the field of radar detection the situation has changed materially in your favour. All the essentials for a successful campaign are to hand. I am sure that you will take up this challenge with the old fighting spirit of the submariner, for this struggle is decisive for our nation's future. The Führer is watching every phase of your struggle. Attack, follow up, sink.

U341 was lost to depth charges from a Canadian B24 of 10 Squadron RCAF on 19 September, but five 'Leuthen' boats contacted ONS18 as the faster ON202 overhauled it, presenting one major shipping conglomeration target. Most of 'Leuthen' confronted only powerful escort forces which had been kept apprised of the group by Ultra and HF/DF detection and decryption of U-boat messages announcing attacks. *U270* launched the first *Zaunkönig* and hit frigate HMS *Lagan*, causing severe damage, the ship towed to the Mersey and declared a constructive loss. It was one of 15 torpedoes fired against warships with seven claimed sunk, a further three 'probables', as well as three freighters destroyed by conventional torpedoes during that first night. The actual result was less impressive: one destroyer heavily damaged, another and a corvette destroyed as well as two freighters, one damaged by a previous attack before sunk after being abandoned.

Heavy fog the following day hindered further attacks, though contact was maintained by hydrophone and radio fixes. Radar-equipped escorts showed no such difficulty in attacking surfaced U-boats, and by late afternoon, as fog dissipated, aircraft systematically attacked the 'Leuthen' boats, several heavily damaged and *U377*'s commander Gerhard Kluth wounded in both arms during fierce firing between the boat and an RAF 10 Squadron B24. That night, 'Leuthen' experienced only limited possibilities in intermittent fog, and after a 90-hour battle, the attack was broken off by BdU with three U-boats lost. By their calculations, 12 escort vessels had been destroyed and three probably, as well as nine freighters sunk totalling 46,500 tons, and another two damaged. In fact, three escorts had been sunk, another a constructive loss, and six merchants sunk for 36,422 tons, with one other damaged.

The largest obvious discrepancy lay with the exaggerated success against escorts resulting from *Zaunkönig*. Rather than a deliberate intention to inflate success, this overestimation resulted from a crucial flaw in its operation. With a maximum range of 5.7 kilometres, the T5 possessed a short arming range only 400 metres from the firing boat. Once the acoustic sensor was live and the torpedo armed, it would search for the loudest propeller, possibly that of the launching U-boat. Captains were ordered to dive to 60 metres immediately after firing, most opting to go deeper to withstand potential depth-charge retaliation. Once fully submerged, the cacophony of sound detected through hydrophones could easily mistake actual hits with other explosions. Not until the following year would BdU begin to question the validity of wildly successful sinking reports; until then the *Zaunkönig* was hailed as 'entirely successful'.[5]

But this taste of victory predictably turned sour. Operational 'Leuthen' boats were reinforced to form 'Rossbach', eventually numbering 21 U-boats. Plagued by aircraft, three convoys reported by B-Dienst were rerouted around 'Rossbach's' patrol line while U-boats took damage. *U731* was bombed, its commander Werner Techand and five men wounded by strafing. As Techand broke for home, lookouts spotted the destroyer screen for SC143, shadowing with dubious assistance from a BV222 flying boat that transmitted incorrect navigation information and a beacon signal for only 15 minutes. Over two days and nights 'Rossbach' attempted to get closer, though only two freighters were sighted amid several destroyers. A single merchant and Polish destroyer were sunk, while six U-boats were lost to British, Canadian and American aircraft as they vainly attempted to fight back with anti-aircraft fire. 'Rossbach' morphed into 'Schlieffen' which attacked ONS20; a single straggler was sunk, but five U-boats were lost to escorting aircraft and warships. As the battle had unfolded, officers in BdU were divided over whether orders for U-boats to remain surfaced and fight attacking aircraft should remain in force, the *'Schlieffen'* line widely scattered with no mutual support possible between boats. Dönitz ruled that the order stand, and catastrophic losses and severe damage resulted.

This mistake was soon exposed, and as surviving U-boats were reshuffled several more times, they were ordered to submerge in daylight. Finding nothing except relentless air patrols, the final groups were dissolved, and U-boats withdrawn to between Northern Ireland and Scotland. There, BdU created multiple small mobile U-boat groups, constantly moved to complicate Allied tracking. Though several convoys were sighted, the small number of U-boats in each group – generally three – prevented attacks against strong escorting forces. By 7 January 1944, they were dissolved and U-boats ordered to operate independently, the tactical patrol line discontinued unless the unlikely prerequisite of firm Luftwaffe reconnaissance could be provided.

West of Spain, *'Schill'* group was formed for a single night action. Comprising ten U-boats, *'Schill'* included three flak boats – *U211*, *U441* and *U953* – whose reduced fuel capacity made them unsuitable for North Atlantic missions. Initially, this patrol line appeared effective when *U262* located MKS28 and launched a submerged attack on three large ships and a destroyer, claiming four hits with two probable freighters and a destroyer sunk (by *Zaunkönig*), but actually destroying only Norwegian freighter *Hallfried*. It was to be *'Schill's'* sole success.

Luftwaffe aircraft reported MKS30 combining with SL139 on 15 November and *'Schill'* was reinforced and split into three patrol lines. Luftwaffe bearings of varying reliability were passed to the U-boats which attacked three days later. Forewarned by Ultra decryption of the impending threat, escort ships destroyed four U-boats for minor damage to two merchants, and by 20 November contact was lost, a shadowing Fw 200 and Ju 290 both shot down.

Klaus Hartmann's *U441* had taken a pounding once again from aircraft and was forced to abort, with BdU soon ordering reconversion of all 'aircraft-traps' to their original state. The idea had become outmoded as air power was too great, their torpedo and fuel capacity too low and flak weaponry nearly matched by all enlarged *Wintergarten* configurations. Continuation of action against Gibraltar convoy traffic was attempted by the group 'Weddigen' (not to be confused with the flotilla of the same name), *U262* passed overhead by ships of MKS31 just before dawn on 26 November and surfacing inside the convoy, later reporting three ships torpedoed, although none were hit according to British records. Ordered to submerge by day due to intense aircraft activity, 'Weddigen' lost four U-boats with no successes before being dissolved on 6 December.

Group 'Borkum' was drawn up in a patrol line 400 miles west-northwest of Cape Ortegal to intercept expected KMS convoy traffic but becoming involved with Luftwaffe operations supporting several incoming blockade runners. The first, *Osorno*, had departed Batavia heavily laden during October and led the way towards Biscay. Informed by Ultra, the Allies launched Operation *Stonewall* using air and naval units already on Biscay patrol to find and sink them, destroying outbound *Pietro Orseolo* near the Breton coast.

Osorno was sighted by Luftwaffe reconnaissance on 22 December amid hailstorms and heavy seas, as was US Navy Task Group TG 21.15, including carrier USS *Card*. As German destroyers and torpedo boats sailed to meet the blockade breaker, 'Borkum' was vectored towards the Americans, *U275* sinking escorting destroyer USS *Leary* with a *Zaunkönig* torpedo on the morning of Christmas Eve and USS *Card* narrowly missed by torpedoes from *U415*. HMS *Hurricane*, escorting convoy OS62/KMS36 which 'Borkum' had originally intended to intercept, was sighted that evening and sunk by a *Zaunkönig* from *U415*.

They were the only successes 'Borkum' achieved and *U645* was lost, posted as missing, fate unknown. With the subsequent dissolution of 'Borkum' on 13 January, so ended U-boat attempts to intercept convoys headed north between Spain and the Azores. *Osorno* eventually entered the Gironde River and reached Bordeaux under Ju 88 escort, striking a submerged wreck but run aground to save the cargo, subsequently unloaded by lighter. Incoming blockade breaker *Alsterufer* and three others within the South Atlantic – *Rio Grande*, *Weserland* and *Burgenland* – were all sunk by the US Navy with assistance from Enigma intelligence and exhaustive aerial reconnaissance. Following the failure of all but one ship of this third wave of blockade runners, use of large freighters was prohibited from 18 January 1944, smaller capacity U-boats used thereafter.

Disappointing though *Monsun* had been, Penang's U-boats were reinforced, Dommes having handed command of *U178* over to his First Watch Officer, Wilhelm Spahr, and now ashore acting as a de facto flotilla leader. Receiving operational orders from BdU, Dommes passed them onto the commanders in harbour, for all other matters deferring to Naval Attaché Paul Wennecker. Not until December 1944 was Dommes named *Chef im Südraum*, assuming control of all Kriegsmarine installations in the south Orient, exercising his new command from Singapore. Jürgen Oesten, commanding officer of *U861* which was later despatched to Penang, remembered that: 'Relations with the Japanese were reasonably good. We were the only white people running around free, which was a bit of a problem for the Japanese as they had established a sort of racial war in order to improve their position with the native population.'[6]

During September and October, four Type IXD-2s that had accompanied Dommes' *U178* into the Indian Ocean arrived home. The fifth, Robert Bartels' *U197*, was sunk by aircraft on 20 August south of Madagascar. After rendezvousing with *U181* to pass over Enigma settings for the latter's return journey, Bartels elected to remain within the area, a transmission from *U181* triangulated and an RAF Catalina despatched from Natal to investigate. The Catalina found *U197* running surfaced and dropped six depth charges as gunners exchanged fire, with obvious damage inflicted and *U197* visibly listing to port, running at reduced speed.

Bartels dived but a thick oil slick betrayed the boat's position and *U197* resurfaced, flak weapons manned once again. Radioing his predicament to BdU, *U181* and Kentrat's *U196* were ordered at full speed to Bartels' aid. However, *U197*'s distress messages had been made in such haste that they sent conflicting coordinates 250 miles apart. By this time, another 265 Squadron Catalina had arrived, strafing the German gun crews and straddling the boat with six shallow-set depth charges. *U197* rolled over and sank, the last depth charge lodged on deck and exploding as it went down, upwelling oil marking the end of Bartels and his 66 men.

The return of the four remaining U-boats broke records of U-boat endurance, the shortest voyage, by Robert Gysae's *U177*, at 184 days, the longest Kentrat's *U196*, on patrol for a total of 225 days, nearly eight months. Lüth's experience of his marathon voyage in command of *U181* resulted in his now-famous lecture 'Problems of Leadership in a Submarine', presented at a convention of Naval Officers at Weimar on 17 December 1943 before he was transferred to command of Gotenhafen's 22nd U-Training Flotilla. Lüth was reputedly highly pedantic about the conduct of his men, which he supervised with an almost puritanical zeal, revealed within his lecture:

> There is no constant change between day and night, for the lights have to burn all the time inside the boat. There are no Sundays and no weekdays, and there is no regular change of seasons. Therefore life is monotonous and without rhythm, and the captain must attempt to compensate for these disadvantages as far as possible... I never had to contend with sexual problems on board, not even during the mission which lasted seven and one half months. To be sure, I have not permitted the men to hang pictures of nude girls on the bulkheads and over their bunks. If you are hungry you wouldn't paint bread on the wall.

Nonetheless, despite occasional mockery from his fellow officers for his somewhat intrusive and devoutly National Socialist supervision of his men, Lüth's crew appear to have maintained undiminished admiration for their captain, and *U181* remained combat effective throughout the longest voyages. Jürgen Oesten would also later undertake long-distance patrolling of the Indian Ocean aboard *U861*:

> On long-distance trips it is all the more essential to keep up a good and careful, direct contact with each member of the crew. It helps to publish a good weekly newspaper and in our case

the medical officer together with the wireless operators did a good job. Music helps as well and certain competitions and games.[7]

From that first wave of Type IXD-2 commander, as well as Lüth, Hartmann also departed his boat to Aix-en-Provence as FdU Mediterranean, while Robert Gysae became head of the 25th U-Training Flotilla. Only Kentrat remained with his boat following this epic voyage. However, despite their remarkable endurance, results had been paltry, and the U-boats were not fully refitted until the following year. Between them they had destroyed 25 ships (claiming 36) – the most, ten, by Lüth while Kentrat achieved a miserable two. Despite doubts regarding the wisdom of such operations, five U-boats had either already departed for Penang or were preparing to leave: *U848*, *U849*, *U510*, *U850* and *U172*. The experienced Wilhelm Rollmann in *U848* sank British freighter *Baron Semple* on 2 November northwest of Ascension, but three days later was spotted by a US Navy Liberator of Ascension-based VP-107 and depth charged, inflicting enough damage to prevent the U-boat submerging. With heavy bomber reinforcement and despite frantic anti-aircraft defence, *U848* was finally sunk, leaving 20 survivors visible in the water. Twenty-eight days later, a single delirious man, Hans Schade, was picked up by light cruiser USS *Marblehead*, dying within 48 hours.

By the year's end, only *U510* remained; four boats and 207 men were lost before reaching the Cape of Good Hope. Heinz-Otto Schultz's *U849* was destroyed on 25 November by depth charges from another Liberator of VP-107; *U172* was sunk on 13 December after refuelling from auxiliary tanker Type XB *U219* and surprised by aircraft. Although the tanker escaped, Hermann Hoffmann's *U172* was damaged by aircraft from USS *Bogue* and depth charged by destroyers. *U172* was forced to surface and a brief gun battle followed, during which Hoffmann himself manned a machine gun and killed an American sailor. Hopelessly outgunned, the crew abandoned ship and Hoffmann and 45 survivors were rescued as prisoners. Klaus Ewerth's *U850* was the last to be sunk, attacked by several Avengers and Wildcats of USS *Bogue*'s VC-19 on 20 December and hit by a 'Fido' homing torpedo, debris and body parts later recovered from a large pool of floating oil. The attack had come 25 minutes after a congratulatory radio message from Dönitz informed Ewerth that his wife had given birth to their fifth child.

Alfred Eick's *U510* refuelled successfully from *U219* on 24 November west of the Cape Verde Islands but narrowly escaping American pursuit after transmitting a sighting of *Osorno*. Rounding the Cape during mid-January, *U510* refuelled again from *Charlotte Schliemann* before sailing north to the Gulf of Aden. There Eick attacked convoy PA69 travelling from the Persian Gulf and sank British tanker *San Alvaro* and American *E.G. Seubert* as well as damaging Norwegian tanker *Erling Brövig*. During March, *U510* roved the Arabian Sea and destroyed two more freighters, a small sailing vessel and 249-ton minesweeping whaler HMS *Maaløy* near Ceylon, entering Georgetown harbour on 5 April. Eick was awarded the first Knight's Cross given in Malaya.

Wilhelm Spahr took his new command *U178* from Penang on 27 November 1943, loaded with 107 tons of tin ingots and 2 tons of tungsten welded within the keel and 30 tons of crude rubber, packed within the bilge, living quarters and superstructure of the boat. Unwilling to let offensive possibilities pass, Dönitz ordered *U178* to operate against shipping off the Indian sub-continent before heading to Bordeaux, an entire month spent with no targets until Spahr sank American Liberty ship *José Navarro* 200 miles west of Trivandrum. It was to be the arduous voyage's sole success.

As things stood at the beginning of 1944, the Penang U-boats were barely ready for return journeys. Dockyard capacity was limited and torpedoes in short supply. Nevertheless, *U532*, *U168*, *U188* and *U183* were ordered to embark similar cargoes as *U178* as well items such as opium, wolfram and quinine, and return to France via combat patrols in the Indian Ocean.

Junker's *U532* headed towards Ceylon, torpedoing two ships before making its way to rendezvous with *Charlotte Schliemann* to take fuel vital to the journey. Lüdden's *U188* hunted east of Aden and sank five ships by the month's end, adding Chinese freighter *Chung Cheng* and four cotton-carrying Arab dhows with torpedo, gunfire and ramming during February. As the dhows sank, Pich's *U168* sailed to patrol southwest of India before fuelling from *Charlotte Schliemann* and rounding the Cape to the Atlantic. The last, Schneewind's *U183*, also sailed for operations south and southwest of mainland India.

The limited-range Type IXCs required refuelling, and after *U532* reached *Charlotte Schliemann* on 11 February, bad weather prevented resupply and they sailed southward to a rearranged rendezvous 600 nautical miles distant in calmer seas, losing sight of each other in periodic blinding squalls. Aware of the tanker's presence through Ultra, the Royal Navy despatched Catalinas to shadow, while destroyer HMS *Relentless* and cruiser *Newcastle* reached the meeting point and sank *Charlotte Schliemann*. Meanwhile, *Brake* had recently sailed from Singapore with fuel, lubricating oil and provisions for 12 U-boats and was hurriedly despatched to meet *U532*, *U168* and *U188*. Lüdden replenished first, taking fuel and supplies despite rough seas, *U188* also requiring lubricating oil due to overheating diesels.

U188 remained nearby as picket boat while the others attempted resupply, *Brake's* captain curtailing attempts in deteriorating weather as they all travelled together towards the southwest. Lüdden's war diary records events three hours later:

> 1210hrs. Smoke feather bearing 140°T. With it 2 aircraft.
> Artillery fire from the direction of the smoke feather. Vessel still not distinguished. Am positioned about 500 meters behind *Brake*. Dived because I have no torpedoes. On board from 12.19 to 13.50 hours 148 artillery impacts and 14 heavy detonations were counted. In the boat some heavy concussions, because we are in the direct vicinity of *Brake*.[8]

The aircraft originated from carrier HMS *Battler*, again guided to the rendezvous by Ultra. Supported by cruisers HMS *Suffolk* and *Newcastle* and destroyers HMS *Roebuck* and *Quadrant*,

Operation *Covered* had been organized to specifically sink the supply ship, risking discovery of the Ultra secret by again using Enigma codebreaking to direct tactical advantage. *Roebuck* sighted *Brake* at a range of 13 miles and opened fire, the German crew scuttling while both U-boats dived to safety, Pich's *U168* later rescuing 135 German crewmen. However, the rescue was premature, and aircraft forced a crash dive, *U168* plummeting like a rock as its trim was severely affected by the extra weight, an unexploded depth charge denting the outer casing. Cautiously, *U168* resurfaced after dark, hydrophones detecting clear traces of enemy destroyers nearby. *U168* returned hideously overcrowded alongside *U532* to Jakarta. The destruction of the Indian Ocean tankers assured that neither boat would ever see France again. Only *U188* had taken aboard enough fuel for the voyage to Bordeaux though empty of torpedoes and in dire jeopardy due to lubricating oil problems.

After entering the Atlantic, Lüdden was instructed to contact Gerhard Seehausen's *U66*, one of the oldest Type IXs still in service and desperately short of supplies. Orders to *U68* and *U515* to meet with Seehausen had remained unanswered; both were sunk by aircraft from USS *Guadalcanal* northwest of Madeira during April. *U66* was in bad shape after nearly four months at sea, sinking four ships in the Gulf of Guinea – the last significant U-boat success in that area. Fuel and rations were extremely low, and the inexperienced medical officer Wolf Loch discovered that a packing error had provided only one small bottle of vitamin pills; as a result, the crew began to exhibit classic symptoms of scurvy. Awaiting resupply, *U66* was forced to spend time surfaced as the aged batteries were incapable of holding a full charge. *U66* was cornered by Americans on 6 May:

> 0518hrs: Lüdden [*U188*] not met. Supplying impossible since [we have been] D/Fed constantly since the 26th... Central Atlantic worse than Biscay...
> 0615hrs: Plane keeping in touch.
> 0622hrs: Being attacked by destroyer.

With *U66* unable to dive, action against USS *Buckley* (part of Task Group 21.11 centred around carrier *Block Island*) resulted in the two vessels becoming interlocked with men even fighting hand-to-hand aboard the American's decks. Gerhard Seehausen and 23 of his men were killed in the fierce combat as the two vessels traded gunfire before *U66* went under.

With *U188* also suffering problems – the transmitter inoperative and engine lubricant of the wrong viscosity – Lüdden pressed on to France. Only by mixing cooking fat with the oil did the U-boat manage to limp into port on 19 June. Carrying intelligence documents for Dönitz, Lüdden was ordered to Berlin, but his convoy was ambushed by the French Resistance, emboldened by the approach of American troops. He was captured and the documents taken, including information detailing U-boat approach channels to Penang, Singapore and Jakarta. Although Lüdden later escaped and was rescued by Waffen SS troops, the loss of the documents was a blow to Dönitz.*

With both tankers sunk within the expanse of the Indian Ocean, Dönitz once again considered the probability of Enigma having been compromised. As Günter Hessler later wrote, 'Treason, compromise of the U-boat codes, or interception of radio traffic to Japan may have been contributory causes, but nothing definite could be established.'[9] Nonetheless, BdU immediately ordered current code keys discarded and an 'emergency procedure' of every boat setting Enigma rotors to match initial letters of the addresses, forenames and surnames of their chief radio operator and Third Watch Officer. Allied codebreaking was barely affected. In Whitehall, Churchill was furious that the Enigma secret had been wielded by the Admiralty in what he considered a clumsy manner, despite destruction of the two Indian Ocean tankers thwarting return of three U-boats laden with cargo, and forcing *U183* to also return to Penang.

While the destruction of *Charlotte Schliemann* could have been merely fortunate for the Allies, the sinking of *Brake* stretched

---

* Lüdden, awarded the Knight's Cross during this last patrol, was later transferred to BdU Staff, responsible for artillery and navigational matters. He was mortally injured during an accidental fire aboard the training ship *Daressalam* on 13 January 1945.

credulity. The Admiralty's prepared cover story for the latter was that U-boat transmissions near the refuelling sight excused an anti-submarine sweep, though the story was weak at best. As a result, decrypted transmission of a meeting between *U801*, damaged by American carrier aircraft, and U-tanker *U488* for resupply west of Cape Verde led to strict Allied instructions to remain clear of this meeting so as not to compound the potential problem. Though Royal Navy forces withdrew, Admiral King refused to do so, and Task Group 21.11 sank *U801* and the Type VIIF *U1059* that was carrying a cargo of 39 torpedoes for Penang. King and First Sea Lord Sir Andrew Cunningham exchanged heated messages over the American's refusal to follow instructions, though King correctly maintained that *Block Island* was just one of many hunter-killer groups sweeping the Atlantic, thereby not betraying the Ultra secret.

On 4 May, the last Type XIV U-tanker, *U490*, departed Kiel bound for Penang. By stationing within the Indian Ocean, Wilhelm Gerlach's tanker could resupply those Type IXCs now trapped in Malaya. On 12 June, guided once again by decrypted Enigma messages, Task Force 223 centred on escort carrier USS *Croatan* was despatched to find and sink the U-boat. Despite Gerlach being extremely cautious during his voyage into the Atlantic, a briefly transmitted weather report to BdU on 11 June was detected by HF/DF and *U490* hit by Hedgehog projectiles fired by destroyer USS *Frost*. Subsequent Hedgehog and depth-charge attacks by USS *Frost*, *Huse* and *Inch* forced *U490* to the surface, illuminated by searchlights and fired upon until the crew abandoned ship and scuttled, all 60 men rescued. It was the end of the U-tankers.

Chapter Eleven

Total Commitment

'The Atlantic is my first line of defence in the West...'
Adolf Hitler, 5 June 1943

Although individual U-boats still sailed to North America, the Caribbean, Brazil and West Africa – maintaining an average monthly presence of one to two boats within the operational zone – successes were slight, as everywhere they confronted heavily escorted convoys and near constant air patrols. Perhaps the most satisfying kill, made on 29 May by Detlev Krankenhagen's *U549* bound for Brazil, was the sinking of carrier USS *Block Island* from Task Group 21.11. The American force had been put onto *U549*'s trail by Enigma intelligence, Avenger and Wildcat aircraft hounding the boat the previous day and night. Krankenhagen hit *Block Island* with three T3 torpedoes, a *Zaunkönig* then used to damage escorting USS *Barr* during depth-charge attacks. The carrier sank within one and a quarter hours, six Wildcat fighters already aloft forced to head for the Canary Islands, ditching that night, and only two crews later rescued. By then, Krankenhagen was gone, his boat lost with all hands to American depth charges.

The American 'hunter-killer' task forces had been an inspired use of US Navy power, and on 4 June Task Force 233 of five destroyer escorts and carrier USS *Guadalcanal* achieved the remarkable distinction of capturing *U505* intact as the boat returned from West Africa. Enigma intelligence sent by Knowles' F-21 U-boat

tracking room had warned of *U505*, *U190* and *U155* all close to
the Gulf of Guinea coastline. Interestingly, Knowles' estimation of
exactly where *U505* was, was off by 267 miles; BdU's estimation
was off by 452.

Using HF/DF, USS *Guadalcanal* homed relentlessly on *U505*
until the boat was detected by USS *Chatelain*, depth charged and
damaged, Harald Lange surfacing his U-boat whereupon two
Wildcat fighters began strafing. Ordering *U505* scuttled, Lange
was hit by machine-gun fire and shrapnel in both knees and legs
and lost consciousness. His First Watch Officer, Paul Meyer, was
also badly wounded, and it appears that panic gripped the crew
as they attempted to exit through heavy gunfire. Chief Engineer
Josef Hauser failed to set scuttling charges, later claiming that
he believed the boat was sinking when he left, though two men
attempted to fulfil Lange's scuttling order but were foiled by
jammed valves on the diving cells and an American boarding party
that replaced a sea strainer removed to flood the boat. Led by
Albert David, the boarding party from USS *Pillsbury* secured *U505*
despite the potential danger of scuttling explosives going off at any
second. *U505* was towed to Bermuda; a half-ton of documents
and equipment was retrieved, an intelligence bonanza including
a working Enigma machine, cypher material, charts, engineering
manuals and the *Addressbuch* enabling double enciphering of
grid references. With the German crew isolated from others, and
Americans sworn to secrecy, the capture was never discovered by
BdU and Enigma's fall was complete.

In conference with Hitler during March, Dönitz had related his
plan to use U-boats 'more sparingly' except in the case of invasion,
because of severe casualties. During 1943, 244 U-boats had been
lost to all causes, 90 more than the total lost between the outbreak
of war and end of 1942. Already during January and February
1944, 37 more had been lost and interim countermeasures failed
to slow down this horrendous attrition. Dönitz maintained that,
though the outlook remained bleak, U-boat operations could never
come to a standstill, as not only would morale never recover, but,
as he emphasized to his own officers, every aircraft engaged on

ASW work was one less bombing Germany. In this he was largely mistaken, many of the aircraft involved being unsuitable for standard bombing missions, and the number of B24s engaged having no substantial impact on heavy bomber missions over Germany and occupied Europe.

On the Eastern Front, within the Black Sea, Rosenbaum had deftly operated his small flotilla, though attempts to form small patrol lines and hunt Soviet tanker traffic largely failed. Regular skirmishes with Soviet landing and patrol craft occurred as 30th U-Flotilla supported the German retreat to the Crimean Peninsula. Minelaying before Soviet harbours and attacks on Soviet destroyers engaged in shore bombardment yielded little confirmed results, although, in conjunction with Luftwaffe raids, caused Stalin to tighten his paranoid grip on Soviet naval forces, disallowing use of major surface ships without his express permission. By this, the flotilla's strategic goal was at least somewhat achieved.

By 1944, the aged Type IIB U-boats and their crews had become increasingly fatigued by combined bad weather, Soviet air power and constantly bad war news. On 8 April 1944, Soviet landings on the Crimean Peninsula began and with it another general German retreat. Within one month, 90,260 Axis soldiers and 15,435 wounded had been evacuated by sea from Crimea to Constanta, with Sevastopol falling to the Soviets on 9 May. Two days later, Rosenbaum embarked for a routine flight to meet with Brinkmann and discuss Crimea's fall, the aircraft suffering mechanical failure immediately once airborne and crashing, killing all on board. Temporary control passed to Clemens Schöler of Rosenbaum's staff, before Klaus Petersen, former captain of *U9*, assumed control in July 1944.

At the other extreme of the Eastern Front, lines in Finnmark had barely moved since the early days of *Barbarossa*, though increased British air and submarine activity around the Norwegian coast repeatedly stirred fears in Berlin of Allied invasion. On 16 February, orders were issued to create an anti-invasion force, effectively tying 21 U-boats to the *'Mitte'* group that lay inactive and unused spread between Narvik and Stavanger under the tactical command of

Viktor Schütze (serving as FdU Training Flotillas) and subject to the depredation of Coastal Command attacks, ironically in support of the impending invasion of Normandy. Another flotilla had been formed during the previous year. The 13th U-Flotilla had been created in Trondheim by the administrative transfer of 12 U-boats, which remained operationally unaffected and still under FdU Norway direction, the post now held by veteran commander Reinhard Suhren. Trondheim increasingly became the focal point for Arctic boats while the 11th U-Flotilla at Bergen generally functioned as a transit point for U-boats headed west.

The Arctic had been a steady drain on Dönitz's U-boats throughout 1943. Establishing weather stations in remote locations, minelaying near Soviet harbours, skirmishing with British and Soviet naval forces and operating in support of futile surface force forays into the Arctic occupied them until resumption of convoying from Britain during November 1943. However, as well as U-boats failing to impede the convoy, battleship *Scharnhorst* was sailed into action against JW55B during atrocious weather conditions and sunk off the North Cape.

With *Tirpitz* in repair following a British midget submarine attack, Kriegsmarine Norwegian strength resided now with U-boats, and during December, in conference with Hitler, Dönitz finally agreed to reinforce the Arctic, the overall strength of the 11th U-Flotilla to be raised to 24. Although group operations continued against Arctic convoys, victories were few and casualties high.

In the Mediterranean, the 29th U-Flotilla reacted with little energy to the fresh crisis of Allied landings at Anzio in January 1944 that attempted to outflank German positions. Under Werner Hartmann's direction as FdU Mediterranean, both *U223* and *U230* attacked invasion shipping and claimed two destroyers, a patrol vessel, three LSTs and an LCF sunk. The reality was that during January, not one vessel was destroyed by U-boat, the 'fire-and-forget' weaponry resulting in over-zealous claims. To the south, on 15 February Horst Fenski's *U410* sank freighter *Fort St Nicolas* headed for Salerno east of Capri, lightly damaged by retaliatory depth charges. Three days later, Fenski sank the first ship bound for Anzio destroyed by U-boat when he torpedoed destroyer HMS *Penelope*, which sank in 40 seconds with 417 men killed. Two nights later, Fenski also sank *LST348* in a surfaced attack, a single 3-inch shell fired towards *U410* as it retreated at speed. Docking successfully in Toulon on 28 February, *U410* was destroyed along with *U380* by USAAF bombing 11 days later.

Scattered ships were sunk throughout the Mediterranean over the weeks that followed, ranging from Algerian waters by newly arrived *U969* to the Anzio beachhead and on to the Lebanese coast, where *U453* sank sailing vessels by gunfire and ramming. By the end of May, ten reinforcing U-boats had arrived within the Mediterranean thus far during 1944, but 11 had been sunk. Despite its occasional successes in action, the 29th U-Flotilla exerted no real influence on Allied operations, less even than an exhausted and overstretched Luftwaffe that was also reliant on new technology – guided glide and rockets bombs – revitalizing largely obsolete equipment. On the evening of 19 May, Dierk Lührs sank 7,147-ton British freighter *Fort Missanabie* from convoy HA43 south of Taranto. Lührs bottomed his boat at 180 metres and all but essential lights were doused, with crew members ordered to lie down to conserve oxygen. As dawn broke overhead, *U453* rose off the bottom and crept away, later located by destroyers HMS *Liddesdale*, *Tenacious* and *Termagant* at noon, beginning a 12-hour chase that, despite evasive turns and twice use of Bold capsules, caused such severe damage that *U435* surfaced and scuttled, one man killed by British gunfire in the water. As Lührs was taken prisoner, he was not to know that his success against HA43 was the last ship sunk by a Mediterranean U-boat.

While phantom invasion was feared in Norway, actual invasion finally broke on the French coast. Despite Hitler's statement to Dönitz in June 1943 that he would rather fight a war in the Atlantic than on the shores of Europe, one year later the long-awaited second front opened in Normandy with Operation *Overlord*, its naval component named *Neptune*. Since April, all Type VIICs in France had ceased offensive patrols, instead being fitted as quickly as possible with *Schnorchels*, extended flak weaponry and the latest

radar detectors and torpedoes. Dönitz formed group 'Landwirt',
an anti-invasion group held at six hours' readiness, similar to 'Mitte'
in Norway.

Of somewhat indeterminate size due to U-boats undergoing
work, when Allied forces stormed ashore in Normandy, 36 U-boats
answered the 'Landwirt' call to arms. In Brest 15 U-boats were
available, known as the 'Holzbein' group, though possessing only
eight boats equipped with a Schnorchel. These were instructed to
immediately sail for Seine Bay and engage the enemy fleet. The
remaining seven were initially ordered to 'proceed surfaced at night
at high speed' to the English coast near Plymouth, though, as
Eberhard Godt wrote within the BdU War Diary, 'This means the
last mission for those boats without Schnorchel.' 'Landwirt' U-boats
from the other ports were formed into a reconnaissance line along
the 200-metre curve at the western Channel entrance.

All 'Landwirt' boats were provided with detailed instructions
by FdU West Hans-Rudolf Rösing, whom Dönitz designated
Director of Operations in the case of an invasion. From Rösing
and subsequent briefings by 1st U-Flotilla commander Werner
Winter arose the controversial 'ramming order' claimed by some
to have been given to 'Landwirt' skippers. According to captains
Herbert Werner (U415) and Heinz Marbach (U953), Rösing ended
his briefing with instructions that U-boats were to 'attack and sink
invasion fleet with the final objective of destroying enemy ships by
ramming'.[1] This emotive topic continues to elicit debate, and it is
possible that confusion stemmed from Dönitz's 'Order of the Day'
in which he stated:

Every enemy vessel which serves the landing, even if it ferries
only half a hundred sailors or a tank, is a target demanding
the total commitment of the boat. It is to be attacked even if
one's own boat is put at risk. When it is a matter of getting
at the enemy landing fleet, no thought must be given to the
danger of shallow water or possible mine barriers or any other
consideration. Every man and every weapon of the enemy
destroyed before the landing reduces the enemy's chance of

success. But the U-boat which inflicts losses on the enemy at the landing has fulfilled its highest task and justified its existence, even though it stays there.

The rhetoric of 'total commitment' was nothing new in the Wehrmacht and had been used with U-boats fighting against the *Torch* invasion, but it was open to misinterpretation. I asked Rösing in Kiel during a visit in 2001 directly about the supposed order he had given:

> That is true, and it's not true. Well, when they were sent out, I went to Brest to speak to the commanders. And, Dönitz had said 'you must fully risk your boats – you must take large risks.' And it may be that somebody said 'even to ram', maybe the situation is that you do this too. But of course, this was not the order. No, Dönitz was not a friend of suicidal missions.[2]

However unintentional, the commitment of *'Landwirt'* was hopeless. Of the 15 Brest boats, only five came anywhere near the invasion fleet: *U629*, *U373*, *U441*, *U740* and *U821* were all sunk; *U256*, *U413*, *U415* and *U963* returned with damage, and *U269* was forced to divert to St Peter Port, Guernsey and sunk on 25 June after putting to sea for a fresh attempt. Coastal Command saturated the western end of the Channel with Operation *Cork* sweeps, and on 10 June Rösing was ordered to halt sailings for the invasion front and pull back all surviving U-boats not equipped with a *Schnorchel* to the defensive line established on the 200-metre curve. Coastal Command's offensive sweep covered every part of the *Cork* area, from southern Ireland to the mouth of the Loire, with aircraft every 30 minutes, denying U-boats time to charge batteries, and three days later those without *Schnorchels* were recalled to harbour and prepared for defence against unlikely landings in Brittany. The only successes *'Landwirt'* had were the crippling of frigate HMS *Goodson*, later declared a total constructive loss, and severe damage to four Liberty ships of convoy EMC17 headed to Utah Beach, all inflicted by *U984*. The U-boat's commander, 23-year-old Heinz

Sieder, was awarded the Knight's Cross after his successful return to Brest, lost to unknown causes during their next mission, the wreck later found lying southwest of Brighton. During the entirety of June, only five merchants were sunk within the immediate invasion area and five others struck mines laid off British harbours.

Five days after the invasion had begun, two U-boats south of Nova Scotia, two in the Caribbean and two in the Gulf of Guinea, were ordered to break off operations and return to France, or Norway, if sufficient fuel remained. Eleven U-boats sailed from Norway to reinforce the attack on *Neptune* shipping, seven destroyed during transit. Meanwhile, the '*Mitte*' U-boats held for a phantom invasion were whittled to six by Dönitz, with the remainder posted to the Arctic or Baltic where Soviet forces pushed into Estonia. As D-Day had exploded in Normandy, 32 U-boats had been under Reinhard 'Teddy' Suhren's command within the Arctic, and by August, with Allied troops firmly ashore in France, and escort ship allocation reduced, Murmansk convoys recommenced, with JW59 taking Suhren and his staff by surprise.

Suhren committed five boats of the '*Trutz*' group, with two reinforcements joining them. They sank sloop HMS *Kite* as it travelled at only 6 knots while attempting to untangle the pipes of its foxer decoy, only 14 men rescued, while one of the boats racing from Narvik – Hans-Jürgen Stahmer's *U354* – blundered into a carrier group embarked upon Operation *Goodwood*, a planned air strike against *Tirpitz*. Firing a spread of FAT torpedoes at close range, Stahmer hit escort carrier HMS *Nabob* in the stern and frigate HMS *Bickerton*, killing 38 men and causing the latter to be abandoned and scuttled. *U354* was kept underwater by aircraft as a skeleton crew aboard *Nabob* restored power, the carrier later reaching Rosyth and scrapped. Stahmer's victory was fleeting; *U354* was sunk northeast of the North Cape by depth charges from escort ships two days later. Despite wild claims of success attributed to T5 and FAT torpedoes, JW59 did not lose a single merchant ship, although returning convoy RA60 lost two steamers torpedoed by Wolfgang Ley's *U310*.

In Normandy, German lines crumbled and American forces reached Avranches on 4 August – the gateway to Brittany and the Atlantic U-boat bases. U-boats in Brest, Lorient and Saint Nazaire began relocating south to La Pallice and Bordeaux, while, from Angers, FdU West was also forced to evacuate and move to La Rochelle with a mobile radio truck. British and Canadian air and naval forces tightened their grip on Biscay in a concerted attempt to destroy not only U-boats at sea, but escorting vessels that shepherded them to and from harbour. It was devastatingly successful. The U-boat bunkers were repeatedly bombed, though only superficial damage resulted to all but Brest, where the roof was finally breached, albeit with no damage inflicted on any U-boats. The towns surrounding the bunkers were virtually levelled.

American forces placed Brest under siege from 6 August, the deep-water port a strategic Allied objective, held by a mixed bag of Wehrmacht troops stiffened by paratroopers of 2nd *Fallschirmjäger* Division. The battle that followed lasted until 17 September and was hugely destructive in both human lives and the city and its environs. With the port's surrender, 1st U-Flotilla commander Werner Winter and an undetermined number of flotilla personnel from this and 9th U-Flotilla passed into captivity. Ironically, Brest – its harbour clogged with obstructions sunk by the Germans – had lost all significance by then, as Antwerp had also been liberated, providing a deep-water supply hub closer to the front line.

With every French U-boat port under threat of land attack, all but Bordeaux were declared 'fortresses', ordered held to deny their use to the enemy while U-boats evacuated to Norway. Imperative had been placed on *Schnorchel* installation of those boats hitherto unequipped and only four were left in French harbours – *U123* and *U129* in Lorient, *U178* and *U188* in Bordeaux – all immobilized by lack of batteries, and scuttled. Lorient, Saint Nazaire and La Rochelle were defended once again by scratch formations, including men from the U-boat flotillas whose boats had been destroyed, or staff and personnel simply trapped by the rapid Allied advance. Rather than repeat the horrific battle of Brest, Allied command placed the ports under siege, all three only surrendering in May 1945; Saint Nazaire was last, three days after the unconditional German surrender was signed at Reims.

The Atlantic ports had been trapped in a vice as Allied troops also advanced from the south of France. During the second half of 1944 within the Mediterranean, only four U-boats left port for offensive patrols, achieving nothing against stifling air and naval power. Allied forces penned at Anzio had broken out, and Operation *Dragoon* put Allied troops ashore in Provence on 15 August, opposed only by *U230*, which ran aground on the Saint Mandrier Peninsula east of Toulon and was scuttled, the crew captured the following day. Toulon and Marscilles were both captured by the Allies on 27 August, Gunter Jahn, head of the 29th U-Flotilla, among the prisoners taken. Amid the detritus of scuttled and bombed U-boats left behind, French troops found four dissembled sections of a Type XXIII U-boat in Toulon. The post of FdU Mediterranean was dissolved, and in the Aegean Sea, the scuttling of *U565* and *U596* in Salamis harbour marked the end of the 29th U-Flotilla as German troops began their difficult withdrawal from Greece.

In Norway, with the influx of U-boats from France, Suhren's position of FdU Norway became FdU Norwegian Sea following the arrival of Rösing who remained FdU West, responsible for logistical support of U-boats outside of Arctic waters and gradually assigned greater operational control. *Tirpitz* was repeatedly damaged by air raids until 12 November, when RAF Lancasters carrying Tallboy bombs caused the great ship to capsize, eradicating the final German surface threat as morale began to crack among the U-boat men. During October, *U995*'s commander Walter Köhntopp was threatened with court martial for alleged cowardice after evading air attack by remaining submerged and reportedly stating the boat's position as 'hopeless'. The humanitarian Suhren consulted with the head physician at Narvik's Kriegsmarine Hospital and arranged for Köhntopp to be certified as medically unfit and transferred ashore to the flotilla staff, his place taken by zealous Hans-Georg Hess.

While August and September had been devastating for U-boats in western Europe, the six overworked Type IIs of 30th U-Flotilla were also ground beneath the enemy's heel. Constanta harbour was now directly attacked by Il-2 ground attack 'Sturmoviks', and on 20 August one such raid damaged *U18* and *U24* with bomb splinters and sank the 'Iron Cross boat' *U9* with a direct hit. Rendered non-operational, *U18* and *U24* sailed only once more, to be scuttled southeast of Cape Tuzla. Three days after the air raid, King Michael I mounted a coup d'état in Romania, deposing the Antonescu dictatorship and deserting the Axis cause.

Romanian ships were now legitimate targets, and command of the remaining three U-boats passed directly to *MGK Süd*, while Brinkmann and Petersen organized evacuation from Romania. *U23* sailed to within 800 metres of Sevastopol harbour, but found no Soviet ships, returning to position east of Constanta, while *U20* occupied a new operational area east of Sulina and *U19* lay off the Danube delta. Bulgaria also wavered on leaving the Axis powers, though BdU ordered the boats to remain on station, exhausting offensive capabilities before scuttling off the Bulgarian coast if still German occupied.

Rudolf Arendt's *U23* attacked Constanta harbour on 1 September, firing three torpedoes at Romanian warships, hitting destroyer *Regina Maria* in the stern and sinking 2,686-ton steamer *Oituz* on the shallow seabed. Leaving the scene, Arendt deployed an EMS mine before sailing southeast.* The flotilla's final attack was made by Willy Ohlenburg's *U19* early the following day, sinking 441-ton Soviet minesweeper *BTSC-410 Vzryv*. Travelling in company with Romanian minelayer *Admiral Murgescu*, the Soviets accused the Romanian Navy of treachery and complicity in the sinking and punitively seized the Romanian fleet.

As the remnants of the 30th U-Flotilla in Constanta joined the hurried retreat towards Germany, the three active boats were ordered to scuttle. With no chance of reaching German-held shoreline during the fluid land battle, all three sailed for Turkish territorial waters and were abandoned and sunk within sight of land, their crews interned by Turkish authorities for the remainder of the war. The 30th U-Flotilla ceased to officially exist in October 1944.

---

* The EMS 'periscope-drift-mine' resembled a U-boat periscope, encouraging an enemy vessel to ram and detonate the 14-kilogram warhead.

During August, *U862* with *U861* and *U198*, under new commander Burkhard Heusinger von Waldegg, had a brief rash of success in and around the Mozambique Channel despite Royal Navy Force 65, built around the carrier HMS *Battler*, hunting them; *U198* was sunk shortly thereafter. Following his arrival in Penang with *U862*, Heinrich Timm reported dwindling targets and improving ASW tactics within the Indian Ocean and suggested an ambitious thrust into the Pacific towards southwest Australia, an area Timm had sailed as a merchant seaman. BdU added *U168* (finishing repairs in Jakarta) and *U537* (in Surabaya) to the operation, and Helmut Pich took *U168* to Surabaya for battery trials before beginning the mission. Details of his scheduled departure and arrival times, intended speed and route were passed to Japanese authorities by radio signal, in turn intercepted and immediately decoded by Allied intelligence who, as well as breaking the Enigma code, had long been reading Japanese cyphers. Dutch submarine *Zwaardfish* intercepted *U168* and hit it with three torpedoes out of six, with 27 survivors, including Pich, taken prisoner. Werner Striegler's *U196* was ordered to replace Pich in Singapore, for removal and replacement of the keel cargo.

Peter Schrewe's *U537* departed on 9 November, the Japanese naval picket at Surabaya radioing details of departure times, course, and the U-boat's route, including estimated times passing specific landmarks. American Fleet submarine USS *Flounder* was waiting and hit *U537* with a stern salvo at only 1,000 yards. There were no survivors. *U196*, ordered by BdU first to meet with inbound *U510* in the Indian Ocean before heading to Australia, departed on schedule on the last day of November and disappeared to unknown causes. Only Timm in *U862* reached the Pacific, sailing as far as Gisborne Harbour, New Zealand, in a 90-day patrol that narrowly missed New Zealand coaster *Pukeko* with torpedoes near Napier but sank two Liberty ships: *Robert J. Walker* southeast of Sydney and the only vessel destroyed by U-boat within the Pacific; and *Peter Silvester* west of Perth and the last ship sunk by Far Eastern U-boats.

The establishment of Penang's U-boats proved an exercise in futility, Georgetown abandoned by U-boats after Liberators from RAF 159 Squadron from Kharagpur, India, laid 60 mines in the port's approach channels during the night of 27 October. Japanese conventional minesweeping capability was extremely low; against acoustic and magnetic mines it was non-existent. German personnel withdrew to Jakarta and Surabaya, the former declared the primary combat base for Far Eastern U-boats in late November.

Type VIIF *U1062* had arrived in Penang successfully on 19 April with its load of torpedoes and spare parts for the U-boat base, but only eight more U-boats would complete the voyage successfully. During 1944, 15 were lost attempting to make the journey, two were forced to abort back to France, and the last U-boat bound to the East – Type XB *U234* – departed Kiel in March 1945 and would surrender to the US Navy at the end of May.

Of those planning a reciprocal voyage to Europe, after *U188*'s June 1944 arrival, only Jürgen Oesten's *U861* reached Trondheim on 19 April 1945 and Alfred Eicke's *U510* entered besieged Saint Nazaire on 24 April 1945. Ottoheinrich Junker's *U532*, which had departed Jakarta on 13 January, sailed into Liverpool harbour to surrender on 10 May. Regarding their transportation value, U-boats safely transported 611.4 tons of valuable cargo from east to west – 0.58 per cent of the 104,552 tons shipped by surface blockade breaker. According to historian Jürgen Rohwer, during 34 patrols German U-boats destroyed 133 ships, totalling around 687,500 tons, within the Indian Ocean. By comparison, Japanese submarines sank a confirmed 596,840 tons; the attention of the Imperial Japanese Navy focussed on the Pacific.

At sea there was little that U-boats could now do to heavily impact fighting on continental Europe, but that's not to say that their threat had completely diminished. Complacency within the Allied ranks was quickly punished as *U486* displayed in a December patrol that destroyed a freighter near Plymouth, and troopship and two frigates near Cherbourg. The sinking of troop transport *Léopoldville* on Christmas Eve was particularly devastating; 763 men of the US 66th Infantry Division were killed and the combat worth of the division was so shaken that they were posted to stand opposite the dormant front line surrounding Lorient and Saint Nazaire's fortress cities until the war's end.

While new midget submarines and explosive motorboats of the *Kleinkampfverbände* (small battle units) prepared for operations in the Scheldt estuary before Antwerp, conventional U-boats began operating close inshore in British waters, Dönitz hoping to prolong the battle until the electro-boats could enter service. Within the Baltic several Type XXI and Type XXIII U-boats were beginning 'working up' trials. Unexpected problems and defects caused by the bombing of German industry and the transport system complicated assembly times for vessels designed to be built in modular sections and then assembled at one central shipyard location. This dislocation, combined with inevitable design flaws and innovations, kept the boats training within the Baltic, being heavily mined by Allied bombers. Bomber Command mined the Skagerrak and Kattegat and the southern coast of Norway, forcing U-boats sailing from Germany to proceed surfaced where Liberators attacked by night, Mosquitoes and Beaufighters hounding them by day.

The 'inshore campaign' by which Dönitz hoped to stalemate the Allies began in September 1944, a handful of Type IX boats trying this new tactic against Canada and the northern portion of the United States, while 120 Type VIIs were sent to the British coast, commanders granted considerable leeway in deciding whether to launch operations in what were sure to be heavily contested waters. Radio silence became the norm, as no centralized BdU coordination was required. Initially, the North Channel and Irish Sea yielded the greatest results, the U-boat combat zone soon extended to the English Channel.

Amid strong tidal streams, often confusing bottom topography and many wrecks strewn around the British Isles, U-boats found a certain degree of shelter from ASDIC, which had been reduced to 50 per cent effectiveness at best. Aircraft, their biggest killer for over a year, were almost completely useless, unable to detect *Schnorchel* heads if the U-boat was trimmed as low as possible for functionality. U-boats frequently bottomed in shallow water and awaited hydrophone detection of convoy traffic, rising to attack, and then bottoming once more amid the jumbled seabed of rocks and wrecks.

Disturbed by this unexpected reversal, fresh defensive minelaying in northern and southern approaches to the Irish Sea was undertaken by the British, designed to force U-boats offshore if not sink them. Sonobuoys, first successfully used in July 1942, were heavily deployed by Coastal Command, frequently in conjunction with MAD (Magnetic Anomaly Detector) gear, although in shallow waters it displayed the inability to distinguish between sources of magnetic variance, i.e. wreck or U-boat. However, used in combination with sonobuoys, the MAD allowed an aircraft to localize sonobuoy contacts, which could provide confirmation that the contact was, indeed, a submarine.

The sudden loss to the Allies of both radio direction finding and Enigma code-breaking due to the lack of U-boat radio transmissions contributed to an initial decrease in U-boat sinkings. Radar had been largely nullified by U-boats remaining submerged, and radar detection equipment mounted on *Schnorchel* heads allowed submerged boats to detect incoming Allied search aircraft and dive.

This invisibility, however, was instantly lost once an attack had been launched. Allied methods of hunting a U-boat to exhaustion were as effective as ever once the enemy had betrayed its presence, although due to a lack of radio reporting, subsequent losses that swiftly began to overtake the inshore U-boats were not yet appreciated in Berlin. Into 1945, presumed effectiveness of the inshore offensive ensured fresh departures from Norway through to March; 27 U-boats had sailed into action during February, the highest commitment to the offensive to date, from which 16 were sunk. Of the 24 that sailed during March, 15 were destroyed. Despite this high concentration of U-boats, successes were slight and overclaiming rife. For example, on 21 February Karl-Hermann Schneidewind recorded within *U1064*'s KTB that he had attacked and sunk three ships in the North Channel, totalling an aggregated 17,000 tons. In fact, only 1,564-ton Icelandic steamer *Dettifoss* from convoy UR155 had been sunk. Additionally, *U1203* sank just a single ship during ten and a half weeks at sea, the 580-ton British ASW trawler HMT *Ellesmere*, rather optimistically claimed by Sigurd Seeger as a 5,000-ton freighter.

Despite this miserable return, 31 January 1945 marked a seminal moment, when new boat *U2324* joined the inshore campaign – the first Type XXIII to sail operationally, bound for the Firth of Forth. Hans Hass took seven days to bring *U2324* to his allocated patrol area, launching an attack on 18 February against a small coastal convoy at only 400 metres' range. Firing both torpedoes, Hass missed due to a gyro angling failure and returned, dejected, to Norway.

Hass had demonstrated the major flaw in the Type XXIII as an offensive weapon. Though fast and agile underwater, the small U-boat possessed only two torpedoes, loaded from outside and therefore single-shot weapons; less even than the Type II U-boat with which Germany had begun the war. Comparing the Type IID and Type XXIII is interesting. The Type IID carried five torpedoes and was capable of a range of 5,650 surfaced nautical miles, but only 56 submerged, with a surfaced top speed of 12.7 knots and 7.4 submerged. The Type XXIII carried two torpedoes and was capable of a range of 2,600 nautical miles surfaced, 194 submerged and top speeds of 9.7 knots surfaced and 12.5 submerged. Undoubtedly, the newer design was more mobile and effective as a submerged weapon of war, but despite its greater likelihood of survival compared with the Type II, the Type XXIII carried no more weaponry than a *Seehund* midget submarine.

By the time of *U2324*'s return, a second Type XXIII had begun active service, Fridtjof Heckel taking *U2322* from Kristiansand on 6 February to the Firth of Forth. After one failed shot, Heckel attacked convoy FS1739 south of Berwick on 25 February and hit Danish ship *Egholm* sailing for the British Ministry of War. The 1,317-ton freighter sank in 25 metres of water, and the Type XXIII had finally achieved victory in combat. Only two more Type XXIIIs would sink anything before the war's end.

Within the Arctic, the front line had finally moved after nearly four years of war. Exhausted by battle against the Soviets, Finland signed an armistice with effect from 19 September 1944. German troops were to be expelled from Finland and the Wehrmacht evacuated troops from Finnmark in a scorched earth retreat, establishing a new defensive line at Lyngenfjord with mountains creating a natural barrier east of Tromsø. Kirkenes was lost to the Finns as was Hammerfest, abandoned in October, and U-boats moved to Kilbotn.

Convoys JW61 and RA61 were both opposed by U-boat groups that, despite claims, hit only frigate HMS *Mounsey*, which suffered ten men killed but returned to Kola Inlet for temporary repair. Similar results were achieved from those convoys that followed to the end of 1944 while losses remained high. The last of the Norwegian flotillas – 14th U-Flotilla – was formed during December in Narvik under the command of Knight's Cross holder Helmut Möhlmann, former skipper of *U571*. It would number only eight U-boats on strength during its brief existence.

Willi Dietrich in *U286* made the final successful torpedo attack within Arctic waters as part of the '*Faust*' group when he torpedoed frigate HMS *Goodall* at the entrance to the Kola Inlet only 7 miles from Murmansk. The ship's magazine exploded, blowing away the forepart of the vessel and killing the commander James Vandalle Fulton and 111 other men. Dietrich's victory was short-lived; *U286* was sunk with all hands that same day by depth charges from British frigates HMS *Loch Insh*, *Anguilla* and *Cotton*.

Within the Baltic, large numbers of U-boats took part in the frantic evacuation of soldiers and civilians from East Prussia during the closing days of the war, while others mounted a final defence against Soviet Baltic naval forces with torpedoes and mines. Alongside surface ships of every description, U-boats rescued nearly 2,000 people from before the vengeful Red Army, some as individuals aboard cramped Type II training boats, others carrying 120 Luftwaffe flak artillerymen aboard a large Type XXI. Eventually, the chaos of the war's end overtook them all. Hitler committed suicide in his Berlin bunker on 30 April after naming Dönitz his successor. To him was left the final act of surrender. On 4 May he ordered his men to cease fire.

My U-boat men!

Six years of U-boat war lie behind us. You have fought like lions.

A crushing material superiority has forced us into a narrow area. A continuation of our fight from the remaining bases is no longer possible.

U-boat men! Undefeated and spotless you lay down your arms after a heroic battle without equal. We remember in deep respect our fallen comrades, who have sealed with death their loyalty to the Führer and Fatherland.

Comrades! Preserve your U-boat spirit, with which you have fought courageously, stubbornly and imperturbably though the years for the good of the Fatherland.

Long live Germany!

Instructed to surrender all U-boats intact to Allied forces, complete with weapon loads, 156 entered captivity as per instructions. A further 216 U-boats – some not yet commissioned – were scuttled in defiance as part of Operation *Regebogen*, originally a BdU initiative though 'cancelled' following the Allied surrender demands.

In France, the three besieged U-boat ports surrendered. Bernard Geismann, formerly of *U107*, had been acting as flotilla supply officer for Ernst Kals, commander of the 2nd U-Flotilla and naval troops trapped in Lorient. After months of trench warfare, Geismann was unwilling to go meekly into captivity.

On the evening of 7 May, 1945, I received the radio message from Germany that from 8 May there would be an armistice on all fronts. I personally handed this radio message to *Kapitän zur See* Kals in the officers' bunker. On the morning of 8 May a Feldwebel I knew came and persuaded me and 14 other sailors to flee the fortress in a boat that had been prepared. So, we got out of Lorient on the day of the surrender. After 32 hours of sailing we arrived in Santander, Spain. There we were welcomed in a friendly manner and later moved on to El Ferrol. However, in August 1945 we German soldiers were extradited to England and taken to prison camp in Edinburgh.[3]

Dönitz's U-boat war had lasted from the very first day of conflict with Britain, with torpedoes against *Athenia*, to the last and the sinking of *Avondale Park* on 7 May 1945. Despite the heroism of his men in action, U-boats had never come close to achieving their stated goal of determining the war's outcome through destruction of merchant shipping tonnage, only occasionally reaching his theoretical targets and never able to maintain that pressure. Numerically inferior at the outset, by the time Dönitz possessed his desired numbers, his technology was outdated, his crew inexperienced, his best men prisoners, dead, or physically and mentally spent. The vaunted Type XXI, in which he pinned hope of reversing the war at sea, could not live up to expectations. It was a flawed machine that, though pointing the way for future submarine design, was too hurried into service to have been successful, possessed of enough design faults to render them vulnerable. Only two sailed on war patrols, *U3008* and *U2511*, the latter captained by veteran 'Adi' Schnee, who claimed making a simulated attack after the cease fire order on cruiser HMS *Norfolk* and its destroyer screen before escaping undetected, although recent research throws doubt on this. Regardless, the Type XXI was too little and too late; several were lost to shipyard bombing raids or aircraft attacks.

Statistically, of 1,394 wartime commanders of U-boats commissioned into the Kriegsmarine – including those in training – 847 (60 per cent) failed to sink a single ship. The majority of those that were successful in either destroying a ship or causing it to be declared a constructive loss accounted for between one and five ships (399 commanders, 29 per cent); a further 66 (5 per cent) sank between six and ten ships, while 82 (6 per cent) destroyed over ten vessels. In the Royal Navy's post-war analysis of U-boat logs, they summed up these findings as 'most of the shipping casualties were inflicted by a large body of low performance individuals.'[4]

Many U-boat fates continue to be revised as wrecks are found and documents scoured once again. But these are the locations and causes of U-boat losses, not the result. In total, 749 U-boats were lost in action during the Second World War, with 26,971 men killed. This comprised nearly three-quarters of the fighting force assembled by Dönitz for his U-boat war.

Was Dönitz's overall 'tonnage-war' strategy unsound? No, though it proved unattainable. There was never any doubt that interdiction of Britain's maritime supply provided the only hope for German victory at sea. Indeed, upon the outbreak of war in 1939, *Grossadmiral* Raeder had recorded an entry within the SKL War Diary in which he stated:

> Today the war against England and France, which the Führer had previously assured us we would not have to confront until 1944 and which he believed he could avoid up until the very last minute, began... As far as the Kriegsmarine is concerned, it is obvious that it is not remotely ready for the titanic struggle against England... [Our] surface forces, moreover, are so weak and so few in numbers compared to the British fleet that the only course open to them, presupposing their active employment, is to show that they know how to die gallantly and thereby to create the basis for an eventual rebirth in the future.[5]

With such a bleak, though accurate, assessment, Germany's sole possibility for success lay in the U-boats. During the First World War, Germany had faced a similar situation with the Imperial Navy's surface fleet rendered impotent after the inconclusive Battle of Jutland. After flirting with unrestricted submarine warfare at various points but continually restraining this policy due to diplomatic pressure from the United States, the Kaiser finally allowed a full unrestricted campaign to begin on 1 February 1917, fought by 105 front-line U-boats: 69 in the Atlantic and off the Flanders coast, 23 in the Mediterranean, ten in the Baltic and three at Constantinople. The results were spectacular, as U-boats destroyed 25 per cent of all Britain-bound shipping and reduced that nation's supply of wheat to a six-week stockpile. The climactic month of April 1917 witnessed 413 ships destroyed totalling 873,754 tons, a figure never surpassed in either world war. Ultimately, it was not the predicted American declaration of war on 6 April 1917 that defeated the U-boats, but the belated introduction of mercantile convoying. This defensive measure, beyond all else, robbed U-boats of their ability to inflict the fatal wound as they continued to operate individually in action, rather than collectively as Dönitz planned. Ultimately, those U-boats were only finally beaten by Germany's internal collapse in October 1918, with 178 U-boats lost during the war but an operational fleet of 171 remaining at the time of the November armistice, and another 149 in construction. Ironically, the Allies' mistaken belief that they had mastered U-boats in combat, rather than through the power of convoying, invited a punishing reminder by Karl Dönitz beginning in 1939.

However, as we have seen, Dönitz lacked the strength to deliver a crippling blow to Great Britain. The accepted narrative points to the collapse of the U-boat campaign in May 1943, as if the North Atlantic remained the sole arena of combat for Dönitz's U-boats. Certainly, it was the centre point of his battle – the '*Schwerpunkt*' as he called it – but it was not his only chosen region for attack; more than once – before 1943 – he curtailed operations within this area, as North Atlantic convoys were not Britain's sole lifeline. The South Atlantic offered Dönitz huge possibilities, and he long harboured a desire to attack South Africa's merchant choke points, as well as the lightly defended Indian Ocean. Operations off the United States, Caribbean and Gulf of Mexico provided a bonanza of targets to his second-generation of gifted U-boat officers such as Albrecht Achilles, Reinhard Hardegen and Reinhard Suhren. Yet, as always, he was hamstrung by a lack of operational U-boats. Combined with poor Luftwaffe reconnaissance cooperation, the problem of target acquisition remained staggeringly difficult in most theatres of action, barring where the enemy thoughtfully provided a brightly lit background which silhouetted steamers for U-boats to shoot at, as off the United States in early 1942. And yet, once again, numbers never favoured Dönitz. He attacked the United States – the greatest western industrial power – with an initial wave of just six U-boats.

Furthermore, just as the US Navy also discovered to its cost in their Pacific submarine campaign, faulty weaponry exacerbated the chances of ever-moving U-boat operations out of their perpetual operational deficit. Torpedoes were shockingly defective due to nothing more than negligence. Minelaying became the most effective U-boat weapon during the early months of the war – a dangerous and unpopular task for U-boat crews, with none of the immediate gratification provided by a successful torpedo attack. Morale barely survived this ordeal.

The decision to despatch U-boats to the Mediterranean is frequently cited as disastrous. Hindsight would say that it was indeed a poor choice, though not one of Dönitz's design. Though they swiftly bloodied the Royal Navy within the Mediterranean, the introduction of U-boats to this theatre was a flawed part of a campaign woefully mismanaged by Hitler from its instigation. The possibilities of success in North Africa – severing of the Suez Canal and potential pressure on already pro-Axis Middle Eastern countries – appear beyond Hitler's conception, as evidenced by his unwillingness to sanction the invasion of Malta and lack of emphasis on supplying the Afrika Korps. Instead, he reinforced failure when the point of potential triumph had irrevocably passed, and relegated U-boats to anti-invasion defence – something for which they were patently unsuited. This unsuitability was demonstrated once again in the waters off Normandy in June 1944, when U-boats were destroyed in large numbers as part of their 'death ride' against Operation *Overlord*. It was a disastrous use of outmoded machinery.

Hitler had ignored the Mediterranean because of his fixation on the Soviet Union, though U-boats in action at both extremities of the Eastern Front, and within the Baltic Sea, achieved little to affect the course of the war. Despite the destruction of PQ17 and sporadic sinkings of other Arctic freighters, the course of the titanic struggle on land remained largely unaffected. Likewise within the Black Sea. Although the presence of six small U-boats hampered deployment of major Soviet surface naval units, it could not stem the tide of a resurgent Red Army from 1943 onwards.

The fact that the same types of U-boat with which Germany entered the war were still the operational core at the end shows

an inability to admit technological inferiority. In the same way
as that stubborn – and arrogant – belief in the superiority of the
Enigma coding machine over all enemy attempts at decryption,
the conviction that adaptations such as increased flak weaponry,
bubble decoy dischargers and the *Schnorchel* would allow Type
VII and IX U-boats to remain viable in combat was greatly
mistaken. By the time that Dönitz finally mustered the number
of combat U-boats he had long coveted, the U-boat war had
been essentially lost and his best captains either dead or ashore,
frequently nursing frayed nerves from months of arduous combat.
Stubborn belief in the power of Walter's flawed machinery and
then the Type XXI and XXIII electro-boats almost mirrored
Hitler's fixation with his V1 and V2 'wonder-weapons' which
he believed would change the face of war. Allied air power and
the dislocation of German manufacturing infrastructure, not
to mention RAF mining of Baltic training grounds, ensured
that no Type XXIs would be fully committed to action, while
the Type XXIII was too limited a weapon to exert great effect.
Despite almost miraculous efforts by Albert Speer as Armaments
Minister, German production was unable to meet Dönitz's hopes
for a new generation of U-boat.

The U-boat war between 1939 and 1945 – fought from the first
day to the last and in all of the world's oceans except the Southern
Ocean – was doomed to fail from the outset. At no point did it
actually threaten to decisively sever Britain's maritime trade arteries,
though there were momentary, fleeting successes. Of course,
statistics will never convey the terror of a convoy attack at sea, with
exploding torpedoes, burning ships and drowning men. Nor do
they convey what it must have been like to be trapped in a sinking
U-boat falling to the ocean's bottom which could be several miles
below. They do not, however, lie. The popular image of U-boats
coming close to starving Britain into submission belongs to the
First World War, not the Second. As Jürgen Oesten once told me:

> We needed to start the war with 300 U-boats... so it was quite
> clear that our chances were less than limited. In addition, we

have been working with a rate of more than 50 per cent losses right from the beginning. We were not at all prepared for this sort of fight, as Hitler was too stupid, he thought he could play around in Europe without Britain's interference.

Dönitz was a good naval officer, as such, and therefore this submarine war was carried through to the bitter end. His handicap was that he could be influenced by emotions and Hitler was able to let him swim in a soup of emotions, disregarding the actual facts.[6]

It seems a fitting epitaph to the Kriegsmarine's U-boat war.

Select Bibliography

Arendt, Rudolf, *Letzter Befehl: Versenken!*, Ullstein Verlag, 2003.

Barnett, Correlli, *Engage the Enemy More Closely*, Hodder & Stoughton, 1992.

Bauer, Arthur O., *HF/DF An Allied Weapon against German U-Boats 1939–1945*, Diemen, 2004.

Blair, Clay, *Hitler's U-Boat War*, Volumes 1 & 2, Weidenfeld & Nicolson, 1999.

Brustat-Naval, Fritz and Teddy Suhren, *Nasses Eichenlaub*, Koehlers Verlag, 1983.

Burdick, Charles B., *'Moro': The Resupply of German Submarines in Spain, 1939–1942*, Cambridge University Press, September 1970, Central European History, Vol. 3, pp. 256–284.

Carroll, Francis M., *Athenia Torpedoed*, Naval Institute Press, 2012.

Caulfield, Max, *Tomorrow Never Came*, W.W. Norton and Company, 1958.

Churchill, Winston, *The Second World War*, six volumes, Cassell & Co., 1954.

Conn, Stetson and Byron Fairchild, *The Framework of Hemisphere Defense*, Center of Military History, United States Army, 1989.

Cremer, Peter, *U333: The Story of a U-boat Ace*, Grafton Books, 1986.

Director of Operational Analysis (Royal Navy), *The U-Boat Logs, 1939–1945: Part 3, Operations Outside the Atlantic Theatre*, Ministry of Defence, London, 1966.

Dönitz, Karl, *Ten Years and Twenty Days*, Weidenfeld & Nicolson, 1958.

Enders, Gerd, *Auch kleine Igel haben Stacheln*, Koehler Verlag, 1984.

Frank, Norman, *Search, Find and Kill*, Grub Street, 1995.

Gasaway, E.B., *Grey Wolf, Grey Sea*, Ballantine Books, 1970.

Hadley, Michael, *U-boats Against Canada*, McGill, Queen's University Press, 1985.

Hessler, Günter, *The U-boat War in the Atlantic, 1939–1945*, HMSO, London, 1989.

Hirschfeld, Wolfgang, *The Secret Diary of a U-Boat*, Leo Cooper, 1996.

Högel, Georg, *Zwischen Grönland und Gibraltar*, Amazon Books on Demand, 2005.

Lohmann W. and H.H. Hildebrand, *Die Deutsche Kriegsmarine 1939–1945*, three volumes, Podzun Verlag, 1956.

Maiolo, Joseph A., 'Deception and Intelligence Failure: Anglo-German Preparations for U-boat Warfare in the 1930s', *Journal of Strategic Studies*, Vol. 22, 1999, pp. 55–76.

Metzler, Jost, *The Laughing Cow*, William Kimber, 1955.

Moeller, Kevin M., *The Italian Submarine Force in the Battle of the Atlantic*, Fort Leavenworth, US Army Command and General Staff College, 2014.

Morison, Samuel Eliot, *History of United States Naval Operations in World War II*, Little, Brown and Company, 1956.

Mulligan, Timothy, 'The German Navy Evaluates Its Cryptographic Security, October 1941', *Military Affairs*, Vol. 49, 1985, pp. 75–79.

Paterson, Lawrence, *Hitler's Grey Wolves*, Greenhill Books, 2004.

Paterson, Lawrence, *Otto Kretschmer*, Greenhill Books, 2018.

Paterson, Lawrence, *U-Boats in the Mediterranean*, Chatham Publishing, 2007.

Raeder, Erich, *Grand Admiral*, De Capo, 2001. First published by US Naval Institute 1960 as *My Life*.

Rohwer, Jürgen, *Axis Submarine Successes of World War Two*, Greenhill Books, 1999.

Rössler Eberhard, *The U-Boat*, Cassell & Co., 2001.

Sebag-Montefiore, Hugh, *Enigma*, Weidenfeld & Nicolson, 2000.

Ships of the Royal Navy; Statement of Losses During the Second World War, HMSO, London, 1947.

Speer, Albert, *Inside the Third Reich*, Book Club Associates, 1971.

Stevens, David, *U-Boat Far from Home*, Allen & Unwin, 1997.

Tarrant, V.E., *The U-Boat Offensive 1914–1945*, Arms & Armour Press, 1989.

Terraine, John, *Business in Great Waters*, Leo Cooper Ltd, 1989.

Topp, Eric, *The Odyssey of a U-Boat Commander*, Praeger Publishing, 1992.

Warnock, Timothy A., *Air Power versus U-Boats*, Air Force History and Museums Programme, 1999.

Werner, Herbert, *Iron Coffins*, Henry Holt and Co., 1969.

Wynn, Kenneth, *U-boat Operations of the Second World War*, Volume 1 & 2, Chatham Publishing, 1998.

www.uboat.net.

www.uboatarchive.net.

www.fold3.com (Admiralty War Diaries).

Notes

INTRODUCTION

1   https://www.thecourier.co.uk/fp/news/local/fife/1291387/ve-day-75th-anniversary-u-boat-attack-led-to-pointless-deaths-off-fife-in-final-minutes-of-second-world-war/.

CHAPTER ONE

1   Karl Dönitz, *Ten Years and Twenty Days*, p. 7.
2   Letter from Werner Lott (*U35*) to Earl Mountbatten of Burma, 9 September 1974.
3   FdU KTB 19 August 1939.
4   FdU KTB 16 August 1939.

CHAPTER TWO

1   Max Caulfield, *Tomorrow Never Came*, p. 53.
2   Georg Högel, *Zwischen Grönland und Gibraltar*, p. 90.
3   SKL KTB 1 October 1939.
4   BdU KTB 31 October 1939.
5   Albert Speer, *Inside the Third Reich*, p. 272.
6   BdU KTB 21 January 1940.

CHAPTER THREE

1   Lawrence Paterson, *Otto Kretschmer*, p. 91.
2   BdU KTB 15 May 1940.

3   SKL KTB 25 June 1940.

4   Interrogation report *U76* survivors, Admiralty Naval Intelligence Division, N.I.D. 08409/43.

5   Karl Dönitz, *Ten Years and Twenty Days*, p. 101.

6   Letter from Bernard Geismann, 20 February 2002.

7   Högel, *Zwischen Grönland und Gibraltar*, pp. 131–132.

8   Figures from *Ships of the Royal Navy; Statement of Losses During the Second World War, 3 September 1939 to 2 September 1945*, HMSO, 1947.

9   E.B. Gasaway, *Grey Wolf, Grey Sea*, p. 60.

10   Narrative by Captain Finn Skage of Snefjeld, National Archives, Kew, quoted on the exhaustively researched www.warsailors.com (https://www.warsailors.com/singleships/snefjeld.html).

11   Interview with Otto Kretschmer, *The World at War*, BBC television, 1973.

12   BdU KTB 20 October 1940.

13   Lawrence Paterson, *Otto Kretschmer*, p. 134.

14   *The Defeat of the Enemy Attack on Shipping*, Naval Staff History, Historical Section, Admiralty, 1957, Appendix 6, p. 302.

15   BdU KTB 13 December 1940.

16   Karl Dönitz, *Ten Years and Twenty Days*, p.137.

CHAPTER FOUR

1   Email from Jürgen Oesten to author, 15 June 2002.

2   BdU KTB 9 October 1940.

3   BdU KTB 28 August 1940.

4   BdU KTB 21 December 1940.

5   HMS *Vanoc* after action report.

6   Letter from Otto Kretschmer, 18 June 1989.

7   Royal Navy Interrogation Report, C.B. 04051 (26) 'U556; Interrogation of Survivors', August 1941, Naval Intelligence Division.

8   Royal Navy Interrogation Report, C.B. 04051 (27) 'U651; Interrogation of Crew', September 1941, Naval Intelligence Division.

9   BdU KTB 14 April 1941.

10   Jost Metzler, *The Laughing Cow*, p. 99.

11   *U69* KTB 21 May 1941.

12   BdU KTB 21 June 1941.

CHAPTER FIVE

1   Letter to Mac MacGowan from David Balme, held at Royal Navy Submarine Museum.
2   Karl Dönitz, *Ten Years and Twenty Days*, p. 153.
3   Letter to the author from Erich Topp, 6 November 2001.
4   Sub-lieutenant D.E. Balme, R.N. Report on Operation *Primrose*.
5   Admiralty War Diary, Monday 25 August 1941.
6   BdU KTB 12 August 1941.
7   Admiralty Report C.B. 4051 (31); '*U 570*' Interrogation of Crew.

CHAPTER SIX

1   Interrogation Report *U501*, Naval Intelligence Division, C.B. 4051 (30), October 1941.
2   *U552* KTB 31 October 1941.
3   KTB *U66* 24 September 1941.
4   KTB *U66* 24 September 1941.
5   KTB *U66* 24 September 1941.
6   BdU KTB 28 September 1941.
7   Letter dated 24 October 1941, quoted in Hugh Sebag-Montefiore, *Enigma; The Battle for the Code*, from Microfilm Reel 40 at the Ministry of Defence.
8   BdU KTB 22 November 1941.
9   *UA* KTB 1 December 1941.
10 Wolfgang Hirschfeld, *Diary of a U-boat*, pp. 101–102.
11 Royal Navy Report of Interrogation of Crew of *U95*, November 1941.
12 *U331* KTB 25 November 1941.
13 Naval Historical Society of Australia, *HMS Barham – A Survivor's Account of Sinking*. https://www.navyhistory.org.au/author/mcdoi/.

CHAPTER SEVEN

1   Wolfgang Frank, *Die Wölfe und Der Admiral*, Gerhard Stalling Verlag, 1953, p. 285.
2   BdU KTB 10 December 1941.
3   ESF War Diary January 1942, uboatarchive.net.
4   *U123* KTB 26 March 1942.

5   *U123* KTB 15 January 1942.

6   Peter Cremer, *The Story of a U-boat Ace*, p. 68.

7   Fritz Brustat-Naval and Teddy Suhren, *Nasses Eichenlaub*, p. 99.

8   *U156* KTB 22 February 1942.

9   Winston Churchill, *The Second World War*, Vol. IV, p. 108.

10   Preliminary Report by the Chief of Staff, Naval Staff
     (*Vizeadmiral* Fricke on the conference with the Führer on
     22 January 1942).

11   'Destruction of German submarine', Report of A9/DD147,
     15 April 1942.

12   BdU KTB 26 March 1942.

13   *U507* KTB 16 May 1942.

14   Navy Department, *United States Naval Administration in World
     War II; History of Convoy and Routing*. Washington, D.C., 1939–
     1945, p. 58.

15   Interview with Jürgen Oesten.

CHAPTER EIGHT

1   Lawrence Paterson, *Second U-Boat Flotilla*, Pen & Sword Books,
     2003, p. 179.

2   *U156* KTB 6 July 1942.

3   BdU KTB 11 June 1942.

4   Admiralty War Diary, 11 December 1942.

5   Figures from www.uboat.net reflect the most current thought on a
     slightly variable tally.

CHAPTER NINE

1   Norman Franks, *Search, Find and Kill*, p. 217.

2   Winston Churchill, *The Second World War*, Vol. IV, p. 554.

3   Karl Dönitz, *Ten Years and Twenty Days*, p. 322.

4   Royal Navy Report, 'Interrogation of Survivors from *U187*'
     (C49073) 406 8/43, held at Royal Navy Submarine Museum.

5   BdU KTB 6 March 1943.

6   Correlli Barnett, *Engage the Enemy More Closely*, p. 610.

7   BdU KTB: Message 1769, 'To All Boats' 24 May 1943.

8   BdU KTB 5 August 1943 Addendum.

CHAPTER TEN

1   David Stevens, *U-Boat Far from Home*, p. 149, Reiffenstuhl diary
    entry 9 December 1944.
2   *U196* KTB 6 August 1943.
3   Herbert Werner, *Iron Coffins*, pp. 154–155.
4   BdU KTB 7 September 1943.
5   BdU KTB 24 September 1943.
6   Letter from Jürgen Oesten, 15 June 2002.
7   Email from Jürgen Oesten to the author, 17 November 2002.
8   *U188* KTB 12 March 1944.
9   Günter Hessler, *The U-boat War in the Atlantic*, Vol. III, p. 61.

CHAPTER ELEVEN

1   Herbert Werner, *Iron Coffins*, p. 213.
2   Interview with Hans-Rudolf Rösing, October 2001.
3   Letter from Bernard Geismann, 4 March 2002.
4   *The U-Boat Logs, Part 2: Operational Performance & Degradation*,
    Directorate of Operational Analysis (RN), Ministry of Defence,
    August 1966, p. 11.
5   SKL War Diary, 3 September 1939.
6   Jürgen Oesten in Hamburg, 19 June 2002.

Index